# Criminal Law in Greece

# Criminal Law in Greece

**Ilias G. Anagnostopoulos**
**Konstantinos D. Magliveras**

This book was originally published as a monograph in the International Encyclopaedia of Laws/Criminal Law.

Founding Editor: Roger Blanpain
General Editor: Frank Hendrickx
Volume Editors: Frank Verbruggen & Vanessa Franssen

Wolters Kluwer

*Published by:*
Kluwer Law International B.V.
PO Box 316
2400 AH Alphen aan den Rijn
The Netherlands
E-mail: lrs-sales@wolterskluwer.com
Website: www.wolterskluwer.com/en/solutions/kluwerlawinternational

*Sold and distributed by:*
Wolters Kluwer Legal & Regulatory U.S.
920 Links Avenue
Landisville, PA 17538
United States of America
E-mail: customer.service@wolterskluwer.com



ISBN 978-94-035-3857-0

e-Book: ISBN 978-94-035-3867-9
web-PDF: ISBN 978-94-035-3877-8

# The Authors

*Ilias G. Anagnostopoulos*, born in Piraeus in 1956, graduated from the School of Law of the National and Kapodistrian University of Athens (1978) and received a Doctor Juris degree from the University of Frankfurt am Main, Germany (1982). He is a Professor of Criminal Law and Criminal Procedure at the same School of Law, where he started his academic career as a Lecturer (1989).

His numerous publications in Greek, English, and German cover various aspects of financial crime, European and international criminal law, the reform of criminal procedure, fundamental rights and crime policy.

Ilias was called to the Athens Bar in 1983 and heads Athens-based law firm Anagnostopoulos focusing on white-collar crime and criminal risk management. Since 2013 he chairs the Hellenic Criminal Bar Association. Memberships include the Experts Committee of the Hellenic Ministry of Justice, the High-Legal Council with the Bank of Greece, the European Criminal Bar Association (founding member).

Ilias Anagnostopoulos is the author of Part II of this book.

*Konstantinos D. Magliveras*, born in Athens in 1963, graduated from the School of Law of the National and Kapodistrian University of Athens. He graduated LLM from Exeter University, LLM from the University of East Anglia, and D.Phil. from Oxford University. He has carried out postdoc research at Erasmus Universiteit, Rotterdam. He is an attorney at law, member of the Athens Bar Association.

He has written and published extensively in the fields of, *inter alia*, international criminal law, including money laundering and trafficking in human beings, international(ized) criminal courts and tribunals; and human rights and fundamental freedoms. In 2018, he participated and appeared as *amicus curiae* before the Appeals Chamber of the International Criminal Court in the case of *Al Bashir*. He is a member of the International Law Association's Committee on Nuclear Weapons, Non-Proliferation and Contemporary International Law.

Konstantinos D. Magliveras is the author of the General Introduction, Part I and Part III of this book.

# Table of Contents

# List of Abbreviations

| | |
|---|---|
| Art. | Article |
| Arts | Articles |
| CC | Civil Code |
| CCP | Code of Criminal Procedure |
| CETS | Council of Europe Treaty Series |
| CISA | Convention on the Implementation of the Schengen Agreement |
| CJEU | Court of Justice of the European Union |
| EAW | European Arrest Warrant |
| EBRD | European Bank of Reconstruction and Development |
| ECHR | European Convention of Human Rights and Fundamental Freedoms |
| ECtHR | European Court of Human Rights |
| ed | editor |
| eds | editors |
| EP | European Parliament |
| EPPO | European Public Prosecutor's Office |
| ETS | European Treaty Series |
| EU | European Union |
| EU Charter | Charter of Fundamental Rights of the European Union |
| EuCLR | European Criminal Law Review |
| Eucrim | The European Criminal Law Association's Forum |
| FATF | Financial Action Task Force |
| FD | Framework Decision |
| FEK | Fyllo Efimeridos Kyverniseos (Greek Government Gazette – Official Gazette) |
| FIU | Financial Intelligence Unit |
| GRECO | Group of States Against Corruption |
| ICC | International Criminal Court |
| ICCPR | International Covenant on Civil and Political Rights |

## List of Abbreviations

| | |
|---|---|
| ILM | International Legal Materials |
| JC | Judicial Code |
| LNTS | League of Nations Treaty Series |
| OECD | Organisation for Economic Co-operation and Development |
| OJ | Official Journal of the European Union |
| OSCE | Organisation for Security and Co-operation in Europe |
| para. | paragraph |
| paras | paragraphs |
| PC | Penal Code |
| RIDP | Revue International de Droit Pénal |
| StraFo | Strafverteidiger Forum |
| TFEU | Treaty on the Functioning of the European Union |
| THB | Trafficking in Human Beings |
| UN | United Nations |
| UN Doc. | United Nations document |
| UNESCO | UN Educational, Scientific and Cultural Organisation |
| UNGA | United Nations General Assembly |
| UNIDROIT | International Institute for the Unification of Private Law |
| UNSC | United Nations Security Council |
| UNTS | United Nations Treaty Series |
| USA/US | United States of America |
| ZIS | Zeitschrift für Internationale Strafrechtsdogmatik |
| ZStW | Zeitschrift für die gesamte Strafrechtswissenschaft |

# Preface

The first edition of this monograph came out just as this century had dawned. Since then, many things have changed in Greek society. This reality has also been reflected in numerous important changes that have taken place in the field of substantive and procedural criminal law. After all, essential characteristics and tendencies prevailing in a particular society should be reflected in its criminal laws and procedures, so that the latter constitutes a faithful mirror of societal values, principles, and morals. But the world as a whole has radically changed over the last 25 years. New global and regional criminal law treaties and conventions have been adopted, often regulating matters for the first time. Moreover, the European Union, of which Greece has been a Member State since 1981, has been very active in producing secondary legislation in the criminal law area. As a result, developments in Greek criminal law and procedure have also been influenced by the treaties ratified by Greece and by EU law. But the most significant development has no doubt been the promulgation of a new Penal Code (PC) and a new Code of Criminal Procedure (CCP) in the summer of 2019, following a rather arduous drafting process, which in total lasted for some ten years.

Based on the above considerations, the present authors have attempted not only to offer a detailed presentation of the new PC and CCP, while also noting important changes from the abrogated Codes, but also to record the global and regional legal instruments, which have been accepted and applied by Greece, as well as the applicable European Union legislation. At the same time, the authors have tried to read the Greek criminal legislation from a critical point of view and record issues of concern, when they were deemed pertinent.

The law is stated as the authors understood it to be in November 2020; where possible, subsequent amendments have been taken into account.

# General Introduction

## §1. The General Background of the Country

### I. Geography and Climate

*1.* Greece is a relatively small country lying in the southeast of Europe. It covers an area of *circa* 132,000 square kilometres and borders by land Albania, Northern Macedonia (formerly, the Former Yugoslav Republic of Macedonia), Bulgaria and Turkey, and by sea Italy, Libya, Cyprus and Egypt.

Geographically speaking, Greece could be divided in the mainland and over 2,000 islands. The mainland is divided into six main regions: Thrace, Macedonia, Epirus, Thessaly, Sterea Ellada and the Peloponnese. There are five large groups of islands: the Ionian Islands, the Cyclades, the Dodecanese, the islands of the Eastern Aegean Sea and the Sporades. The vast part of continental Greece is mountainous, and there are some 40 mountains with an elevation exceeding 2,000 meters (the Smolikas peak at the Pindus mountains, whose length is 230 kilometres, has an elevation of 2,637 meters). Large flat areas suitable for agriculture are principally to be found in Thessaly, the Peloponnese and Macedonia.

*2.* Greece enjoys a typical Mediterranean climate with very warm summers and cold winters. For example, the average temperature in Athens ranges from 9.2 degrees Celsius in January to 27.2 degrees in July. Such variation in temperature can also be seen in the city of Thessaloniki, where the average temperature of 5.5 degrees in January rises to 25.9 degrees in July. During the winter months, the peaks of many mountains are snow covered.

### II. Population

*3.* According to the most recent data, the estimated population of Greece was 10,678,632 on 1 January 2021, having reached an all-time high of 11,123,393 inhabitants on 1 January 2011. June 1996 data, the Greek population stood at 10,475,878 inhabitants.[1]

1. For details, *see* the website of the Hellenic Statistical Authority at: https://www.statistics.gr/en/statistics/pop. For concise figures, *see:* https://www.statistics.gr/en/statistics/-/publication/SPO18/- and the website of the European Commission, at: https://eacea.ec.europa.eu/national-policies/

During the Second World War and the country's triple military occupation by German, Italian and Bulgarian forces, where mass executions were perpetrated, Greece suffered considerable human losses. However, the country enjoyed a very large population increase between the 1950s and the 1970s, and this was despite large emigration waves during the same period. The trend of an augmenting population was slowed down considerably in the 1980s and even more in the 1990s and was overturned at the beginning of the twenty-first century, even though births through artificial insemination have increased considerably. Families with no children or with only one child have become a common phenomenon. During the last decade, the number of deaths has exceeded the number of births. Thus, in 2019 there were 86,440 births and 119,446 deaths, while for 2021 the figures were, respectively, 85,303 and 143,329. The diminishing population in Greece could be attributed to a combination of demographic, societal, economic and other factors. These include a preference for one child families; many deaths among people in the reproduction period due to road traffic accidents;[2] a large number of young people emigrating to pursue undergraduate and postgraduate studies, mainly to other European Union (EU) Member States; and since 2010, a mass emigration to almost all parts of the world on account of the monetary and debt crisis which has plagued the country and which continues to have adverse microeconomic and macroeconomic consequences for the Greek economy.

## III. Economy: The Monetary and Debt Crisis of 2010 and the Transformation of the Greek Society and Economy

*4.* Traditionally, Greece has been an agricultural country, even though the total arable areas are less than 25% of the territory. In past times, there were attempts towards industrialization and the setting up of heavy industry (e.g., shipyards) but they have not been very successful. Several reasons have contributed to this, including the lack of abundant natural resources; the lack of sustainable long-term investments as well as of foreign direct investment; the lack of a significant domestic market able to absorb local production; the lack of funds committed to research and development; the lack of adequate competition and the existence of oligopolistic practices in many sectors of the economy; an anachronist and ailing public administration incapable of following European and world developments and prone to corruption; an ever-changing taxation system, etc. However, Greece used to have several large industries in textiles, cement, food processing, chemicals, etc. However, nowadays most of them have ceased production, or have become bankrupt or have transferred production to other countries attracted by lower production costs and/or more favourable taxation. This has resulted in Greece importing goods which were once domestically produced, thus deteriorating the balance of payments.

---

eurydice/content/population-demographic-situation-languages-and-religions-33_en and at: https://ec.europa.eu/eurostat/web/population-demography/demography-population-stock-balance/database.

2. *See* Overseas Security Advisory Council, Bureau of Diplomatic Security, U.S. Department of State, *Greece 2019 Crime & Safety Report*, 25 Feb. 2019, where it is noted that 'Greece has one of the highest rates of per-capita traffic fatalities in the EU', at: www.osac.gov.

*5.* In October 2020, the National Statistical Authority announced that the revised GDP for 2019 was EUR 183,606 billion, an 1.9% increase compared to 2018. Services are the largest sector in the economy (its share is well over 50% of the GDP), with agriculture and industry following. Tourism and shipping are the leading sectors in services, while the once vibrant banking sector, with high profile presence in Southeastern European countries, the Balkans and Turkey, has been diminished to the point of almost becoming extinct. It is estimated that in 2018 the tourism industry's direct contribution to the GDP amounted to EUR 21.6 billion (11.7%) and that it further augmented in 2019.[3] Another traditional source of foreign income has been emigrants' remittances. According to the Migration and Remittances Factbook 2016, published by the World Bank, in 2013 the stock of Greek emigrants was slightly over 1 million; in 2008 inward remittance flows stood at USD 2,687 billion, while in 2014 and in 2015 they remained unchanged at USD 735 million per year.[4] Finally, ever since Greece joined the European Economic Community in 1981, it has relied extensively on EU funding. Indeed, Greece is presently the second largest net recipient (after Poland).

*6.* The monetary and debt crisis which has plagued Greece since 2010 has led to the most significant changes in its economy and society.[5] To overcome the crisis, Greece resorted, on the one hand, to the International Monetary Fund (IMF)[6] and, on the other hand, to the European Union (EU) and its Member States for urgent financial assistance. As regards the IMF, its financial support was provided in the form of a three-year EUR 30 billion Stand-By Arrangement (SBA), this being the IMF's standard lending instrument.[7] As regards the EU, a total amount of EUR 241.6 billion was lent to Greece during the three so-called programmes. In particular, during the first programme, which lasted from May 2010 to March 2012, EUR 52.9 billion were disbursed as bilateral loans from the other Member States to Greece. During the second programme, which was active from March 2012 until June 2015, the European Financial Stability Facility lent EUR 141.8 billion to Greece. And during the third programme, which ran from August 2015 to August 2018, EUR 46.9 billion were disbursed as loans from the European Stability Mechanism (ESM). The reason why there were finally three 'programmes' is the following: the third programme was considered necessary because the execution of the second one had not solved the debt crisis, while the second programme was deemed essential because the first one, notwithstanding the additional IMF assistance, had proven inadequate to resolve the original crisis, which had in the meantime worsened.

---

3. For relevant figures, *see* the OECD data, at: https://data.oecd.org/greece.htm.
4. At: https://openknowledge.worldbank.org/handle/10986/23743.
5. Generally, *see* P. Siani-Davies, *Crisis in Greece*, Oxford: Oxford University Press, 2017.
6. *See* International Monetary Fund, *Greece: Request for Stand-By Arrangement*, IMF Country Report No. 10/111, May 2010, at: https://www.imf.org/external/pubs/ft/scr/2010/cr10111.pdf.
7. *See* International Monetary Fund, *IMF Survey: Europe and IMF Agree €110 Billion Financing Plan with Greece*, IMF Survey online, 2 May 2010, at: https://www.imf.org/en/News/Articles/2015/09/28/04/53/socar050210a.

*7.* The timely disbursement of the EU loans and the funds under the IMF SBA was subjected to specific conditions and requirements being met promptly and in full. Given that the total amount of the loans extended to Greece exceeded by far the loans previously disbursed to any other State facing a debt crisis, there were many arduous conditions attached. The fulfilment of these conditions demanded that unprecedented changes be made to the Greek society and economy, where decades-long arrangements were overturned literally overnight.[8] In particular, during the 2010–2018 period, the Greek Parliament approved and the President of the Republic promulgated fifteen reform packages, which resulted in very extensive reforms, in the financial sector, in the administration of the State, in the labour market, in the tax system, in the pensions system, etc.[9] Moreover, austerity measures were constantly adopted, which primarily concerned slashes in salaries and in pensions, closing or merging public entities, etc. This situation led, according to the Organisation for Economic Co-operation and Development (OECD), to one in three Greeks living below the line of poverty.[10] The question of the constitutionality of the legislative instruments adopted during the debt crisis eventually came up. In the beginning, almost all were found to be in compliance with the Constitution but, later on, several laws were held to be unconstitutional by the country's highest courts. At the time of writing, there was still pending litigation before them.

There have also been complaints lodged with the ECtHR, principally arguing that the measures implemented by Greece to respond to the economic/debt crisis were in violation of Article 1 of Protocol No. 1 to ECHR,[11] which protects the right of property.[12] Thus, in *Koufaki and Adedy v. Greece*, the ECtHR declared the applications inadmissible as being manifestly ill-founded. In particular, the reduction of the first applicant's salary did not risk her to be exposed to subsistence difficulties incompatible with Article 1 of Protocol No. 1, while, for as long as the Greek Parliament did not overstep the limits of its margin of appreciation, it was not for the Court to say whether the domestic legislation had chosen the best means to address the country's fiscal problems or whether the legislative power should have been used differently.[13] In *Mamatas and Others v. Greece*, the applicants, who were private individuals holding Greek State bonds, argued that their forcible participation in the scheme to reduce the Greek public debt by exchanging their bonds for other

8. Generally, *see* A. Verde, 'The Greek Debt Crisis: Causes, Policy Responses and Consequences' in P.D. Posta & L.S. Talani (eds), *Europe and the Financial Crisis*, Houndmills: Palgrave Macmillan, 2011, 143–164.
9. *See* D. Diliagka, *The Legality of Public Pension Reforms in Times of Financial Crisis – The Case of Greece*, Baden-Baden: Nomos, 2018.
10. *See also* UN Human Rights Council, *Report of the Independent Expert on the effects of foreign debt and other related international financial obligations of States on the full enjoyment of all human rights, particularly economic, social and cultural rights, Cephas Lumina*, Mission to Greece (22–27 Apr. 2013), UN Doc. A/HRC/25/50/Add.1, 7 Mar. 2014.
11. ECHR was signed on 4 Nov. 1950, entered into force on 3 Sep. 1953. Greece ratified it under Legislative Decree 2329/1953. In 1969, the military regime in power in Greece at the time denounced the Convention. Following the restoration of democracy in July 1974, it was ratified again under Legislative Decree 53/1974, FEK 1974 A' 256, which also ratified Protocol No. 1.
12. Generally, *see* I. Pervou, 'Human Rights in Times of Crisis: The Greek Cases Before the ECtHR, or the Polarisation of a Democratic Society' (2016) 5 *Cambridge International Law Journal* 113–138.
13. ECtHR, Application nos 57665/12 and 57657/12, *Koufaki and Adedy v. Greece*, Decision of 7 May 2013.

debt instruments of lesser value (a practice known as 'haircut' on bonds) had breached Article 1 of Protocol No. 1. The Court held that, even though this forcible participation amounted to an interference with the applicants' right to respect for their property, this interference pursued a public-interest aim, namely, to preserve economic stability in Greece and to restructure the national debt, at a time when the country was engulfed in a serious economic crisis. It followed that the applicants had not suffered any special or excessive burden, in view, particularly, of the wide margin of appreciation that Greece enjoyed in that sphere and, therefore, there was no violation of Article 1 of Protocol No. 1.[14] It becomes apparent from these cases that the ECtHR placed a lot of significance to the margin of appreciation, which, however, is a rather elusive concept open to very broad interpretation.

*8.* The loans extended to Greece do not appear to have resolved its perennial debt problem.[15] In 2020, government debt as a percentage of GDP reached 252%, a staggering increase compared to, say, 1997 when it stood at 199%.[16] In absolute figures, the amount of the debts owed today by Greece is higher than that owed in the summer of 2015, when the country came very near to declaring officially a sovereign default.[17] While it would not have been the first time that Greece would have defaulted,[18] it would have been the first developed world country participating in a regional economic integration organization (namely, the European Union) not to have served its foreign debt. Even though default was finally avoided, the dependence of Greece on third states for its apparent survival, a fact which has characterized and influenced the country since its independence in the 1830s, will no doubt persist in the foreseeable future.[19]

---

14. ECtHR, Application nos 63066/14, 64297/14 and 66106/14, *Mamatas and Others v. Greece*, Decision of 21 Jul. 2016.
15. Generally, *see* European Commission, Commission Staff Working Document, Country Report Greece 2020 Accompanying the document Communication from the Commission, 2020 European Semester: *Assessment of progress on structural reforms, prevention and correction of macroeconomic imbalances, and results of in-depth reviews under Regulation (EU) No 1176/2011*, SWD(2020) 507 final, 26 Feb. 2020.
16. *See* The World Bank Data, *Central government debt, total (% of GDP) – Greece*, online, at, https://data.worldbank.org/indicator/GC.DOD.TOTL.GD.ZS?locations=GR.
17. *See* BBC, *The Greek debt crisis story in numbers*, 10 Jul. 2015, at: https://www.bbc.com/news/world-europe-33407742; The New York Times, *Explaining Greece's Debt Crisis*, 17 Jun. 2016, at: https://www.nytimes.com/interactive/2016/business/international/greece-debt-crisis-euro.html; Council of Foreign Relations, *Greece's Debt 1974–2018*, at: https://www.cfr.org/timeline/greeces-debt-crisis-timeline.
18. *See* L. Tsoulfidis & M. Zouboulakis, 'Greek Sovereign Defaults in Retrospect and Prospect' (2016) 14 *South-Eastern Europe Journal of Economics* 141–157, at: http://www.asecu.gr/Seeje/issue27/issue27-tsoulfidis-zouboulakis.pdf.
19. Generally, *see* C. M. Reinhart & C. Trebesch, *The Pitfalls of External Dependence: Greece, 1829–2015*, The Brookings Institution, Economic Studies Program, Brookings Papers on Economic Activity, vol. 46(2), Fall 2015, pp. 307–328.

## IV. Historical Background, Political System and Administrative Structure

*9.* Greece, the successor to the Byzantine Empire, gained her independence from the Ottoman Empire under the London Protocol of 1830, by virtue of which France, Great Britain and Russia recognized it as an independent state. This Protocol and the subsequent Treaty of London of 24 April/7 May 1832 envisaged that Greece will be ruled as a monarchy and bestowed unlimited powers on the monarch. The Greek Crown was offered to and accepted by Prince Frederick Otto, son of Ludwig the First, King of Bavaria. He was deposed in 1862, having promulgated the first written Constitution in 1844. The same year, the Crown was offered to Prince George of Denmark. During his reign, the Constitution of 1864 came into effect, which was considered one of the most liberal if not the most liberal Constitution in Europe at the time. It was revised in 1911. The post-World War II Constitutions of 1952 and 1975 could be considered as an evolution of the 1864 Constitution. The Constitution of 1975 was amended in 1986, in 2001, in 2008, and, lastly, in November 2019.[20]

*10.* According to Article 1 of the 1975 Constitution, as currently in force, Greece is a parliamentary democracy with the President of the Republic embodying the sovereign. Article 26 thereof sets out the classic trichotomy of state authority into the legislative branch (carried out by the Parliament and the President of the Republic), the executive branch (carried out by the Government) and the judiciary (carried out by the civil, penal, administrative and special courts).

*11.* In pursuance to Article 101 of the Constitution, the administrative structure of Greece is based on the one hand, on the decentralized system and, on the other hand, on the prevailing economic, social and geographical conditions. Moreover, the administration of all regional affairs is entrusted to the so-called organizations of regional self-government (or local government agencies), which enjoy administrative independence. Traditionally, they have been structured into two levels, the first constituted of municipalities and communes and the second constituted of prefectures. At the end of the twentieth century, the system was overhauled, and smaller communes were compulsorily merged into larger communes. At almost the same time, several functions and powers were shifted from the Government to the local authorities. In 2011, more radical changes were implemented, which restructured the local government's administrative organization and established seven so-called Decentralised Administration Authorities.[21] In a nutshell, under the pre-2011 system there existed 1,037 communes and municipalities, which under the new system were merged into 325 (and, as of 2019, 332) municipalities (first-level local authorities); 54 prefectures which became 13 regions (second-level local authorities), while

20. For translation in English and in French, which include all amendments, as well as in German which amendments up to 2008, *see* https://www.hellenicparliament.gr/en/Vouli-ton-Ellinon/To-Politevma/Syntagma/.
21. *See* Act 3852/2010, New Architecture of Decentralised Administration and Self-government – The Kallikrates Programme, FEK 2010 A' No. 87.

the 13 Regions of the previous system were replaced by the aforementioned seven Decentralised Administration Authorities.[22]

*12.* The existence and unhindered operation of political parties is safeguarded by the Constitution. According to Article 29(1) thereof, Greek citizens, who have the right to vote, may freely establish and participate in political parties. The operation of political parties is determined by Acts of Parliament, which are adopted in plenary sessions (Article 72(1) of the Constitution). The organization and the activities of political parties must serve the unhindered operation of the democratic regime. Political parties receive on a yearly basis financial assistance from the State budget, the amount of which is based on the number of votes that each party received at the last national (general) elections.[23] The total amount of the financial assistance for 2020 has been set at EUR 13.5 million, which should be regarded as disproportionately high for a country that was on the brink of sovereign default. With a paltry turnout of 57.78%, the last general elections took place on 7 July 2020, which returned the following six political parties being represented in Parliament: *Nea Dimokratia* (it received 39.85% of the votes); *Synaspismos Rizospastikis Aristeras* (31.53%); *Kinima Allagis* (8.10%); *Kommounistiko Komma Elladas* (5.3%); *Elliniki Lysi* (3.70%); and *MERA 25* (3.44%).[24] Greek politics have always been dominated by political families, whose members have served as Presidents of the Republic, Prime Ministers, Ministers, members of Parliament, Mayors, etc. This is perhaps a symptom of a country which has not managed to integrate itself fully into the mentality and the temperament of the Western European democracies. It is extremely difficult to be elected member of Parliament if one does not belong to an established political party.

## V. Crime Statistics for Greece

*13.* According to data prepared by the World Bank, in 2017 the number of intentional homicides per 100,000 people in Greece stood at 0.7. In the period between 1990 and 2017, the line for murders in Greece reveals that presently the number is at its lowest level ever, having peaked in 1997 when it stood at 1.9.[25] As regards the rate of assaults and major assaults (as recorded by the Greek Police), in 2006 it stood at 66.7 per 100,000 people, of which the rate for rapes stood at 2.4 (a significant increase from 1996 when the rate was only 1.3), and the rate for robberies

22. Generally, *see* Council of Europe, Directorate General of Democracy and Political Affairs, *Structure and operation of local and regional democracy: Greece – Situation in 2012*, Strasbourg, January 2013.
23. *See* OECD, *Integrity in Political Finance in Greece*, OECD Public Governance Reviews, OECD Publishing Press, 2018. The following publication also contains references to the situation in Greece: Yves-Marie Double, *Fighting Corruption: Political Funding*, Thematic review of GRECO's Third Evaluation Round, Council of Europe, no date, at: https://rm.coe.int/16806cbff2.
24. For further details, *see* the webpage of the Hellenic Ministry of the Interior, at: https://ekloges.ypes.gr/current/v/home/en/. *See also* OSCE, Office for Democratic Institutions and Human Rights, *Greece Parliamentary Elections October 2019*, ODIHR Needs Assessment Mission Report, Warsaw, 24 May 2019, at: https://www.osce.org/odihr/elections/greece/420839?download=true.
25. *See* https://data.worldbank.org/.

was at 23.4. Also for the year 2006, the rate for burglaries was 292.3, the motor vehicle theft rate was 138.6 (almost the same rate was recorded in 1996), the rate for drugs related (including drugs trafficking) offences stood at 74, and, finally, the rate of attrition in the criminal justice system for all offences stood at 2.174 (all figures per 100,000 people).[26] Comparing the total number of criminal offences committed in the years between 2003 and 2007, the relevant figures have remained more or less the same and have ranged between 4,008 in 2003 and 3,927 in 2007 per 100,000 people.[27] However, comparing the total number of criminal offences committed in the years between 2007 and 2011, one observes a continuous trend towards diminishing criminality. Thus, in 2008 there were 3746 offences recorded, in 2009 there were 3436 offences, while the figures for 2010 and 2011 were, respectively, 2954 and 1716 offences per 100,000 people, a most notable change of minus 55% between 2007 and 2011.[28]

*14.* During the same period, a surge in economic crime has been recorded. Thus, the cases of fraud increased from 9 in 2007 to 17 in 2011 (an 85% change), while the cases of corruption increased from 0.7 in 2007 to 1.0 in 2011 (a 50% change) having previously peaked in 2009 with 1.6 cases per 100,000 people.[29] It should also be noted that tax evasion has always been ripe in Greece and ranks much higher than in most other EU Member States. There is also a very extended underground economy (also referred to as 'shadow economy' or 'black economy'), which again is much larger than in other EU states.[30] The extended underground economy is linked to the widespread tax evasion and arguably the one funnels the other. The number of reports confirming tax evasion reached 327 in 2015, 215 in 2016, 236 in 2017, while in the period from January 2018 to April 2018 there were 103 reports. Of these reports, those exceeding EUR 50,000 in tax evasion were 294 for 2015, 186 for 2016, 196 for 2017 and 87 for the first four months of 2018.[31] According to the Secretary-General of the OECD, 'two out of three euros from VAT are lost due to tax evasion' in Greece.[32] While tax evasion is a plague for the Greek economy, successive governments have resorted to tax amnesties and/or leniency schemes as

26. *See* S. Harrendorf, M. Heiskanen & S. Malby (eds), *International Statistics on Crime and Justice*, European Institute for Crime Prevention and Control, HEUNI Publication Series No. 64, Helsinki, 2010.
27. *See European Sourcebook of Crime and Criminal Justice Statistics 2010*, 4th ed., Den Haag, 2010, at: https://www.unodc.org/documents/southeasterneurope/cards-bih-prosec./BiH_Doc_2_European_Sourcebook_2010.pdf.
28. *See* European Sourcebook of Crime and Criminal Justice Statistics 2014, 5th. ed., 2nd revised printing, Helsinki, 2017, at: http://wp.unil.ch/europeansourcebook/files/2018/03/Sourcebook2014_2nd_revised_printing_edition_20180308.pdf.
29. *Ibid.*
30. During the period 2000–2016, it is estimated that the shadow economy in Greece ranged between 28.1% and 32.2% of GDP, *see* B. Kelmanson, K. Kirabaeva, L. Medina, B. Mircheva & J. Weiss, *Explaining the Shadow Economy in Europe: Size, Causes and Policy Options*, International Monetary Fund Working Papers WP/19/278, November 2019, pp. 25–26.
31. *See* European Parliament, *Tax collection in Greece: State of play – June 2018*, PE 614.518, 19 Jun. 2018, at: https://www.europarl.europa.eu/RegData/etudes/IDAN/2018/614518/IPOL_IDA(2018)614518_EN.pdf.
32. *See* 'OECD chief: The only Grexit is from the bailout', *Euractiv*, 30 Apr. 2018, at: https://www.euractiv.com/section/economy-jobs/news/oecd-chief-the-only-grexit-is-from-the-bailout/.

a method to generate additional tax revenue and supplement the often depleted State coffers and/or to mitigate disproportionately harsh sanctions for alleged tax offences.[33] Only some of these tax amnesties have been successful, and these are principally because their terms were very generous to tax-liable individuals and entities.[34] While tax evasion and the underground economy are invariably viewed as socio-economic problems,[35] they also pose significant challenges to the criminal justice system. If the adopted criminal law initiatives to curb them prove to be ineffective or happen to be 'too little too late' or lack active implementation (from the stage of prosecution of the alleged tax evaders to the stage of forceful execution of the criminal sanctions ordered, including the sequestration of tainted property of the convicted persons), the effects will be felt by the national economy. In addition, they will shake even more the average citizen's trust to the domestic criminal justice system and, more generally, to the rule of law.[36]

Anecdotal evidence shows that Greek citizens are very wary of State institutions and question whether they are able and willing to fight large-scale economic crime promptly and effectively. Presently, there is a National Strategic Plan for Combating Corruption, whose implementation covers a period of three years (July 2018 to July 2021), and which has the benefit of the aims and action of the previous Strategic Plan that ran between 2015 and 2018. At an institutional level, in August 2019 a new entity was created, the National Transparency Authority (NTA), pursuant to Act 4622/2019,[37] which was formed by amalgamating six relevant entities, namely the General Inspector of Public Administration, the General Secretariat for the Fight against Corruption, the Body of Inspectors for Health and Welfare Services, the Body of Inspectors of Public Works, the Body of Inspectors – Controllers of Public Administration and the Body of Inspectors – Controllers for Transports. According to its first annual report, the NTA is a modern and innovative public organization, which strives, *inter alia*, to restore citizens' trust in institutions.[38] In recent years, its

---

33. *See* e.g., Arts 57–61 of Act 4446/2016, which concerned the 'voluntary disclosure of taxable information of past years', FEK 2016 A' 240. While it used to be the case that Acts of Parliament dealt with and regulated a specific subject matter, since 2010 a trend has developed whereby the same Act regulates issues that are unrelated to each other. Thus, Act 4446/2016 also dealt with the Bankruptcy Code, the Code of Administrative Procedure, the Code of Criminal Procedure, electronic transactions, etc.
34. *See* generally, V. Argyropoulou, '"Coming in from the Cold" The Latest Tax Amnesty in Greece and Lessons for the Future' (2018) 24 *University of California, Davies Journal of International Law and Policy* 125–134.
35. *See* G.L. Vousinas, 'Shadow Economy and Tax Evasion. The Achilles Heel of Greek Economy. Determinants, Effects and Policy Proposals' (2017) 20 *Journal of Money Laundering Control* 386–404.
36. Tax morale and the rule of law have been identified as two of the important determinants of Greece's shadow economy, *see* A. Bitzenis, V. Vlachos & F. Schneider, 'An Exploration of the Greek Shadow Economy: Can Its Transfer into the Official Economy Provide Economic Relief Amid the Crisis?' (2016) 50 *Journal of Economic Issues* 165–196. *See* further the project on 'Rule of Law and State Reform in Greece', which was carried out at the Max Planck Institute for Comparative Public Law and International Law, at: https://www.mpil.de/de/pub/forschung/archiv/rule-of-law-and-state-reform.cfm.
37. FEK 2019 A' 133.
38. *See* National Transparency Authority, *Annual Report 2019*, 14, at: https://aead.gr/images/essays/ANNUAL_REPORT_18.09.2020_ENGLISH_VERSION_FINAL.pdf.

principal activities concerned the supervision of the anti-smoking legislation and the measures taken vis-à-vis the COVID-19 pandemic. Finally, Greece has ratified the Agreement for the Establishment of the International Anti-Corruption Academy as an International Organization, which was signed in Vienna, Austria, on 2 September 2010.[39]

## §2. Criminal Law, Criminal Justice and Criminal Science

### I. Definitions of Criminal Law

#### *A. Criminal Law*

*15.* In line with several other European continental legal systems, in Greek law, criminal law is defined as a branch of public law, which deals, on the one hand, with the commission of criminal offences and, on the other hand, with the institution of criminal proceedings against the alleged perpetrators. The ultimate aim is to inflict on the convicted offender an array of appropriate measures of a punitive nature (criminal sanctions), which, depending on the nature of the offence committed, may also include security measures.

The fact that criminal law is considered to be part of public law stems from the idea that its rules are not concerned with regulating the relations between the individuals concerned (i.e., the perpetrator and the victim) but with the duty that the State imposes upon the perpetrator to repair the damage he has inflicted upon society by committing the offence which is attributable to him. To put it otherwise, criminal law is a compendium of compulsory and binding legal provisions regulating the relations between the State and those individuals (or natural persons),[40] who have allegedly committed one or more criminal offences and who are later convicted by a duly constituted criminal court of justice for having carried them out. As it is alleged that the perpetrator has, without good cause, broken the equilibrium with the State and has caused a rift in the society at large, the State is empowered to investigate the allegations, and, if they are proven to be true, to pronounce his guilt and to impose appropriate and proportionate sanctions. The latter could have different aims and purposes and could serve different needs. Thus, they may not only seek to punish the perpetrator, or to repair the rift in the society, but also to act as deterrent to other individuals, who might have considered or may consider in the future to commit the same or similar offences. Generally speaking, the taking of these measures aims, *inter alia*, at showing to the public at large that 'crime does not pay', to use the Victorian era adage in Great Britain. Any organized society as well as the institutions that impose its norms and rules would, undoubtedly, prefer to avert criminal conduct in all its manifestations, even if the perpetrators are absolutely willing to accept the full consequences of their criminal acts.

39. Ratified under Act 4287/2014, FEK 2014 A' 198.
40. Note that by using the term 'individuals' and 'people' one means the whole population residing at any given moment in the Greek territory, namely citizens as well as aliens, who may be in legal residence or in illegal residence, asylum seekers, etc.

Even though this is a perfectly acceptable equation (whoever has broken the rules assumes full responsibility for the offending action and suffers without protestation the threatened sanctions), organized societies prefer that the life, the work and the behaviour of the populace are based on morality and on the principles and ideals which have over time developed and approved by the society. Indeed, moral values have preceded the adoption of criminal legislation. Even today, the moral standards accepted by the society at large define to a large extent the content of the criminal statutes and determine which offences should be abolished and which acts/behaviour should be criminalized. The fundamentally moral nature of criminal law has been emphasized in literature.[41] Even though the words 'criminal' and 'immoral' are not always synonymous, it should be accepted that all criminal acts involve, depending each time on the applicable circumstances, a larger or smaller degree of immorality. Alternatively, an immoral act or behaviour does not always constitute the commission of a criminal offence. As has been argued, people 'refrain from conduct for the moral reasons that make it wrong, without reference to the fact that the conduct is criminal'.[42]

*16.* The existence and application of criminal law does not mean that individuals, legally incorporated persons, companies, undertakings, etc., are deprived of other legal means to redress offenders. These means are primarily contained in the Civil Code (CC) and, more particularly, in Book II (Law of Contract), Chapter Thirty-Nine ('Unlawful Acts', Articles 914–938). The definition of unlawful acts (which are akin to the German *unerlaubte Handlungen*, to the Anglo-Saxon notion of *tort* and *tortious acts*, and to the Latin notion of *delictum*) is given in Article 914: 'Whoever, acting culpably and in contravention of the law, causes damage to a third person, is obliged to offer restitution (reparation) to such third person.' One could thus talk of civil, as opposed to criminal, offences. A fundamental difference between criminal offences and unlawful acts is the nature of the means of redress to which, on the one hand, the State and, on the other hand, the victim of the offence are entitled to. Whereas in the former case, the State has the power to impose measures of a punitive nature (depending on the circumstances these could take the form of imprisonment, confinement in a penitentiary, pecuniary sanctions, etc.), in the latter case, natural and legal persons are endowed with the right to demand restitution (reparation), which usually takes the form of monetary compensation.[43]

This difference could be explained as follows: The taking of measures of a punitive nature (including criminal sanctions) is the exercise of a specific power, of a

---

41. *See*, *inter alia*, A.W. Mewett, 'Morality and the Criminal Law' (1962) 14 *The University of Toronto Law Journal* 213–228; N. Walker, 'Morality and the Criminal Law' (1964) 11 *The Howard Journal of Criminal Justice* 209–219; and, more recently, A. Duff et al., *Criminalization: The Political Morality of the Criminal Law*, Oxford: Oxford University Press, 2014.
42. *See* J. Edwards, 'Theories of Criminal Law', *The Stanford Encyclopedia of Philosophy*, Winter 2019 Edition, at: https://plato.stanford.edu/archives/win2019/entries/criminal-law/.
43. Generally, *see* S. Alexiadis, 'Victim Offender Reconciliation Schemes in the Greek Justice System' in H. Messmer & H.-U. Otto (eds), *Restorative Justice on Trial: Pitfalls and Potentials of Victim-Offender Mediation – International Research Perspectives*, NATO Science Series D, Vol. 64, 1992, pp. 309–316.

given authority which is held by the State and is exercised by its properly constituted organs. According to Article 1(3) of the Constitution, which is a manifestation of a genuine, Western style, democracy, all powers emanate from the people, exist for the welfare of the people and that of the Greek Nation, and may only be exercised as the Constitution itself dictates. When it comes to punitive measures and criminal sanctions, Article 96(1) of the Constitution stipulates that the punishment for having committed a criminal offence as well as the ordering of all measures envisaged in the criminal statutes shall be entrusted to the ordinary criminal courts. Thus, the Constitution, by transferring said powers to criminal courts, prevents and prohibits individuals from inflicting punitive measures themselves upon other individuals, even if the latter happen to be (criminal) offenders. It is in this way that the Constitution prevents not only arbitrary punishment but also situations which could compromise the rule of law. The victims of offences must entrust the resolution of their conflict with the alleged offenders to the criminal courts. The Constitution strictly forbids them to resolve any such dispute by themselves. In other words, they are prohibited from taking the law into their own hands. If they happen to do so, they would have committed an offence themselves and will be prosecuted. Generally speaking, the alleged victims of a criminal act have two options on how to react: they could entrust the resolution of the conflict to the State and its competent organs (namely, the criminal courts) and also seek themselves to be awarded restitution/satisfaction by the court of justice competent to hear civil actions.

### *B. Substantive Criminal Law*

*17.* The term 'substantive criminal law' covers what most people refer to as 'criminal law'. It could be understood as the totality of mandatory legal rules which are laid down by the State to determine which human acts or omissions (behaviour) are of criminal interest and which punishment (punitive measures/sanctions) should be inflicted on the (convicted) offender, under which conditions, and subject to which exceptions and limitations. These mandatory rules are primarily to be found in the Penal Code but also in the various special criminal statutes.

### *C. Criminal Procedure*

*18.* The existence of substantive criminal law alone does not lead to the imposition of sanctions on the convicted perpetrator. That is so because, although the substantive criminal law does stipulate the nature of the sanctions to be inflicted and their severity, it does not entail the relevant procedures to be applied. To put it otherwise, substantive criminal law is concerned with the theoretical but not with the practical aspects of dealing with the commission of (criminal) offences, which are, by definition, of a procedural. As Greek law subscribes to the codification of legal rules, norms and processes, it is the CCP which contains the relevant regulations. In effect, it is in this Code that all stages following the commission of an offence are laid, namely the investigation of the facts surrounding the commission of the offence, the prosecution of the alleged perpetrator and the trial against him/her. And should the latter be convicted, the CCP lays down the rules pertaining to the infliction of penal sanctions, the right of appeal and the procedure for cassation.

### D. *Criminal Offences*

*19.* This term denotes those manifestations of human activity (acts) or those omissions which the State has determined that they constitute attacks against society at large or threaten its equilibrium and, for this reason, envisages the imposition of criminal sanctions against the perpetrators. As is later explained (*infra* paragraph 173), the Penal Code has categorized criminal acts into misdemeanours and serious crimes. The Penal Code avoids using these terms unless this is dictated for the clarity of the provision. On the contrary, it sets out the objective constitutive elements of each and every criminal act and threatens a specific sanction, the severity of which denotes whether the State regards it as a misdemeanour or a serious crime.

The definition of 'criminal offence' is given in Article 14(1) of the Penal Code as follows: 'Crime is an act, which is unlawful and attributable to the perpetrator and punishable by law'. Since this definition breaks down the term 'crime' into two elements (unlawfulness and culpability), whenever the Penal Code (only rarely it must be said) refers to 'crime', the term is used with a specific and technical meaning. Admittedly, this meaning does not always correspond to the term 'criminal offence', which, however, is used in this monograph to denote the act of committing a specific offence.

## II. The New Penal Code: Characteristics of Greek Criminal Law

*20.* On 11 June 2019, a new Penal Code was promulgated and came into effect on 1 July 2019.[44] On the same day, a new CCP was promulgated;[45] its analysis is to be found in Part II of this monograph. The overhaul of the old Penal Code, which was originally promulgated in the 1950s and had been revised on far too many occasions, proved to be a rather tedious and cumbersome process. Not all sectors in the Greek society were happy with the final draft. They considered it to reflect in some respects the ideological orientation of the regime then in power (a coalition government between a left/far-left party (*Synaspismos Rizospastikis Aristeras*) and a right/far-right party (*Aneksartitoi Ellines*)). The fact that the new Penal Code was promulgated on the very same day that the Parliament was dissolved for the July

44. Under Act 4619/2019, FEK 2019 A' 95. For highly critical comments on some of its basic institutions and provisions alongside a comparison with the German Penal Code, *see* K. Vathiotis, 'Konvergenzen und Divergenzen zwischen dem neuen griechischen StGB und dem deutschen StGB im Bereich der Strafrechtsdogmatik' (2019) 131 *Zeitschrift für die gesamte Strafrechtswissenschaft* 1205–1227.
45. Under Act 4620/2019, FEK 2019 A' 96.

2019 general elections to take place,[46] contributed to its being regarded as quite controversial. *Nea Dimokratia*, the main opposition party in Parliament before the 2019 snap general elections, vowed to overturn various provisions of the new Penal Code if it were elected government. In the new Parliament, whose inaugural session took place on 17 July 2019, *Nea Demokratia* enjoyed a majority of members and, faithful to its pre-election promises, it promptly commenced the procedure for amending the Penal Code which had entered into force only sixteen days earlier. Act 4623/2019, which was adopted in August 2019,[47] brought about some significant changes to the new Penal Code. Thus, it suspended the operation of those provisions which stipulate the imposition of community service as one of the primary criminal sanctions due to the lack of proper infrastructure, while, in those misdemeanours, where the ordering of community service is the only sanction envisaged, it substituted it with the imposition of a monetary penalty.

Further changes to the new Penal Code were made in November 2019 under Act 4637/2019.[48] It amounted to a mini revision of the new Penal Code given that the text of almost thirty provisions was amended, often significantly. Arguably, most of the amendments did not concern improvements to the text of the new Penal Code, which were considered necessary because several legal gaps had been revealed. Rather, they reflected the quite different stance that, compared to the previous regime, the new government had on many political and societal matters. Notwithstanding that in a democratic country, a new government is within its rights to undo legislative initiatives of the previous government, the Penal Code should be considered a legislative text of such importance that its content should remain stable and change whenever imperative developments require it and not revised to accommodate the dogma of the one or the other political party. Otherwise, the rule of law cannot but suffer and, if the rule of law is undermined, democracy and the enjoyment of human rights and fundamental freedoms will suffer as a result.

The new Penal Code and the new CCP have not been translated into any foreign languages. Generally speaking, Greek authorities only seldom translate domestic legislative instruments. A very good translation of the old Penal Code in English was published in 2017, preceded by an informative introduction.[49] It is still a useful publication, but readers should be warned that the new Penal Code differs considerably from the version used for the translation.

---

46. Under Presidential Decree 56/2019, FEK 2019 A' 97. It should be noted that the President of the Republic could have postponed the promulgation of the new Penal Code until after the general election.
47. Act 4623/2019 of 9 Aug. 2019, Regulations of the Ministry of Interior, provisions on digital governance, pension arrangements and other urgent issues, FEK 2019 A' 134. The changes to the Penal Code are to be found under the 'other urgent issues' provisions (Arts 95 et seq. of Act 4623/2019).
48. Act 4637/2019 of 18 Nov. 2019, Amendments to the Penal Code, the Code of Criminal Procedure and related provisions, FEK 2019 A' 180. Further changes were made under Acts 4855/2021, 4871/2021, 4947/2022, 5002/2022 and 5039/2023.
49. E. Billis (ed.), *The Greek Penal Code*, English translation by V. Chalkiadaki and E. Billis, Berlin: Duncker & Humblot, 2017.

*21.* Was it necessary to have gone through this revision process or could the old Penal Code have been modernized by adopting targeted amendments? The Explanatory Memorandum, which accompanied the draft new Penal Code when it was introduced to Parliament, was adamant that a new one was required. It gave the following reasons:

> During the period of this validity, the Penal Code has received far too many amendments in order either to regulate new circumstances or to implement a criminal justice policy on the basis of circumstantial incidents. [Greek criminal law theorists were] concerned by certain changes, which were apparently adopted as urgent legislative interventions but without being harmonized with the general principles of the Penal Code. The same is true as regards the adoption of analogous stipulations by virtue of special laws. Especially following the distinctive influence that the Constitution of 1975 has had upon the legal system, it was obvious that the Penal Code was in need of a fundamental modernization but also of an 'ideological discolouration' in order to conform both to a contemporary criminal justice policy but also to protect citizens[50] from the abuse of criminal suppression and the application of the principle of the rule of law ... Thus, in parallel to maintaining the democratic and liberal characteristics of the Penal Code, it was necessary to rationalize and to renew it for the purpose of reflecting the needs of a contemporary social rule of law and the challenges that it faces. The latter made it imperative to construe a system of criminal sanctions, which reflects the contemporary beliefs on punishment, to abolish offences, which do not protect existing and important public goods for the society at large, to rehabilitate [the principle] of proportionality, which was often breached through ad hoc amendments, ... and, to the extent possible, to perfect the Penal Code from a legislative point of view.

Moreover, the Explanatory Memorandum laid down the basic principles, which should guide the interpretation and application of the new Penal Code and, by necessary implication, the criminal law system as a whole, including the CCP. There are eleven such principles, most of which reflect rights and obligations which are stipulated in and secured by the Constitution: (a) the principle of the legality of crime and punishment;[51] (b) the principle of the respect and protection of the value of human beings;[52] (c) the principle of proportionality; (d) the principle of culpability; (e) the principle of democracy; (f) the liberal principle; (g) the principle of

---

50. It was probably wrong to refer only to 'citizens' because the Greek Constitution makes it rather clear that the rule of law applies to whomever resides within the territory of the country at any given moment. Moreover, the question of the application of criminal law upon aliens but also the protection that criminal law as well as the associated human rights norms offer to aliens should be expressly addressed by the legislator, especially given the not insignificant number of third-country nationals living in Greece with often an illegal/irregular status. Presumably, these are issues to be dealt with by the legislator and not left to the courts to decide on a case to case basis.
51. *See* Art. 7(1) of the Constitution. *See* further Art. 5(3) of the Constitution: 'Personal liberty is inviolable. No one shall be prosecuted, arrested, imprisoned or otherwise confined except when and as the law provides'.
52. *See* Art. 2(1) of the Constitution: 'The respect and the protection of the value of human beings constitute the primary obligation of the State'.

equality;[53] (h) the principle of the social state;[54] (i) the principle of leniency; (j) the principle of the subsidiary nature of criminal law; and (k) the principle of the rule of law.[55]

As it will become apparent by reading this part of the monograph, in the new Penal Code a score of provisions, including whole Chapters, were abrogated or merged. However, the provisions in the new Penal Code were not renumbered to reflect this state of affairs. Consequently, there is no continuity in the numbering of the provisions currently in force, e.g., the provision following Article 191A is Article 207, and the one following Article 397 is Article 404. The decision to maintain the numbering of the provisions of the old Penal Code was made in an effort to facilitate the transition to the new regime and to ensure continuity in case law and legal doctrine.

*22.* Before examining some particular characteristics of the Greek criminal law, it is instructive to mention that, even though the Penal Code uses terms and words which have a specific (legal) meaning and content, when it sets out the principal rules of criminal law or when it describes the constitutive elements of criminal acts it also uses everyday words and terms (jargon) from other disciplines. It follows that there is a need for the Penal Code to offer suitable definitions for the latter. The relevant provision on definitions, Article 13, lays down the definition of only seven terms: civil servant (state employee/officer); relative/next of kin; document; bodily/physical violence; commission of offences by profession; information system; and digital data. Several of these terms are elaborated later in this monograph. However, on an ad hoc basis the text of the Penal Code gives the definition of certain criminal acts or the content of legal terms having a special meaning in its context. Suffice it to mention Article 310, which defines the offence of severe bodily harm, Article 322, which offers the definition of abduction (kidnapping), and Article 149, which defines the term 'state secret'.

*23.* The Greek Penal Code envisages two separate types of criminal sanctions: (a) punishment in the form of punitive measures/penalties; and (b) security measures. The former constitutes the principal type of criminal sanctions, whereas the latter operates as a substitute to or as complimentary measure. Security measures have two specific aims. The first is to substitute punitive measures when, for several reasons, penalties may not or cannot be inflicted on the offender. The second is to complement punitive measures, when the personality of the offender renders the punitive measures imperative (e.g., a drug addict or an alcoholic).

*24.* In certain cases, the Penal Code endows the sentencing court of justice with a considerable margin of appreciation to decide whether they should relieve the offender of all criminal sanctions. Thus, in the offence of bodily injuries, the court

53. *See* Art. 4(1) of the Constitution: 'Greeks are equal before the law, and Art. 4(2) thereof: 'Greek men and women have equal rights and obligations'.
54. *See* Art. 25(1) of the Constitution: ' … the social rule of law is under the guarantee of the State'.
55. *Ibid.*

may not punish the offender, if the court is convinced that he acted out of 'justifiable indignation' on account of an act, which had been committed by the victim against the offender or before him just before the latter perpetrated the offence and which act was particularly cruel or harsh (Article 308(4)). And, if the bodily injuries were suffered with the consent of the victim and the very act of inflicting them does not contradict *bonos mores*, the illegal nature of the offence shall be negated (Article 308(3)). Equally, in the offences of minor theft, minor embezzlement or minor fraud, the court has the discretion not to punish the offender, if he acted out of a pressing and immediate need to use or consume what was stolen, acquired by fraud, or embezzled (Article 377 and Article 387). In these cases, the offences committed retain their criminal nature, but the Penal Code confers upon the sentencing court the discretion not to impose the threatened punishment (*in casu*, payment of a monetary penalty or provision of a community service). However, this margin of appreciation does not extend to the Public Prosecutor, who is obliged to bring the case before the competent criminal court and let it decide whether discretion should be exercised or not.

## III. Overview of the Criminal Justice System

### A. *The Police*

*25.* Unlike other European countries, in Greece there is a unified police force, which is called the Hellenic Police. There used to be two separate police forces, one responsible for large cities (Urban Police) and the other for the countryside (Gendarmerie) but they were amalgamated in 1984. According to Act 2800/2000, the Hellenic Police are a law enforcement agency responsible, *inter alia*, for preventing the commission of criminal offences, investigating the commission of offences, apprehending alleged offenders, restoring law and order, etc. However, the Hellenic Police have also been entrusted with the following activities and functions: serving criminal court judgments and orders to appear before criminal courts, keeping order during sports events and other athletic games, guarding politicians, VIPs, and other persons of interest, issuing national identity cards and passports, etc. These side-tasks take up considerable human resources, which presently are only ill afforded. In 2000, a Directorate of Internal Affairs commenced its operation under Act 2713/1999. More recently, the Hellenic Police Intelligence Division (HPiD) was established to serve as the central intelligence hub, especially as regards the perpetration of serious crimes, organized crime as well as terrorist activities.[56]

### B. *The Prosecution Service*

*26.* *See infra* at paragraphs 344 et seq.

56. Under Act 4249/2014 (FEK 2014 A' 73), as amended by Art. 231 of Act 4281/2014 (FEK 2014 A' 160). HPiD operates pursuant to the regulations of Art. 27 of Presidential Decree 178/2014 (FEK 2014 A' 281).

### C. *Investigating Judges and Judicial Councils*

*27.* *See infra* at paragraphs 422 et seq. and 323 et seq.

### D. *Trial Courts*

*28.* *See infra* at paragraphs 311 et seq.

### E. *The Penitentiary System*

*29.* *See infra* at paragraphs 549 et seq.

### F. *The Bar*

*30.* Greece does not have a unitary system of Bar Associations. Currently, there are 63 Bar Associations. As a rule, the capital of each (of the old) prefectures is the seat of a Bar Association. To practice law in Greece, one must first become a member of one of the Bar Associations. He then possesses the title of 'lawyer'/'attorney at law'. According to Article 1 of the Code of Lawyers, attorneys at law have a legal status of freelance public officers.[57] This also explains the fact that, before being able to offer his services as a lawyer, one must already have been appointed as an attorney at law by virtue of a decision signed by the Minister of Justice and published in the Official Gazette. The possession of a law degree, even a higher (postgraduate) law degree, does neither confer the right to practice law as a legal professional nor to use the title of 'lawyer'. One must first become an apprentice lawyer for a period of eighteen months, then pass successfully written public exams (there used to be oral exams as well) and, finally, be admitted to a Bar Association. Apprentice lawyers do not enjoy any specific privileges and, as a rule, may not appear before courts on their own.

When one is first admitted to a Bar Association, one may appear only before Justices of the Peace and the Courts of First Instance, whether civil, criminal or administrative. When at least four years have lapsed and provided that he has made enough court appearances, he may apply to become an 'Appeal Lawyer'. This gives him the right to appear before all courts, except for highest courts of the land, namely the Supreme Civil and Criminal Court (*Areios Pagos*), the Supreme Administrative Court (*Conseil d'état*), the Court of Auditors, and the Supreme Special Court. To this end, one must spend at least four more years and apply to become a so-called *Areios Pagos* Lawyer, i.e., an attorney at law who has the power to appear before the highest courts. This division of lawyers according to seniority aims at protecting clients from having inexperienced lawyers handling their cases.

57. The Code was promulgated as Act 4194/2013 (FEK 2013 A' 208) and was lastly amended under Act 4745/2020 (FEK 2020 A' 214). The previous Code had been adopted in the 1950s (Legislative Decree 3026/1954).

Another restriction, prohibiting attorneys at law to practice law and to appear before courts of justice which were located in the territory of another Bar Association, was abolished as part of the package of measures imposed by Greece's creditors during the aforementioned debt crisis of the 2010s. These measures were meant to loosen up the strict regulation that characterized certain professions in Greece, including that of attorneys at law.

## §3. Historical Background

*31.* Greece has a very long and distinguished history, even though the modern Greek State has a history of less than 200 years. It was established as an independent State in 1830[58] after a ten-year Liberation War (or War of Independence) against the Ottoman Empire. Greece's long and distinguished history is usually broken down into five epochs: Ancient Greece; the Roman period; the Byzantine era; the Ottoman Empire period; and Modern Greece. Greek legal history could be traced as far back as the writings of Homer (Iliad and Odyssey) around the eighth century B.C.[59] In subsequent periods, the legal systems in place were that of the Greek cities-states,[60] while in the case of the Roman period and the Ottoman period that of the conqueror. The names of famous legislators from Ancient Greece have survived to this day, e.g., Solon and Dracon (the term 'draconian law' is named after him). As regards the Byzantine era, which historically largely coincided with the Middle Ages in the West, the legal system was a continuation and development of Roman law with many inputs from the civilization that flourished in Byzantium (with Constantinople as its capital city) and the eventual use of the Greek language by the judiciary, the executive and the legislative.[61]

*32.* During the War of Independence, which broke out in March 1821, the representatives of revolted Greeks adopted three constitutional texts, whose provisions and political system were meant to apply to those regions that would be liberated from the Ottoman Empire. The most developed was the so-called Political Constitution of Greece. It was approved in May 1827, five months before the famous naval

58. *See* Protocole (No. 1) tenu à Londres le 3 Février 1830, relatif a l'indépendance de la Grèce. It was concluded between Russia, France and Great Britain. According to Art. 5 of the Protocol, both the Sublime Porte (Ottoman Porte) and the Greek government were obliged to issue acts of amnesty for the respective population. *See also*, Arrangement between Great Britain, France, Russia, and Turkey for the Definitive Settlement of the Continental Limits of Greece, signed in Constantinople on 21 Jul. 1832.
59. Generally, *see* M. Gagarin, *Early Greek Law*, University of California Press, 1989.
60. *See, inter alia*, A. Biscardi, *Diritto Greco Antico*, Milan: Giufrre, 1982, Ch. VIII; M. Gagarin & D. Cohen (eds), The Cambridge Companion to Ancient Greek Law, Cambridge: Cambridge University Press, 2005; P.J. Perlman (ed.), *Ancient Greek Law in the 21st Century. Ashley and Peter Larkin Endowment in Greek and Roman Culture*. Austin: University of Texas Press, 2018.
61. *See* Z. Chitwood, *Byzantine Legal Culture and the Roman Legal Tradition, 867–1056*, Cambridge: Cambridge University Press, 2017; B.H. Stolte, 'The Law of New Rome: Byzantine Law' in D. Johnston (ed.), *The Cambridge Companion to Roman Law*, Cambridge: Cambridge University Press, 2015, 355–373; B.H. Stolte, 'Not New but Novel. Notes on the Historiography of Byzantine Law', *Byzantine and Modern Greek Studies* 22 (1998) 264–279.

Battle of Navarino. The Constitution of Troizina, as it is better known, was one of the most liberal constitutional texts of the first half of the nineteenth century. It was, among others, influenced by the French Declaration of the Rights of Man and Citizen (1789). In some respects, it was more progressive than the contemporary Constitution of Belgium which was promulgated in February 1831. For example, it prohibited slavery, it banned the trade in slaves and it provided that whoever was regarded as a slave or was bought as a slave was a free person as soon as he stepped onto Greek soil, regardless of gender and religion. Because of its liberal and democratic content, the Constitution of Troizina contained several legal principles and norms, which later became the cornerstones of criminal law and criminal procedure all over the world.[62] In particular, the following principles were included: personal freedom is guaranteed; no one may be prosecuted unless envisaged in the legislation; no one may be arrested unless there was an arrest warrant issued by a judge; no one shall be deprived of the competent judge, he being the judge provided for in the legislation; no penalty shall be imposed and executed but only as prescribed by law; the retroactive application of legislation is prohibited; and, finally, the accused is always considered innocent (presumption of innocence).

*33.* When the modern Greek State was created in the early 1830s, very few of the institutions and organizations that are necessary for a country to function existed (e.g., courts of justice, police force, postal services, financial institutions, etc.). One of the existing institutions was the Greek Eastern Orthodox Church, which for several centuries had been, *inter alia*, involved in the settlement of certain disputes through the operation of ecclesiastical courts. Moreover, the new State had no Constitution (the first Constitution was promulgated in 1844). Arguably, this was against the wishes of the population for whom the Constitution signified the embodiment of sovereignty. The following abstract from the Preamble of the Constitution of Troizina is characteristic: '… the Greek nation declares before God and men its political existence and independence and [through this Constitution] introduces the fundamental principles of its polity'. The new State also lacked written legislation. For obvious reasons, the legal system of the Ottoman Empire could not continue to apply, since the Byzantine law of the pre-Ottoman conquest era (mid-15th century AD) was outdated and fragmented.

Since the early eighteenth century, legal science in Continental Europe had promoted the concept of codes and codification, namely statutes which would not regulate specific issues or a range of associated issues but would deal with a field of law in its entirety. The (mostly foreign) jurists who were entrusted with formulating the legislation for the modern Greek State were strongly influenced by the concept of codes as legal rules and institutions grouped together in a rational manner. As regards specifically criminal law, the first Greek Penal Code was promulgated in January 1834 during the reign of Otto of Wittelsbach, Prince of Bavaria and King

62. For example, the prohibition of the non-retroactivity of criminal law, the principle that no one shall be deprived of his natural judge, the principle that no one shall be arrested without a prior order issued by a judge; generally, *see* K. Magliveras, 'The Protection of Human Rights in the Constitution of Troizina and the Constitution of Belgium of 1831: A First Comparative Analysis' in S. Perrakis (editor), *Rencontres Internationales de Nafplion*, XVI Period 2021, Athens: I. Sideris Publishers, 2022, 185–196.

of the Hellenes. It was drafted in German by Georg Ludwig von Maurer, a Bavarian jurist, on the basis of the Bavarian Penal Code of 1813, as it had been amended in 1822, in 1827, and in 1831. Afterwards, it was translated into Greek and was published in the Official Gazette in both Greek and German (as was at the time the case with all statutes). However, two years later it was decreed that only the Greek text, as had in the meantime been revised, will apply.

As regards the CCP, it was also prepared by von Maurer and followed the principles of French and Bavarian criminal procedure. It was published in March 1834 and entered into force in January 1835. Before the CCP, the so-called Organisation of Courts of Justice and Notaries Public had been published in February 1834. It followed the relevant French legislation in force at the time (Loi du 20 avril 1810 relative à l'organisation de l'ordre judiciaire et l'administration de la justice), and it established the following court structure (in ascending line): Justices of the Peace, Courts of First Instance, Appeal Courts and a Supreme Court of Justice (cour de cassation), which was named 'Areios Pagos' after the *Areios Pagos* of the antiquity, namely a rocky place near the Acropolis of Athens, where a body of nine rulers of the Athenian city-state met and functioned as a judicial body adjudicating cases of premeditated murder, arson, sacrilege, etc.[63] This court structure has remained unchanged until today.

*34.* The 1834/1836 Penal Code underwent many amendments and, by 1910, it had become obvious that a new Code had to be drafted. The following year, a three-member legislative committee was appointed to perform this task. However, it proved to be a difficult task. Finally, a new Penal Code was issued forty years later with Act 1492/1950. Thus, the 1834/1836 Penal Code had a life span that exceeded 110 years. Together with the Penal Code, a new CCP was adopted (Act 1493/1950), which was based on the draft that had been finalized before Second World War, in 1934. Both these Codes had been written in the so-called Katharevousa language, which was conceived in the late eighteenth century as a form of simplified Ancient Greek that took into consideration the language spoken by the people (the so-called Demotic Greek or Dimotiki). Until 1976, when 'Dimotiki' became by law the official language of the country, 'Katharevousa' was used in Acts of Parliament, in court judgments, and, generally, in official and public sector documents. The 1950 Penal Code, as had in the meantime been amended, was published in 'Dimotiki' in 1985,[64] while the CCP in 1986.[65]

## §4. Sources of Criminal Law, Classifications and Techniques of Criminal Law

*35.* There are in total six domestic and international sources of criminal law in Greece. Three of them are classified as domestic sources (the Constitution, the Penal

63. *See* The Kosmos Society, *Law and Courts in Ancient Athens: A Brief Overview*, 20 Sep. 2018, at: https://kosmossociety.chs.harvard.edu/law-and-courts-in-ancient-athens-a-brief-overview/.
64. Under Presidential Decree 283/1985, FEK 1985 A' 106.
65. Under Presidential Decree 258/1986, FEK 1986 A' 121.

Code, the CCP, and the Special Penal Statutes) and three as international sources (international agreements, treaties and conventions, European Union legislation, and decisions of international organizations). The various techniques are explained when examining the relevant sources.

## I. The Constitution

*36.* The Constitution of 1975, as amended and presently in force.[66] The relevant provisions are principally to be found in Part II of the Constitution, which sets out the various civil and social rights enjoyed by the population. The State must guarantee and protect them and, where necessary, promote them. In particular, these provisions are (in the order of appearance): Article 5A (all persons have the right to information, as specified by law); Article 6 (no one shall be arrested or detained without a justified arrest warrant, issued by a court of justice and served at the time of arrest or detention – the maximum duration of pre-trial detention may not exceed specific limits); Article 7 (there is no crime and no penalty shall be imposed without a law that was in force before the act was committed – torture, any physical injury, harm to health, or exercise of psychological violence, as well as any other insult to human dignity are prohibited and punishable – those who were convicted, detained or otherwise deprived of their personal liberty unjustly or illegally shall be compensated); Article 8 (no one shall be deprived without his will of the judge appointed by law – judicial commissions and extraordinary courts, by any name, may never be established); Article 9 (the individual's private and family life is inviolable – searches in a residence may not be carried out, except when and as prescribed by law and always in the presence of members of the judiciary); Article 9A (all persons have the right to be protected from the collection, processing and use, especially by electronic means, of their personal data, as specified by law); Article 19 (the privacy of letters and the freedom to respond or communicate in any other way is absolutely inviolable – judicial authorities must observe secrecy and are not bound by it only for reasons of national security or for the investigation of particularly serious offences); Article 20 (everyone has the right to the provision of legal protection by the courts of justice). Most of these provisions are also included and elaborated in the Penal Code, the CCP, and other criminal statutes.

Other relevant provisions can be found in:

(a) Section B of Part III of the Constitution, e.g., Article 47 stipulating that the President of the Republic has the right to pardon, convert or mitigate the sentences imposed by the courts, while amnesty may be granted only for political offences and never for common offences crimes and Articles 49 and 50 on the special responsibility of the President of the Republic.

66. *See* The Constitution of Greece, as revised by the parliamentary resolution of 25 Nov. 2019 of the IXth Revisionary Parliament, at: https://www.hellenicparliament.gr/en/Vouli-ton-Ellinon/To-Politevma/Syntagma/.

(b) Section C of Part III, e.g., Article 60 providing that for as long as a parliamentary term is ongoing, no Member of Parliament shall be prosecuted or arrested or imprisoned or otherwise restricted without the permission of the House.
(c) Section D of Part III, e.g., Article 85 regulating the responsibility of Ministers and Article 86 setting out the procedure for prosecuting members of Government (these cases are adjudicated at first and last instance by a Special Court of Justice).
(d) Section E of Part III regulating the judiciary, especially Articles 93–100A on the organization and jurisdiction of the courts, and Article 97 providing that the ordinary criminal courts are responsible for punishing the perpetration of offences and for taking all measures laid down in criminal laws.

Finally, Article 120, the very last provision of the Constitution, reads as follows:

1. …
2. Respect for the Constitution and for laws that comply with it as well as loyalty to the Motherland and to the Republic are a fundamental obligation of all Hellenes.
3. The usurpation, in any way, of popular sovereignty and the powers that derive from it shall be prosecuted as soon as the legal authority is restored, at which point the statute of limitations for the criminal offence begins.
4. The observance of the Constitution is left to the patriotism of Hellenes, who are entitled and obliged to resist by any means against anyone who attempts to overthrow it by force.

## II. The Penal Code and Code of Criminal Procedure

*37.* The Penal Code of 2019 and the Code of Criminal Procedure of 2019, as presently in force. These Codes are analysed in the present monograph.

## III. Special Penal Statutes

*38.* The Penal Code is not meant to regulate exhaustively all criminal behaviour and to set out the constitutive elements and punishment of all offences. While theoretically speaking, this could have been feasible, it might not have been desirable given that (a) the Penal Code would have to be in a constant process of amendment and revision, and (b) the regulation of certain offences with complex criminal intent (e.g., tax evasion, smuggling, trafficking in narcotics, insider trading) might not have been possible within the confines of the Penal Code, whose provisions need to be concise. The need to regulate criminal behaviour, which is not envisaged in the Penal Code, has been addressed through the adoption of special penal statutes. Sometimes, their purpose is to implement into the Greek legal order the provisions of ratified multilateral treaties of a criminal law nature (e.g., the Rome Statute establishing the ICC (1998))[67] or to comply with EU legislation. It is also the case that, at the same time, a single statute that amends the Penal Code and/or the CCP may also include other provisions which, however, do not form part of either Code. One such example is Act 2929/2001 titled 'Amendment of provisions of the Penal Code and of the Code of Criminal Procedure and other provisions for the protection of citizens from punishable acts of criminal organizations.'[68] It brought changes and introduced new provisions in the Penal Code and the CCP but also regulated other aspects of organized criminality, e.g., the liability of legal persons and enterprises and the protection of witnesses. As far as the latter provisions are concerned, it should be regarded as a special penal statute.

Presently, there are special penal statutes in force which were promulgated more than a century ago, e.g., Act 146/1914 on unfair competition.[69] The Ministry of Justice has never codified them. The thematic areas that they currently regulate include, *inter alia*, the following: aliens; privacy of electronic communications; antiquities/cultural property; personal data; non-prompt payment of salaries; stock exchange offences; smuggling; (human) transplants; narcotics; money laundering; weapons/ammunition/explosives; the environment; bankruptcy offences; racism and hate speech; and tax evasion. Some of the special penal statutes are examined in Chapter 6 of Part I of the present monograph. The provisions of the General Part of the Penal Code apply, *mutatis mutandis*, to all special penal statutes, except if the latter contain different stipulations.

## IV. International Agreements, Treaties and Conventions

*39.* These legal instruments are binding on the Greek legal order when they have been ratified in accordance with the relevant provisions of the Constitution (Articles 28 and 36) and when they have entered into force. Ratified treaties take precedence over conflicting laws, including the Penal Code and the Code of Civil Procedure. Whether they also take precedence over the Constitution is a matter of contention. However, Constitutional provisions should not deliberately go against a ratified treaty. For example, if a future amendment to the Constitution were to negate the presumption of innocence, it should be treated as a direct contravention of Article 6(2) ECHR (1950) and of Article 14(2) ICCPR (1966).[70] Both provisions have the same wording: 'Everyone charged with a criminal offence shall have the right to be presumed innocent until proved guilty according to law.' Greece is a contracting party to most global and regional treaties and conventions pertaining to criminal law. Details on many of them as well as on the Acts of Parliament that have ratified them are given in the present monograph and are not repeated here for reasons of space.

67. Concluded under UN auspices on 17 Jul. 1998, entered into force on 1 Jul. 2002, 2187 *UNTS* 3; (1998) 37 *ILM* 999. Greece ratified it under Act 3003/2002, FEK 2002 A' 75.
68. FEK 2001 A' 141.
69. As lastly amended by Act 3784/2009, FEK 2009 A' 137.
70. Concluded under UNGA auspices on 16 Dec. 1966, entered into force on 23 Mar. 1976, 999 *UNTS* 171. Greece ratified it under Act 2462/1997, FEK 1997 A' 25.

It should be noted that in most instances, Acts of Parliament perform only the purpose of being the so-called instrument of ratification and do not transpose the individual provisions of the ratified treaty into the Greek legal order or do not harmonize the latter with the former or implement the former into the latter. Thus, the actual transposition/harmonization/implementation might require a subsequent Act of Parliament. However, even if such an Act is never promulgated, given that Article 28(1) of the Constitution recognizes that ratified treaties rank higher than statutes, theoretically speaking, any conflicting provisions in the domestic criminal legislation will no longer be valid. The invalidity must be recorded by a judgment rendered by a court of justice. However, the following question arises: if someone has been prosecuted for an offence, whose constitutive elements, pursuant to a ratified treaty, are different from those under the Greek Penal Code/special penal statutes, should the criminal court, on its own initiative, examine the different constitutive elements and give precedence to the ratified treaty or should the accused raise the issue of conflict himself? In theory, the entire domestic legislation must be consistent with all ratified treaties and will all the international obligations that Greece has assumed as a contracting party. Whether this is indeed the case is a matter of contention.

## V. European Union legislation

*40.* Greece became the tenth Member State of the European Economic Community (the predecessor of the EU) on 1 January 1981. All EU legislation – both primary (the Treaty on European Union and the Treaty on the Functioning of the European Union) and secondary – is binding on Greece and takes precedence over conflicting domestic law. The supervision of the compatibility of Greek legislation (including criminal statutes) with EU law (the so-called infringement proceedings) has been entrusted to the European Commission,[71] the EU's executive arm. The finding of infractions has been entrusted to the Court of Justice of the EU. On many occasions, it has found Greece to be in breach of EU law.

Secondary EU law takes the form of either regulations or directives. The former are binding legislative acts and must be applied in their entirety to all (presently twenty-seven) Member States. The latter are legislative acts that set out goals that all Member States must achieve. They must be transposed in the domestic legal systems of the twenty-seven Member States, but it is up to each Member to determine how to reach these goals. It should be noted that the EU does not have a general competence to legislate in the area of criminal law. Criminal law remains within the domain of the Member States. However, the EU is allowed to legislate in those areas where the commission of offences affects or could affect the principal goal of the EU, namely the attainment and the operation of an economic and monetary union (EMU). Thus, Article 83(1) TFEU provides that the European Parliament (EP) and the Council may, by means of directives, establish minimum rules concerning the definition of criminal offences and sanctions in those areas of particularly serious

71. Generally, *see* European Commission, Report from the Commission, *Monitoring the application of European Union law*, 2021 Annual Report, 15 Jul. 2022, COM(2022) 344 final.

crime having a cross-border dimension (i.e., from one Member State to another). Article 83(1) lists these areas as follows: terrorism, trafficking in human beings and sexual exploitation of women and children, illicit drug trafficking, illicit arms trafficking, money laundering, corruption, counterfeiting of means of payment, computer crime and organized crime. The EU considers that criminal law measures are fundamental rights-sensitive and that, unavoidably, they interfere with the individual rights of suspects, victims or witnesses. Therefore, the acts to be adopted must respect fundamental rights and freedoms, as guaranteed in the EU Charter and in the ECHR, as revised and presently in force. References to the latter instruments are made elsewhere in the monograph.

The incorporation of EU legislation into Greek law is regulated in Act 1338/1983, as amended and currently in force. It provides that EU directives are incorporated into national law either by a formal law (an Act of Parliament) or by a regulatory act, namely a presidential decree or a ministerial decision and always within the deadline specified in each directive. As is the case with other legal systems, presidential decrees can be issued only on the basis of an authorizing provision in a statute. Of particular interest is Article 5 of Act 1338/1983, which provides that with the presidential decrees, issued in accordance with Article 4 thereof, offences may be punished as a misdemeanour under the Penal Code as long as this is necessary for the effective implementation of EU acts, provided that the specific offence to be created does not constitute a criminal offence under current Greek legislation. If the relevant offences are to be punished as serious crimes, an Act of Parliament must be promulgated.

To exemplify the above, reference will be made to Act 4689/2020,[72] which transposed into Greek legislation five EU Directives with a criminal law nature, namely Directive 2016/800,[73] Directive 2017/1371,[74] Directive 2017/541,[75] Directive 2016/1919[76] and Directive 2014/57.[77] Additionally, it amended Act 3363/2008 'European Unit of Judicial Co-operation (EUROJUST), Joint Investigation Teams and other provisions'[78] to apply the provisions of Regulation 2018/1727.[79] Act 4689/2020

72. FEK 2020 A' 103.
73. Directive (EU) 2016/800 of the European Parliament and of the Council of 11 May 2016 on procedural safeguards for children who are suspects or accused persons in criminal proceedings, O.J. L 132, 21.5.2016, p. 1.
74. Directive (EU) 2017/1371 of the European Parliament and of the Council of 5 Jul. 2017 on the fight against fraud to the Union's financial interests by means of criminal law, O.J. L 198, 28.7.2017, p. 29.
75. Directive (EU) 2017/541 of the European Parliament and of the Council of 15 Mar. 2017 on combating terrorism and replacing Council Framework Decision 2002/475/JHA and amending Council Decision 2005/671/JHA, O.J. L 88, 31.3.2017, p. 6.
76. Directive (EU) 2016/1919 of the European Parliament and of the Council of 26 Oct. 2016 on legal aid for suspects and accused persons in criminal proceedings and for requested persons in European arrest warrant proceedings, O.J. L 297, 4.11.2016, p. 1.
77. Directive 2014/57/EU of the European Parliament and of the Council of 16 Apr. 2014 on criminal sanctions for market abuse (market abuse directive), O.J. L 173, 12.6.2014, p. 179.
78. FEK 2008 A' 99.
79. Regulation (EU) 2018/1727 of the European Parliament and of the Council of 14 Nov. 2018 on the European Union Agency for Criminal Justice Cooperation (Eurojust), and replacing and repealing Council Decision 2002/187/JHA, O.J. L 295, 21.11.2018, p. 138.

introduces into the Greek legal system several serious crimes, including those envisaged in Article 23. This provision, which implements Directive 2017/1371, stipulates that whoever, during the execution of an organized plan that was carried out in the territory of at least two EU Member States, incurred a loss of value added tax (VAT) resources exceeding EUR 10 million by using false or inaccurate VAT returns or by submitting statements with the purpose of fraudulently concealing the non-payment of VAT, shall be punished with confinement in a penitentiary of at least ten years and a fine of 1,000 daily units. Reference to other EU secondary law instruments is made elsewhere in the present monograph.

## VI. Acts (Decisions) of International Organizations

*41.* Apart from the EU, Greece participates in several other European international organizations as well as in global organizations, namely the United Nations and its Specialized Agencies. In some instances, the acts and the decisions, which are approved by these international organizations, can be binding upon the Greek legal order. This is particularly the case with the UN Security Council when it acts pursuant to Chapter VII of the UN Charter in conjunction with Article 25 thereof. To give an example, Security Council Resolution 1373(2001) decided, *inter alia*, that all States shall prohibit their nationals or any persons and entities within their territories from making any funds, financial assets or economic resources or related services available, directly or indirectly, for the benefit of terrorist organizations or individuals for any purpose, even in the absence of a link to a specific terrorist act.[80] The compulsory application of such UN Security Council decisions (resolutions) is regulated under Compulsory Act 92/1967 and is explained elsewhere in the present monograph.

80. *See also* UNSC Resolution 2368(2017) of 20 Jul. 2017 and Resolution 2462(2019) of 13 Jun. 2019.

# Part I. Substantive Criminal Law

## Chapter 1. General Principles

### §1. The Principle of Legality

#### I. Limitation on Penalization

*42.* In line with criminal tradition in Continental Europe, the principle *nullum crimen nulla poena sine lege* (the principle of legality) is of paramount importance to the Greek criminal law.[81] This principle is enshrined in Article 7(1) of the Constitution, which reads: 'There shall be no crime nor punishment shall be inflicted unless it is provided by a legal statute in force before the commission of the act and defining its constitutive elements. In no case shall punishment be inflicted, which is heavier than what was provided at the time the act was committed.'

This constitutional provision is in line with the principle of legality enshrined in global and regional human rights instruments, e.g., in Article 11(2) of the Universal Declaration of Human Rights (1948),[82] in Article 7 ECHR (1950) and in Article 15(1) ICCPR (1966). More recently, this principle was reaffirmed in Articles 22 and 23 of the Statute of Rome establishing the ICC (1998), and in Article 49 of the EU Charter.[83] Pursuant to Article 28(1) of the Constitution, ratified international conventions, which have entered into force, form an integral part of Greek domestic law and prevail over any contrary provision.

*43.* One of the more specific doctrines flowing from Article 7(1) of the Constitution is that criminal law must always be in writing, must be approved by Parliament, must be promulgated and published as envisaged in the Constitution.[84] This means that the creation of offences and the imposition of criminal sanctions may

81. All references in this Part of the monograph are to the new Penal Code, unless otherwise stated. References to the male gender imply the female gender as well, unless otherwise indicated or becomes obvious from the text.
82. Adopted by the UNGA on 10 Dec. 1948 as Resolution 217A.
83. O.J. C 326, 26.10.2012, p. 391.
84. *See* Art. 42 of the Constitution, which stipulates that the President of the Republic promulgates and publishes the laws which have been approved by Parliament within one month of the vote, although there is no stipulation which will the consequences be in case of failure. The President of the Republic is empowered to send back to Parliament any law it has been approved by it, explaining the reasons for the referral. If the not promulgated law is approved again by Parliament (this time it requires the absolute majority of the total number of members (currently 300)), the President of the Republic is obliged to promulgate and publish it within ten days.

never be based on customary law or be the result of judge-made law. If EU secondary law instruments envisage the creation of offences in the domestic legal systems of Member States, in Greece this requires an Act of Parliament. In particular, the Act will establish the relevant offences, will lay down their constitutive elements, will prescribe the punishment to be imposed, and will specify whether prosecution will be ex officio or only possible after a criminal complaint has been lodged by the victim/s. For example, Act 4679/2020 implements into Greek law the EU Directive on trademarks[85] and the Directive on the enforcement of intellectual property rights.[86] Article 45 of this Act criminally punishes (with imprisonment and monetary penalties) anyone who uses trademarks in violation of its provisions, or who sets in circulation, possesses, imports/exports goods bearing the trade mark owned by third parties, or who breaches a registered trade mark with a sign that is identical to the trade mark of the goods or services in question, etc.[87]

*44.* Since the late 1980s and early 1990s, the international community has witnessed a considerable expansion in the creation of criminal offences through multilateral treaties, which have been invariably negotiated and concluded in the context of international and regional organizations. As far as Greece is concerned, these organizations include, *inter alia*, the United Nations, the Council of Europe, the Organisation of Economic Co-operation and Development (OECD), and the Organisation of the Black Sea Economic Organisation (BSEC). Under these global and regional agreements, contracting parties undertake the obligation to establish in their domestic legal orders all the offences laid down therein. These treaties concern a large array of criminal acts, which are characterized by their transnational nature and the fact that often the alleged perpetrators might not be located in one State, but the offences are perpetrated in the territory of another State or States. To offer examples of this international criminal law making, Greece has signed, ratified and/or acceded to international treaties and conventions which aim at:

(a) combating bribery and corruption, including the Convention on Combating Bribery of Foreign Public Officials in International Business Transactions, which was negotiated under the auspices of OECD;[88] the UN Convention against Corruption;[89] the Council of Europe Criminal Law Convention on

85. Directive (EU) 2015/2436 of the European Parliament and of the Council of 16 Dec. 2015 to approximate the laws of the Member States relating to trademarks, O.J. L 336, 23.12.2015, p. 1.
86. Directive 2004/48/EC of the European Parliament and of the Council of 29 Apr. 2004 on the enforcement of intellectual property rights, O.J. L 157, 30.4.2004, p. 1.
87. Act 4679/2020, Commercial trademarks – Incorporation of Directive (EU) 2015/2436 to approximate the laws of the Member States relating to trademarks and of Directive 2004/48/EC on the enforcement of intellectual property rights, and other provisions, FEK 2020 A' 71.
88. Signed on 17 Dec. 1997, entered into force on 15 Feb. 1999. Greece ratified it under Act 2656/1998, FEK 1998 A' 265, and deposited the instrument of ratification on 5 Feb. 1999. For a report of the Convention's application in Greece, *see:* https://www.oecd.org/fr/daf/anti-corruption/conventioncontrelacorruption/2386896.pdf.
89. It was adopted by the UNGA on 31 Oct. 2003, opened for signature in December 2003, entered into force on 14 Dec. 2005, 2349 *UNTS* 41. Greece signed it on 10 Dec. 2003 and ratified it pursuant to Act 3666/2008, FEK 2008 A' 105. Generally, *see* United Nations Office on Drugs and Crime, Country Review Report of Greece, *Review by Ireland and Gabon of the implementation by Greece of*

Corruption,[90] and Additional Protocol;[91] the Council of Europe Civil Law Convention on Corruption;[92] and the Council of Europe Agreement establishing the Group of States against corruption;[93]

(b) combatting organized crime and its manifestations, including the UN Convention against Transnational Organized Crime,[94] and its three supplementary Protocols: the Protocol on Human Trafficking,[95] the Protocol on Migrant Smuggling,[96] and the Protocol on Trafficking of Firearms;[97] and the Agreement among the Governments of the Black Sea Economic Co-operation Participating States on Co-operation in Combatting Crime, in particular in its Organized Forms,[98] with its Additional Protocols of 2002[99] and of 2004;[100]

(c) combating international terrorism and its various forms, including the Convention on the Prevention and Punishment of Crimes against Internationally Protected Persons, including Diplomatic Agents;[101] the International Convention for the Suppression of Terrorist Bombings;[102] the International Convention for

---

*Articles 15–42 of Chapter III. 'Criminalization and law enforcement' and Articles 44–50 of Chapter IV. International cooperation of the United Nations Convention Against Corruption for the review cycle 2010–2015*, at: https://www.ministryofjustice.gr/wp-content/uploads/2020/02/UNCAC-EN.pdf. *See also* the Declaration Against Corruption and Bribery in International Commercial Transactions, adopted on 16 Dec. 1996 as UNGA Resolution 51/191.

90. Signed on 27 Jan. 1999, entered into force on 1 Jul. 2002, ETS No. 173. Greece ratified it under Act 3560/2007, FEK 2007 A' 103.
91. Additional Protocol to the Criminal Law Convention on Corruption, signed on 15 May 2003, entered into force on 1 Feb. 2005, ETS No. 191. Greece ratified it under Act 3560/2007, FEK 2007 A' 103.
92. Signed on 4 Nov. 1999, entered into force on 1 Nov. 2003, ETS No. 174. Greece ratified it under Act 2957/2001, FEK 2001 A' 260.
93. The Agreement is composed of three documents: Committee of Ministers Resolution (98)7 of 5 May 1998 authorising the partial and enlarged Agreement establishing the 'Group of States against Corruption – GRECO'; Resolution (99)5 of 1 May 1999 establishing the 'Group of States against Corruption – GRECO'; and the Statute of GRECO which is appended to Resolution (99)5.
94. Adopted by the UNGA on 15 Nov. 2000, entered into force on 29 Sep. 2003, 2225 *UNTS* 209. Greece signed it on 13 Dec. 2000, ratified and implemented it by virtue of Act 3875/2010, FEK 2010 A' 158.
95. Protocol to Prevent, Suppress and Punish Trafficking in Persons, Especially Women and Children, entered into force on 25 Dec. 2003, 2237 *UNTS* 319. Greece ratified and implemented it by virtue of Act 3875/2010, FEK 2010 A' 158.
96. Protocol against the Smuggling of Migrants by Land, Sea and Air, entered into force on 28 Jan. 2004, 2241 *UNTS* 507. Greece ratified and implemented it by virtue of Act 3875/2010, *supra*.
97. Protocol against the Illicit Manufacturing of and Trafficking in Firearms, their Parts and Components and Ammunition, entered into force on 3 Jul. 2005, 2326 *UNTS* 208. Greece ratified and implemented it by virtue of Act 3875/2010, *supra*.
98. Signed on 2 Oct. 1998, entered into force on 4 Oct. 1999. Greece ratified it under Act 2925/2001, FEK 2001 A' 138. BSEC legal instruments are reproduced at: http://www.bsec-organization.org/charter.
99. Signed on 15 Mar. 2002. Greece ratified it under Act 3334/2005, FEK 2005 A' 92. The UNGA 'took note' of the Protocol's entry into force in Resolution 59/259, 'Cooperation between the United Nations and the Black Sea Economic Cooperation Organization', 23 Dec. 2004.
100. On combatting terrorism, adopted on 3 Dec. 2004, entered into force on 16 Oct. 2005. Greece ratified it under Act 3452/2006, FEK 2006 A' 70.
101. Concluded under UN auspices, opened for signature on 14 Dec. 1973, entered into force on 20 Feb. 1977, 1035 *UNTS* 167. Greece ratified it under Act 1368/1983, FEK 1983 A' 89.
102. Concluded under UN auspices on 15 Dec. 1997, opened for signature on 12 Jan. 1998, entered into force on 23 May 2001, 2149 *UNTS* 256. Greece ratified it under Act 3116/2003, FEK 2003 A' 48.

the Suppression of the Financing of Terrorism;[103] and the Additional Protocol on Combatting Terrorism to the Agreement among the Governments of the Black Sea Economic Co-operation Participating States on Co-operation in Combatting Crime, in particular in its Organized Forms.[104] It should be noted that even though Greece had notified its willingness to accede to the Prüm Treaty,[105] it still has not become a contracting party,[106] and that it has signed but not ratified the Council of Europe Convention on the Prevention of Terrorism;[107]

(d) combatting THB, namely the aforementioned Protocol on Human Trafficking appended to the UN Convention against Transnational Organized Crime;[108] the Council of Europe Convention on Action against Trafficking in Human Beings;[109] and, specifically concerning women, the Convention on the Elimination of All Forms of Discrimination against Women;[110] and

(e) combatting narcotic drugs, namely the UN Convention against Illicit Traffic in Narcotic Drugs and Psychotropic Substances.[111] Greece has signed but not ratified the Council of Europe Agreement on Illicit Traffic by Sea, which implements Article 17 of the UN Convention against Illicit Traffic in Narcotic Drugs.[112]

Regarding much older international treaties, which deal with criminal law matters and are still in force, suffice to mention that Greece is a contracting party to the International Convention for the Suppression of the Traffic in Women and Children,[113] and to the International Convention for the Suppression of Counterfeiting

103. Adopted by the UNGA on 9 Dec. 1999, opened for signature on 10 Jan. 2000, entered into force on 10 Apr. 2002, 2178 *UNTS* 197. Greece ratified it under Act 3034/2002, FEK 2002 A' 168.

104. Signed on 3 Dec. 2004, Greece ratified it under Act 3452/2006, FEK 2006 A' 70.

105. Convention between the Kingdom of Belgium, the Federal Republic of Germany, the Kingdom of Spain, the French Republic, the Grand Duchy of Luxembourg, the Kingdom of the Netherlands and the Republic of Austria on the stepping up of cross-border cooperation, particularly in combating terrorism, cross-border crime and illegal migration, signed on 27 May 2005, entered into force on 1 Nov. 2006, 2617 *UNTS* 3. The Convention is based on EU Council Decision 2008/615/JHA of 23 Jun. 2008 on the stepping up of cross-border cooperation, particularly in combating terrorism and cross-border crime, O.J. L 210, 6.8.2008, p. 1. The Decision is binding on Greece.

106. *See* Council of the European Union, Press Release, 2807th Council Meeting, Justice and Home Affairs, Luxembourg, 12–13 Jun. 2007, 10267/07 (Presse 125), p. 13.

107. Opened for signature on 16 May 2005, entered into force on 1 Jun. 2007, CETS No. 196.

108. *See* K. Magliveras, *Combating Trafficking in Persons: The Role and Action of International Organisations*, Athens: Ant. N. Sakkoulas Publishers, 2007, pp. 57 et seq.

109. It was opened for signature on 16 May 2005, entered into force on 1 Feb. 2008, ETS No. 197, 2569 *UNTS* 33. Greece ratified it under Act 4216/2013, FEK 2013 A' 266. *See* Magliveras, *ibid.*, pp. 27 et seq.

110. It was opened for signature on 18 Dec. 1979, entered into force on 3 Sep. 1981, 1249 *UNTS* 13. Greece ratified it Act 1342/1983, FEK 1983 A' 39.

111. It was opened for signature on 20 Dec. 1988, entered into force on 11 Nov. 1990, 1582 *UNTS* 95. Greece ratified it under Act 1990/1991, ΦΕΚ 1991 A' 193.

112. It was signed on 31 Jan. 1995, entered into force on 1 May 2000, ETS No. 156.

113. It was concluded under the auspices of the League of Nations on 30 Sep. 1921, entered into force on 15 Jun. 1922, 9 *LNTS* 415. Greece ratified it under Legislative Decree of 20 Oct. 1922, which also ratified the International Agreement for the suppression of the 'White Slave Traffic' (signed on 18 May 1904, entered into force on 18 Jul. 1905) and the International Convention for the Suppression of the White Slave Traffic (signed on 4 May 1910).

Currency.[114] The question of counterfeited currency is of particular importance for the Greek legislation, because Greece participates in the third stage of the European Monetary Union and is part of the Eurozone, which has the euro as the single common currency. In 2006, Greece notified the contracting parties of the Convention for the Suppression of Counterfeiting Currency that it had given the European Police Office (Europol) a mandate to combat euro counterfeiting and that it will be Europol which shall perform the central office functions within the meaning of Articles 12 to 15 thereof.[115]

*45.* The principle of legality of Article 7(1) of the Constitution cancan further be found in Article 1 of the old Penal Code, which reads, 'No punishment is inflicted apart from those acts for which the law has expressly stipulated the punishment prior to their perpetration.' This article was rephrased in Article 1 of the new Penal Code. Admittedly, the wording in the old Penal Code did not exhaust all the parameters of the *nullum crimen nulla poena sine lege* principle, as laid down in the Constitution. However, since Greek law does not perceive the existence of a criminal offence without the stipulation of a specific penalty for it, the incomplete wording in the old Penal Code had not given rise to any particular difficulties. The formulation of Article 1 in the new Penal Code is explained *infra* at paragraph 59.

*46.* The insistence on a written criminal law has been one of the traditional differences between Continental and Anglo-Saxon (or common law) legal systems. This contrariety, which is explained by the different ways in which the two legal systems have evolved over the centuries,[116] has increasingly been bridged as common law countries proceed with the codification of criminal law. Although both systems have their advantages and disadvantages, we live in an epoch where legal rules change at an alarming speed, and the fact that the Anglo-Saxon criminal law can be revised by judicial decisions without necessitating lengthy legislative amendments is undoubtedly of considerable value in ensuring that it is kept up to date with new

114. It was concluded under the auspices of the League of Nations on 20 Apr. 1929, entered into force on 22 Feb. 1931, 112 *LNTS* 371. Greece ratified it under Act 5016/1931.
115. *See* Council Act of 26 Jul. 1995 on the establishment of a European Police Office (Europol Convention), O.J. C 316, 27.11.1995, p. 1, transposed in Greek law under Act 2605/1998, ΦΕΚ 1998 A' 88; and Council Decision 2005/511/JHA of 12 Jul. 2005 on protecting the euro against counterfeiting, by designating Europol as the Central Office for combating euro counterfeiting, O.J. L 185, 16.7.2005, p. 35. Note that all contracting parties to the Europol Convention participating in the Eurozone (i.e., those EU Member States having adopted the euro as their single currency) have entered into identical notifications. Presently, Europol operates under a different legal basis: *see* Regulation 2016/794 of the European Parliament and of the Council of 11 May 2016 on the European Union Agency for Law Enforcement Cooperation (Europol) and replacing and repealing Council Decisions 2009/371/JHA, 2009/934/JHA, 2009/935/JHA, 2009/936/JHA and 2009/968/JHA, O.J. L 135, 24.5.2016, p. 53, *see* in particular Art. 4(4) thereof. Regulation 2016/794 has been amended under Regulation (EU) 2022/991 of the European Parliament and of the Council of 8 Jun. 2022 amending Regulation (EU) 2016/794, as regards Europol's cooperation with private parties, the processing of personal data by Europol in support of criminal investigations, and Europol's role in research and innovation, O.J. L 169, 27.6.2022, p. 1.
116. Generally, *see* O.F. Robertson., T.D. Fergus, W.M. Gordon, *An Introduction to European Legal History*, Oxon: Professional Books Limited, 1985, 208–257.

developments in society. However, it is also true to say that the Anglo-Saxon system has inherent negative points, since the protection of civil liberties and legal certainty might not be always adequately safeguarded and of course a lot depends on the quality of the judicial decisions, especially those of the highest courts.

## II. Legality and Interpretation

*47.* According to Article 7(1) of the Constitution, punishment may not be inflicted on the basis of an analogous application of a criminal statute, which has not been specifically promulgated to apply to the case under consideration. This doctrine relates to the legal gaps (*lacunae*) which a Penal Code inevitably entails. These gaps fall into two categories.

First, those which the legislator left unregulated either because the legislator could not have envisaged the future development of criminal law or because it was the outcome of a deliberate choice. Thus, the legislator was aware of the gaps and chose not to address them.

Second, those gaps which the legislator has deliberately left unregulated because they refer to post-legal notions for which it is preferable to endow the judge with a measure of discretion to decide their application on a case-by-case basis. Often this is referred to as the margin of appreciation, a term which is mere translation of 'marge d' appréciation', a concept of French administrative law advanced by the Conseil d'état.

It should be emphasized that this second category does not refer to legal gaps in the strict sense of the word but reflects the legislator's choice. The offences of committing lewd lascivious acts (Articles 337 (insulting sexual dignity) and 353 (insulting sexual decency) of the Penal Code) exemplify this point. Their definition at the time the old Penal Code entered into force in the early 1950s would have rendered their application meaningless in the twenty-first century, given the intervening radical transformation of the Greek society, technological advances, etc. Indeed, both provisions were fundamentally revised under Act 1419/1984 to keep abreast of the Greek society's evolution at the time. They were again reformulated under the new Penal Code.

*48.* Greek criminal law does not recognize the existence of gaps of the first category. Thus, if a particular act has not been expressly characterized as a criminal offence, this denotes that it was not the intention of the legislator to penalize it. Therefore, the ability of judges to create new criminal offences on the basis of consistent case law is severely restricted.

However, Greek criminal law does permit the existence of gaps of the second category. Indeed, this is in line with the existence of a codified system of criminal law, whose provisions cannot be revised at will but nevertheless have to keep up with societal developments. This is best achieved by allowing judges to interpret criminal statutes in accordance with ever-changing social circumstances or with the prevailing circumstances and needs. Whether judges actually take advantage of this possibility and whether their interpretation truly reflects the prevailing situation at any given moment are valid considerations which the legislator should perhaps take into consideration in future amendments of the criminal statutes.

*49.* Whereas Greek criminal law does prohibit the analogous application of a criminal provision to establish or to increase criminal liability (*in malam partem*), it does permit such application, if it were to lead to the exclusion or mitigation of criminal liability (*in bonam partem*). For example, the provision of Article 308(3), which prevents the attribution of guilt to the perpetrator of bodily injuries, provided that the victim has consented, and the act does not contradict *bonos mores*, could be applied by analogy to cases where the victim of verbal injury (Article 361), or defamation (Article 362) has also given his consent (on consent, *infra* paragraphs 236 et seq.).

*50.* Prohibiting the application of criminal law by analogy as a means to establish or increase criminal liability should be regarded as a cornerstone of all liberal democratic States and Greece is one of them. If the opposite were to happen, the rule of law would be left seriously wanting. A 'good' illustration is Article 15 of the Penal Code of the Russian Soviet Federative Socialist Republic of 1926. It stated that, if a criminal offence was not included in the Penal Code, its basis and limits of responsibility were to be determined by application of those provisions in the Penal Code, which laid down criminal acts which were most similar in nature. Using this provision, which was finally abolished under Article 3 of the USSR Principles of Criminal Law of 1958, Soviet courts were able to create new and increased penalties for existing offences.[117]

Furthermore, it should be noted that we are not concerned here with instances where anomalous domestic situations may demand to apply criminal statutes by analogy to avoid impunity, as was the case, for instance, during the Second World War. Thus, during the Nuremberg Trials, US Justice Robert H. Jackson maintained in his closing arguments that the conviction of Nazi war criminals necessitated the application of the doctrine of punishment by analogy 'to enable conviction for acts which no statute forbade'.[118]

## §2. The Principle of the Individual Guilt (*Mens Rea*)

*51.* All offences require a certain state of mind, a *mens rea*, which is the connecting factor between the criminal offence and the perpetrator. A person commits an offence when his mind has determined to proceed with a kind of behaviour, which the legislator has deemed to be illegal (and not solely immoral). The requirement of *mens rea* denotes that a person can only be punished for a criminal offence if his mind is legally blameworthy. This principle derives from the more general

117. *See* H.J. Berman, 'Analogy' in F.J.M. Feldbrugge et al. (eds), *Encyclopedia of Soviet Law*, 2nd Revised Edition, Dordrecht: Martinus Nijhoff, 1985, 47–48.

118. *See* Chief of Counsel for Prosecution of Axis Criminality, *Nazi Conspiracy and Aggression*, Supplement A, United States Government Printing Office, Washington, 1947, p. 7, at: http://www.nizkor.com/hweb/imt/tgmwc/tgmwc-19/tgmwc-19-187-01.shtml.

principle of guilt, which precludes the imposition of punishment for a criminal offence until and unless the offender is to be blamed for its commission; in other words, the element of culpability must always be present (*nullum crimen sine culpa*). In the Greek legal order, the principle of guilt can be found in two provisions. The first is Article 2(1) of the Constitution stipulating that the State shall respect and protect human dignity. This provision should be read together with Article 7(2) of the Constitution. The second provision is Article 14(1) of the Penal Code which defines what should constitute a criminal offence, namely an illegal act *attributable* to the perpetrator and punishable by law.

*52.* Since Greek criminal law applies the principle of the individual guilt, it does not recognize strict or objective liability. Article 34 of the Penal Code stipulates that an act cannot be criminally attributed to the perpetrator, if, at the time he committed the criminal act, he was unable to realize the illegality of his behaviour due to a mental disorder or disturbance of consciousness (*infra* paragraph 144). Therefore, although the act was undoubtedly of a criminal nature, the perpetrator was incapable of apprehending such notions as illegality, culpability, etc. and, in effect, his mind was not in a state of being 'legally blameworthy'. However, there are exceptions to this rule. Article 35(1), for example, refers to bringing oneself to the state of disrupted conscience to commit the offence (*infra* paragraph 145). The old Penal Code included another exception, namely Article 193, which concerned instances where the perpetrator brought himself to a state of excessive drunkenness and in such state committed an offence which was not premeditated. According to the Explanatory Memorandum of the new Penal Code, Article 193 was deleted because it had been criticized as being a provision which led to the punishment of a person just because he got drunk.

In case Article 34 of the Penal Code is applicable, the gravity of the criminal behaviour or the dangerous personality of the offender is irrelevant. Since insanity (note that the Penal Code does not use this term, preferring the more socially acceptable term 'mental disruption') is treated as an absolute exception to the attribution of criminal liability, even if the most hideous crimes had been committed, the offender cannot be held responsible. Notwithstanding that the imposition of criminal sanctions is not possible in these circumstances, the Penal Code does contain provisions on the obligatory ordering of measures against such a perpetrator to protect the society from any criminal acts which he may commit in the future. These take the form of security and/or protective measures (*infra* paragraph 229).

## §3. The Principle of Proportionality

*53.* With regard to determining the right sentence for the convicted offender, the principle of proportionality applies. Thus, Article 79(1) of the Penal Code obliges the judge to take into account the gravity of the committed criminal offence and the degree of the offender's culpability when determining the sentence. The 'gravity' of offences is determined by three elements laid down in Article 79(2:): (1) the damage that the offence caused or the risk it caused, (2) the nature, the kind and the object of the offence, as well as (3) the relevant circumstances which surrounded the preparation or perpetration of the offence (time, place, instrumentalities, means, etc.). Under the old Penal Code, Article 79(2) also referred to the degree of *dolus* as a criterion for calculating the severity of the offence. However, in the new Penal Code, it has become a criterion for calculating the degree of culpability.

The principle of proportionality is widely applied. It is expressly stated in Article 25(1) of the Constitution and has application in other branches of domestic law (e.g., administrative law) but also in public international law and in the law of the European Union.

## §4. Corporate Liability

*54.* Greek criminal law does not contain provisions dealing with the liability of legal persons (companies/enterprises/undertakings, or 'legal persons' under EU law) and the punishment of offences committed by them. This should be regarded as distinct from the liability of those natural persons, who are responsible for the operation and administration of legal entities. However, the ever-increasing involvement of private enterprises in the economic life of a country and the transborder operation of companies (mostly in the form of multinational corporations) have raised the question of their criminal (as opposed to their civil and/or administrative) liability. Examples could be offered from environmental law, where violations often affect directly the right to life. The question posed here is 'what should be the criminal treatment of a company that has, e.g., polluted a river or the sea or other parts of the ecosystem or has caused harm to the health of the people living in the vicinity of its factories?' Provided that the procedural problems with prosecuting companies are overcome, the only punishment which could realistically be inflicted are non-custodial penalties, notwithstanding the imposition of other penalties in the form of administrative sanctions. Two things should be clarified here. The first is that we are not concerned with the severity of the criminal sanctions but only with their nature, i.e., custodial sentences/imprisonment versus monetary penalties/administrative sanctions. The question of the severity is rather subjective; which is more severe: one month of imprisonment for the company's executives or a penalty of EUR 100 million? The second is that we are not concerned with cases where it has been shown that the members of the Board of Directors and/or the senior management of a company and/or the principal shareholder/s bear individual criminal responsibility, i.e., they are liable irrespective of their company's liability. Clearly, in such cases it would be possible to impose custodial sentences upon them. Presumably, this will be an instance where a company's 'human element' (if this term could be used) will be punished.

*55.* To offer an example of a legislative provision concerning the imposition of administrative sanctions for criminal acts perpetrated by a company (legal person), reference will be made to Article 8 of Act 2803/2000 on the ratification of the Convention Concerning the Protection of the Financial Interests of the European

Communities.[119] It stipulated that if a legal person had acquired any benefit, which derived from the criminal offences stipulated in the Act, and such benefit could be attributed to the responsibility of any natural person, who acted either on his own behalf (i.e., in his individual capacity) or collectively as a member of any organ of the legal person in question, a range of administrative sanctions shall be imposed. These sanctions included (a) an administrative fine not exceeding three times the value of the benefit acquired by the company, (b) the temporary or permanent prohibition of the company carrying out its activities, and (c) the temporary or permanent exclusion of the company from public benefits or assistance. The Convention has been replaced by the Directive 2017/1371 (the so-called PIF Directive),[120] which was adopted to implement Article 325 TFEU concerning the protection of EU financial interests.[121] Greece implemented Directive 2017/1371 by virtue of Act 4689/2020.[122]

*56.* The reason why incorporated entities may not be held criminally liable is because Greek criminal law subscribes to the idea that only natural persons (individuals) are capable of committing offences. In particular, the criminal system is founded on the principle of individual culpability. This is also manifested in Article 7(1) of the Constitution, which, as has been explained, understands crimes as acts committed by a natural person that have been penalized by virtue of the existence of a statute, which must have been promulgated before the acts were committed. It follows that, pursuant to Greek criminal law, a legal person (company) does not have a 'guilty mind': *actus reus* is reserved only for natural persons and, therefore, '*nulla poena sine actu*'. Thus, the criminal responsibility referred to in the previous paragraph as the 'human element' of a company may not be transferred from individual (natural) persons to a company and thus become corporate liability. This would have violated the very fundamentals of the criminal system.

*57.* Since the late 1980s and early 1990s, the UN and the Council of Europe have adopted several treaties asking contracting States to consider criminalizing certain acts, which are committed by companies and, to that end create, new offences in their domestic legal orders. At the same time, EU legislation expects that Member States treat specific acts as criminal offences, including acts that are committed

119. *See* Council Act of 26 Jul. 1995 drawing up the Convention on the protection of the European Communities' financial interests, O.J. C 316, 27 Nov. 1995, p. 48. The Convention came into force on 17 Oct. 2002.

120. Directive 2017/1371 of the European Parliament and of the Council of 5 Jul. 2017 on the fight against fraud to the Union's financial interests by means of criminal law, O.J. L 198, 28 Jul. 2017, p. 29.

121. Generally, *see* M. Kaifa-Gbandi, 'The Protection of the EU's Financial Interests by Means of Criminal Law in the Context of the Lisbon Treaty and the 2017 Directive (EU 2017/1371) on the Fight against Fraud to the Union's Financial Interests' (2018) 13 *Zeitschrift für Internationale Strafrechtsdogmatic* 575–582.

122. Act 4689/2020, Transposition in the Greek legislation of Directives (EU) 2016/800, 2017/1371, 2017/541, 2016/1919, 2014/57, ratification of the Memorandum of Administrative Cooperation between the Ministry of Justice of the Hellenic Republic and the Ministry of Justice and Public Order of the Republic of Cyprus, amendments to Act 3663/2008 to implement Regulation (EU) 2018/1727, and other provisions, FEK 2020 A' 103.

by legal persons. Principally, they concern the perpetration of economic crime, sometimes referred to as 'white-collar crime', e.g., insider dealing (insider trading), money laundering, corruption, organized crime, financing terrorist acts, etc.

*58.* As regards the relevant treaties concluded in the context of the Council of Europe, Greece is a contracting party to several of them, including the Convention on Laundering, Search, Seizure and Confiscation of the Proceeds from Crime,[123] the Convention on Laundering, Search, Seizure and Confiscation of the Proceeds from Crime and on the Financing of Terrorism (2005, mentioned *infra*), the aforementioned Criminal Law Convention on Corruption, and the Convention on Cybercrime.[124] Greece is not a contracting party to the Council of Europe Convention on Insider Trading[125] and to the Convention on the Protection of Environment through Criminal Law, which so far has been ratified only by Estonia.[126] These and the other international treaties mentioned elsewhere in this monograph create various obligations and duties. Greece, like all other contracting parties, must not only implement them domestically but must also ensure and supervise their fulfilment and observance.

---

123. Signed on 8 Nov. 1990, entered into force on 1 Sep. 1993, ETS No. 141. It entered into force for Greece in June 1999.
124. Convention on Cybercrime, Concerning the Criminalisation of Acts of a Racist and Xenophobic Nature Committed through Computer Systems, signed on 23 Nov. 2001, entered into force on 1 Jul. 2004, ETS No. 185, and Additional Protocol, signed on 28 Jan. 2003, entered into force on 1 Mar. 2006, ETS No. 189. Greece ratified both instruments under Act 4411/2016, FEK 2016 A' 142. This Act, additionally, harmonized Greek legislation to the provisions of Directive 2013/40/EU of the European Parliament and of the Council of 12 Aug. 2013 on attacks against information systems and replacing Council Framework Decision 2005/222/JHA, O.J. L 218, 14.8.2013, p. 8, and amended other domestic legislative instruments, completely unrelated to the regulation of cybercrime. That the same Act of Parliament approved an international treaty, and thus became the instrument of ratification which was notified to the Secretary-General of the Council of Europe, and, moreover, on the one hand, transposed an EU Directive into Greek law and, on the other hand, amended unrelated domestic law, should be considered problematic.
125. Signed on 20 Apr. 1989, entered into force on 1 Oct. 1991, ETS No. 130. Only eight Council of Europe Member States are contracting parties.
126. Signed on 4 Nov. 1998, not yet into force, ETS No. 172.

# Chapter 2. Scope of Application of Criminal Statutes

## §1. Principles Concerning the Temporal Scope of Criminal Statutes

### I. Prohibition of Retroactivity

*59.* The legal principle prohibiting the retroactive application of criminal law (*nullum crimen nulla poena sine lege*) is of fundamental importance and is considered a constitutional principle. As has already been explained, Article 7(1) of the Constitution stipulates that no offence shall exist and no punishment shall be inflicted if it is not laid down in a criminal statute which was promulgated before the perpetration of the criminal act and provided that such statute sets out the constitutive elements of the offence. It is interesting to note that while several constitutions of other states have no specific provision concerning the principle of the non-retroactivity of criminal law, all contemporary Greek Constitutions have had one. As has also been explained, this prohibition can be further found in Article 1 of the Penal Code. Under the old Penal Code, the article concerned solely the *nulla poena sine lege* principle. In the new Penal Code, Article 1 has been reformulated: 'A crime does not exist without a statute which must be applicable before the commission of the act and which stipulates its constitutive elements as well the penalty to be inflicted for it.'

*60.* From the prohibition of retroactivity flows another prohibition, namely the retroactive application of a subsequent law which augments the severity of the punishment. This principle, which is not expressly stated in Article 1 of the Penal Code but follows by necessary implication, denotes that it is not allowed to inflict a penalty which is more severe than the penalty that was provided by the law at the time of the criminal act.

The principle of non-retroactive application of criminal law has two consequences. First, the alleged perpetrator may not be prosecuted, if at the time he committed the act, the latter did not constitute an offence and was not punishable, but the act became subsequently a criminal offence and, consequently, a criminal penalty may now be inflicted. Second, if the act was punishable at the time it was committed and, before the prescribed procedure was completed before the competent criminal court, the legislator promulgates a new stricter statute, the latter cannot be applied. On the contrary, should the alleged preparator, who now has the legal status of a defendant, be found guilty, the earlier sanction shall be inflicted, even though at the time of sentencing it was no longer applicable. Thus, it could be argued that repealed criminal statutes remain in force until all criminal prosecutions brought under them have reached the procedural stage of res judicata. What constitutes 'more severe punishment' is a question to be decided by the sentencing criminal court on a case-by-case basis.

## II. Retroactivity of the Milder Statute

*61.* The aforementioned legal principles lead to the additional conclusion that the defendant will benefit from a subsequent statute if it happens to be more lenient for him. This was expressly laid down in Article 2(1) of the old Penal Code: it stipulated that, if from the moment the criminal act was perpetrated and until the criminal procedure had reached the stage of res judicata more than one legal provision had been in force, the criminal court was obliged to apply the one which was more favourable to the defendant. The new Penal Code retained this formulation but added that the court shall apply the legal provision, which *in the case in question* is more favourable to the defendant (emphasis added). In practice, the new formulation of Article 2(1) directs the criminal court to even apply a combination of legal provisions if this would lead to a more favourable treatment of the defendant. Based on the revised Article 2(1), the court is obliged to search and impose the criminal sanction that will prove to be the most advantageous to the defendant in question. Presumably, failure to do so is a ground for appeal. While this leniency might not be what the society at large expects of the criminal justice system and its treatment of offenders, it is in fact in compliance with the principle of retroactivity of the milder statute.

*62.* Pursuant to Article 2, the notion of a 'milder statute' is understood as a legal provision that leads to the more lenient treatment of the defendant. Which provision or which combination of provisions operates in favour of the defendant at any given moment is a question that could be manifested in many ways. This includes instances where the subsequent statute does no longer regard the perpetrated offence as criminal, i.e., it abolishes the act's criminal nature, where lighter penalties than the existing ones are introduced (e.g., confinement in a penitentiary of up to ten years instead of confinement for at least ten years); where in order to prosecute the alleged offender a prior criminal complaint must have been lodged by the alleged victim, i.e., prosecution is not allowed when brought by the State without the alleged victim's consent being manifested by his lodging a criminal complaint; where the statute of limitations for the criminal act allegedly perpetrated has been reduced and consequently the prosecution must be terminated, etc.

By virtue of Article 2(2), the principle of the retroactivity of the milder sanction has been broadened to cover instances where a subsequent statute terminates the criminal nature of the perpetrated act. In these cases, the execution of the criminal sanctions imposed and of any security measures imposed shall cease. Article 2(2) applies automatically in the sense that, if the perpetrator has been sentenced to imprisonment, he must be immediately set free and he is not required to wait for a court decision confirming it. An issue which follows from Article 2(2) is to ascertain the consequences of a statute that was promulgated after the conviction and provides a lighter sentence for the same criminal offence. Strictly speaking, there are no favourable consequences for the convicted person who finds himself in this situation, since the Penal Code does not envisage it. The legislator might provide it in a future amendment of the Penal Code to improve the position of convicted persons.

*63.* The application of the 'milder statute' does not raise any problems when the new statute contains only provisions that are more lenient for the defendant. However, there may be cases where it contains both favourable and unfavourable provisions: for example, whereas previously the commission of a certain offence incurred a term of imprisonment between a minimum of three months and a maximum of five years, these limits were amended to six months and three years respectively. In this example, the new provision is at the same time more favourable because the maximum term of imprisonment was reduced but also unfavourable because the minimum term was increased. Although this situation is not expressly addressed in the Penal Code, it can be solved as follows: if the court takes the view that the appropriate criminal sanction for the defendant in question is the maximum laid down in the legislation, the court must apply the provisions of the new statute, it being the most lenient for the defendant. However, if the court imposes the minimum term of imprisonment, the court is bound to apply the sentencing provisions of the earlier statute, even though it has been repealed. Finally, if the court imposes a sanction which lies between the minimum and maximum limits, the court will have to use its discretion, as no statute is milder than the other. In doing so, it should be guided by the clear wish of the legislator, namely that the offence in question should overall attract a more lenient term of imprisonment than before. In such instances, it is expected that the higher-ranking courts, including the Criminal Division of Areios Pagos, will provide lower courts with the necessary guidance.

## III. The Extent of the Prohibition Against Retroactive Criminal Law

*64.* Under the old Penal Code, there were two exceptions to the principle permitting the retroactive application of the milder criminal statute, but they were both abolished in the new Penal Code. The first exception concerned the so-called statutes of temporary application. These were legal instruments whose temporal duration was determined at the time of promulgation or whose enforcement was triggered by the existence of certain extraordinary circumstances, such as war, outbreaks of infections or calamities. According to Article 3 of the old Penal Code, such statutes would continue to be enforced even after their termination, provided that the criminal acts created under them were committed at the time they were still in force. Additionally, Article 3 stipulated that the provision of Article 2(1) was applicable in this case. Thus, if from the time that the criminal act was perpetrated and until a res judicata judgment was pronounced, several statutes of temporary application had been enforced, the court had to must apply the one which is the most favourable to the defendant.

*65.* The second exception concerned security measures (*infra* paragraphs 289 et seq.). By virtue of Article 4(1) of the old Penal Code, the security measures envisaged in Articles 69, 71 to 74 and 76 thereof were imposed in accordance with the statute which was in force at the time the case was heard. Moreover, Article 4(2) stipulated that, if after security measures had been imposed, a subsequent statute abrogated the act's criminal nature, the measures ordered were not automatically revoked. However, the court that ordered them had the discretion, after hearing the opinion of the public prosecutor, to decide whether they should be retained or not.

## §2. Principles Concerning the Applicability of Criminal Statutes with Respect to Space

### I. The Four Principles of Criminal Jurisdiction

*66.* A criminal offence may be committed either in the territory of one of the nearly 200 countries that make up the international community and either against a national of that country or against a foreigner. Greek criminal law applies the traditional four principles of jurisdiction in international criminal law:

(a) The territorial principle (Greek criminal law shall apply to all offences perpetrated on Greek territory, regardless of whether the perpetrator was a Greek or a foreign national).[127]
(b) The principle of active personality (Greek criminal law shall apply to offences committed by Greek nationals, even if they were perpetrated in another State (i.e., it is of no relevance in which State they were actually perpetrated).
(c) The principle of passive personality (Greek criminal law shall apply to offences that were committed by foreigners in another State, but violate the interests of Greek nationals).
(d) The principle of universal jurisdiction (Greek criminal law shall also apply to certain offences, which the international community has considered to be atrocious or particularly heinous or dangerous for the world at large, notwithstanding the nationality of the perpetrator, the nationality of the victim and the place where these offences were perpetrated).

*67.* The application of these four principles of jurisdiction could give rise to issues of conflict when Greek courts, alongside courts of one or more third States, claim to have jurisdiction over the commission of a particular offence. To resolve this conflict, the Penal Code has adopted the territorial principle as the main basis for the jurisdiction of Greek courts. The other three principles shall be applied only in the instances specifically laid down in the Penal Code.

Pursuant to Article 5(1), Greek criminal statutes apply to all criminal acts that have been committed within the territory of the Greek State, even if they were committed by aliens. The new Penal Code added the following provision to Article 5(1): 'The Greek criminal statutes shall also apply to any act of participation that was carried out within the territory of the Greek State, if the principal act, for which the Greek criminal courts have no jurisdiction, is punishable pursuant to the Greek criminal statutes.' This new provision presumably caters for those transnational

---

127. For a comparative treatise on the territorial principle among European countries with references to the old Greek Penal Code, *see* G.E. Langemeijer, 'Le principe de territorialité' in J.M. van Bemmelen & D. Wiersma (eds), *Le Droit Pénal International – Recueil d'Études en Hommage à van Bemmelen*, Leiden: Brill, 1965, 174.

crimes with multiple constitutive elements that are carried out in stages and where principal (larger) offence presupposes the prior commission of certain participatory criminal acts by persons who are different from the final perpetrators. Invariably, all or some of these participatory acts are carried out in States different than the State where the principal offence was perpetrated.

*68.* Greek territory comprises the land that lies inside the outside borders of the country, the territorial waters, the aerial space and the sub-terrain thereof. According to Article 5(2), vessels and aircraft registered in Greece are also regarded as 'Greek territory' regardless of where they were located at the time the offence was committed and provided that, in pursuance of the applicable rules of international law, they are not subjected to a foreign legal system.

## II. Extraterritorial Criminal Jurisdiction

*69.* The application of the other principles of criminal jurisdiction (active personality principle, passive personality principle, and universal jurisdiction) inevitably gives rise to the application of Greek criminal law to offences perpetrated outside the Greek territory, in other words, to extraterritorial criminal jurisdiction.

The principle of active personality (also known as the nationality principle) is envisaged in Article 6(1): Greek criminal law will apply to serious crimes and misdemeanours that were committed in a foreign State by a Greek national, subject to the condition that the offence is punishable under the law of the State where the offence was committed (the principle of double criminality), unless it was perpetrated in a 'politically unconstituted' country. However, there are exceptions to this rule. For example, Article 348D stipulates that the provisions of Articles 339, 342, 348, 348A, 348B, 348C, 349 and 351A, which deal with acts of fornication with and pornography of underaged persons, shall apply to offences committed by Greek citizens abroad, even if they were not punishable under the legal system of the State where perpetrated. Moreover, the fifth paragraph of Article 187, which deals with establishing and operating criminal organizations, stipulates that paragraphs (1) to (4) thereof apply also applies when the relevant offences have been carried out abroad by a Greek national or were aimed against a Greek citizen or a legal person headquartered in Greece or against the Greek State even if they were not punishable pursuant to the legislation of the State where the offences were committed.

*70.* According to Article 6(2), an alien shall be prosecuted, if he was a Greek national at the time the offence was perpetrated. In order to avoid situations where a foreign national assumes the Greek citizenship to preclude his prosecution, the same provision stipulates that an alien offender, who obtained Greek citizenship after the offence was perpetrated, shall also be prosecuted. In these cases, Article 6(3) requires that the victim or the government of the State where the criminal act was committed has requested the prosecution of the alleged offender. However, this requirement concerns only misdemeanours even if, pursuant to the Greek laws, they are prosecuted ex officio. Under the old Penal Code, the prosecution of the offence of Article 154 (acts of violence against foreign diplomats accredited to Greece) required the prior request of the victim. The new Penal Code abolished this requirement. However, the prosecution of the offence of Article 155 (disgracing or destroying symbols or emblems of a foreign sovereign state, which maintains peaceful relations with Greece and is recognized by it) is only possible if the foreign government has requested it.

Generally speaking, a criminal prosecution can start in two ways: either the public prosecutor himself brings a criminal action against an individual or a group of individuals or the alleged victim (*in casu* the victim is not an individual, but a sovereign State legally represented by the government in power) lodges himself a criminal complaint with the public prosecutor and the latter, being convinced of the validity of the complaint, brings a criminal action. Criminal complaints are regulated in Articles 115–116. In a nutshell, the person who directly suffered from a culpable act is entitled to lodge a criminal complaint. If this person has not reached the age of 13 or has been placed under judicial guardianship, this right may only be exercised by his legal representative. If he is between 13 and 18 years old, both the victim and the legal representative can lodge it. Who the legal representative of underaged persons will be is a question addressed in the Book IV (Family Law) in the Civil Code. In case two or more persons have the right to lodge a criminal complaint, they can exercise this right autonomously, i.e., independently from one another. According to Article 115(4), the right to lodge a criminal complaint is inherited as follows: first to the surviving spouse or to the person who had co-habited with the deceased person until his death as well as to his children and, should they not exist or should they be the perpetrators of the crime, to his parents. Two brief observations: (a) the wording of this provision seems to suggest that the parents can never be the perpetrators of the crime, and (b) there seems to be no good reason why the siblings should not inherit this right if no other relatives are alive.

Even though the wording of Article 154 does not expressly stipulate that such acts must have taken place within the Greek territory, arguably a foreign national, who has burned the flag of his country in the State of citizenship and then migrates to Greece, may not be prosecuted in Greece, because the Penal Code does not grant Greek courts with jurisdiction over him, while burning a flag is not an offence to which the principle of universal jurisdiction applies.

Finally, it should be noted that, according to Article 156, the above offences against foreign States shall be prosecuted only if Greece maintains diplomatic relations with the foreign State in question and the principle of reciprocity (i.e., that the foreign State's legislation also punishes violent acts directed against Greek diplomats, the Greek flag, etc.) is present both at the time the offence was perpetrated and at the time the alleged offender is tried. Whether or not Greece maintains diplomatic relations with a foreign State is a question of fact. It depends on several considerations, including with which foreign countries Greece strives to have diplomatic relations or not, the obligations which Greece must observe by virtue of its participation in international organizations, etc. It follows that Greece may, for example, be obliged to terminate diplomatic relations with a third State in order to comply with a decision adopted by the UN Security Council pursuant to Chapter VII of the UN Charter or if so determined by the Council of the European Union to further the objectives of its Common Foreign and Security Policy.[128] Equally, Greece may have to refuse to recognize a State which declared its independence if the Security Council has regarded it as a violation of the peremptory rules of public international law.

*71.* The provision of Article 7 (passive personality principle) is even more far-reaching than Article 6. It provides that criminal statutes shall be applied to serious crimes or misdemeanours, which were committed abroad by a foreign national, provided that they are aimed against a Greek national and are punishable in accordance with the law of the State where committed. Article 7 could also be understood as a manifestation of the principle of protection, meaning the legislator wishes to protect the interests of Greek nationals on all occasions and irrespective of the State where these were violated. As is the case with Article 6, the prosecution for misdemeanours under Article 7 requires a prior request by the victim or by the government of the State where the misdemeanour was committed. The new Penal Code added the following provision to Article 7: the term 'Greek citizens' also includes, on the one hand, the *foetus*, which, when born alive, will acquire the Greek nationality, and, on the other hand, the legal persons which have their seat in Greece.

*72.* The principle of universal jurisdiction (or principle of the protection of universal (global) interests) is enshrined in Article 8. In particular, as regards the offences set out in Article 8, the Greek criminal legislation shall be applied against both nationals and aliens irrespective of the legislation of the State where they were perpetrated. While it is not expressly stipulated in Article 8, it should be accepted that the nationality of the victims is of no consequence. The new Penal Code brought about changes in the list of the offences included in Article 8 in an apparent effort to modernize it. Among others, the following offences were deleted: trade in slaves (Article 323 of the old Penal Code); illegal circulation and trafficking in pornographic and lewd publications;[129] journeys taken to foreign States by persons who committed sexual or other lewd acts against minors in their territory (the so-called sexual tourism, Article 323B of the old Penal Code);[130] etc.

---

128. *See* Arts 21–46 of the Treaty on European Union and Arts 205–222 TFEU.

129. *See also* Arts 29 and 30 of Act 5060/1931 on the Press, General Violations of Honour and Other Similar Offences, as currently in force. *See* further Art. 14 of the Constitution: the seizure (confiscation) of newspapers and other publications before or after distribution is prohibited but seizure by order of a public prosecutor is exceptionally allowed, *inter alia*, in the case of obscene publications which are obviously offensive to public decency (*infra* paras 229 and 231). Greece's obligations in this area emanate from the International Convention for the Suppression of the Circulation of and Trade in Obscene Publications, signed in Geneva on 12 Sep. 1923, entered into force on 7 Aug. 1924, 27 *LNTS* 217, ratified by Greece under Act 4311/1929. The International Convention was amended by the Protocol signed in Lake Success, New York, on 12 Nov. 1947, entered into force on the same day, 46 *UNTS* 169. The Protocol was ratified by Greece under Act 2306/1953. Greece never became a party to an earlier relevant treaty, the Agreement for the Suppression of the Circulation of Obscene Publications of 1910, which was amended by the Protocol signed on 4 May 1949, 47 *UNTS* 159.

130. *See also* Communication from the Commission of 27 Nov. 1996 on combating child sex tourism, COM/96/0547 final, O.J. C 3, 7.1.1997, p. 2.

The offences now covered by Article 8, which is titled 'Offences abroad which are always punished in accordance with the Greek laws', fall into two groups: the first group (lit. (a) to (f)) includes those which are considered to infringe on national essential interests; the second group (lit. (g) to (k)) enumerates those offences for whose prosecution there exists a strong global interest. The Article 8 offences are the following (in the order of appearance):[131]

(a) High treason, and offences against the international status of the Greek State (Articles 134–137, Articles 138–152, *infra* paragraphs 180 et seq. and paragraphs 183 et seq.).
(b) Offences relating to service in the armed forces and the obligation of Greek males to perform compulsory military service, which still exists in Greece.[132]
(c) Offences perpetrated by persons having the status of civil servants in the Greek State or the status of employees in an organ or an organization (institution) of the European Union, whose seat is in Greece (Articles 235–260, *infra* paragraph 207).[133] The definition of a civil servant is given in Article 13(a) as the person to whom, even temporarily, the execution of a public service, of a municipal service, of a community service or of a service to any other legal person governed by public law, has been lawfully entrusted. This definition may not include, as a rule, those employed by legal persons, which are governed by private law but are wholly owned by the Greek State and to which the State has entrusted the performance of acts or activities of public interest.
(d) Offences directed against or addressed to a civil servant of the Greek State or against Greek nationals, who are in the employment of an organ or an organization (institution) of the European Union, provided that such offences were carried out while these persons were executing their service or are related to the execution of their duties.
(e) Perjury committed during proceedings pending before the courts and other public Greek authorities (Articles 224 et seq., *infra* paragraphs 205 et seq.).
(f) Acts of terrorism.

131. For the treaties creating obligations to Greece in respect of the offences laid down in Art. 8, *see also infra* para. 44.
132. These offences were regulated under Arts 202–206 of the old Penal Code. According to the Explanatory Memorandum, they were deleted because such provisions are not to be found in contemporary penal codes, while the matters relating to the compulsory service in the armed forces are regulated in the Military Penal Code. *See* further Art. 4(6) of the Constitution: 'Every Greek capable of bearing arms is obliged to contribute to the defence of the Fatherland as provided by law'.
133. *See, inter alia,* Convention drawn up on the basis of Art. K.3 (2) (c) of the Treaty on European Union on the fight against corruption involving officials of the European Communities or officials of Member States of the European Union, O.J. C 195, 25.6.1997, p. 2; Directive 2017/1371 of the European Parliament and of the Council of 5 Jul. 2017 on the fight against fraud to the Union's financial interests by means of criminal law, O.J. L 198, 28.7.2017, p. 29, which repealed and replaced the Convention drawn up on the basis of Art. K.3 of the Treaty on European Union, on the protection of the European Communities' financial interests, O.J. C 316, 27.11.1995, p. 49. Generally, *see* Art. 235(1) of the Treaty on the Functioning of the European Union: the EU and the Member States are obliged to counter fraud and any other illegal activities affecting the former's financial interests by adopting measures, which shall act as a deterrent and shall be capable of affording effective protection both in the Member States and in all EU institutions and agencies.

(g) Piracy.
(h) Offences relating to the currency (Articles 207 et seq., *infra* paragraphs 201 et seq.).
(i) Illegal trafficking in narcotic drugs.
(j) Trafficking in human beings.
(k) Any other offence for which special provisions or international treaties, which have been signed and ratified by the Greek State, stipulate the application of Greek criminal legislation.

*73.* The Penal Code does not contain a list of the relevant international treaties. Thus, theoretically speaking, whether acts, activities and behaviour, which are criminalized under a specific international treaty, fall into the ambit of Article 8(k) is a question to be each time interpreted by the criminal courts. However, the meaning of this provision is not that Greek courts will have jurisdiction over any offence laid down in a ratified international treaty, but only those treaties that expressly stipulate the application of the contracting parties' domestic criminal legislation or ask parties to create criminal offences domestically (e.g., the aforementioned UN Convention against Illicit Traffic in Narcotic Drugs and Psychotropic Substances (*infra* paragraph 44) or the International Convention for the Protection of All Persons from Enforced Disappearance).[134] Thus, even though, as already explained, Greece has ratified the Rome Statute establishing the ICC, not all criminal acts, which are laid down in Articles 5 et seq. of the Rome Statute (titled 'Crimes within the jurisdiction of the Court') come by definition under the ambit of Article 8(k) of the Penal Code. And this is because the Rome Statute does not envisage the application of the domestic laws of contracting parties. To ascertain which of the crimes laid down in the Rome Statute have been incorporated as substantive criminal law into Greece's domestic legal order, one should compare Articles 5 et seq. with the provisions of Act 3948/2011, which is titled 'Adaptation of the Provisions of Domestic Law to the Statute of the International Criminal Court (ICC) which Was Ratified Under Act 3003/2002.'[135] This is also what has happened in Germany, which adopted a specific legislative instrument, the International Criminal Code (*Völkerstrafgesetzbuch*), with effect from 1 July 2002.[136]

According to Article 2 of Act 3948/2011, its substantive law provisions shall be applied to Greeks and aliens, when the relevant offences have been perpetrated in the Greek territory, or against the Greek State or against a Greek citizen abroad. It

---

134. Adopted by the UNGA on 20 Dec. 2006, entered into force on 23 Oct. 2010, 2176 *UNTS* 3, ratified under Act 4268/2014, FEK 2014 A' 141.

135. FEK 2011 A' 71. In addition, Act 3948/2011 regulates the procedural relationship between Greece and the ICC, as regards cooperation, arrest and surrender of wanted persons, etc. These issues had not been addressed in the instrument of ratification, namely Act 3003/2002. There are currently 123 State parties to the ICC.

136. English translation at: https://germanlawarchive.iuscomp.org/?p=758. For Australia, *see* G. Triggs, 'Implementation of the Rome Statute for the International Criminal Court: A Quiet Revolution in Australian Law' (2003) 25(4) *Sydney Law Review* 507. An intriguing question, which cannot be elaborated here, is whether the repudiation of the ICC Rome Statute by a contracting party would also render inapplicable the corresponding substantive law provisions in its domestic legislation; *see* generally, K.D. Magliveras, 'The Withdrawal of African States from the ICC: Good, Bad or Irrelevant?' (2019) 66 *Netherlands International Law Review* 419–439.

follows that Act 3948/2011 does not share the spirit of universality that characterizes the ICC, whose aim is to ensure, within the confines of the principle of complementarity, that there will be no impunity for war crimes, crimes against humanity, acts of genocide, etc. Thus, the Greek legislator could have stipulated, in the true spirit of the ICC, that Greek courts will be competent to try all criminal acts laid down in the Rome Statute even though there was no link with the Greek State and nationals. Arguably, the Greek State might have feared that domestic courts would have to deal with the prosecution of crimes allegedly perpetrated by foreigners in a third State and that such foreigners might be citizens of a State with which Greece maintains close economic and military relations (e.g., with the USA). In short, Greece, and not the country of nationality, might become the jurisdiction to try offences allegedly perpetrated by nationals of 'friendly' nations, a fact that would complicate its foreign relations. Three observations ought to be made. First, these are political, not legal considerations. Second, the so-called *forum shopping* though debatable is not an unacceptable practice internationally. Third, for many years now, other European States, including Belgium and Spain, have embraced universality for gross violations of international law. The Greek legislator has clearly not followed the spirit of universality which distinguishes several European countries.

### A. *The Effects of Criminal Penal Procedures in Foreign States and the Execution of Criminal Sanctions Imposed Abroad*

*74*. The effects on the Greek legal system of crimes committed abroad are regulated in Articles 9–11 of the Penal Code.[137] Article 9 lays down the principle that offences, which were perpetrated abroad, shall not be prosecuted before Greek criminal courts, if one of the following three instances is present.

First, if the offender was tried abroad and was acquitted or, in case he was convicted, he has fully served the criminal penalty inflicted. The latter provision, which should also be understood as a manifestation of the *non bis in idem* principle (*infra* paragraph 359), has been interpreted rather restrictively by Greek courts.[138] Thus, the latter tend not to apply Article 9, if the charges against the alleged offender were dropped as the result of 'plea bargaining' between him and the prosecution and not on the basis of a criminal court judgment. However, since the new CCP has introduced the procedure of plea bargaining principally for financial and economic crimes (*infra* paragraphs 507 et seq.), the stance of courts will have to change (at least) as far as these crimes are concerned. Given that the typology of criminal offences differs, and sometimes considerably, between national legal systems, it would be helpful if the Ministry of Justice published guidelines on this matter.

---

137. Generally, *see* W. Gruetzner, 'Les effets dans un état européen des decisions pénales rendues dans un autre état européen' in Institut d'Etudes européennes, *Droit Pénal Européen*, Bruxelles: Presses Universitaires de Bruxelles, 1970, 357, with references to the old Greek Penal Code.
138. Generally, *see* G. Coffey, 'Resolving Conflicts of Jurisdiction in Criminal Proceedings: Interpreting *ne bis in idem* in Conjunction with the Principle of Complementarity' (2013) 4 *New Journal of European Criminal Law* 59–81.

Finally, Greek courts do not regard release on parole as a fully served custodial sentence unless and until the whole time of the parole has lapsed.

Second, if, in accordance with the applicable foreign law, the prosecution of the offence has been time-barred or the inflicted criminal sanction was time-barred or pardoned.

Third, if, in accordance with the applicable foreign law, for the offence to be prosecuted, it is required that the victim has filed a criminal complaint, and this was never lodged or was lodged but was subsequently revoked.

The provision of Article 9 may not be applied to any of the acts laid down in Article 8. Prosecution in Greece shall not be allowed if a res judicata judgment or other decision has been delivered by a court of justice or other competent judicial authority in an EU Member State concerning the same criminal act.[139] The application of the *non bis in idem* principle in relation to criminal sanctions inflicted is modified if the convicted offender is later prosecuted and convicted in Greece for the same offence. Thus, Article 10 stipulates that, if the penalty imposed abroad has been wholly or partly serviced, it shall be deducted from the penalty to be imposed by Greek courts. The right not to be tried or punished twice, as a manifestation of *non bis in idem* principle, must be observed by Greece since it is enshrined in the European Convention of Human Rights and Fundamental Freedoms (ECHR) (Article 4 of Protocol 7 thereof) as well as in Article 50 of the Charter of Fundamental Rights of the European Union (EU Charter).[140]

Although the provision of Article 10 implies that the decisions of foreign criminal courts are recognized and taken into consideration by Greek courts, this should be qualified by the provision of Article 11, which is titled 'Recognition of foreign criminal judgments'. Should a Greek national be convicted in a foreign State for an offence which, according to Greek criminal laws, leads to the imposition of accessory penalties (*infra* paragraphs 279 et seq.), the competent Greek court is expressly authorized to inflict them. Equally, it may impose the security measures (*infra* paragraphs 289 et seq.), which are stipulated in Greek criminal statutes, to anyone convicted or acquitted in a foreign State. The only exception concerns res judicata judgments or decisions, which have been rendered by a court of justice or other competent judicial authority in an EU Member State, as already explained. It follows that accessory penalties may be imposed only upon Greek nationals, whereas

139. *See also* Council Framework Decision 2009/948/JHA of 30 Nov. 2009 on prevention and settlement of conflicts of exercise of jurisdiction in criminal proceedings, O.J. L 328, 15.12.2009, p. 42. This instrument aims at preventing situations, where the same person is subject to parallel criminal proceedings in different Member States in respect of the same facts, which could result in the final disposal of those proceedings in two or more Member States. Therefore, it seeks to prevent an infringement of the principle of *non bis in idem*, as stated in para. 3 of the Preamble.

140. As regards the EU legal order, this principle also operates as a ground allowing Member States to refuse judicial cooperation in criminal matters, *see* e.g., Art. 3 of Council Framework Decision 2002/584/JHA of 13 Jun. 2002 on the European arrest warrant and the surrender procedures between Member States – Statements made by certain Member States on the adoption of the Framework Decision, O.J. L 190, 18.7.2002, p. 1, and Art. 11 of Directive 2014/41 of the European Parliament and of the Council of 3 Apr. 2014 regarding the European Investigation Order in criminal matters, O.J. L 130, 1.5.2014, p. 1.

security measures upon both Greek nationals and foreigners. This different treatment should be attributed to the fact that Greek criminal law does not regard security measures as punishment per se but rather as a means to protect the society at large from the offender's violent or dangerous personality.

## §3. Principles Concerning the Applicability of Criminal Statutes with Regard to Persons

*75.* Notwithstanding that criminal law provisions are of general application, both Greek law and public international law afford protection to certain categories of persons by stipulating that they are immune from the instigation of criminal proceedings against them. The rationale of granting such immunities is primarily based on the important or special nature of the office which these persons hold. Generally speaking, these immunities are only valid for the duration of holding office and for the offences allegedly perpetrated during that time.

### I. Immunities Based on Domestic Public Law

*76.* Traditionally, persons holding high public offices have been immune from criminal prosecution, including the Head of State, the Prime Minister and Ministers, as well as members of Parliament. As far as the President of the Republic is concerned, Article 49(1) of the Constitution stipulates that he shall bear no responsibility whatsoever for acts relating to exercising his duties, with the exception of the serious crime of high treason (Article 134, *infra* paragraph 180) and the intentional breach of the Constitution. This provision has been further elaborated in Act 265/1976 on the responsibility of the President of the Republic, which contains the modalities for the criminal prosecution and removal from office.[141] Act 265/1976 divides the acts which the President of the Republic carries out into two categories: those which are directly related to the exercising of official duties and those which are not relevant to the office (the Presidency). As regards the former, he shall incur criminal liability only for high treason, which is defined as overthrowing or forcefully changing the constitutional order, and for the intentional breach of the Constitution, which is defined as deliberately acting against the Constitution with the intent to cause serious disruption to the proper functioning of the State. As regards the latter acts, he shall assume criminal responsibility in full.[142]

*77.* The criminal liability of the members of the government is set out in Article 86 of the Constitution, which deals only with criminal acts and omissions relating to the exercise of their duties. Article 86, which covers those who are currently members of government, those who used to be members of government as well as deputy ministers, was one of the provisions changed in the latest amendment of the

141. FEK 1976 A' 6.
142. *See* P. Spyropoulos & T. Fortsakis, *Constitutional Law in Greece*, 3rd ed., Alphen aan den Rijn: Wolters Kluwer, 2017, paras 202 et seq.

Constitution in November 2019. Crucially, according to Article 86, the power of prosecution lies with Parliament itself. It follows that even a preliminary judicial inquiry may not take place without the Parliament's prior express authorization. According to the procedure laid down in Article 86, which arguably is cumbersome and complicated, a special court comprising thirteen judges from the country's highest-ranking courts shall be established to try the alleged offences perpetrated by members of government. These judges shall be drawn by the Chairperson of the Parliament in a public ballot. Such a special court is also the competent judicial organ to hear the criminal allegations against the President of the Republic. The modalities are contained in Act 3126/2003 on the criminal responsibility of ministers as amended, which replaced Act 2509/1997, which in its turn had replaced Legislative Decree 802/1971. The latter dates from the era of the military dictatorship in Greece (1967–1974). The criminal responsibility of ministers was first envisaged in Article 83 of the Constitution of 1844 and was first regulated in the namesake Law of 1876.

*78.* The protection afforded to members of Parliament is laid down in Articles 60–62 of the Constitution. They enjoy a general immunity from prosecution in relation to acts, omissions and other deeds, which are directly related to their office. The only exception is the offence of slander (Article 362, *infra* paragraphs 233–234), for the prosecution of which the Parliament must give its consent (Article 61 of the Constitution, titled 'non-criminal liability of members of Parliament'). This immunity extends to offences carried out by members of Parliament for the duration of a legislative period, except for *in flagranti delicto* serious crimes. Thus, they may not be prosecuted, arrested or imprisoned without the Parliament's authorization. In particular, Article 62(1) of the Constitution, which was one of the provisions revised during the November 2019 amendment, stipulates that:

> For the duration of the term of office, a member shall not be prosecuted, arrested, imprisoned or otherwise restricted without the permission (authorization) of [the other members of Parliament] … this permission must be given by the Parliament if the request of the public prosecutor's office concerns an offence which is not related to the performance of [the accused member's] duties or his political activity. The Parliament, under the responsibility of its chairperson, must rule on the request within three months after the prosecutor's request for prosecution was forwarded to the Chairperson.

*79.* Finally, Article 151 of the old Penal Code should be mentioned, a provision of a rather vague wording, which had received little attention by commentators. It stipulated that anyone, while acting as the legal representative (agent) of the Greek State or of an allied State, contracted affairs of his principal in a deliberate manner, which could have caused damage to the principal, faced confinement in a penitentiary. Although apparently Article 151 had never been applied in practice, it could have served as a legal basis for prosecuting, for example, a Minister of Minister Affairs, or an ambassador and other State officials, who deliberately entered into agreements with third States, even though they were aware of the damaging effects to the Greek State's interests. Even though the new Penal Code deleted Article 151, it should be noted that Article 50 of the Vienna Convention on the Law of Treaties (1969)[143] stipulates that, if the expression of a State's consent to be bound by a treaty has been procured through the corruption of its representative directly or indirectly by another negotiating State, the former State is entitled to invoke such corruption to invalidate its consent to be bound by the treaty in question. Presumably, these instances of corruption would have to be prosecuted under domestic criminal law.

## II. Immunities Based on Public International Law

*80.* Greece has signed and ratified both the Vienna Convention on Diplomatic Relations of 1961[144] and the Vienna Convention on Consular Relations of 1963.[145] Therefore, Greece is obliged to afford foreign-accredited diplomats as well as to consular officials the immunities which have traditionally been guaranteed under public international law and are laid down in these two treaties. Greece has not signed the European Convention on State Immunity.[146] Greece has ratified the Convention on the Privileges and Immunities of the United Nations (1946),[147] and the Convention on the Safety of United Nations and Associated Personnel.[148] It should be noted that the privileges and immunities stipulated in the UN Convention of 1946 have been taken over by several other international organizations in which Greece participates as a Member State, e.g., the Organization of the Black Sea Economic Co-operation.[149]

*81.* An interesting case of immunities concerns the relationship between Greece and the European Bank of Reconstruction and Development (EBRD). Greece is a founding member of the EBRD. As a result of the sovereign debt crisis that Greece has experienced since 2010 (*supra* paragraphs 4 et seq.), on 25 November 2014, it requested that it be granted the status of recipient country under the Agreement establishing the EBRD.[150] The reason for the request was for Greece to be able to

143. Greece ratified it under Presidential Decree 402/1974, FEK 1974 A' 141. Under Act 1981/1991, FEK 1991 A' 187, Greece also ratified the Vienna Convention on the Law of Treaties between States and International Organisation or Between International Organisations of 1986, UN Doc. A/CONF.129/15, which has not yet entered into force.
144. Singed on 18 Apr. 1961, entered into force on 24 Apr. 1964, 500 *UNTS* 95. Ratified under Legislative Decree 503/1970, FEK 1970 A' 108.
145. Signed on 24 Apr. 1963, entered into force on 19 Mar. 1967, 596 UNTS 261. Ratified under Act 90/1975, FEK 1975 A' 150.
146. Signed in Basel on 16 May 1972, entered into force on 11 Jun. 1976, ETS No. 74. Presently, ratified by eight Council of Europe Member States.
147. Signed on 13 Feb. 1946, entered into force on 17 Sep. 1946, 1 *UNTS* 15. Greece ratified it under Act 412/1947, FEK 1947 A' 213.
148. Singed on 9 Dec. 1994, entered into force on 15 Jan. 1999, 2051 *UNTS* 363. Greece ratified it under Act 2584/1998, FEK 1998 A' 45.
149. *See* the Additional Protocol on the Privileges and Immunities of the Organization of the Black Sea Economic Cooperation, signed on 30 Apr. 1999, entered into force 1 May 2004. Greece ratified it under Act 2933/2001, FEK 2001 A' 150.
150. Signed on 29 May 1990, entered into force on 28 Mar. 1991, (1990) 29 *I.L.M.* 1077. Greece ratified it under Act 1942/1991, FEK 1991 A' 48.

receive EBRD funding, grants and technical assistance. The request was accepted in the course of 2015. While Chapter VIII of the Agreement establishing the EBRD (Articles 44–55) deals specifically with its immunities, privileges and exemptions, the fact that it was to embark on operating in Greece and have a Resident Office in Athens apparently necessitated a further, bilateral, Agreement, which was concluded in 2015.[151] Of direct interest is Article 17 of the Bilateral Agreement, which contains stipulations on the privileges and immunities of the Bank's personnel located in Greece, their dependents and household staff. These stipulations, which are in addition to those provisions laid down in Chapter VIII, treat these individuals as diplomatic agents in accordance with the aforementioned Vienna Convention of 1961, even though the latter and the protection it affords are not mentioned in Chapter VIII. It follows that the EBRD staff located in Greece may enjoy more rights and privileges compared to other staff located in another EBRD Member State.

Finally, in February 2019, the Ministry of Foreign Affairs put to public consultation the text of a draft law, which provided for the recognition of an array of privileges and immunities to the Delegations of the International Committee of the Red Cross and the International Federation of Red Cross and Red Crescent Societies in Greece. The draft law was apparently never introduced to Parliament.

---

151. *See* Agreement Between the Hellenic Republic and the European Bank of Reconstruction and Development Regarding Cooperation and the Activities of the European Bank of Reconstruction and Development in the Hellenic Republic, done in Tbilisi (Tiflis) on 14 May 2015, entered into force on 13 Nov. 2015. Greece ratified it under Act 4341/2015, FEK 2015 A' 142, *UNTS* No. I-55018. For details on EBRD activities in Greece, *see* https://www.ebrd.com/greece.html.

# Chapter 3. General Principles of Criminal Liability

## §1. Introduction: The Basic Elements of Criminal Offences

*82.* One could view criminal offences from two different perspectives. The former could be defined as each and every act which the law punishes with the infliction of criminal sanctions. The latter, and this is exactly the perspective with which this Chapter is concerned, could be defined as the human behaviour, which violates those rights that are protected by the law[152] and which are enjoyed by individuals or of the society at large, in such a grave manner that the behaviour becomes dangerous and socially unacceptable. However, for such a behaviour to be characterized as a criminal offence, and not simply as morally unacceptable behaviour, it must be (a) attributed to the culpability of a specific individual, who becomes the perpetrator of the criminal act under the former (objective) perspective, and (b) regarded as criminal under the applicable laws.

*83.* From the above, it follows that a criminal offence consists of the following four basic elements:

(a) The Material or Physical Element (*Actus Reus*). A criminal offence is the result of an outgoing human behaviour. In other words, it constitutes the external manifestation of an individual's inner (esoteric) world, which few people might be able to fully understand.
(b) The Element of Unlawfulness. The offence must not only lead to the violation of legitimate interests (to be also understood as privileges/rights/freedoms) but must also be of such a magnitude that it could reasonably be regarded as an unacceptable instance of anti-social behaviour. As the imposition of criminal sanctions by itself entails the violation of the perpetrator's rights and freedoms, which are protected by law, through, e.g., the deprivation of life, property, honour, etc., the principle of proportionality must always apply between, on the one hand, the criminal offence perpetrated, and the threatened punishment, on the other hand. The principle of proportionality is inherent in any legal system subscribing to the rule of law.
(c) The Moral or Mental Element (*Mens Rea*). The criminal behaviour must be attributed to the specific culpability of the perpetrator, who must have his faculties intact to realize the illegality of his acts and behaviour before, during and after the commission of the offence. This element signifies that the perpetrator must be capable of being the bearer of *culpa*, that has acted either intentionally or on the basis of punishable negligence and that has not been prevented from acting differently (*infra* paragraphs 118 et seq. 'Grounds of Justification and Grounds of Excuse').

---

152. The term 'rights protected by law' translates the Penal Code's term *ennoma agatha*; in German the relevant term is *Rechtsgut*. *Ennoma agatha* is an overarching legal term covering not only rights and privileges but also other non-tangible notions such as the environment, collective values, public goods, and interests.

(d) The Element of Legality (*Nullum Crimen Nulla Poena Sine Lege*). As has been explained, this element denotes that the specific act must have already been regarded by the legislator to constitute a criminal offence and for the perpetration of which the legislator has already envisaged the infliction of a specific sanction.

The definition of the culpable offence given in Article 14(1) ('Crime is an unlawful act attributable to the perpetrator and punishable by the law') corresponds to these four elements: (i) an act; (ii) the illegal/unlawful nature of the act; (iii) the attribution of the act to the perpetrator's *culpa*; (iv) the act is criminalized under the applicable legislation. The new Penal Code has not altered this definition.

## §2. The Material or Physical Element (*Actus Reus*)

### I. Description

*84.* The presence of the material or physical element is indispensable for a criminal act to be committed. It is manifested in society through the voluntary conduct of the person committing the act. According to Article 14(1) and (2), the term 'conduct' could be expressed in two different ways: it could either take the form of an act (positive action) or of an omission (lack of action). The example of Article 307 will be given: it threatens the imposition of a term of imprisonment of up to one year or a monetary penalty on anyone, who does not save a third person whose life is threatened or endangered, even though he does not have to endanger his own life or health. Here, the criminal offence committed is the omission to prevent the materialization of a specific danger, namely the failure to save the third person's life. For the criminal legislator, it is irrelevant whether the offender has any moral obligation to save another person's life, to do so constitutes a legal obligation and, in its turn, its non-observance constitutes culpable behaviour (a criminal omission) punishable with criminal sanctions.

### II. Explication

*85.* It is a general proposition in the legal systems of all States that criminal statutes find no application to ideas, thoughts, emotions, sentiments, etc., which do not result directly in the carrying out of an act or an omission. This is true, irrespective of the intensity of the ideas and sentiments. For example, the thought of D to murder his neighbour, because he has an adulterous affair with D's wife, is indifferent to the criminal legislator for as long as D does not actually commit the murder or at least does not proceed with culpable preparatory acts. Thus, these inner thoughts would become of interest only after one or more of the constitutive elements of the relevant criminal act have been carried out. It follows that the application of criminal law commences the moment these inner thoughts have been externalized and have become actual acts or omissions resulting in negative consequences for one or more individuals, which become victims, or for the society at large.

*86.* There are two basic circumstances which surround the commission of criminal offences, namely place and time. As far as the former is concerned, Article 16 envisages that a criminal act may be manifested or materialized in the following two different places. The first is the place where the offender perpetrated wholly or partly the culpable act or omission. The second is the place where the consequences of the culpable act or omission have taken place or, in the case of attempt, the place where the consequences would have taken place had the offender's intent been fully materialized. That the place, where the criminal act was committed, might never be established is of no consequence, provided that the place where the offence's effects materialized becomes known. For example, if it is established that someone died in a specific place on account of fatal wounds inflicted upon him, there is no need to also ascertain the place where the attack took place.

*87.* As far as time is concerned, Article 17 stipulates that the crucial point is the time at which the offender committed the criminal act or, in the case of omissions, the time at which he ought to have acted. The time at which the consequences of the criminal act or omission were manifested or materialized is, as a rule, irrelevant to the legislator. The fact that the crucial element is the time when the act/omission was perpetrated is of importance when the statute of limitations is applied (Articles 111–112).[153] However, this formulation creates the following gap: because of their nature or because of the offender's *dolus*, there might be offences whose consequences will materialize at an unknown time in the future, often many years later, when their commission could have very well been time-barred. A good example of such offences is the (often deliberate) violation of the rules and regulations applicable to the construction of buildings. To faithfully observe all the relevant rules is of particular importance in Greece, as it is among the ten most earthquake-prone countries in the world. In the past, there have been cases where it was revealed that during the construction of buildings, which collapsed during an earthquake causing the death of people, the applicable rules had been breached. Thus, on 7 September 1999, an earthquake which shook the Attika region and whose epicentre was only 18 kilometres from the centre of Athens, resulted in the death of at least 111 people. After autopsies were carried out, it was revealed that 102 of them died as a result of the collapse of buildings, including three factories.[154] Breaching the applicable construction rules and regulations is an offence punishable, pursuant to Article 286 of the old Penal Code, with confinement in a penitentiary. In 2014, Article 286 was amended[155] to reflect the very large periods of time which could lapse between the construction of a building and the manifestation of criminal acts perpetrated during construction. Consequently, the statute of limitations was amended to commence with the death, or the grave bodily injuries suffered by the victims, but was capped

153. Note that Greece is not a party to the United Nations Convention on the Non-Applicability of Statutory Limitations to War Crimes and Crimes against Humanity, signed on 26 Nov. 1968, entered into force on 11 Nov. 1970, 754 *UNTS* 73.

154. Generally, *see* 'Greek earthquake: Buildings collapse as powerful tremor shakes Athens', *BBC News*, 19 Jul. 2019, at: https://www.bbc.com/news/world-europe-49047793.

155. Under Art. 13 of Act 4315/2014, FEK 2014 A' 269.

at twenty-five years from the breach of the applicable rules. In the new Penal Code, the statute of limitations was increased to thirty years, which should be considered among the stringent in the world.

## III. Acts, Omissions and Causation

### A. *Offences of Act*

*88.* As has been explained, the term 'act' in criminal law is understood as an outgoing human behaviour; it takes the form of externally manifesting the perpetrator's inner world. In effect, only human behaviour is punishable and, therefore, acts committed by animals are indifferent to the criminal legislator. However, under the previous Penal Code a person was criminally liable for acts committed by animals, which he owned, or which were under his supervision. In particular, Article 435 envisaged a range of relevant petty offences, namely neglecting to take the necessary measures required to avoid the occurrence of damage caused by dangerous animals, keeping dangerous wild animals without the required police authorization and turning dogs against people. As already mentioned, Article 468 of the new Penal Code abrogated all petty offences.

*89.* Although it is a general principle of criminal law that the victim of an offence may only be another human being, a person may be criminally liable when his actions are directed against animals with the intention to cause harm. The culpability of such acts should not be understood to mean that the criminal law confers rights upon the animals themselves; it does not elevate animals to the status of being recipients of rights *stricto sensu*.[156] However, the life, health and well-being of animals are protected by special statutes, namely Act 1197/1981 and Act 4039/2012 as amended, which establish, *inter alia*, the criminal offences of abandoning, abusing, torturing or killing animals.[157] Moreover, Article 285 of the Penal Code, which is titled 'Violation of measures for the prevention of diseases', criminalizes the transmission of diseases to human beings or to animals.

*90.* The State is mandated to protect the environment.[158] This obligation is laid down in Article 24 of the Constitution, which was amended in 1986 and in 2001.

156. *See* N. Kanellopoulou Malouchou, 'De la protection des animaux (en droit Grec): Vers un droit subjectif fondamental?' (2017) VII *Revue Méditerranéenne de Droit Public* 163.
157. Note that there is a world-wide movement advocating that animals and other creatures of nature should be endowed with certain basic rights offering them a degree of protection. In this respect, *see* C.D. Stone, Should Trees Have Standing? – Toward Legal Rights for Natural Objects, re-issued as *Should Trees Have Standing? And Other Essays on Law, Morals, and the Environment*, Dobbs Ferry: Oceana Publications, 1986.
158. For developments in Greek environmental law, *see* E. Tsioumani, 'Greece' (2015) 26 *Yearbook of International Environmental Law* 391–395; E. Tsioumani, 'Greece' (2017) 28 *Yearbook of International Environmental Law* 347–349; M. Ntona & E. Asimakopoulou, 'Greece' (2020) *Yearbook of International Environmental Law*, https://doi.org/10.1093/yiel/yvz030; and E. Asimakopoulou,

This Constitutional duty was rather belatedly implemented by virtue of Act 1650/1986 on the protection of the environment. Article 2 of Act 1650/1986 defines 'pollution' as the presence in the environment of elements, which could have adverse consequences on, *inter alia*, live organisms and ecosystems. Moreover, Article 28(1) thereof threatens the imposition of a term of imprisonment between three months and two years as well as a pecuniary penalty to anyone causing pollution to or downgrading the environment. As regards the protection of the marine environment, specific legislation was adopted under Act 743/1977, as amended, and under Act 4037/2012,[159] as lastly amended under Presidential Decree 113/2019.[160]

As a Member State of the European Union, Greece is obliged to implement promptly and in their entirety the relevant EU rules on environmental protection.[161] These rules are principally contained in Directive 2004/35/EC,[162] as last amended by Regulation 2019/1010.[163] Moreover, Greece has ratified a large number of relevant international and regional treaties and conventions, including the following: the Convention of Long-range Transboundary Air Pollution (concluded in 1979);[164] the Convention on the Protection and Use of Transboundary Watercourses and International Lakes (1992);[165] the Convention for the Protection of the Mediterranean Sea Against Pollution (Barcelona Convention, 1976);[166] the Vienna Convention for the Protection of the Ozone Layer (1985);[167] the United Nations Convention on Climate Change (1992);[168] the Kyoto Protocol to the United Nations Convention on Climate Change (1998);[169] the Basel Convention on the Control of Transboundary Movements of Hazardous Wastes and their Disposal (1989);[170] the Stockholm Convention on Persistent Organic Pollutants (2001);[171] the Convention on Wetlands of

---

'Greece' (2022) *Yearbook of International Environmental Law*, https://doi.org/10.1093/yiel/yvac054. *See also*, WWF, *Environmental Legislation in Greece 10th Annual Review – Summary*, September 2014, at: www.wwf.gr.

159. Act 4037/2012, Adaptation of the Greek legislation to the provisions of Directive 2005/35/EC of the European Parliament and of the Council of 7 Sep. 2005 on ship-source pollution and on the introduction of penalties for infringements (L255), which was amended by Directive 2009/123/EC of the European Parliament and of the Council of 21 Oct. 2009 (L280) and other provisions, FEK 2012 A' 30.
160. FEK 2019 A' 218.
161. *See* further, Commission Staff Working Document, *The EU Environmental Implementation Review 2019 Country Report – Greece*, SWD(2019) 138 final, 4 Apr. 2019, at: https://ec.europa.eu/environment/eir/pdf/report_el_en.pdf.
162. Directive 2004/35 of the European Parliament and of the Council of 21 Apr. 2004 on environmental liability with regard to the prevention and remedying of environmental damage, O.J. L 143, 30.4.2004, p. 56.
163. Regulation 2019/1010 of the European Parliament and of the Council of 5 Jun. 2019 on the alignment of reporting obligations in the field of legislation related to the environment, O.J. L 170, 25.6.2019, p. 115.
164. 1302 *UNTS* 217, ratified under Act 1374/1983, FEK 1983 A' 91.
165. 1936 *UNTS* 269, ratified under Act 2425/1996, FEK 1996 A' 148.
166. 1102 *UNTS* 27, ratified under Act 855/1978, FEK 1978 A' 235. Greece has also ratified the Protocols to the Barcelona Convention.
167. 1513 *UNTS* 293, ratified under Act 1818/1988, FEK 1988 A' 253.
168. 1771 *UNTS* 107, ratified under Act 2205/1994, FEK 1994 A' 60.
169. 2303 *UNTS* 162, ratified under Act 3017/2002, FEK 2002 A' 117.
170. 1673 *UNTS* 57, ratified under Act 2203/1994, FEK 1994 A' 58.
171. 2256 *UNTS* 119, ratified under Act N. 3447/2006, FEK 2006 A' 52.

International Importance Especially as Waterfowl Habitat (Ramsar Convention, 1971);[172] and the Convention on International Trade in Endangered Species of Wild Fauna and Flora (CITES, 1973).[173] Finally, Greece has ratified conventions, which have been concluded under the auspices of the International Maritime Organisation (IMO) and concern the protection of the seas from pollution, e.g., the International Convention for the Prevention of Pollution of the Sea by Oil (OILPOL, 1954), superseded by the International Convention for the Prevention of Pollution from Ships,[174] including the Protocol of 1978 (MARPOL73/78).[175]

### B. *Offences of Omission*

*91.* Generally speaking, offences of omission (*delicta ommissionis*) could be divided into two categories: genuine/authentic and non-genuine/non-authentic. The former category is understood as offences where the culpable act committed was to abstain from or to avoid carrying out an action, even though a criminal statute imposed the obligation to do so. Two factors characterize genuine/authentic offences of omission: the omission per se must be envisaged in the criminal statutes and must be punished separately. Apart from the offence of failing to save one's life (Article 307, *supra* paragraph 84), other examples include the following: (a) breaching the obligation to subsistence, provided that this duty has been imposed by law and has been recognized by an executory title (this will usually be a final court judgment), regardless of whether the title is only a temporary one (Article 358); (b) if an accident has taken place, omitting to offer the assistance, which was requested and which could have been offered without incurring any risk (Article 288(2)); and (c) omitting to reveal promptly to the competent authorities any reliable information, which has come to one's attention concerning a third party's plan to commit a serious crime or the fact that such party had started with its commission (Article 232).

*92.* Non-genuine/non-authentic *delicta ommissionis* are offences in which the punishable criminal behaviour is the omission of the offender to prevent their consequences, even though he had a 'special legal obligation' to do so. Contrary to the genuine/authentic offences of omission, these are not laid down in criminal statutes, and no separate punishment is inflicted. Article 15 states that, in those cases where the law requires the materialization of a specific consequence for the constitution of an offence, the fact that it was not omitted is punishable in the same manner as if it had resulted by the commission of an act, provided that the offender had a 'special legal obligation' to prevent its materialization.

---

172. 996 *UNTS* 245, ratified under Legislative Decree 191/1974, FEK 1974 A' 350. Greece has declared ten sites as wetlands of international importance with a total surface area exceeding 163,000 hectares.
173. 993 *UNTS* 243, ratified under Act 2055/1992, FEK 1992 A' 105.
174. 1340 *UNTS* 61.
175. Under Act 1269/1982, FEK 1982 A' 89.

*93.* In the past, the Penal Code did not specify the sources of this 'special legal obligation'; legal doctrine and case law regarded the law, contracts, and previous dangerous acts of the perpetrator as the main sources of such obligation. Article 15, in its present formulation, lays down these three sources:

(a) The law at large (and thus not only the criminal statutes). For example, parents have the obligation of subsistence of their underage children, which is based on the special relationship existing between them, as laid down in the Civil Code.[176] It follows that, if a parent knowingly omitted to fulfil this duty and the child consequently died, he should be responsible for the serious crime of murder by omission (Article 299 in conjunction with Article 15). In other words, even though the parent did not physically perpetrate the act of murder, the fact that he owed a specific duty to his child, whose omission led to the same consequence (the child's death), is treated by the legislator as if the actual act of murder had been perpetrated.

(b) Contractual obligations. For example, the contract between a factory guard and the company owning the factory gives rise to the special duty of the guard to do anything possible to save, in case of danger, the company's property.

The provision of services by medical doctors and by lawyers gives rise to certain duties, which have their foundation in these two legal bases. Thus, from a contract to provide medical services derives the special duty of doctors to protect their patients' life.[177] Equally, lawyers have a special duty not to act in a way which would be detrimental to the interests of their clients.[178] Finally, reference should be made to Article 233: it punishes with a term of imprisonment of up to three years or with a monetary penalty any lawyer, who knowingly causes damage to his client's interests either directly (e.g., by recommending a course of action which is adverse to the client's interests) or indirectly (e.g., during litigation offering his services to the other side as well).

(c) The offender's prior dangerous and unlawful behaviour. For example, the driver of a vehicle, who has caused grave bodily injuries to a third person, is under a special legal obligation to bring him promptly by the best available means to the nearest hospital. Should he, despite being aware that the victim's life is threatened, desert the victim, who later dies as a result of the injuries suffered, the Penal Code treats the driver as having caused his death by positive action. For this reason, he will be prosecuted for the offence of intentional murder. As in the aforementioned example of the father who omits to feed his child, the

---

176. *See* Civil Code, Book IV (Family Law), Art. 1390.
177. *See* e.g., Arts 13 et seq. of Compulsory Law 1565/1939, On the Code of Practice of the Medical Profession, which was abrogated under Act 4512/2018, FEK 2018 A' 5. *See also* the Code of Medical Deontology, which is embodied in Act 3418/2015, FEK 2015 A' 287.
178. *See* Arts 5, 35, 37, 38 and 140 of the Code of Lawyers, which is embodied in Act 4194/2013, FEK 2013 A' 208. *See* further, Arts 36–37 of the Code of Lawyers' Professional Ethics of 4 Jan. 1980. *See also* the Charter of Core Principles of the European Legal Profession & Code of Conduct for European Lawyers, 2019 Edition, which has been adopted by the Council of Bars & Law Societies of Europe, at: https://www.ccbe.eu/fileadmin/speciality_distribution/public/documents/DEONTOLOGY/DEON_CoC/EN_DEON_CoC.pdf.

driver has perpetrated a serious offence by omitting to carry out a special legal obligation, namely to bring the victim to the nearest hospital.

In reality, the driver has two legal obligations vis-à-vis the injured victim. The first is to save him from the danger threatening his life (Article 307). This is a duty of general application, in the sense that it applies to everyone who was in the vicinity of the accident and could but failed to help the victim. The second duty (to bring the victim promptly to hospital) applies only to the driver and, therefore, it is a specific duty. In these circumstances, criminal law does not afford the offender a choice of which of the two legal obligations to observe; he must always fulfil the latter.

*94.* Road accidents are further regulated in the Code of Road Traffic, whose provisions should be construed as *lex specialis.*[179] Article 43(2) thereof, which is titled 'Behaviour in the case of an accident', enumerates the various obligations imposed on the vehicle driver, who has caused a road accident resulting in death or bodily injuries. First, he must afford all necessary assistance to the victim. Second, he must inform the nearest police authority and remain in the accident area until their arrival. Third, he must refrain from making any changes in the accident area which could obstruct the Police. Non-compliance with these duties is threatened with a term of imprisonment of at least three months. Moreover, if the driver's behaviour leads to the death of the victim or to grave bodily injuries, Article 43(4) thereof threatens a term of imprisonment of between six months and five years, unless his offence is punishable by a heavier sentence under a different criminal provision, as well as the compulsory revocation of the driving license.

*95.* The aforementioned three legal bases of non-genuine *delicta ommissionis* should not be understood as necessarily mutually exclusive; in other words, criminal liability might be founded on more than one basis. Taking the example of the father, the liability incurred for the child's death due to his omission to feed him is founded on civil law as well as criminal law provisions. However, neglecting to feed the child constitutes in itself dangerous criminal behaviour and, therefore, his liability may also be based on the fact that he omitted to take his child to the hospital in order to save his life, assuming, of course, that death was caused by malnutrition.

## *C. Causation Offences*

*96.* The question of causation arises in the so-called offences of result. These are crimes (e.g., homicide, abortion, fraud, damage to another's property, etc.), which are manifested not only through the perpetration of a culpable act but, moreover,

179. Ratified under Act 2696/1999, FEK 1999 A' 57, as currently in force and lastly amended by Act 5039/2023, Measures to support relatives of the victims and those affected by the 28 Feb. 2023 Tempe train accident, pension provision, arrangements to enhance transportation safety, provisions to enhance development, interventions to modernize tourism legislation and other emergency provisions, FEK 2023 A' 83.

there is a requirement that the act has led to a specific consequence. To put it otherwise, that a change in the outside world has taken place, which is attributable to a culpable act. It follows that, in these instances, the mere existence of a criminal act and a consequence is not sufficient to establish criminal jurisdiction: there must also be an objective connecting point (causation) between the two so that the consequence has been the result of the specific criminal behaviour. That such causation exists is not necessarily the determining factor for imputability. This may only be concluded, if it is shown, that the alleged offender was responsible for causing the consequence as well. In the case of the 'offences of result', the process of ascribing imputability to a specific perpetrator is a two-part test. First, it must be established that the causation between the criminal act and the consequence does exist. If this requirement is satisfied, the second test is to determine whether the alleged perpetrator was also responsible for it, i.e., show intent or punishable negligence.

*97.* To furnish an example: A driving with intent at high speed in a densely populated area causes bodily injuries to pedestrian B, who is carried to the hospital and stays overnight only for observation as his injuries did not necessitate to be operated. The following morning the hospital is destroyed by fire leading to the death of B. Is A responsible for the death of B and may he be prosecuted? Clearly, there is causation between the behaviour of A (driving recklessly and realizing the associated risks) and the fact that B was injured. In these circumstances, the behaviour of A was the necessary condition which led to the injuries suffered by B, because, if A had not driven at high speed, B would not have been injured (*conditio sine qua non*). Moreover, there is causation between the consequences of the behaviour of A and the death of B, in the sense that, if A had not injured B, the latter would not have been hospitalized and he would not have died as a result of the fire (*conditio sine qua non*). Notwithstanding the existence of causation in both instances, this does not give rise to criminal responsibility for A because, as has been explained, intent or punishable negligence must also be shown to establish criminal responsibility. In the present example, the burning down of the hospital was an act outside the sphere of influence of A. Thus, the second test is not satisfied and, consequently, A may only be prosecuted for having caused bodily injuries to B.

*98.* The theory of *conditio sine qua non* has always been prevalent in Greek criminal law. However, its application before the introduction of the old Penal Code differed because it was not required to show criminal responsibility vis-à-vis the perpetrator: the existence of causation was adequate to prosecute the alleged perpetrator. This could lead to cases of injustice because the offender might have been prosecuted for the heavier consequences of his criminal act even though he did not act with that intention. In conclusion, the demand that criminal responsibility must be shown in the case of 'offences of result' negates such an unacceptable application of *conditio sine qua non*.

## IV. Classification of Offences from the Point of View of the Material Element

### A. Momentary and Continuous Offences

*99.* Momentary offences are those acts or omissions which are perpetrated at a given time. The fact that the completion of their commission might have taken a certain period of time is of no relevance, as these offences expire the moment they are carried out. Momentary are the offences of fraud (Article 386), theft (Article 372), inflicting bodily injuries (Articles 308 et seq.), rape (Article 336), etc.

*100.* Continuous offences are those acts or omissions whose perpetration creates a lasting illegal situation. That these offences were carried out in the first place and were culpable does not exonerate their perpetrators from criminal responsibility for as long as they are considered to be continued to be carried out. On account of their very nature, omissions constitute continuous offences, e.g., the illegal confinement of a person (Article 325) or the failure to fulfil the obligation to subsistence (Article 358). Notwithstanding the temporal duration of a continuous offence, it always constitutes a single offence and, therefore, it may be punished only once. For example, in the case of the father, who neglects to feed his children, he did not commit the punishable offence of Article 358 each and every time he had the obligation to subsistence.

*101.* The distinction of offences into momentary and continuous is of practical importance in the following instances:

(a) In the application of the statute of limitations. In the case of continuous offences, the statute of limitations may commence only after the act or omission has been materialized in full (expired). The example of the offence of breaching the rules and regulations concerning the construction of buildings leading to death of persons many years later has been given above.
(b) In the case of defence (*infra* paragraphs 121 et seq.). Defence is a justifiable excuse only for as long as the offence is being carried out and may not be invoked after the offence has been completed because it would then become retaliation/reprisals.
(c) In the case of accomplice liability. A person may be an accomplice only if he had participated before or during the perpetration of the offence.
(d) In the enforcement of the legal principle *mala fides superveniens nocet*. This rule is applied only in the case of a continuous offence.
(e) In the application of the most recent criminal statute. If the commission of a continuous offence commenced when a particular criminal statute was in force and continued while different statutes were in effect, the alleged offender will be tried according to the most recent one, irrespective of whether an earlier statute might have been milder for the alleged offender in question.

*B. Occasional and Habitual Offences: Committing Offences 'As a Profession'*

*102.* This is another categorization of offences and concerns both momentary and continuous offences. The distinction centres on the typology of the criminal behaviour shown by the perpetrator, *in casu* the habit of committing offences of a certain type. This behavioural pattern is of interest to the criminal legislator because it reveals particular characteristics of his personality which ought to be taken into account. The old Penal Code envisaged several instances where the repeated commission of the same type of offence was to be treated as aggravating circumstances, invariably leading to the imposition of more severe criminal sanctions, going as far as confinement in a penitentiary. Several of them were removed in the new Penal Code. Suffice to mention forgery (Article 216(3) of the old Penal Code); pimping (Article 349(3)); theft (Article 374(e)); fraud (Article 386(3)); and receiving or handling in goods obtained by committing a criminal act (Article 394(4)). As far as the new Penal Code is concerned, the commission of the same offence 'by profession' constitutes aggravating circumstances, *inter alia*, in the following criminal acts: abortion (Article 304(2)); assisting sexual intercourse with a minor (Article 348(1)); extortion (Article 385(3)); child pornography (Article 348A(4)(a)); and loan sharking (Article 404(2)). As is made explicit in these provisions, heavier penalties are to be imposed because the offender acted 'as a profession', i.e., with an intention to acquire illegal income on a regular basis.

## §3. The Moral or Mental Element (*Mens Rea*)

### I. Subjective Guilt or Culpability

*103.* *See supra* paragraphs 19, 51–52.

### II. Intent

*104.* According to Article 27(1), the notion of intent could be defined as the psychological state of a human being (person), who, although fully aware of the circumstances (elements) which, pursuant to the criminal statutes, constitute the commission of an illegal act or omission, wishes, aims at or accepts that their results will be materialized. Thus, the notion of intent is made up of two components: the mental and the volitional (*sciens et volens*). For intent to exist, it is irrelevant whether the alleged offender was aware that his act or omission was unlawful. The term 'intent', as used in the criminal statutes, should be distinguished from its use in everyday life, where it is usually understood as *dolus malus*. Whether the offender was aware of the illegal nature of his act or not is an indifferent consideration for the criminal legislator to the extent that it concerns the existence of *dolus*. On the contrary, such awareness is taken into account for the purposes of imputation and accusation.

## A. *Types of Intent with Reference to Their Consequences*

*105.* The notion of intent is manifested in the following three variations:

(1) Purpose (or direct intent of the first degree). The offender acts in order to bring about the consequences of his illegal behaviour. In these cases, the materialization of the consequences is exactly what the offender has been aiming at; for example, by shooting B (the act), A had intended to kill him (the result) and his mind was framed accordingly.
(2) Direct Intent (or direct intent of the second degree – *dolus directus*). The offender visualizes the materialization of the constitutive elements of a crime as the necessary consequences of his behaviour and, importantly, accepts it. In these cases, the offender recognizes that the commission of the offence will be a necessary side effect of his intended aim. For example, A sets his house alight (the act) to defraud the insurance company by cashing in the fire insurance policy (the aim), even though he knows and accepts that his actions will cause the death of his invalid mother, who is confined in her bed and cannot move without assistance (the side effect). It should be noted that in the old Penal Code, the commission of fraud relating to an insurance policy was a separate criminal act envisaged in Article 388. The new Penal Code abrogated this provision and effectively included it in the general offence of fraud, whose constitutive elements are laid down in Article 386 (*infra* paragraph 246).
(3) Indirect or Eventual Intent (*dolus eventualis*). The offender is aware or visualizes as probable the materialization of the constitutive elements of a criminal act as a result of this action but, nevertheless, accepts it. In these cases, the offender recognizes that, as a probable side effect of his intended aim, a criminal act may be committed. For example, A shoots at B (the act) in order to scare B off his property (the aim), notwithstanding that the shooting could potentially lead to causing B bodily injuries (the side effect). A does accept this probability and carries out the shooting. The main difference between direct and indirect intent lies into the varying degree of apprehension that the offender has as regards the possibility and the probability that, through the acts he has resolved to carry out, he will commit a criminal offence.

## B. *Degrees of Intent*

*106.* The above-mentioned three variations of intent lead to the question of whether the criminal legislator demands that all intentional offences are committed by the same degree of *dolus*. As a general proposition, it could be argued that, unless the criminal statutes prescribe a specific degree of intent to be attributed to the alleged offender, any of the three variations will be sufficient to establish culpability.

The Penal Code invariably uses various terms to describe intent, including 'deliberately', 'knowingly' and 'with the aim to'. The first term denotes that any variation of intent will be sufficient (e.g., Article 348A (pornography of minors)). The second term denotes that the offender must have acted with direct intent of the first or of the second degree (e.g., Article 229(1) (lodging a criminal complaint against a third person who has committed no offence); and Article 231(1) (offering refuge to a criminal)). Finally, the third term denotes that a supplemental mental element in the form of direct intent of the first degree is required to establish the culpability of the offender's acts (e.g., Article 370(1) (breaching the confidentiality of correspondence); and Article 372 (theft)).

### C. *The Distinction Between Premeditated and Non-premeditated Intent*

*107.* Premeditated intent exists when the offender is at full mental and psychological peace with himself which allows him to think rationally and to decide freely the commission of the criminal act which he has contemplated. On the contrary, the notion of non-premeditated intent comes into play when the offender is in a state of mental or psychological anguish and, in effect, his ability to reach sound decisions may, for this reason, have been diminished.

The importance of this distinction is best manifested in determining the severity of the punishment to be inflicted for intentional homicide. Article 299 envisages two types of intentional homicide: homicide and heat-of-passion homicide. The latter covers the killing of another person, which was decided and carried out while the offender was under mental or psychological anguish. In the former case, the threatened penalty is life-long confinement in a penitentiary or confinement for at least ten years (Article 299(1)). In the case of heat-of-passion homicide, it is confinement in a penitentiary for between 5 and 15 years (Article 299(2)).

## III. Negligence

### A. *Definition*

*108.* The Penal Code contains a general self-standing definition of negligence, which is applied to all relevant offences. According to Article 28, negligence is defined as the lack of attention (care), which the offender 'owed' under the circumstances and which he could have exercised and, because of which, he either did not envisage the criminal consequences of his action or he did envisage them but believed that they would not materialize.

*109.* Arguably, this definition suggests that the notion of negligence comprises the following three elements:

(1) The element of error (misapprehension) in the commission of the offence. This denotes that the offender either did not envisage that his behaviour would lead to the materialization of the criminal consequence or, although he did envisage it, he nevertheless thought he would be able to avoid it.

(2) The element of lack of attention or prudence required under the circumstances. This denotes that the non-realization or the belief (hope) that the consequences would be averted were the result of the lack of attention (prudence) which the offender could and should have exercised.
(3) The element that the result must be foreseeable. This is the connecting factor between the first and second elements and it is required under Article 28. This element operates as a *conditio sine qua non*: if the offender had shown the required attention, he would have envisaged the criminal consequences, or he would not have hoped to avoid them. The crucial question, namely which was the particular result that had to be foreseen, may only be answered on a case-by-case basis. The judge must place himself in the position of the offender and determine whether he could and should have envisaged, for example, that bodily injuries (Article 314) or death (Article 302) would result from digging a large and deep hole in the pavement in front of his house to undertake maintenance work without properly fencing it and illuminating it during the night. In such an instance, we are not concerned with whether the act constitutes an offence per se but whether the act (or omission for that matter) has consequences which give rise to criminal liability, irrespective of the characterization of the act as an offence.

### *B. Types of Negligence*

*110.* There are two types of negligence: (a) negligence without realization of the risk involved (absentmindedness – the offender does not foresee the consequences of his criminal act) and (b) negligence with realization of risk (recklessness – the offender foresees the consequences but believes or hopes that he will be able to avoid them). For example, A, driving in a densely populated area, does not exercise the degree of attention required under the circumstances and, therefore, does not realize that pedestrian B is at the same time crossing the road. A runs B over and causes his death. The lack of care on behalf of A prevented him from realizing the risk involved. On the contrary, in the second type of negligence, A foresees the possibility of running B over, but he is so certain of his driving abilities that he does contemplate the possibility that he will not be able to avoid hitting B.

*111.* The degree of attention (care), which had to be shown at a given moment, will ultimately depend on the personal circumstances, the capabilities and the skills of the offender. Certain categories of people must show a stricter degree of care than the 'man in the street' when exercising their professional duties on account of the special nature of their profession or because of their specific qualifications or skills that their employment entails or demands.

### *C. Evaluation of Negligence*

*112.* It could be argued that negligence has two aspects: an external and an internal one. Under the former aspect, negligence is understood as a manifestation of the behaviour of a human being and has as its object the incorrect (defective) commission of an act. Under the latter aspect, it results in criminal responsibility and has as its object the lack of attention (care), which was consequential of an externally incorrect behaviour. On the basis of this distinction, the definition of negligence in Article 28 might create the impression it covers only the internal aspect. However, it is true to say that the Penal Code does not completely ignore the external aspect. Reference will be made to Article 302 (negligent homicide) and to Article 314(1) (causing negligent bodily injuries or harm to one's health). Since these two provisions expressly refer to the consequences caused by negligent behaviour (respectively, death and bodily injuries/health harm), they do take into consideration its external aspect.

Finally, reference should be made to Article 29, which is titled 'culpability arising from the outcome (result)'. It stipulates that, when the law provides that a certain act is punishable by a more severe penalty if it leads to a specific outcome, which constitutes a self-standing (independent) crime of negligence, such penalty shall be imposed on the perpetrator only if the outcome may be attributed at least to his negligence and provided that the crime is not more severely punished in accordance with another provision. The provision of Article 29 is expressly mentioned in Article 42(3), which regulates attempts (*infra* paragraphs 156 et seq.): if the person, who attempted a crime, which is punished by a more severe penalty when the crime has a specific outcome, causes on account of his culpability this result, he shall be punished with the penalty envisaged for the crime having a specific outcome but reduced as per Article 83 (*infra* paragraphs 156 et seq.).

## IV. The Required Form of Guilt

*113.* In accordance with Article 26, serious crimes are punishable only if they have been perpetrated with intent; misdemeanours are punishable, if they have been committed with intent and, where expressly provided for, as a result of negligence. The Penal Code punishes certain offences with varying severity, depending on whether they were committed intentionally or negligently. This is consistent with the principle of proportionality. The relevant provisions include Article 264(1) and (2) (arson), Article 265(1) and (3) (arson in forests), and Articles 299 and 302 (homicide).

# Chapter 4. Justification, Excuse and Other Grounds of Impunity

## §1. General Principles

*114.* It is a general principle of the criminal law of most, if not, all nations that the commission of a criminal act does not necessarily lead to the prosecution of the offender and, if found guilty, to his punishment. Penal Codes enumerate, invariably in an exhaustive fashion, those grounds which would cancel the wrongfulness (culpability) of a criminal act or omission. In these instances, it is acknowledged that a criminal act has been perpetrated but, for reasons of natural law or of procedural fairness or for some other reason, the State has decided to forfeit its right to prosecute the alleged offender, despite the wish of the victim to see the alleged offender tried.

*115.* The grounds of impunity, which are envisaged by the Penal Code, fall into two groups: those negating the unlawful (culpable) nature of a criminal act or omission (grounds of justification, Articles 20–25) and those negating the imputability of an offence to a certain person (grounds of excuse, Articles 30–35). Moreover, the former could be categorized as general or specific and relate either to the offence or to the person of the alleged offender. Thus, general grounds concerning offences would be necessity and defence. As examples of specific grounds, the following provisions could be mentioned: the justifiable infringement of professional secrecy (Article 371(4)); the consent of the victim in the case of bodily injuries/health harm provided that it is not in conflict with *bonos mores* (Article 308(3)); and the termination of pregnancy (abortion) which was carried out to save a pregnant woman's life or with her consent in some other cases (Article 304(4)). General grounds concerning the person of the alleged offender include defence, whereas specific ones include superior orders.

*116.* Over and above the grounds of justification, which are expressly laid down in the Penal Code, Article 20 stipulates that the unlawful nature of an offence is negated, if the act was undertaken while exercising a right or while fulfilling a duty provided for by law. Thus, the bailiff, who opens by force the door of the warehouse belonging to A in order to enter in it and sequestrate his property, is not acting unlawfully, as he does so in execution of a court order delivered against A. Under Greek law, bailiffs are obligated to execute court orders and judgments when so requested by a person holding a legal title.

*117.* A rather interesting case concerning the application of Article 20 came before the Court of Appeal of Piraeus in 1993. A, in order to ensure that her son B inherits her late husband C, produced a birth certificate of B claiming that C was his father. Relatives of C sued A for the pecuniary damage which they suffered as a result of the change in the succession line (they would have also inherited C if B had not existed). The court acquitted A on the basis of the birth certificate. Later, the relatives claimed that the birth certificate was forged and demanded that criminal proceedings be brought against the mother. The Court of Appeal refused to do so invoking Article 20 in conjunction with the fact that, under Article 224 (*infra* paragraphs 205 et seq.), the defendant does not have a duty to tell the truth, while the natural law right of self-preservation should also be guaranteed. In the present case, the court was careful to say that it did not accept that the defendant was exercising a right of telling lies.[180]

## §2. Grounds of Justification

*118.* The Penal Code envisages three general grounds of justification, namely superior orders (Article 21), defence (Article 22), and necessity (Article 25).

### I. Superior Orders

*119.* According to Article 21, an act is not unlawful, if the person carries it out to execute an order, which was legitimately given to him by a competent authority, provided of course that the proper procedure was followed, and the relevant regulations were applied. This ground of superior orders may only be invoked, if the person in question was deprived by law of the opportunity to examine its legality and, by necessary implication, its validity. For example, during a demonstration, A, the commanding officer of a riot police platoon, orders B, a platoon member and hierarchically inferior to A, to fire plastic bullets at the demonstrators. B, in executing the order received, shoots and causes grave bodily injuries to C, one of the demonstrators. B should not, as a rule, incur any criminal liability. Although he has committed an offence, he was not in a position to question the legality of the order given to him. However, legally speaking, an offence was committed (grave bodily injuries) and, therefore, somebody should be made answerable. The solution, which was given in Article 21 of the old Penal Code and was carried on in the new Penal Code, has been to regard A as the personification of the public authority which gave the order and, consequently, as the person who should be criminally liable. Hence, A should be the person to be prosecuted. It could of course be the case that A, in his defence, will himself invoke superior orders claiming that the order was given to him by the Deputy Chief of the Police, and so on.

However, the new Penal Code added a new paragraph two to Article 21, according to which the defence of superior orders shall not be applied if the order was manifestly unconstitutional (e.g., because the demonstrators were peacefully exercising their respective constitutional right) or illegal. It follows that, in the example given above, B may no longer proceed with executing the order knowing that, if its execution leads to the perpetration of criminal acts, he will be exonerated since the culpability of his acts will pass on to A, and so on. On the contrary, B will now have to reach a decision of his own based on how he himself interprets the (superior order) he has received. Thus, he may either execute it and possibly face a criminal trial later on, if a state prosecutor were to deem that the order was manifestly unconstitutional or illegal or refuse to execute it, in which case, he could possibly face solely disciplinary action.

180. Court of Appeal of Pireaus, Decision No. 211/93, (1994) 44 *Poinika Chronika* 533 (in Greek).

*120.* Article 21 should not be examined only in relation to the police forces[181] and *mutatis mutandis* to the armed forces[182] but also as regards civil servants as a whole. In a democratic state, which subscribes to the rule of law, civil servants must have the right and be afforded the opportunity to question the legality of the orders given to them. This is precisely laid down in Article 25(3) of the Code of Civil Servants, which is embodied in Act 3528/2007:[183] should an order be manifestly unconstitutional or illegal, the civil servant, who was ordered, is obliged not only to refuse to execute it for also to promptly report it to the competent public authority.[184] What at any given moment constitutes or does not constitute a manifestly unconstitutional or illegal order is subject to the personal opinion of the civil servant. However, civil servants are expected to act in an objective manner and not according to their personal beliefs. Therefore, the Explanatory Memorandum clearly states that, in order to refuse to execute an order, the latter must directly contravene the letter of a specific legal provision and not be considered unlawful just based on the interpretation of a legal provision.

Despite this clarification, Article 25(3) also stipulates that if an order, which is manifestly contrary to legislative provisions or regulatory acts, contains grounds that are urgent and concern the general interests of the State, or when the refusal to execute the first order, which was manifestly contrary to such provisions, was followed by a second order setting out urgent grounds pertaining to the general interests of the State, the civil servant is obliged to execute the order and to report it at the same time to the higher-ranking authority. If the order was given by a Minister, the report must be addressed to the Prime Minister. Arguably, this formulation leaves much to be desired and a lot will depend on balancing, on the one hand, the (perceived) interests of the State and, on the other hand, the rights, freedoms, privileges, etc., which were breached as a consequence of executing the order. At the end of the day, it will be a court of justice which will adjudicate this balancing. However, the basic principles and axioms that run through any democratic public administration based on the rule of law (e.g., the principle of legitimate expectations, the duty to give reasons, the assumption of liability in the cases of wrongdoing, proportionality, a good and transparent administration, the scrutiny that Parliament must exercise, etc.) need to be taken into account, as appropriate.

It is submitted that, depending on the circumstances, there may be other restrictions placed on hierarchically inferior officers when they are executing superior orders. Thus, even if an inferior officer is not, for whatever reason, in a position to question the legality of an order, he should refuse to obey it, if it emanated from an authority which was unconstitutionally established (e.g., a para-military organization) or from a regime which came into power from the unconstitutional overthrow of the legitimate government, from a *coup d'état*, etc. Equally, if executing the order

181. As regards the Greek Police, *see* Art. 2(4) of Presidential Decree 120/2008, Disciplinary Law of Police Personnel, FEK 2008 A' 182.

182. *See*, in particular, Art. 53 of the Military Penal Code, which is embodied in Act 2287/1995, FEK 1995 A' 20, as lastly amended by Act 4637/2019, FEK 2019 A' 180.

183. FEK 2007 A' 26, as last amended under Act 4714/2020, FEK 2020 A' 148.

184. Note that the previous legislative regime regarding civil servants, Presidential Decree 611/1977, covered instances where the order given was only manifestly illegal, *see* Art. 71 thereof.

would involve action, which is clearly prohibited by the legislation, for example, torture, inhuman and degrading treatment or other violations of human dignity (Article 137A, *infra* paragraph 182).[185]

## II. (Self-) Defence

### A. *Posing the Problem*

*121.* Under Greek criminal law, the legal foundation of defence is the so-called principle of the superior interest. This is a notion which, as the following illustration shows, is not always readily identifiable. Suppose that A, a robber armed with a shotgun, enters a bank and, after he has immobilized both employees and customers, starts to collect banknotes out of the cash drawers. B, an employee of the bank entrusted with its security, manages to set himself free, shoots and kills A. If B is prosecuted for the death of A, should he be acquitted on the ground that he acted in defence? To put it otherwise, should the unlawfulness of his act be lifted, because he tried to secure a 'superior interest'?

The question, which must be averred in this example, is to ascertain which was the 'superior interest' that B defended. Was it to prevent A from leaving the bank with the proceeds of his crime and, consequently, to avoid the bank suffering a financial loss? Surely, the bank's pecuniary damage (which could anyway have been covered under a suitable insurance policy) may not be considered as an interest superior to a man's life. On the contrary, the 'superior interest' should lie in the damage which A caused to the rule of law, the basis of every civilized society. A, by using the shotgun as a weapon to threaten others and, possibly, to inflict bodily injuries to them, or even to cause their deaths, has violated the enjoyment of their rights and freedoms. Therefore, he has breached the legal *status quo* of the society, which A has accepted by living in it. This should be the 'superior interest' that B tried to defend, while by committing criminal acts A was not upholding any 'superior interest'.

*122.* Normally, superior interests are not to be protected by private citizens. This is a function which the law invariably entrusts to the police force and similar authorities. However, as the police cannot always be present whenever superior interests are threatened or violated, their protection, and by necessary implication, the rule of law, may sometimes have to be left to private citizens. The latter, as they attempt to defend it, may commit offences, whose criminal nature is negated.

185. *See also* Art. 7(2) of the Constitution: 'Torture, any bodily maltreatment, impairment of health or the use of psychological violence, as well as any other offence against human dignity are prohibited and punished as provided by law'.

## *B. Position under Greek Law*

*123.* Article 22(2) defines defence as 'the necessary violation', which a person commits against another person, who is attacking him or a third person, so as to protect himself or the third person from an unlawful and present attack which is directed against them. It follows from the wording of Article 22(2) that it is a provision of general application and does not find application only in the case of specific offences. Moreover, it is irrelevant whether the person who commits the violation, acts to protect himself (self-defence) or somebody else. Article 22(2) would appear to be in conformity with Article 2(2)(a) ECHR, which stipulates that deprivation of life is not violating the Convention, if it has resulted from the use of force which is no more than absolutely necessary in order to defend any person from unlawful violence.

## *C. Conditions*

### 1. Conditions Relating to Attack

*124.* There are four conditions which would have to be present for a criminal act to be regarded as an attack justifying defence:

(a) The existence of an attack. The term 'attack' should be understood as human behaviour which threatens a right enjoyed by a third person and which is protected by law at the time the attack materializes.

(b) The attack must be present. This condition requires that the attack (aggression) is imminent or has commenced but has not yet been completed. The duration of the attack does not have to coincide, from a temporal point of view, with the duration of the offence. For example, A enters the house of B with the intention to steal a valuable object. Although the act of removing the object constitutes the offence of theft (Article 372, *infra* paragraph 239), the attack is still present if B, returning to his house, sees A running down the street carrying the stolen object. Even though the constitutive elements of the offence of theft have already been completed (the object is now in the possession of the thief who wishes to bring it into his ownership illegally), the attack against B is still present. Therefore, he –and indeed any other person, since the attack is considered to be directed against all members of the society– may still exercise the 'necessary violation' against A. In these circumstances, the act of 'defence' is understood as the indispensable action to which B (or any other individual) was forced to resort so as to terminate the consequences of the perpetrated offence, namely the loss of the (right to) property on the object.

(c) The attack must be unlawful. The behaviour which constitutes the act of the attack must be in breach of a legal provision, which was valid and in force at the time it was carried out.

(d) The attack must have been directed against the person, who acted in defence, or against any third party. The latter, broadly defined, would denote the society at large.

2. Conditions Relating to Defence

*125.* There are three conditions which would have to be present for an otherwise criminal act to be regarded as defence:

(a) The act of defence must be carried out solely in order to safeguard existing rights, freedoms, privileges, etc., which are protected by the law.
(b) The act of defence should aim at violating rights which the attacker enjoyed under the law. It is generally accepted that such acts may exceptionally violate rights, freedoms, etc., enjoyed by a third person. They usually take the form of property rights. For example, A uses the vehicle, which he has borrowed from B, for the purpose of transporting the goods which he stole from C. Since the vehicle is used to further the consequences of the attack, C may cause damage to the vehicle, if this is necessary to prevent A from escaping in it with the stolen goods. For as long as A is with the stolen goods in B's vehicle, the attack is considered to be ongoing. In these circumstances and in accordance with the provisions on necessity (*infra* paragraphs 130 et seq.), C should not bear any criminal responsibility for the damage caused to the vehicle.
(c) The violation of the rights, freedoms, privileges, etc., of the attacker must be 'necessary'. Article 22(3) supplies the parameters, according to which, the degree of necessity will be evaluated in each case. These parameters are: the degree of the dangerousness of the attack; the nature of the damage which was threatened to take place; the intensiveness of the attack and the means by virtue of which it materialized; and all other relevant circumstances (e.g., the methods which were available to the person invoking the right to defence). Exceeding what was necessary under the circumstances leads to the criminal responsibility of the person claiming to have acted in defence and will be dealt with pursuant to the provisions dealing with emergency situations in defence.

*126.* As has previously been mentioned, even though the Penal Code does not expressly lay down that the right of defence is an absolute one, its wording leads to the conclusion that it may be invoked/exercised in relation to any criminal act. Notwithstanding this conclusion, the following question must be asked: are there any instances where the person who suffered the attack should have considered acting in a different way, thus avoiding resorting to defence? Different answers have been given. According to one opinion, defence is precluded if the person under attack could have reasonably avoided it, presumably by not causing any harm to himself, to members of his family, etc. A second opinion, which would appear to be the most appropriate, claims that defence is always necessary, because it is a means to protect not only individual rights but also, and this is far more important, the rule of law. A third opinion argues that the violation, which the attacker suffers, is justified only if retreating from the defence would have resulted in diminishing the dignity of the person being attacked. This submission is based on rather subjective criteria and should, therefore, be avoided.

*127.* Notwithstanding that the act in defence is allowed to cause more serious harm than the averted attack, there should be a degree of proportionality between the attack (aggression) and the defence; in other words, defence has its upper limits, and the legislator should not allow the defending person to go beyond them. Therefore, Article 23 prescribes that acts of defence perpetrated by surpassing the degree, which was necessary in the circumstances, are punishable, as constituting offences by themselves. If such acts were committed intentionally, the perpetrator shall be punished with a lighter penalty (mitigating circumstances, Article 83, *infra* paragraphs 156 et seq.). If they were done negligently, the punishment to be imposed is that of the negligently committed offence. However, if the defending person went beyond the upper limits as a result of fear, panic or similar psychological situations, he bears no criminal responsibility.

Since the defending person, by exceeding the upper limits, commits an offence per se, it is now the attacker who finds himself in the position of exercising his right to defence. This is a situation where roles are reversed. The former attacker becomes the defending person and *vice versa*. Theoretically speaking, this state of affairs could continue *ad infinitum*. However, the intervention of the state through its law enforcement organs should avoid such eventualities. It should be noted that there are no legal presumptions of (self-) defence under Greek criminal law.

### *D. Prohibited (Self-) Defence*

*128.* According to Article 24, if someone deliberately caused the attack of a third person in order to carry out against him a culpable act under the guise of defence, he shall not be relieved of the penalty laid down in the legislation. As it becomes obvious, Article 24 caters for those cases, where an offence is perpetrated under the pre-text of (self-) defence. For example, A, being aware of how short-tempered B is, constantly provokes him hoping to cause his violent reaction (attack) and inflict upon him bodily injuries (Article 308) under the guise of acting in self-defence. A will not only be prosecuted but will also have to endure the acts to which B will resort to defend himself from the attack perpetrated by A.

## III. Legitimate Resistance Against Unlawful Acts of Civil Servants

*129.* The Penal Code does not stipulate if, and under which conditions, defiance of unlawful acts carried out by civil servants, or, more generally, by agents of a public authority, is permissible. However, aspects of such a situation are regulated in Article 120(4) of the Constitution, which stipulates that the observance of its provisions rests with all Greek citizens, who have not only the right but also the obligation to resist with any means anyone attempting to negate the Constitution. Evidently, the Constitution refers to instances of a coup d'état or when the State institutions have collapsed or when the State apparatus deliberately acts unconstitutionally or undemocratically, violates the rule of law, cancels the enjoyment of protected civil rights and fundamental freedoms, etc. It should be accepted that the duty laid down in Article 120(5) is attached to all Greek nationals and may be exercised collectively.

## IV. Necessity

### A. Necessity as a Justification

*130.* According to Article 25, an act is not illegal, if it is carried out by a person in order to avert a present danger, which threatens him or his property or a third person and may not be avoided by employing other means. Arguably, there is a strong resemblance between necessity and defence. What distinguishes them is that, in the case of necessity, the present and inevitable danger is not caused by an attack of another person and that the violation (the old Penal Code used the term 'damage') inflicted must be considerably inferior to the violation, which would have resulted had the danger materialized. For example, A is on a holiday with his invalid brother B. When A realizes that the hotel room where B stays is on fire, he breaks down the door and the windows to gain access to the room and save his life. A has committed the misdemeanour of causing damage to another's property (Article 378). However, the element of necessity (i.e., the immediate danger threatening the life of B) and the fact that the danger was present and inevitable, while it could not have been averted in another way, justify the violation (pecuniary damage) which was caused. The legal foundation of necessity is the principle of superior interests (*supra* paragraph 122): the life of B was an interest superior to the property of the hotel owner.

### B. Conditions

*131.* For necessity to justify the illegal nature of an act, all the following nine conditions must be met:

(1) Existence of danger. Unlike the notion of 'danger' in the case of defence, which is understood as human behaviour, here it means any situation, which could violate (the welfare, the personality, etc.) of a person or his property.
(2) The danger must be present and inevitable.
(3) The perpetrator was not in a position to avert the danger by employing some other means.
(4) The danger must threaten legitimate interests, the bearer of which is the person invoking necessity, any other person, the society at large, or the State.
(5) The violation must be considerably inferior to the violation, which was threatened, and which would have been caused had it been allowed to materialize. Article 25 stipulates that the degree of inferiority required should be calculated by reference to the 'nature and importance' of the violation caused. The term 'nature' denotes the material element involved; for example, private property is materially inferior compared to life. The term 'importance' denotes the element of intensiveness; for example, inflicting simple bodily injuries is less intense than severe bodily injuries.
(6) The violation caused must be necessary under the circumstances. The person invoking necessity is not allowed to use any means to protect the superior interest. On the contrary, he must employ those which will cause the less harm.

(7) The person, who is threatened by the danger, should not be under a legal duty to expose himself to the danger. This condition is expressly laid down in Article 25(2). For example, the captain of a sinking vessel is under the legal duty to leave the vessel last and only after he has done everything that is humanly possible to save the lives of passengers and crew.
(8) The person invoking necessity should be conscious of the present and inevitable danger and his acts should be directed at averting the danger and that alone.
(9) The danger must not have been caused through the fault of the perpetrator.
(10) The upper limits of necessity may not be exceeded.

If any of these requirements are not met, Article 25(3) stipulates that the provision of Article (exceeding the upper limits of defence, *supra* paragraph 120) shall be applied.

### *C. Prohibited Necessity*

*132.* If someone causes the violation in order to inflict damage to a third person under the guise of necessity, he shall be punished for having intentionally committed the offence. What has been said in relation to prohibited (self-) defence (*supra* paragraphs 121 et seq.) applies here as well.

### *D. Conflict of Interests*

*133.* Conflict of interests could be defined as a situation of necessity, where a person, who is under the obligation to fulfil a certain legal duty, may do so only if he does not observe another legal duty, the non-fulfilment of which would lead to his prosecution. It follows that the conflict of interests concerns acts of omission for which there was a 'special legal obligation' (Article 15, *supra* paragraphs 92 et seq.) to prevent the materialization of their consequences. The difference between necessity and conflict of interests is that in the latter case damage was caused to fulfil a specific duty, a situation which would ordinarily not have taken place in the former case. Unlike necessity, which requires that the inflicted damage must be substantially inferior to the threat, in the case of conflict of interests, the illegal nature of the act is negated even if the fulfilled legal duty equals (in terms of significance) the non-fulfilled one.

*134.* The legal duties involved in a typical conflict of interests situation concern either a conflict between more duties demanding the taking of certain action or a conflict between duties requiring action and those which demand that the person in question omits the taking of certain action. The former will be manifested in one of the following two instances. First, when the fulfilled legal duty ranks higher than the non-fulfilled one. For example, a surgeon chooses to operate on a patient, whose life is at imminent risk and not another patient, whose operation can be postponed without any major risk to his life. Second, when the relevant legal duties are all of equal value. For example, in a sinking vessel, a father chooses to save his own child and not the life of a third person. In this example, his omission is not unlawful, even though he had a legal obligation to save the life of the third person (Article 307, *supra* paragraphs 84, 91 and 93).

*135.* Conflict of interests as a ground for negating the criminal nature of an offence was not regulated in the old Penal Code but was introduced in the new Penal Code as Article 33, which is titled 'Inability to escape performing a wrong'. In particular, an act shall not be imputable to the perpetrator, if, at the time it was carried out, he was unable to comply with what was the right thing to do on account of a personal insurmountable dilemma due to a conflict of interests, provided, however, that the damage (violation) caused by the act is by type and importance proportionate to the violation which was threatened. As mentioned in the Explanatory Memorandum, Article 33 attempts to resolve the so-called tragic moral dilemmas, namely situations of conflict of interests, which are extremely difficult to be directly weighed in comparison, as the aforementioned example with the duty to protect the life of others. Evidently, in these cases, moral principles as well as philosophical ideals come into play. However tragic as these dilemmas might be, the criminal legislator does not regard them as being able to cancel the wrongfulness of the act. Thus, the act remains criminal in nature, and the perpetrator hopes that it will not be imputable to him.

However, there might be cases where the criminal legislator has chosen to regulate conflict of interests in a different way. For example, in the case of breaching professional secrecy (Article 371, *infra* paragraph 235), the act shall not be regarded as illegal and the perpetrator shall not be punished, if he aimed at fulfilling a duty or at safeguarding a justified important public or private interest and he could not have acted otherwise.

### *E. Consent of the Victim*

*136.* The Penal Code does not contain a general provision on consent. However, there are two cases where the consent of the victim expressly negates the illegal nature of the offence committed. The first concerns the misdemeanour of inflicting bodily injuries. According to Article 308(3), the criminal nature of the damage inflicted will be negated, if the bodily injuries were inflicted with the victim's consent and do not contradict *bonos mores* (*supra* paragraph 35).

*137.* The second case concerns the act of abortion or, to use the Penal Code's phraseology, the 'artificial termination of pregnancy'. According to Article 304(1), to perform an abortion is punishable with confinement in a penitentiary of up to ten years, unless the pregnant woman has given her consent. On the contrary, when the pregnant woman has consented, the person who performed the abortion shall be punished with a term of imprisonment up to three years or a monetary penalty (Article 304(2). In both cases, the pregnant woman herself does not commit a criminal act. However, if she is in her twenty-fourth week of pregnancy and she herself performs an abortion or allows a third person to do so, Article 304(3) envisages as punishment a term of imprisonment of up to six months or a monetary penalty. In this instance, the fact that the pregnant woman gave her consent is of no relevance because the legislation has determined that pregnant women have no right to terminate the pregnancy. According to the Explanatory Memorandum, in these circumstances, the act of abortion 'is considered particularly harsh and therefore intolerable'.

The above provisions raise the question if, provided that consent has been given, there are instances where the act of abortion may not be culpable. The fourth paragraph of Article 304 stipulates that, if any of the following three conditions are met, the artificial termination of pregnancy, which was performed by a gynaecologist–obstetrician with the participation of an anaesthesiologist in a fully equipped hospital, shall not be regarded as an illegal act:

(a) the twelfth week of pregnancy has not been completed; or
(b) the pregnancy is the consequence of rape (a serious crime, Article 336), of seduction of a minor (a serious crime or a misdemeanour, Article 339), of incest (a serious crime or a misdemeanour, Article 345) or has resulted from taking advantage of a woman, who was incapable of resisting fornication (a serious crime, Article 338), provided that the nineteenth week of pregnancy has not been completed; or
(c) the embryo was diagnosed with significant anomalies, or the life of the pregnant woman was threatened, or she risked permanent damage to her psychical or mental health. In these cases, the testimonial (confirmation) by a competent medical doctor shall be required. Under the old Penal Code, had the embryo been diagnosed with significant anomalies, an abortion could have been performed only if the pregnancy had not reached the twenty-fourth week. It follows that in this instance, the aforementioned provision of Article 304(3) would not have been applied.

Thus, if none of the above conditions is met, even though the pregnant woman has consented to the abortion, its criminal nature is not negated. The law considers that it has a right to interfere with the private life of pregnant women in an apparent attempt to safeguard the embryo's life. In particular, the Greek legislator takes the view that the decision on abortion is in the personal sphere of the pregnant woman for the first twelve weeks of pregnancy. Notwithstanding ethical or religious considerations, she is at liberty to decide whether she wishes to bear a child and give birth or not. However, after the twelfth week, when, according to scientific research, the embryo has assumed a *quasi*-life of itself, the legislator intervenes regarding, no doubt, that the embryo forms part of the society at large and is entitled to some form of protection. It should be noted that, according to the Greek Civil Code, the embryo can be the bearer of rights,[186] which means that the State has a corresponding obligation of protection.

186. *See* Civil Code, Book V (Succession Law), Art. 1711 stipulating that the *foetus* may become an heir.

*138.* Although, as explained, there are only two instances where the victim's consent expressly negates an act's criminal nature, arguably the consent of the victim might be applied by analogy in other offences as well, including insult (Article 361) and defamation (Article 362). This argument is based on fact that these offences relate directly to the personality of the victim and, therefore, he should be able to give his consent even though the criminal act has already been carried out. Furthermore, there are cases where the consent of the victim not only negates the offence's criminal nature but also its objective constitutive elements and, consequently, there exists no criminally punishable act. These are offences, where the criminal legislator expressly demands, and it is a constitutive element of the underlying offence, that an act has been perpetrated against the will of the victim. This form of consent is referred to as 'acquiescence'. Examples include illegal detention (Article 325); violation of domestic peace (Article 334); and rape (Article 336).

*139.* There are five conditions which must be met for consent to exempt the offender from criminal liability:

(a) The person who consents must be able to offer his consent as regards a culpable act carried out against him.
(b) He does so at his own free will and not as a result of external factors (e.g., threat, violence or deceit).
(c) Consent must be manifested to the external world; in other words, it is not enough that the committed offence is simply tolerated by the victim (e.g., he does not lodge a criminal complaint against the alleged offender).
(d) The offender should be aware that the victim's consent has been given.
(e) The perpetration of the criminal act consented to should not contradict *bonos mores*. Under the fifth condition, the criminal legislator overrules the victim's consent, since it takes the view that certain ethical standards must rank higher than personal volition. Notwithstanding that the Penal Code refers expressly to *bonos mores* only in the case of simple bodily injuries (Article 308(2)), it should be accepted that the same is true in several other offences, where the protection of human dignity is the paramount consideration. For example, the offence of committing minor lewd acts (Article 337): if an employee consents to his employer's lewd acts (which may take the form of sexual harassment in the workplace, *infra* paragraph 231) to avoid being made redundant, the employer will nevertheless be prosecuted, because the victim has been effectively led into offering his consent.

## §3. Grounds of Excuse

### I. Introduction

*140.* According to Greek criminal law, imputability is the disapproval shown by the society for an act committed by a person, who is blamed for it and who, consequently, assumes personal criminal responsibility. Imputability is connected to the more general principle of 'guilt', namely circumstances concerning the personality of the offender and justifying the society's disapproval. The legal basis of these two principles is attributed to Article 2(1) of the Constitution, which orders the State to respect and protect human dignity. It follows that a criminal penalty may not be inflicted, until and unless it can be shown that the offender (or rather the offender's mind) is blameworthy for the commission of a criminal offence. The grounds of excuse are circumstances cancelling the offender's guilt either because, due to his mental health or immaturity, he is not responsible (answerable) for his actions or because unforeseen and unforeseeable events, which he could not have influenced, have rendered his state of mind not blameworthy. Nature dictates that, for a person to perceive the criminal nature of his acts, a certain degree of maturity is required. This degree, which varies from society to society, and from epoch to epoch, must be sufficient so that a person may fully understand the notions of 'good', 'bad', 'evil', 'proper', 'improper', etc. at the time the offence is committed. In the Penal Code, the question of who may be imputable is answered *a contrario*, in other words, it only lays down which persons are not included in the realm of imputability.

## II. Minority: Underaged Persons

*141*. The age of the offender is, by definition, of direct relevance to imputability. In theory, every human being, regardless of age, is in the position to perpetrate an offence. However, not everybody is able to appreciate the criminal (illegal) nature of his acts. This is particularly true in the case of underage offenders. According to Article 121(1), the Penal Code shall be applied and enforced only against those whose age, at the time of the act's perpetration, was between the 12 and the 18 years completed. In Greece, the age for full legal personality and legal capacity is 18. It should be noted that, under the old Penal Code, the minimum age for being made imputable was eight years. The choice of the criminal legislator to increase considerably the minimum age above which a person is capable of imputability but leave the maximum age at 18 is arguably not in line with another change in the legislation, which came into effect in 2016 and concerned participation in the general (parliamentary) elections; according to it, exercising the right to vote was lowered from the 18th to the 17th year of age. Thus, if a 17-year-old is mentally ripe to choose which political party should run the country (a personal decision which has consequences for the society at large) and which specific person should be elected as a member of Parliament, arguably he should also be considered mentally ripe to envision, organize and carry out (at least certain) offences (another personal decision with consequences for the society). Pursuant to Article 126, the criminal treatment of underaged offenders is as follows: if the criminal act was carried out by someone whose age was between 12 and 15 years, the act shall not be imputable, but the criminal court is empowered to order rehabilitative or therapeutic measures against the offender. If the underaged offender has completed his 15th year of age, rehabilitative or therapeutic measures shall be imposed, unless the court deems it necessary to confine him in a correctional institution (the term used in the Penal Code is 'special youth custody facilities'), as laid down in detail in Article 127.

*142.* Over the years, there have been attempts to revise the criminal provisions relating to minors, not least because there was an obligation to bring the domestic legislation in line with the relevant international treaties ratified by Greece. Reference could be made to Act 3189/2003,[187] to Act 3860/2010,[188] and of course, to the provisions of the new Penal Code. However, today, one cannot be certain if the relevant treaties and recommendations, which have been adopted principally under the auspices of the United Nations[189] and the Council of Europe,[190] have been fully implemented in the Greek legal order.

## III. Incapacity for Imputation

*143.* The old Penal Code treated deaf-mute persons very favourably. In particular, Article 33(1) stipulated that they did not bear any criminal responsibility, if the court of justice was satisfied that they lacked the necessary mental ability to perceive the criminal nature of their acts. And even if the court was satisfied that deaf-mute offenders had the necessary mental ability, Article 33(2) directed the sentencing judge to impose a lower punishment, as their condition was enough ground to justify diminished responsibility. The new Penal Code deleted the provision on deaf-mute persons. According to the Explanatory Memorandum, the special care measures for deaf-mute offenders will be regulated in the Penitentiary Code.[191]

*144.* According to Article 34 of the new Penal Code, the incapacity for imputation is only reserved for those offenders, who because of mental or intellectual disorder or because of disturbance of consciousness at the time the act was committed,

187. Act 3189/2003 on reform of juvenile criminal law and other provisions, FEK 2003 A' 243.
188. Act 3860/2010 on improvement of criminal law for juvenile offenders, prevention and treatment of victimization and juvenile delinquency, FEK 2010 A' 111.
189. *See* International Convention on the Rights of the Child, signed on 20 Nov. 1989, entered into force on 2 Sep. 1990, 1577 *UNTS* 3, Greece ratified it under Act 2101/1992. Greece has also ratified the Optional Protocol on the sale of children, child prostitution and child pornography, signed on 25 May 2000, entered into force 18 Jan. 2002, 2171 *UNTS* 227, under Act 3625/2007, FEK 2007 A' 290, and the Optional Protocol on the involvement of children in armed conflict, signed on 25 May 2000, entered into force on 12 Feb. 2002, 2173 *UNTS* 222, under Act 3080/2002, FEK 2002 A' 312. *See* further the United Nations Standard Minimum Rules for the Administration of Juvenile Justice ('The Beijing Rules'), which were adopted under UNGA Resolution 40/33 of 29 Nov. 1985, and the United Nations Guidelines for the Prevention of Juvenile Delinquency ('The Riyadh Guidelines'), adopted under UNGA Resolution 45/112 of 14 Dec. 1990.
190. *See* European Convention on the Exercise of Children's Rights, signed on 25 Jan. 1996, entered into force on 1 Jul. 2000, ETS No. 160; Greece ratified it under Act 502/1997; and Council of Europe Convention on the Protection of Children against Sexual Exploitation and Sexual Abuse, signed on 25 Oct. 2007, entered into force on 1 Jul. 2010, ETS No. 201 under Act 3727/2008, FEK 2008 A' 257. The latter treaty also covers the offence of sex tourism, which, as has been mentioned, has been deleted from the provision of Art. 8 of the Penal Code.
191. Deaf-mute persons come under the protection of the UN Convention on the Rights of Persons with Disabilities, signed on 13 Dec. 2006, entered into force on 3 May 2008, 2515 *UNTS* 3, Greece ratified it under Act 4074/2012, FEK 2012 A' 88. The Convention defines persons with disabilities as 'those who have long-term physical, mental, intellectual or sensory impairments which in interaction with various barriers may hinder their full and effective participation in society on an equal basis with others'.

did not have the ability to realize the illegal nature of their acts or to act in accordance with their own understanding (perception) of illegality. Thus, Article 34 covers what is generally referred to as 'insanity', a generic term covering psychosis, neurosis, organic brain disorders and other instances of retardation. While Article 34 does not explain if this condition should be permanent and incurable or could also be temporary and curable, what is taken into account by the courts is that it existed when the offender perpetrated the offence.

It should be noted that the Penal Code refers to two instances, where the existence of a temporary conscience disorder could justify the infliction of a less severe custodial sentence. These are the serious crimes of predetermined murder (Article 299) and infanticide (Article 303). In the former case, if the court is satisfied that the act was committed as heat-of-passion homicide, instead of the maximum sentence of life confinement in a penitentiary, it shall impose confinement of between five and fifteen years. In the latter case, a mother, who deliberately killed her child either during or after giving birth but while her disorder on account of giving birth was ongoing, shall be punished with confinement in a penitentiary for up to ten years.

*145.* Article 35 deals with instances of deliberate or negligent culpable derangement of conscience (*actio libera in causa*). Thus, anyone who had decided the commission of an offence while in a normal psychological condition but brought himself in a condition of derangement or in a condition of total incapability so as to carry out the criminal act is guilty of perpetrating the offence with intent. Equally, if he had envisaged or could have foreseen that, if he drove himself to such a condition, he might have committed the criminal act, he shall be punished for a negligently perpetrated offence. Finally, if the committed offence is other than the one originally decided, the court shall inflict a less severe sanction pursuant to the provision of Article 83 (*infra* paragraphs 156 et seq.).

*146.* As regards insanity at the time of the trial, this is regulated in Article 80 of the Criminal Procedure Code. It directs the court to suspend proceedings if the court is not about to acquit the defendant. Whether the defendant is insane or not is determined by an expert opinion, which is carried out in a state psychiatric hospital (Article 200 of the Code of Criminal Procedure).

## IV. Intoxication

*147.* If an offender intoxicated himself for the purpose of committing a criminal act, the provision of the aforementioned Article 35 shall apply. The old Penal Code contained two relevant provisions which do not appear in the new Penal Code. The first was Article 193: if someone had committed in the state of deliberate or negligent intoxication an offence, which would have been otherwise imputed to him as a serious crime or misdemeanour, he would have been sentenced, respectively, to a maximum of six months or to a maximum of two years imprisonment. The rationale for the abrogation was that it was not justified that this category of offenders should be treated differently. The second was Article 440, according to which it constituted a petty offence to endanger a person or to violate public order regulations while in a state of intoxication.

## V. Force Majeure and Coercion

*148.* The Penal Code does not expressly refer to force majeure, possibly because it was feared that the insertion of such a general provision would lead to legal uncertainty. However, the case of conflict of interests (*supra* paragraphs 133 et seq.) might be described as a force majeure situation. Coercion has been examined in the context of Article 25 (*supra* paragraphs 130–131).

## VI. Ignorance or Mistake

### A. *Ignorance or Mistake of Law (Legal Error)*

*149.* The Penal Code distinguishes between two instances of ignorance or mistake of law: ignorance of the illegality of a certain act, namely the existence of a statute making an act unlawful (Article 31(1)), and ignorance concerning the criminal nature of an act (Article 31(2)), the so-called excusable legal error. According to the former provision, ignorance of illegality alone is not enough to exclude imputation. According to the latter provision, the criminal act shall not be imputed to the person who committed it, if he was unaware of its unjust nature due to a mistake (error), which he could not have avoided even though he showed the appropriate diligence under the circumstances. In case the offender could have avoided the error (e.g., because he could have shown greater attentiveness but he did not), the criminal act shall be imputed to him but the court of justice may impose a lighter sentence pursuant to Article 83.

The following example illustrates the difference between ignorance of the existence of a criminal statute and ignorance of the unlawfulness of a certain act or behaviour. A Dutch citizen is prosecuted in Greece for consumption of soft drugs. If, in defence, he claims that he was not aware that their consumption was punishable in Greece (Article 31(1)), the court will convict him. However, if he argues that he was not aware that it is prohibited in Greece and the court is satisfied that he showed the appropriate diligence under the circumstances, he should escape sentencing (Article 31(2)). Considering that the criminal laws in the Netherlands and in other European countries (e.g., United Kingdom, Ireland, Germany, etc.) do not criminalize the consumption of soft drugs, the defendant will have a good case to argue.

### B. *Ignorance or Mistake (Error) of Fact*

*150.* In case the offender is not aware of specific facts or circumstances constituting the material elements of an offence, he is not deemed to have had the intention of committing the offence. In effect, the act is not imputable to him as an intentional offence. However, if such ignorance is attributed to carelessness, he shall be prosecuted for negligence (Article 30(1)). Furthermore, if he ignored that aggravating circumstances were present, the court shall impose the ordinary sanction threatened and not the more severe sanction envisaged (Article 30(2)). For example, A illegally entered a building, which is open to the public, with the intent to steal. Even though A illegally removed an object of high scientific importance and value, he was not in the position to be aware of its importance and value. Therefore, he shall be sentenced for theft (Article 373) and not for aggravated theft (Article 374).

## §4. Other Grounds of Impunity

### I. Reporting Criminal Offences to the Competent Public Authorities

*151.* The Penal Code envisages that if the perpetrator of certain offences reports himself or their carrying out to the public authorities (i.e., a public prosecutor, an investigating officer, etc.) promptly, he shall not be punished. This is, for example, laid down in Article 263A(1), which concerns the offences of Article 236 (bribing the civil servants/public sector employees envisaged in Article 13), Article 237 (bribing court judges, jurors and arbitrators but also court judges, jurors and arbitrators accepting bribes), and Article 396 (bribery in the private sector). Moreover, Article 289(2) stipulates that in the case of the so-called common dangerous offences (*infra* paragraphs 214–215), the court may decide not to punish the offender, if, on his own volition, he prevented the danger/risk emanating/resulting from his offence to materialize. Furthermore, pursuant to the first paragraph of Article 187C, if someone who participates in a criminal organization (Article 187) or in a terrorist organization (Article 187A) announces to a public authority that the organization in question plans to carry out a criminal act or if he assists in its dismembering, he shall not be punished. In case the announcement was made by a foreigner, who resides illegally in Greece and an order for his deportation had already been issued, the deportation shall be suspended until a final judgment has been delivered on the criminal acts, which he announced to the authorities, and a residence permit shall be issued to him, without prejudice to the relevant provisions of the legislation on aliens as each time in force.[192] Finally, according to Article 298(2), the provision of Article 289(2) shall apply by analogy to the offences envisaged in Articles 290–293, namely offences committed against the safety of transportation, communications or other public facilities.

### II. Remorse after the Offence

*152.* For certain criminal acts, the Penal Code stipulates that if the offender has shown his remorse (repentance) after perpetrating them but before he was

192. *See* Act 4251/2014, Code of Immigration and Social Integration and other provisions, FEK 2014 A' 80, as lastly amended by Act 4915/2022, FEK 2022 A' 63.

investigated by the authorities as a suspect or before he became a defendant, the culpable nature of his acts shall be negated. These criminal acts are primarily of a monetary nature. As is the case with reporting the commission of offences to the authorities, the favourable treatment of offenders is not stipulated in the Penal Code's provision which criminalizes the act in question. On the contrary, it is stipulated in the so-called general provisions, which are provisions in the Penal Codes whose content applies to a group of offences that are similar in nature.

*153.* Thus, the 'general provisions' in Article 381(2) stipulate that the culpability of the acts envisaged in Articles 372–378, namely some forms of theft and embezzlement, and the damage caused to a third person's property (*infra* paragraphs 237 et seq.), shall be lifted if the offender has willingly returned the stolen property to the rightful owner or if he had offered full satisfaction to the victim by the time he was first investigated as a suspect or when he acquired the status of defendant. And pursuant to the third paragraph of Article 381, he shall be relieved of any sanction if, by the time he has been committed to a criminal trial, he has returned the stolen goods and/or has compensated the owner in full. Moreover, given that several of the offences laid down in Articles 372–378 may only be prosecuted if the victim has already lodged a criminal complaint, the offender is relieved of any criminal sanction if the victim has subsequently withdrawn the complaint. Presumably, the idea here is that, once the victim has been compensated, he might not want to pursue the criminal complaint. Finally, reference will be made to the 'general provisions' in Article 405, which are similar to those in Article 381. In particular, they concern the offences laid down in Articles 386, 386A, 387, 389, 390, 394, 397 and 404, namely some forms of criminal acts directed against the property of a third party (*infra* paragraphs 246 et seq.). *Mutatis mutandis,* the comments made above apply here as well.

## III. Impunity Based on Personal Grounds

*154.* The Special Part of the Penal Code sets out instances where, if certain circumstances of a personal nature are present, the court of justice shall not convict the offender. The first category concerns persons having an intimate relationship with the offender. 'Intimate relationship' is a legal term defined in Article 13(b). It extends beyond traditional family relationships and kinship and covers the following individuals: those connected to the offender by legal kinship, foster parents and foster children, custodial parents and custodial children, the offender's guardians and those who are under the offender's guardianship, spouses, those living together permanently or who have concluded a cohabitation/civil union agreement/contract,[193] those who are engaged to be married, brethren and their spouses or

193. Regulated under Act 3719/2008, FEK 2008 A' 241, as amended by Act 4356/2015, FEK 2015 A' 181; *see also* Arts 1354, 1462, 1463 and 1576 of the Civil Code.

those cohabiting with them as well as those engaged to be married to brethren. Interestingly enough, these individuals come under the ambit of Article 13(b) even if the marriage, the cohabitation or the engagement has been dissolved when the alleged criminal offence was perpetrated.

Two examples will be given. The first is Article 231(2), which stipulates that the misdemeanour of harbouring criminals remains unpunished, if it was carried out to protect one of the persons envisaged in Article 13(b).

The second is Article 232(2), which deals with the misdemeanour of not announcing to the public authorities one's information that a serious crime is being contemplated or has already commenced. Here the omission is not punishable if the announcement would have concerned an Article 13(b) person. However, in certain offences, the fact that the offender was a relative of the victim does not lead to a more lenient punishment or to the non-infliction of criminal sanctions. These offences include negligent homicide (Article 302),[194] and the abduction of minors (Article 324).[195] Finally, reference should be made to Article 345(2), which stipulates that in the case of incest, if it was committed by children or grandchildren or by brothers and sisters, who had not completed their 18th year of age, they may not be punished.

*155.* A second category comprises instances, where the existence of specific circumstances, which directly influenced the offender's behaviour, leads to impunity. The term 'judicial remission of sanctions' is usually used. For example, Article 308(4) provides that in the case of (any degree of) bodily injuries, the perpetrator may be relieved of any punishment, if he inflicted the injuries out of justifiable indignation on account of the victim's earlier acts, provided they were directed against him or were committed before him and they constituted particularly cruel behaviour. The provision of Article 308(4) is applied to the offence of insulting someone by words, deeds or by any other means (Article 361). For other instances falling in this second category, suffice to mention Article 377 (theft of objects of small monetary value committed out of the need for immediate use or consumption), which is also applied in the case of small-scale fraud (Article 387).

194. Note that the new Penal Code deleted the second paragraph of Art. 302, which had stipulated that, should the victim be a relative of the perpetrator, the court may not sentence him, if it was convinced that he had suffered psychological anguish that justified his act.

195. Note that the courts have held that the biological father, who removes his child from the foster parent, is an offender and the same is true when a child, who was not born in wedlock, is removed by his biological father. Presumably, the same culpability exists when it was the biological mother who abducted the child.

# Chapter 5. Incomplete or Partly Perpetrated Offences

## §1. Criminal Attempt

### I. Describing the Problem

*156.* Usually, an intentionally committed offence goes through three consequential but different phases: the internal phase, the phase of carrying out preparatory acts, and the phase of perpetrating the offence (the external phase). The first phase entails conceiving to commit a criminal act and deciding to carry it out. As has been explained, this phase is principally of no interest to the criminal legislator. During the second stage, the future offender undertakes all those acts of a preparatory nature which shall ensure the successful perpetration of the offence, which he has already mentally designed. This stage is also irrelevant to the criminal legislator except for certain criminal behaviour, where the carrying out of preparatory acts constitutes in itself an offence, i.e., separate, independent offences. For example, Article 211 stipulates that whoever plans to commit the offences of counterfeiting banknotes, coins, and other means of payment (Articles 207, 208A and 208B) and for that purpose manufactures or possesses tools, computer software, etc., faces a term of imprisonment of up two years or a monetary penalty. Other examples include the serious crime of high treason (Article 135, where the preparatory acts may be committed through the dissemination of documents, pictures, or the Internet). The third and last phase comprises the attempt (i.e., the perpetrator carries out the necessary acts to immediately commence the offence) as well as the conclusion-materialization (i.e., when all the offence's constitutive elements have been carried out).

### II. Conditions

*157.* Article 42(1) defines attempt as follows: 'Whoever, having already decided to commit a crime, commences to carry out the illegal act envisaged in the legislation, shall be punished, if the crime was not completed, by mitigated punishment (Article 83)'. The use of the word 'crime' denotes both serious crimes and misdemeanours. From this definition, which was formulated anew in the new Penal Code, the following constitutive elements derive:

#### A. *Intent to Commit a Crime*

*158.* In the case of attempt, the intent to commit a serious crime or a misdemeanour differs from the usual element of intent. This is because, in the latter case, the offence's objective basis is covered fully by the subjective basis, in the sense that the element of intent is exhausted when the offender has aimed at exactly what he has been planning to do. On the contrary, in the case of an attempt, the element of intent exceeds the result. To put it otherwise, the person attempting the commission of a crime does not simply wish that his attempt is materialized but rather that the crime is materialized and completed.

*B. Commencement of Execution*

*159.* It is of crucial importance to distinguish between preparatory acts and what Article 42(1) refers to as 'commencing to carry out the illegal act'. The definition of a preparatory act does not usually pose any significant problems: it is an act which precedes in time the actual commission of the contemplated criminal act and serves the purpose of making possible or facilitating the materialization of its constitutive instruments. However, its differentiation from attempt is not always clear. For example, A has set his mind on murdering B. In pursuance of this aim, he purchases a loaded gun, collects detailed information on B's movements and decides on the place where he will assassinate him. Two days later, A is in the vicinity and, as soon as B appears, he aims with the gun, shoots and kills B. The ensuing question is to determine the exact point when the preparatory acts ended and the 'beginning of perpetrating the offence' took place. As explained in the Explanatory Memorandum, the perpetrator commences the criminal act when he has unleashed against a legally protected interest the energy which, in the usual course of events, can cause the culpable damage (fault), if it is not halted/prevented by another act of the same person or by a third person or by a subsequent accidental event.

*160.* Although criminal law theorists have put forward several solutions, arguably the most appropriate is the so-called theory of the impression caused by the offence. According to it, the determinative point should be the time when the perpetrator's acts gave the outside world the impression that an offence is being carried out. These acts should objectively shake the trust that the society has placed in law and order as well as in the security that the domestic legal system provides. This theory is in line with the fact that the Penal Code and, more generally, the criminal legislation do not only protect legitimate interests but also, what can be referred to as, their social environment. When, based on this theory, the society at large perceives that a criminal act is progressing, what the criminal legislation is eager to protect is exactly this environment, whose violation may under no circumstances be tolerated. To return to the aforementioned example of A killing B, a very reasonable conclusion would be that the execution of the offence commenced the moment A raised his gun and took aim at B with the intent to immediately shoot him.

*C. Incompletion of the Offence Independent of the Perpetrator's Will: Voluntary Withdrawal*

*161.* Attempt could be distinguished between finite (i.e., the offender acted in accordance with his plan, but for whatever reason the envisaged criminal result failed to materialize) and non-finite attempt (i.e., the offender did not carry out all the acts he had envisaged and, therefore, not all of the offence's constitutive elements materialized). An example of the former would be that A, intending to murder B, shoots at B but, instead of killing him, he inflicts bodily injuries which do not threaten his life. In the case of the non-finite attempt, A starts shooting at B but, before concluding his intention to murder him, he stops.

*162.* This distinction of attempt relates to the voluntary withdrawal from the commission of an offence, which is expressly regulated in Article 44 of the Penal Code. Voluntary withdrawal is defined as the offender's behaviour where, on his own free volition, he either abstains from any further act, which is necessary for the perpetration of the offence (and this relates to the non-finite attempt) or prevents the criminal consequences, which could have arisen from already concluded criminal acts (and this relates to finite attempt).

The following examples clarify the two forms of voluntary withdrawal. In the first example, A, with the intention of committing the offence of theft, enters the property of another but, before he removes any objects, he changes his mind (i.e., cancels his intention) and walks away. This is the case of abstention from any further criminal act. In the second example, B, knowing that C cannot swim, throws him into the sea with the intention of causing his death by drowning. While C struggles to remain afloat, B (possibly out of remorse) jumps in the sea and promptly saves him from certain death. This is the case of cancelling the criminal consequences of the act.

*163.* According to the Penal Code, the withdrawal must be based only on the offender's own initiative. Article 44(1) stipulates that it should be the result of external factors or obstacles. Thus, in the above example, when A shoots B with the intent to murder him, in case the first shot is unsuccessful and, subsequently, his gun is blocked and A does not complete his act, one cannot speak of voluntary withdrawal because A commenced executing the offence he intended and only abandoned it because his weapon malfunctioned. Under Article 44(2), if the perpetrator of a failed offence does not repeat it immediately of his own volition and not on account of external obstacles, he shall be punished with the penalties envisaged in attempt reduced by half. Moreover, under the third paragraph of Article 44 the same reduced penalty shall be ordered against the offender who, having completed the act, he himself cancelled the materialization of the criminal outcome, while the court has the discretion not to punish the attempt. Finally, if the attempt concerned the commission of an offence whose culpability is lifted in the case of remorse (*supra* paragraph 152), it will not be punished.

*164.* Even though the formulation of Article 44 was amended and broadened in the new Penal Code, the question of voluntary withdrawal in the so-called compound crimes has not been regulated. In particular, the question arises as to how an offender should be treated in case he completed the first stage of a compound crime but voluntarily withdrew from the next stage or stages, whose materialization would have completed all the constitutive elements. For example, in the case of a robbery (Article 380), the offender used physical violence against a third person with the intent to remove from him a valuable object but, when the third person surrendered to him the object under duress, the offender on his own volition did not take possession of it. Therefore, not all the constitutive elements of robbery were carried out. Arguably, since robbery is a compound offence, if the court concludes that, before the offender freely decided to withdraw from completing the crime as originally intended, he had perpetrated other self-standing (autonomous) offences (e.g., bodily injuries (Article 308); disruption of domestic peace (Article 334)), the court may convict and sentence him for these offences. *Mutatis mutandis,* the same argument would apply if the crime of rape were left incomplete due to the voluntary withdrawal of the perpetrator.

### III. Attempting the Impossible

*165.* Article 43 of the old Penal Code concerned the notion of an 'unfitting/inappropriate attempt', namely an act which, according to the mental picture which the perpetrator had depicted, constituted an offence. However, it could not have been perpetrated either because of the object at which it was directed or because of the means which would have been used. To offer an example, A shoots B with intent to murder him but he is already dead (unfitting attempt on account of object) Or A shoots B with the same intent not realizing that the gun is empty (unfitting attempt on account of means used). In the new Penal Code, Article 43 was deleted because, as stated in the Explanatory Memorandum, in these cases the perpetrator was punished because he thought he was committing a crime, while in reality, he was not endangering any legally protected good. It follows that the punishment was solely imposed on account of his *dolus* and, consequently, it would run against basic principles of criminal law. Notwithstanding the legislator's choice to delete it, in the case of serious crimes, arguably the fact that someone conceived them, completed the preparatory acts, commenced materializing his criminal intent and was determined to complete it, shows a disposition which should be of concern, not least because he could be expected to repeat his criminal intent. Following sharp criticism by legal scholars, Article 43 of the old Penal Code has been re-introduced by Article 2 of Act 4855/2021.

### IV. The Punishment of Attempt

*166.* According to Article 42(1), attempt is punished with a less severe penalty as *per* Article 83 (*supra* paragraphs 156 et seq.). Under Article 42(2), the court of justice, assessing all relevant circumstances, has the discretion not to impose any penalty, if the defendant attempted to commit a misdemeanour punishable with a term of imprisonment of less than one year or with a monetary penalty or with community service.

## §2. Participation in the Commission of Crimes

### I. General Remarks

*167.* The constitutive elements of a crime reveal whether more than one person are required to complete an offence (e.g., gang rape (Article 336(3)). It could also be the case that more than one person decided to perpetrate an offence together (complicity or conspiracy). Sometimes, the offender does not commit the criminal act all by himself but employs third persons to aid and abet him during its perpetration: the offender becomes the principal and the third persons become the accessories. If the offender (or offenders) carried out a criminal act, the decision for which was not taken by them but by a third person, the latter becomes the instigator. Finally, one or more third persons may afford assistance or support to the principal either before or after he carried out an offence. The Penal Code criminalizes the behaviour of all these persons.

## II. The Different Types and Degrees of Criminal Participation

*168.* The Penal Code does not accept the notion of the 'uniform principal', namely that all the persons who, one way or another, participated in the commission of an offence should be regarded and treated as principals. On the contrary, it understands the principal narrowly.[196] But there may be instances where it is not readily apparent if the carrying out of the separate constitutive elements of the same offence by different persons should make all of them principals. The case of theft perpetrated by several persons will be given as an example: A cracked open the safe deposit box but it was B who took out the valuables, and it was C who carried them in his car to D; D was the person who had already agreed to convert them into cash, which he had obtained directly from E, who, unknowingly to D, was the person who had persuaded A to use his expertise and open the safe deposit box. The solution is given in Article 45. It stipulates that if two or more persons carried out in common, wholly or partly, the constitutive elements of an offence, each of them shall be punished as co-perpetrator and, therefore, shall be regarded as co-principals.

*169.* It follows that it is of importance to distinguish between the principals and the other categories of co-participants, namely instigators, *agent provocateurs* and accessories. It is important to note that Article 48 stipulates that the latter's culpability is independent of the former's culpability. Instigators may be treated rather harshly considering that they did not actually participate in (physically) carrying out the criminal act: Article 46(1) provides that the principal's penalty shall be imposed on whomever caused another person the decision to carry out the offence, provided that the latter committed it. The rationale behind treating the instigator in this manner is that had he not caused the decision in the former's mind to carry it out, it would not have been perpetrated, and the equilibrium in society would not have been disturbed. The fact that the principal led himself to be persuaded by a third person to commit the offence is rather indifferent to the criminal legislator. However, even if the criminal act was finally not committed, that he was persuaded reveals that the principal had an immoral disposition and a tendency towards acting criminally.

---

196. On the whole, the text of the Penal Code is characterized by a spirit of economy, staying faithful to the ancient Greek adage that to be able to express oneself in as few words as possible is a virtue.

*170.* In the second paragraph of Article 46, the Penal Code refers to a special kind of instigator, the so-called *agent provocateur*, namely, someone, who deliberately caused another person the decision to commit a certain criminal act and did so with the sole aim to apprehend him while he is attempting to carry out the offence or at least a punishable preparatory act. This is also known as entrapment. As the *agent provocateur* intends to prevent the perpetrator from carrying out the offence in full, he shall be sentenced with the penalty threatened for the principal reduced by half. The principal difference between instigation and *agent provocateur*, both being manifestations of participation in a criminal act, is that the instigator's *dolus* is directed towards ensuring that the offence will be carried out, will be completed and not simply attempted. At the same time, the *dolus* of the agent provocateur is directed towards ensuring that the offence will at least be attempted and not remain at the phase of contemplation or of preparatory acts, which are not culpable. The Penal Code does not refer to the case of a person becoming *agent provocateur* in execution of orders given by a State organ and does not also clarify whether it might be invoked as defence.

*171.* The old Penal Code distinguished between direct and simple accessories in accordance with the degree of assistance which they had offered to the principal. This distinction was deleted in the new Penal Code. In particular, Article 47 provides that whoever intentionally offered another person any kind of assistance before the carrying out of the criminal act or during its perpetration shall be punished with a reduced penalty, as laid down in Article 83. This formulation presumably allows the court to evaluate the degree and the nature of the assistance which was offered to the offender and treat the accessory accordingly. However, the court has the discretion to impose the penalty due to the principal, if the accessory offered direct assistance during the perpetration by placing the object of the violation at the disposal of the 'natural principal'. It should be noted that the Penal Code uses the term 'natural principal' only in two provisions: in Article 47 and in Article 112, which deals with the commencement of the statute of limitations.

*172.* Finally, Article 49(1) stipulates that, in those cases where the legislation stipulates that, for an act to be culpable, special skills or a special relationship are required, if these are present only in the person of the perpetrator, the accessories envisaged in Articles 46(1) and 47 shall be punished with a less severe penalty, as provided for in Article 83. However, if such skills or relationships are present only in the person of the accessories, there shall be a reversal of punishment, namely the accessories shall be punished as principals and the principal as accessory.

# Chapter 6. Classification and Survey of Criminal Offences

## §1. General Classification of Criminal Offences

*173.* Under the new Penal Code, offences are divided into two categories according to the level and intensity of the threatened penalties: (a) serious crimes; and (b) misdemeanours. Article 468 abrogated the category of petty offences. This classification of offences is of practical importance in the following areas:

(a) Culpability. According to Article 26, serious crimes and misdemeanours are punished if they were perpetrated intentionally. Misdemeanours shall also be punished if committed negligently but only in those instances expressly stipulated in the criminal statutes.
(b) Statute of limitations. The prosecution of serious crimes is barred after twenty years, if the relevant criminal statute stipulates as punishment confinement in a penitentiary for life, or after fifteen years in any other case, provided that the relevant statute does not provide otherwise. The prosecution of misdemeanours is barred after five years (Article 111). The statute of limitation commences from the day that the criminal act was perpetrated, unless otherwise stipulated (Article 112). It shall be suspended for (a) as long as the relevant legislation stipulates that the criminal prosecution may not commence or continue, and (b) for the duration of the main criminal proceedings and until the sentencing judgment has become res judicata. However, such suspension may not last longer than five years in the case of serious crimes and three years for misdemeanours (Article 113).
(c) In matters that have to do with the CCP, e.g., the competence of the criminal courts to hear different cases.

### I. Ordinary and Political Offences

*174.* Traditionally, ordinary and political offences have been treated differently. Thus, Article 7(3) of the 1975 Constitution provided that the death penalty may never be imposed for political offences. While this provision is of historical only importance in view of the Constitutional amendment of 2001, according to which the death penalty shall not be imposed except for those cases which are envisaged in the legislation and concern serious crimes perpetrated at a time of war (on the abolition of capital punishment in Greece, *infra* paragraphs 264–265), it does reveal the legislator's clear intention to be more flexible towards political offenders. Moreover, pursuant to Article 47(3) of the Constitution (as currently in force), the President of the Republic may grant amnesty to political offences on the basis of a law, which has been approved by three-fifths of the total number of parliamentarians in a plenary session of the Parliament. On the contrary, under Article 47(4) thereof, amnesty for ordinary offences may not be granted even by law. Other relevant provisions include the last sentence of Article 5(2) of the Constitution, prohibiting Greek courts from extraditing foreigners, when extradition is requested only for freedom activities.[197] Finally, Article 97 of the Constitution prescribes that political offences are not prosecuted before ordinary criminal courts but before mixed jury courts of justice.

*175.* Article 62 of the Constitution, as currently in force following the November 2019 amendment, protects members of Parliament who have allegedly committed political offences. This protection takes the form of an exception to the general rule that it is not allowed to prosecute them during Parliament sessions. In particular, Article 62 stipulates that, for as long as Parliament is in session, a parliamentarian may not be prosecuted, arrested or imprisoned without the permission of the Parliament and, additionally, a parliamentarian may not be prosecuted for political offences from the time the Parliament was dissolved and until the proclamation of the next Parliament.

## II. Ordinary and Printing-Press Offences

*176.* Article 14(2) of the Constitution provides that 'The press is free. Censorship and any other preventive measure are prohibited.' The constitutional provisions protecting the press do not, *stricto sensu*, extend to cinema, radio, television, and other similar means of communication (Article 15(1) thereof).

*177.* While Article 14(7) of the 1975 Constitution stipulated that all press offences are considered to be *in flagranti crimine*, the constitutional amendment of 2001 deleted this provision and provided that all matters relating to the civil and criminal liability of the press and other information media shall be laid down in a statute. However, the provision of Article 14(3) thereof has been retained. It prohibits the confiscation of newspapers and periodicals (journals) both before and after circulation, subject to the following exceptions: (a) if offences against Christianity and any other known religion have been perpetrated; (b) if the person of the President of the Republic has been insulted; (c) in the case of publications disclosing information on the composition, the equipment, etc. of the armed forces or on military fortifications; (d) in the case of publications aiming at the violent overthrow of the (legitimate) regime in power or directed against Greece's territorial integrity; and (e) obscene publications (*supra* paragraph 72). The Constitution takes the view that these press offences are so serious that, if they have been committed at least three times within a period of five years, the competent court of justice must order the permanent or temporary discontinuation of the publication of the newspaper/journal in question and, in severe cases, the offender shall be barred from practising the profession of journalist (Article 14(6) of the Constitution).

197. The application of this provision can be questioned if the UN Security Council were to order Greece to extradite specific individuals to another State as it had happened e.g., with Resolution 1044(1996) of 31 Dec. 1996, where the Security Council had ordered the Sudan to extradite to Ethiopia for prosecution three suspects, who were sheltered in the Sudan and who were wanted in connection with the assassination attempt against the then President of Egypt, in Addis Ababa, on 26 Jun. 1995. When the Sudan did not comply, sanctions were ordered against it under Security Council Resolution 1064(1996) of 11 Jul. 1996.

It should be noted that, under the old Penal Code, the grounds for confiscating newspapers and journals laid down in the Constitution were also considered offences. Some of them were deleted in the new Penal Code (e.g., Article 199 which punished the publication of documents, pictures, etc., violating Christianity or any other known religion). Presently, the acts which are punishable are the following: preparatory acts, also through the Internet, deliberately inciting people to high treason (Article 135), and publicly announcing or publishing or spreading State secrets through the Internet (Article 146). The alleged perpetrator of Article 146 does not necessarily have to deliver the State secrets to a specific person or persons, it is sufficient that by uploading on the Internet, it has placed the secret at the disposal of a (undefined) number of people. By necessary implication, State secrets include revealing to third parties, who do not have the necessary security clearance, information concerning the Greek armed forces, the defence lines, etc.

### §2. Survey of Criminal Offences

*178.* The Greek Penal Code is divided into three sections, which are called 'Books'. The first section is the General Part (Articles 1–133). As its title denotes, it contains all those provisions which find application to the specific offences which are set out in the second section, the Special Part (Articles 134–459), but also, more generally, to acts criminalized in other statutes. The third section, which is titled 'Transitional Provisions' (Articles 460–469), lays down the necessary provisions to allow for a smooth passing from the old to the new Penal Code.

## I. An overview of the Criminal Acts Contained in the Special Part of the Penal Code

*179.* The Special Part is divided into 23 Chapters, and several of them are further divided into two or more sub-Chapters. Each Chapter is built around several offences, which have been grouped together on account of the proximity of the behaviour which they criminalize, or, to put it otherwise, because of the proximity of their constitutive elements. Sometimes, at the end of the different Chapters, so-called General Provisions have been inserted, namely specific stipulations which apply to all or most of the offences contained in a given Chapter. Thus, instead of repeating the same stipulation in each and every relevant offence, it was deemed more appropriate (reference to the Penal Code's notion of 'brevity being the soul of wit' has already been made) to insert such 'General Provisions' enumerating the articles to which they are applicable. Generally speaking, they stipulate such matters as whether prosecution will only be possible if the victim has lodged a prior criminal complaint with the authorities or whether the remorse shown by the offender and/or the fact that he compensated the victim of the offence will wholly or partly exonerate him of liability, etc.

*Chapter I. Violations of the Democratic Regime (Articles 134–137A)*

*180.* As had been noted in the previous edition of this monograph,[198] Chapter I, which was titled 'High Treason', had been the object of considerable revision. This is also the case with the new Penal Code, where Chapter I focuses on the violation of the fundamental principles of democracy. Democracy is a protected legal good. The third paragraph of Article 134 enumerates which are the fundamental principles of the democratic regime and which are its institutions: (a) an elected (by Parliament) Head of State; (b) the right of the people to elect (the members of) Parliament through general, direct, free, equal and secret elections within the constitutionally stipulated time periods;[199] (c) the parliamentary system of government; (d) the principle of more than one political parties; (e) the principle of the separation of powers, as laid down in Article 26 of the Constitution; (f) the principle that the legislature, the executive and the judiciary are bound by the Constitution; (g) the principle of the independence of the judiciary; and (h) the application and protection of the rights of the individual laid down in the Constitution. Arguably, the last stipulation should have made an express reference to the global and regional human rights treaties ratified by Greece as well, since, as already explained, under Article 28(1) of the Constitution, they form an integral part of domestic law and prevail over any contrary provision of the legislation.

*181.* The criminal treatment of the violation of the people's will is laid down in Article 52 of the Constitution. It stipulates that its free and unfalsified expression is an expression of popular sovereignty and, therefore, shall be guaranteed by the State, which must ensure it under all circumstances. Criminal sanctions for such violations shall be specified by law. Thus, Article 134(1) of the Penal Code stipulates that anyone, who by using or threatening to use violence attempts to change, permanently or temporarily, the aforementioned principles or institutions or to deprive the executive or the legislative of the authority given to them by the Constitution, shall be punished with confinement in a penitentiary for life or for at least ten years. As regards the commission of preparatory acts, Article 135(1) threatens confinement in a penitentiary for up to ten years. In both cases, the court of justice must impose as an accessory (subsidiary) penalty the deprivation of public office or status. Finally, under Article 135(2), the sanction of the first paragraph is threatened if preparatory acts are carried out in collaboration with a foreign government. The criminal liability of the members of the diplomatic representation of a foreign State, whose government might have assisted in the commission of the crime of high treason, is not laid down in the Penal Code.

*182.* The perpetration of acts of torture and other forms of violation of human dignity, which in the old Penal Code were set out in Articles 134A to 134 D, were merged into Article 137A. Originally, Article 134A had been inserted in 1984, even though Greece ratified the UN Convention against Torture years later, under Act

198. I. Anagnostopoulos & K. Magliveras, *Criminal Law in Greece*, International Encyclopaedia of Laws Criminal Law Series, Kluwer Law International, 2000, para. 172.
199. *See* Arts 51 and 53 of the Constitution.

1782/1988 (*infra* paragraph 543). However, the prohibition of and the punishment for torture, physical injury, damage to health, psychological violence, etc., is expressly stipulated in Article 7(2) of the Constitution. The sixth paragraph of Article 137A defines torture as any deliberate infliction of severe physical pain or mental exhaustion capable of causing serious mental harm as well as any illegal use of chemicals, drugs or other physical or technical means, which aim at bending a person's will. Moreover, pursuant to Article 137A(4), insulting human dignity, even if it is not considered to constitute torture, is punishable, especially when a truth detector has been used or the victim was exposed to prolonged isolation or his sexual dignity was seriously violated.

Even under the present formulation, Article 137A does not cover acts of torture committed by private persons but only by civil servants or members of the armed forces whose duties include the interrogation of persons suspected of having perpetrated culpable acts or disciplinary offences or the execution of penalties or the custody of detainees, etc. Acts, which are committed by one individual against another while carrying out, e.g., the offence of THB do not fall into the scope of the constitutive elements laid down in Article 137A. While it is true that THB is a self-standing offence (Article 323A), it is also the case that it is often difficult to successfully prosecute traffickers. Presently, acts of torture etc., committed by private individuals will be prosecuted, depending on the circumstances, as dangerous or grave bodily injuries (Articles 309–310, both aggravating forms of bodily harm), rape (Article 336), violation of sexual dignity (Article 337) or insult (Article 361).

On the whole, torture, etc., are punishable by confinement in a penitentiary of up to ten years. However, if they were performed with the aggravating circumstances enumerated in Article 137A(3), confinement of a minimum of ten years will be ordered. Finally, pursuant to Article 137A(10), the victim is entitled to demand from the convicted offender and the State compensation (they are both responsible in full) for the damages suffered and monetary satisfaction for psychological ordeal or pecuniary damage.

### *Chapter II. Offending the International Status of Greece (Articles 138–152)*

*183.* This Chapter includes, *inter alia*, the following criminal acts: offences against the territorial integrity of the Greek State (Article 138); exposing the State to war or to armed hostilities or to the risk of countermeasures (Articles 140–141); espionage (Article 148); rendering services to or assisting in any other way enemy forces (Articles 143–144); exposing/revealing /making publicly known State secrets (Article 146). The latter are defined in Article 149 as facts or information, access to which is permissible to only a specific group of people. Such facts and information are characterized as 'secrets' for the specific purpose of not jeopardizing the territorial integrity, the defence capabilities, the international relations or the economic interests of the Greek State or endangering international peace. These offences are mostly punishable by confinement in a penitentiary for life or for a minimum of ten years or for up to ten years. It is interesting to note that, under Article 144(2), if a war has been declared or is about to be declared against Greece, a foreign national who provides means (e.g., arms, ammunition, etc.) and services to enemy forces, shall not be punished, unless, at the time, he was resident in Greece or such means or services originated from Greek territory. This limitation seems problematic if the war or aggression against Greece has been considered illegal under the rules of public international law, for example, pursuant to a resolution of the UN Security Council adopted under Chapter VII of the UN Charter. If the legislator wanted to restrict the extraterritorial application of Greek criminal law, this would have to exclude cases where aliens contributed towards an illegal war/armed conflict being waged against Greece. Moreover, it is a well-known fact that increasingly more and more States (e.g., the USA) deliberately pursue the extraterritorial application of their legislation, including criminal legislation, as a tool of their foreign policy. Indeed, several States and international organizations (e.g., the European Union) have developed the legal notion of 'autonomous sanctions' to inflict measures (also of a punitive nature) on individuals and companies with whom they may have no link whatsoever.

*184.* Thus, it is important to note that the offence of breaching European Union regulations has been included in Chapter II of the Penal Code. In particular, Article 142A stipulates that anyone, who deliberately violates sanctions or restrictive measures, which have been imposed against States or entities or organizations or natural or legal persons on the basis of EU regulations, shall be punished by a term of imprisonment of up to two years (unless a more severe punishment is provided for in other statutes) even if the relevant acts on account of which the sanctions were ordered were not culpable pursuant to the legislation of the country in whose territory they were carried out. EU sanctions invariably take two forms. First, those which implement/execute/give effect to the punitive measures ordered by the Security Council pursuant to Chapter VII of the UN Charter.[200] Second, those, which are ordered, independently of UN action, by the EU itself. The latter, as already mentioned, are often referred to as 'autonomous sanctions'.[201] They are also referred to as 'restrictive measures', but these are not characterized by their punitive nature. Regarding the first set of sanctions, all UN Member States, including all EU Member States, must execute the punitive measures ordered through the applicable domestic procedure. In the case of Greece, Compulsory Act 92/1967[202] stipulates that those Security Council decisions, which concern the total or partial severance of economic relations with a third country and were adopted pursuant to Article 41 of the UN Charter, shall be applied through Royal (now Presidential) Decrees. The latter may also regulate in detail the prohibitions contained in the Security Council

200. Greece ratified it under Compulsory Act 585/1945, FEK 1945 A' 242.

201. On the concept and operation of autonomous sanctions, *see* K. Magliveras, 'Sanctions in Nuclear Non-proliferation Law' in J. Black-Branch & D. Fleck (eds), *Nuclear Non-proliferation in International Law*, Volume V (Legal Challenges for Nuclear Security and Deterrence), Berlin: T.M.C. Asser/Springer, 2020, 129.

202. Compulsory Act 92/1967 on the implementation of the decisions of the Security Council of the United Nations and on the approval and implementation of the recommendations of the Security Council and of the General Assembly, FEK 1969 A' 139. *See*, *inter alia*, Presidential Decree 13/2021, FEK 2021 A' 28 (implementing Security Council Resolution 2491(2019) on smuggling of migrants and trafficking in persons in the Mediterranean Sea off the coast of Libya) and Presidential Decree 10/2020, FEK 2020 A' 11 (implementing Security Council Resolution 2397(2017) on sanctions against North Korea).

decisions and shall set out the necessary domestic measures. Those who violate the provisions of the relevant Presidential Decrees are threatened with a term of imprisonment of up to five years or with a monetary penalty or both. It follows that if an individual were prosecuted for breaching an EU regulation, which was specifically adopted to give effect to a Security Council decision,[203] and the latter also happened to have been implemented in the Greek legal order pursuant to Compulsory Act 92/1967, the natural person in question would be prosecuted for breaching the latter instrument as well.

*Chapter III. Offences Against Foreign States (Articles 153–156)*

*185.* Greece has traditionally been a peaceful country and has always sought to maintain excellent relations with other states. The second paragraph of Article 2 of the Constitution says that much: 'Greece, adhering to the generally recognized rules of international law, pursues the strengthening of peace and justice, and the fostering of friendly relations between peoples and States'. Therefore, the Penal Code criminalizes acts which are perpetrated against the security of third States, or which violate the honour of their diplomatic delegations or their emblems and symbols. For such criminal behaviour to be punishable, Chapter III sets out as prerequisites that the third State maintains peaceful relations with Greece, has been recognized as a sovereign state by the Greek government, and the element of reciprocity is present. Offenders face imprisonment and, in case they violate the emblems of the third State, only a monetary penalty or the provision of community service may be inflicted. Finally, prosecution is possible solely when the foreign government has filed a criminal complaint.

*186.* Chapter III fails to mention whether the emblems of international organizations, whose constitutive instruments have been ratified by Greece, enjoy a protection similar to a third State's emblems. In March 1956, the Athens Representative Office of the United Nations requested that a Greek citizen be punished for illegally removing its emblem. In an advisory opinion delivered on 27 April 1956, *Areios*

203. E.g., Security Council Resolution 1267 (1999) and Resolution 1333 (2000), which concerned the Taliban regime in Afghanistan, were first implemented by virtue of EU Regulation 337/2000, which was replaced by Regulation 467/2001, which was repealed under Regulation 881/2002 of 27 May 2002 imposing certain specific restrictive measures directed against certain persons and entities associated with Usama bin Laden, the Al-Qaida network and the Taliban, O.J. L 139, 29.5.2002, p. 9. Regulation 881/2002 was partly annulled in Case T-318/01, *Othman v. Council and Commission*, Judgment of the Court of First Instance, 11 Jun. 2009, OJ C 180, 1.8.2009, p. 37. It was lastly amended under Commission Implementing Regulation (EU) 2022/873 of 2 Jun. 2022 amending for the 331st time Council Regulation (EC) No 881/2002 imposing certain specific restrictive measures directed against certain persons and entities associated with the ISIL (Da'esh) and Al-Qaida organisations, OJ L 152, 3.6.2022, p. 184. The execution of specific measures ordered under these two Security Council Resolutions were given effect through Council Regulation 2580/2001 of 27 Dec. 2001 on specific restrictive measures directed against certain persons and entities with a view to combating terrorism, O.J. L 344, 28.12.2001, p. 70; it was implemented by Council Decision 2005/930, by Council Decision 2006/379, and by Council Decision 2007/445, which was repudiated under Council Decision 2007/868, O.J. L 340, 22.12.2007, p. 100.

*Pagos* concluded that the Penal Code cannot be applied here; although the UN was an entity with international legal personality, it failed to meet the criteria of a sovereign state under public international law. Shortly thereafter, the UN emblems came to be expressly protected under Legislative Decree 355/1956.

*Chapter IV. Offences Against State and Political Organs (Articles 157–166)*

*187.* The much-reformed Chapter IV in the new Penal Code has been divided into two sub-Chapters. According to its title, the first deals with criminal acts perpetrated against the President of the Republic, against Parliament, against the government and against local government (Articles 157–160A). However, it also covers offences committed by politically exposed persons (PEPs),[204] e.g., when they demand or accept benefits to which they are not entitled (bribes) (Article 159). The second sub-Chapter deals with those criminal acts committed against the electorate (Articles 161–166). It is based on the Constitutional guarantees and protection afforded to parliamentary elections. Thus, Article 51(3) of the Constitution stipulates that 'The Members of Parliament shall be elected through direct, universal and secret ballot by the citizens who have the right to vote' and, more significantly, under Article 52 thereof, the free and unfalsified expression of the popular will constitutes an expression of popular sovereignty and must be guaranteed by all State officers under all circumstances, while the criminal sanctions for violations of this provision shall be specified by law. It follows that the second sub-Chapter is the primary criminal legislation laying down the punitive measures to be inflicted.

*188.* Pursuant to Article 157(1), whoever, by using violence or threatening to use violence, attempts to force the President of the Republic, the Parliament, the government or the Chairperson of a recognized political party to carry out, to omit or to tolerate an act falling within the ambit of their duties shall be punished by confinement in a penitentiary of up to ten years (no pecuniary penalty may be inflicted against such offenders). Regarding bribery, Article 159(1) threatens Prime Ministers, members of government, deputy ministers, members of Parliament, mayors, etc., with confinement in a penitentiary for up to fifteen years and a monetary penalty of up to 1,000 daily units, if they were convicted for having demanded or received directly or through a third person, for themselves or on behalf of a third person, any kind of benefit to which they were not entitled or have demanded such benefit in exchange of their acting or omitting to act in the context of their duties. Pursuant to the fourth paragraph of Article 159, the first paragraph thereof shall be applied when the illegal act has been carried out by members of the legislative organs of international or inter-governmental organizations in which Greece participates as a Member State as well as by members of the European Parliament or the

204. The term 'politically exposed persons' is not used in the Penal Code; however, as it is increasingly used worldwide and is a term, which covers those individuals holding certain prominent public offices or perform prominent public functions, it was considered appropriate to use it here. On PEPs, *see* OECD Financial Action Task Force, *FATF Guidance, Politically exposed persons (Recommendations 12 and 22)*, June 2013, at: http://www.fatf-gafi.org/media/fatf/documents/recommendations/Guidance-PEP-Rec12-22.pdf.

European Commission. As regards these instances, Greek criminal laws shall be applied even if the offence perpetrated abroad is not punishable under the laws of the country where perpetrated.

*189.* To use violence or to threat using violence or otherwise to exploit a working relationship or a relationship of economic dependence so as to prevent someone from exercising his voting right in national elections, municipal elections, elections for the European Parliament, a referendum or to force him casting his vote in favour of or against a specific candidate is a misdemeanour punishable by imprisonment of up to five years, while the sentencing court must order that he be deprived of any offices and positions that he holds (Article 161). But there is another way of directly influencing someone's voting rights, and this is envisaged in Article 165. Thus, whoever, from the commencement of an electorate process and until its end promises or offers to a voter any benefits to which he is not entitled for the purpose of either not exercising his voting rights or exercising them in the way he will be told, shall be punished with imprisonment of up to three years and a monetary penalty. It should be noted that, under Article 51(5) of the Constitution, the exercise of the right to vote for the members of the Hellenic Parliament is compulsory. The obligatory nature derives from the understanding that the status of citizen does not only entail rights but also legal duties and exactly one such duty is to participate as a voter in national elections. In the past, the legislation envisaged penalties for failure to vote: e.g., passports would not be issued to those who did not vote, and they had to pay a fine. Presently, no penalties are imposed. In the July 2019 general election, 42% of registered voters did not vote.

### *Chapter V. Offences Against the Authority of the State (Articles 167–182)*

*190.* Chapter V criminalizes violent behaviour which is addressed towards State officials or public authorities as well as behaviour which violates the decisions of State organs. Article 167 deals with violence against public officials and judges: anyone, who tries to force by using or threatening to use violence a public authority or an official to perform an act which falls within their duties or to omit to carry out a lawful act, shall be punished with imprisonment for up to three years or a monetary penalty. Article 167A, which is a new provision in the Penal Code, specifically deals with influencing court (judicial) officials, other than behaviour which falls into the ambit of Articles 167 and 237. Thus, in all other cases, the attempt to influence or to threat judges, court officers, arbitrators or jurors to carry out an act relating to their duties or to omit to carry out a legal (obligatory) act is punishable by imprisonment of at least one year and a monetary penalty. Under Article 169A, the violation or the refusal to comply with court judgments and orders, which, *inter alia*, regulate family affairs and matters (e.g., communication between parent and child), is threatened with the same punishment as Article 167. Article 169 provides that anyone who, although lawfully asked to do so by a civil servant, refuses, without using force, to offer him the assistance, which is owed pursuant to the legislation, or refuses access in a place where a civil servant attempts to carry out a legitimate action, commits the misdemeanour of disobedience. Offenders are threatened with a term of imprisonment of up to six months or with a monetary penalty.

*191.* Additionally, Chapter V of the Penal Code covers offences relating to violent offences which are committed by or in favour of prisoners and detainees. The following offences are included: deliberately aiding the release of prisoners (Article 172); escaping from prisons (Article 173); and sedition (Article 174). The latter refers to the following criminal behaviour: attempting to escape by using force; attacking prison personnel; or using force against prison officers to compel them to act or desist from acting, which is punishable by a term of imprisonment of at least two years and a monetary penalty. All offences falling into the ambit of Articles 172–174 are treated as misdemeanours. However, the instigator of sedition, as well as those who committed sedition by using weapons, faces confinement in a penitentiary for a maximum period of ten years.

### *Chapter VI. Crimes Against Public Order (Articles 183–197)*

*192.* Based on the assumption that no society may develop and thrive if law and order are not always observed, Chapter VI of the Penal Code criminalizes behaviour which aims at threatening or causing unrest in the society at large. In particular, it creates the misdemeanours of causing disobedience against laws or orders emanating from the State by any means, including the Internet (Article 183); publicly (including through the Internet) inciting the perpetration of crimes or acts of violence risking public order (*ordre publique*); it constitutes aggravated circumstances when these acts are addressed against a group of people or individuals, which are characterized by their race, colour, ethnic origin, religion, physical incapacity, sexual orientation, etc. (Article 184); offering remuneration to a third person to commit a serious crime or a misdemeanour and accepting the same (Article 186); forming or participating in a criminal organization (Article 187); carrying out terrorist acts and/or forming or participating in a terrorist organization (Article 187A); breach of the peace (Article 189); spreading false news causing fear to any number of people, who are subsequently forced to act (or not to act) in a certain way thus damaging the national economy, tourism, the country's defence ability or its international relations (Article 191).

*193.* The aforementioned Articles 187 and 187A have been revised considerably over the last twenty years, and their content has been augmented principally as a result of the legislator implementing and applying in the Greek legal order judicial developments at a global level (e.g., the various UN treaties against organized crime and against international terrorism) and at a regional level (e.g., the various instruments adopted by the European Union, the Council of Europe, etc.). Reference to these legal instruments has already been made. As regards specifically the pertinent rules of EU law, it should be noted that, according to the Explanatory Memorandum, the provision of Article 187A was amended to comply with Council Framework Decision 2008/919/JHA.[205] However, already in 2017, its validity had been terminated, as it was implicitly repealed by virtue of Directive 2017/541.[206] The latter had to be implemented in the domestic legal systems of Member States before 8 September 2018. Therefore, the new Penal Code, which, as mentioned, was adopted in the summer of 2019, and more generally Greek law did not comply with Directive 2017/541 until it was transposed under Act 4689/2020 in May 2020 (*infra*, paragraph 40).

*194.* Article 187(1) defines a criminal organization as follows: an operationally structured organization with permanent criminal activity consisting of three or more persons and aiming at perpetrating several serious crimes. The penalty for those who founded the criminal organization and for those who have joined it is the same: confinement in a penitentiary for up to ten years and a monetary penalty, while the person who administers it is threatened with only confinement in a penitentiary. If several persons have been organized with each other to perpetrate a single serious crime, this will not be regarded as having formed a criminal organization but a criminal union. The latter is treated as a misdemeanour punishable with a term of imprisonment of at least six months. Imprisonment of up to three years shall be imposed if the criminal union intended the commission of a misdemeanour aiming at a monetary benefit, at violating a third person's life, etc. (Article 187(3)). Finally, these provisions shall be applied when the criminal acts were committed abroad by a Greek national or were aimed against a Greek national or against a legal person having a seat in Greece (who is the beneficial owner of the legal person is not of interest) or against the Greek State, irrespective of whether they may not be criminal pursuant to the laws of the State/s were committed.

*195.* Article 187A(1) lays down the definition of an act of terrorism. Two things should be noted: it covers both domestic and international terrorist acts, and the constitutive elements have been intertwined in an apparent effort to be as broad as possible. Thus, by an act of terrorism, the Penal Code denotes those serious crimes or misdemeanours against public order or causing a general danger, which are perpetrated under conditions or in such a way as to cause serious risk to the Greek State or to an international organization for the purpose of seriously intimidating the population or forcibly forcing a public authority or an international organization to perform any act (or to abstain therefrom) or to seriously injure or destroy the fundamental constitutional, political or economic structures of a State (and thus not only Greece) or of an international organization. This definition echoes the text of Article 2 of the draft Comprehensive Convention on International Terrorism, which

205. Council Framework Decision 2008/919/JHA of 28 Nov. 2008 amending Framework Decision 2002/475/JHA on combating terrorism, O.J. L 330, 9.12.2008, p. 21.
206. Directive 2017/541 of the European Parliament and of the Council of 15 Mar. 2017 on combating terrorism and replacing Council Framework Decision 2002/475/JHA and amending Council Decision 2005/671/JHA, O.J. L 88, 31.3.2017, p. 6.

has been negotiated under UNGA auspices with no apparent prospect of conclusion.[207] The inclusion of international organizations as a target of terrorist acts is very interesting given that until today no such act has taken place and, indeed, it remains to be seen how an act of terrorism may destroy the structure of an international organization. While destroying a State's political, economic, etc. structures is something tangible and would affect the population, international organizations are rather intangible. Moreover, it is rather problematic that this provision seems to extend its ambit, according to its wording, to all international organizations and not only to those which have their seat in Greece and/or those in which Greece participates as a Member State. Arguably, for Greek courts to have the competence to try terrorist acts allegedly committed against an international organization there must at least be some connection with the Greek legal order. Otherwise, it is submitted that the competence of Greek courts should be founded on a very extended application of the principle of universal jurisdiction.

As regards the threatened punishment for acts of terrorism, Article 187A(1) does not envisage a sanction per se; on the contrary, offenders shall be punished with the sanction envisaged for each criminal act perpetrated increased as follows: (a) if the threatened punishment is either confinement in a penitentiary for life or confinement for at least ten years, the increased penalty shall be confinement in a penitentiary for life or temporary confinement for at least twelve years; (b) if it is confinement in a penitentiary for at least ten years, it shall be confinement for at least twelve years; (c) if it is confinement in a penitentiary between five and fifteen years, it shall be confinement for at least seven years; and (d) if it is a term of imprisonment, the minimum term shall be increased by one year.

*196.* According to Article 187(A)(2), the manufacture or possession of firearms, explosives and chemical or biological materiel constitutes aggravated circumstances if they serve the goals of the terrorist organization. The fact that the contemplated acts were not actually carried out by the terrorist organization constitutes mitigating circumstances. It is interesting that this provision does not cover all weapons of mass destruction. Whoever causes the decision to a third person to participate in a specific terrorist organization or to commit a certain terrorist act by providing instructions, information or directions to him (recruitment) shall be punishable by imprisonment of between six months and five years, if the act to be carried out constitutes a serious crime and with imprisonment for up to two years if it is a misdemeanour (Article 187A(4)). Finally, a term of imprisonment of up to five years is threatened to anyone, who (a) intends to perform or to contribute in the commission of a terrorist crime; (b) participates in the activities of a terrorist group, even though he was aware that his participation would contribute to its criminal

207. It was first proposed by India in 1996, *see* UNGA Resolution 54/110 of 9 Dec. 1999, which resolved to commence its consideration with a view to its elaboration. On 7 Oct. 2019, the Sixth Committee of the UN General Assembly established a Working Group to finalize the process on the draft Convention, *see* UN Doc. A/74/432, 21 Nov. 2019, para. 5. Discussions are ongoing; for recent action, *see* General Assembly, *Official Records*, UN Doc. A/C.6/76/SR.29, 4 May 2022, Agenda item 111. Finally, *see* the UN Global Counter-Terrorism Strategy, adopted on 8 Sep. 2006 as UNGA Resolution 60/288.

activities; or (c) for the purposes of offering training or attending training on how to carry out terrorist acts, travels to another State/s (Article 187A(7)).[208]

*197.* The latter provision aims at criminalizing the phaenomenon, which was far more prominent in other Western countries than in Greece, of individuals, who, on their own free volition, decided to travel abroad in order to be trained by or to join groups designated as terrorists organizations, e.g., Al Qaeda, ISIS (Da'esh), the al-Nusrah Front, etc. These individuals are usually referred to as 'Foreign Terrorist Fighters' (FTF). According to the Hague – Marrakech Memorandum on Good Practices for a More Effective Response to the FTF Phenomenon, they are 'individuals who travel abroad to a State other than their States of residence or nationality to engage in, undertake, plan, prepare, carry out or otherwise support terrorist activity or to provide or receive training to do so (often labelled "terrorist training")'.[209] The Explanatory Memorandum does not explain which is the legal basis for regarding this behaviour as criminal, especially when the person who underwent training abroad was never involved in the commission of any terrorist-related act. It will be submitted that the legal basis may be operative paragraph 5 of UNSC Resolution 2178 (2014) (it was unanimously adopted pursuant to Chapter VII of the UN Charter on 24 September 2014 at a summit which was presided over by former US President Barack Obama) in conjunction with the first operative paragraph of Security Council Resolution 2396 (2017), also adopted pursuant to Chapter VII on 21 December 2017.[210] Under Article 25 of the UN Charter, Member States have agreed to accept and implement UNSC decisions.

*198.* Finally, as regards the protection and the assistance to be afforded to the victims of terrorism, the Greek legislation has transposed the relevant provisions of the aforementioned Directive 2017/541. Thus, Article 40 of Act 4689/2020 (*infra*, paragraph 40) sets out the content of such protection, which it has subjected to Articles 54–71 of Act 4478/2017.[211] The purpose of Act 4478/2017 was to transpose, *inter alia*, the terms of Directive 2012/29, it being the EU secondary legislation regulating the rights of victims of crime.[212] Pursuant to Article 40(4) of Act 4689/2020, the support services to the victims of terrorist acts are confidential, must be provided free of charge and must be accessible by all victims.

---

208. Note that the aforementioned Act 4689/2020 has augmented the constitutive elements of the following offences to include their perpetration with intent to carry out a terrorist offence: Art. 374 (aggravated theft); Art. 385 (extortion); and Art. 216 (counterfeiting).
209. It was adopted in September 2014 by the Global Counterterrorism Forum, which describes itself as 'an international forum of 29 countries and the European Union', at: https://www.thegctf.org/Working-Groups/Foreign-Terrorist-Fighters.
210. *See also* OSCE Parliamentary Assembly, *Resolution on the Challenges Related to Returning and Relocating Foreign Terrorist Fighters*, adopted at the 28th Annual Session, Luxembourg, 4–8 Jul. 2019, at: https://www.oscepa.org/documents/annual-sessions/2019-luxembourg/3882-luxembourg-declaration-eng/file.
211. FEK 2017 A' 91.
212. Directive 2012/29/EU of the European Parliament and of the Council of 25 Oct. 2012 establishing minimum standards on the rights, support and protection of victims of crime, and replacing Council Framework Decision 2001/220/JHA, O.J. L 315, 14.11.2012, p. 57.

*Chapter VII. Misdemeanours Against Religious Peace (Article 200)*

*199.* Article 13(2) of the Constitution stipulates that every known religion may be exercised freely, without impediments or obstacles and shall be fully protected by law. As the prevailing religion in Greece is Eastern Orthodox Christianity, the Constitution lays down certain prerequisites for the unhindered worship of other recognized religions. In particular, they must not breach public order or *bonos mores,* and there must be no proselytism. Chapter VII comprises of only one provision, Article 200, which punishes with a term of imprisonment of up to two years those who culpably attempt to obstruct or deliberately obstruct a religious gathering or ceremony.

*Chapter VIII. Offences Relating to Military Service and Conscription (Articles 202–206)*

*200.* Greece is one of the remaining Western European countries where male citizens are under the mandatory duty to serve in the armed forces (conscription). This obligation is enshrined in Article 4(6) of the Constitution: 'All male Greek citizens capable of bearing arms are obligated to assist in the defence of the country in accordance with the law.' In the new Penal Code, the whole of Chapter VIII was deleted, because, according to the Explanatory Memorandum, a separate section on conscription is not included in any of the contemporary penal codes, and, moreover, the offences relating to military service are set out in the Military Penal Code.

*Chapter IX. Offences Relating to the Currency, Other Means of Payment and Stamps (Articles 207–215)*

*201.* The international efforts to combat the counterfeiting of currency go back more than ninety years with the conclusion of the International Convention for the Suppression of Counterfeiting Currency and Protocol to which Greece became a contracting party in 1931.[213] To this day, it remains the principal international agreement on currency counterfeiting, which it regards as an extraditable offence. Chapter IX criminalizes the counterfeiting of Greek or any other foreign currency (coins and banknotes) as well as of other means of payment (e.g., credit cards, debit cards, 'travellers' checks, etc.) (Article 207) and the deliberate setting them into circulation (Article 208) as well as the forging of official stamps, which are declaratory of a specific value, with the aim of using them as genuine (Article 208C). It should be noted that, as Greece participates in the Eurozone, it has adopted the euro as its currency, having abolished on 1 January 2002 its previous currency, the drachma,

213. It was concluded on 20 Apr. 1929, entered into force on 22 Feb. 1931, 112 *LNTS* 371. It was discussed by the European Court of Justice in Case C-343/89, *Witzemann v. Hauptzollamt München-Mitte*, Judgment of 6 Dec. 1990, ECLI:EU:C:1990:445.

which lost its status as legal tender. Therefore, Greece must comply with the relevant EU legislation, including Directive 2014/62.[214] Counterfeiting currency and other means of payment and setting them into circulation is a serious crime punishable by confinement in a penitentiary for up to ten years and a monetary penalty. However, if the quantity or the value of the counterfeited currency are small, the relevant offences become misdemeanours. Several people may be involved in the commission of this Chapter's offences, including the forger, the person who actually sets them in circulation and the person who accepts them for payment even though he knows they were forged. Article 208C offences are always misdemeanours. Courts of justice must order the confiscation of all counterfeited or forged currency, other means of payment, counterfeited stamps, etc., as well as the tools and instrumentalities used. Confiscation must be ordered even though no individual has been prosecuted and/or convicted and regardless of whether they were the property of the perpetrator and/or his accomplices (Article 213). All currency confiscated on suspicion of being counterfeited must be sent at once to the National Analysis Centre[215] or to the National Analysis Centre for Coins.[216]

*202.* The wording of Article 207(1), which reads 'Whoever counterfeits or falsifies the currency of any State or issuing authority either during the period before the time of its lawful circulation or while it is being accepted for exchange by the competent institutions … ', raises the following question: whether digital currency or cryptocurrencies (either in the form of stable coins which are usually backed by traditional currency and other securities or in the form of crypto coins (e.g., bitcoin, ethereum, litecoin, etc.), which are not backed) are or should be covered by Article 207(1), even though one cannot falsify a digital currency in the traditional manner as it is not a tangible object. The answer is rather difficult: on the one hand, increasingly more and more companies accept them as a form of payment instead of *fiat* currencies and a number of jurisdictions (e.g., Australia, Japan, etc.) accept them as legal tender. Even though cryptocurrencies have no (centralized) issuing authority, their 'mining' is privately regulated.

214. Directive 2014/62/EU of the European Parliament and of the Council of 15 May 2014 on the protection of the euro and other currencies against counterfeiting by criminal law, and replacing Council Framework Decision 2000/383/JHA, OJ L 151, 21.5.2014, p. 1. Greece implemented it by virtue of Act 4443/2016, FEK 2016 A' 232. *See* further, Regulation (EU) No. 331/2014 of the European Parliament and of the Council of 11 Mar. 2014 establishing an exchange, assistance and training programme for the protection of the euro against counterfeiting (the 'Pericles 2020' programme) and repealing Council Decisions 2001/923/EC, 2001/924/EC, 2006/75/EC, 2006/76/EC, 2006/849/EC and 2006/850/EC, O.J. L 103, 5.4.2014, p. 1.

215. It deals with counterfeited banknotes, it is run by the Greek Police, and forms part of the Counterfeit Monitoring System and of the Counterfeit Analysis Centre. The latter has its seat at the European Central Bank in Frankfurt am Main, Germany.

216. It is part of the National Counterfeit Centre, which is supervised by the Bank of Greece, the central bank of the Hellenic Republic. National Analysis Centres across the Eurozone collaborate with the European Technical and Scientific Centre, which is seated at the French *Monnaie de Paris*.

*Chapter X. Offences Relating to Documents and Records (Articles 216–223)*

*203.* Four different misdemeanours are included in this Chapter: (a) counterfeiting/forging of documents/certificates/records or university diplomas including examination transcripts or other documents, whose purpose is to prove a specific fact or an event, and the deliberate use of the same for unlawful purposes. These include: (a) upward social mobility (Articles 216–217); (b) entering untrue facts into public documents by deceit and/or using them to defraud a third person (Article 220); (c) issuing untrue testimonials by medical doctors, dentists, chemists, midwives, etc. with intent to deceit a public authority or an insurance company or to cause directly a monetary damage to a third person (Article 221); and (d) concealing or destroying documents which are not one's property with intent to cause damage to a third person (Article 222).

*204.* As regards the offences envisaged in Article 216, the following situations are regarded as aggravating circumstances: (a) the perpetrator aimed at obtaining for himself or for another pecuniary benefits by causing damage to a third person, provided that the total benefit or damage caused exceeded EUR 120,000; and (b) that the criminal acts perpetrated were aimed directly against the Greek State or against legal persons which are governed by public law or against local authorities, provided that the total benefit or damage caused exceeded EUR 120,000. Depending on the particular circumstances of each case, the threatened punishment is confinement into a penitentiary for up to ten years and a monetary penalty or confinement for at least ten years and a monetary penalty. The statute of limitations for forged documents/records, which were used to cause damage to the State, is twenty years (Article 216(4)). It should be noted that making use of a fake university diploma to be employed in the public sector is not considered as aggravating circumstance and is treated as a misdemeanour punishable by imprisonment (Article 217).

*Chapter XI. Offences Relating to the Award of Justice (Articles 224–234)*

*205.* This Chapter covers the commission of the following offences: (a) false statements in a court of justice or before investigating magistrates by litigant parties, witnesses, expert witnesses or interpreters (perjury, Articles 224–228); (b) filing untrue criminal complaints with the competent authorities (e.g., the Police) against a third person (Article 229); (c) harbouring/sheltering persons accused of having committed criminal acts (Articles 231); (d) holding back and not revealing to the competent authorities that the commission of serious crimes (not misdemeanours) is being contemplated or that the execution of a serious crime has commenced (not just that preparatory acts have already been undertaken) (Article 232); (e) breach of trust committed by attorneys at law vis-à-vis their clients (Article 233, *supra* paragraph 93); and (f) breaching the secrecy of *in camera* deliberations before courts of justice (Article 234).

*206.* Regarding perjury, unlike other jurisdictions (including common law countries), defendants in Greek criminal cases do not testify under oath. Therefore, they may not be prosecuted for perjury, even if they have deliberately lied. In the new Penal Code, it is a misdemeanour for a witness to deliberately lie while being lawfully examined by a competent State authority, even though he was not under oath. The offender will not be punished, if he later retracts his testimony on his own initiative, provided that no harmful consequences have already taken place (Article 227). Finally, if perjury was perpetrated, the criminal court has the discretion not to convict the offender, if he acted to avoid incriminating himself or a close relative and provided that he did not incriminate a third person. Articles 231 and 232 offenders may also avoid being punished if they acted to protect a person to whom they are related by blood or by marriage relatives, or who is his betrothed, or his foster parents or foster children, etc.

### *Chapter XII. Offences Relating to Service (Articles 235–263A)*

*207.* Chapter XII does not only concern civil servants/employees of the public sector, as this term is defined in Article 13 (*supra* paragraphs 27 and 151), but, depending on the circumstances, it comprises the following categories of persons as well. *First*, employees of an organ or organization (agency) of the European Union having its seat in Greece,[217] and of any other international organization in which Greece participates as a Member State[218] as well as any other person who performs duties corresponding to those carried out by such employees, even if the acts carried out are not culpable under the laws of the State where perpetrated (Article 235(5) and Article 236(4)). *Second*, directors of an undertaking or any other person who has the authority to take decisions on behalf of the undertaking or supervises it (Article 236(3)). *Third*, persons who serve permanently or temporarily with any relationship or status, *inter alia*, in organizations or who are employed in undertakings having any legal form but belong, in whole or in part, to the Greek State, or in local authorities, or in legal persons governed by public law. (Article 237B). *Fourth*, judges and arbitrators, including the members of the Court of Auditors of

217. Although not expressly stated, presumably the Penal Code covers the so-called Agencies of the European Union, namely, legal entities separate from the EU institutions established to perform specific tasks envisaged in EU law. There are two such Agencies located in Greece: (a) the European Centre for the Development of Vocational Training (CEDEFOP), which is seated in Thessaloniki (a new seat agreement with the Hellenic Republic was signed on 21 Nov. 2021). It is regulated under Regulation (EU) 2019/128 of the European Parliament and of the Council of 16 Jan. 2019 establishing the European Centre for the Development of Vocational Training ('Cedefop'), and repealing Council Regulation (EEC) No. 337/75, O.J. L 30, 31.1.2019, p. 90; and (b) the European Union Agency for Cybersecurity (ENISA), which is seated in Athens with a branch office in Heraklion, Crete. It is regulated under Regulation (EU) 2019/881 of the European Parliament and of the Council of 17 Apr. 2019 on ENISA (the European Union Agency for Cybersecurity) and on information and communications technology cybersecurity certification and repealing Regulation (EU) No. 526/2013, O.J. L 151, 7.6.2019, p. 15.
218. *See* the relevant webpage of the Greek Ministry of Foreign Affairs at: https://www.mfa.gr/en/foreign-policy/greece-in-international-organizations/.

the European Union,[219] judges and arbitrators serving in international courts of justice whose jurisdiction has been accepted by Greece,[220] as well as judges, members of jury and arbitrators of other States and always in relation to the carrying out of their judicial duties (Article 237(4)).

*208.* Even though the latter provision does not expressly include the judicial and legal organs operating at the level of the international organizations in which Greece is a Member State, by necessary implication, they should also be covered. They include the Administrative Tribunal of the Council of Europe[221] and the OSCE Court of Conciliation and Arbitration.[222] Finally, for the same reasons, Article 237(4) should apply to the international judicial organs established by multilateral treaties to which Greece is a contracting party, for example, the ECtHR[223] and the ICC.[224] However, it is unclear if Article 237(4) would cover the members of the International Court of Arbitration, which operates under the auspices of the International Chamber of Commerce.[225]

*209.* Chapter XII has been divided into two sub-Chapters depending on whether the accused person has taken advantage of the service for his own (private) benefit (Articles 235–238)[226] or whether he has abused the power of the service (Articles 239–263A).

*210.* The first sub-Chapter deals with demanding or accepting gifts or other benefits for oneself or for another in order to act or to refrain from acting in a matter which relates to one's service and duties (Article 235). This kind of bribery (passive bribery) is punishable by a term of imprisonment of up to five years and a monetary penalty. However, if the act or omission caused by the bribery was contrary to the

---

219. *See* Arts 285–287 TFEU.
220. In January 2015, Greece recognized the jurisdiction of the International Court of Justice as compulsory (Art. 36(2) of the Statute of the International Court of Justice), for the text of the declaration, *see* https://www.icj-cij.org/declarations/gr.
221. Originally called the Appeals Board, it was renamed the Administrative Tribunal pursuant to Resolution (94)11 on the amendment of Arts 59 and 60 of the Staff Regulations and the Statute of the Appeals Board (Appendix XI to the Staff Regulations) modifying the title of the Appeals Board and reducing certain delays in the disputes procedure, adopted by the Council of Europe Committee of Ministers on 5 Apr. 1994. *See* further, Resolution CM/Res(2014)4 amending the Statute of the Administrative Tribunal, adopted by the Committee of Ministers on 11 Jun. 2014.
222. It was established under the Convention on Conciliation and Arbitration within the CSCE, adopted in Stockholm on 15 Dec. 1992, entered into force on 5 Dec. 1994, 1842 *UNTS* 150. Greece ratified the Convention in September 1994.
223. Established under Art. 19 ECHR, as currently in force.
224. Established under the Rome Statute, adopted on 17 Jul. 1998, entered into force on 1 Jul. 2002, 2187 *UNTS* 3.
225. The ICC was founded as a not-for-profit organization under French law in 1919 with the aim to foster the development of world trade. Its present legal status might be equated to that of an international NGO. In 1946 it was granted consultative status in the United Nations, while in 2016 it was granted the status of Observer.
226. Generally, *see* I. Anagnostopoulos, 'Bribery Offences under the New Criminal Code in Greece', *Global Investigations Review*, August 2019.

offender's duties, the legislator treats it as a serious crime punishable with confinement in a penitentiary of up to ten years and a monetary penalty. Moreover, if the offender commits this kind of bribery as a profession, he is threatened with confinement for up to fifteen years and a monetary penalty of up to 1,000 daily units. This more severe punishment can be explained by Greece's efforts to tackle widespread corruption and rampant bribery practices.

*211.* The constitutive elements of active bribery are met when a person offers, promises or supplies to an employee, directly or through another person, any kind of illicit benefit for himself or for another person, so as to cause the employee's action or omission relating to his service and duties and irrespective of whether it will be concluded in the future or has already been concluded. It is punishable with a term of imprisonment of up to three years or a monetary penalty (Article 236(1)). However, if the action or omission contravened the employee's duties, this is regarded as a serious offence and, therefore, the offender shall be punished with confinement in a penitentiary of up to eight years and a monetary penalty (Article 236(2)). It is of some importance to note that originally the provision of Article 236(2) in the new Penal Code treated it as a misdemeanour and threatened a term of imprisonment of between three and five years and a monetary penalty. However, the November 2019 amendments (Act 4637/2019, *supra* paragraph 20) turned it into a serious crime, as indeed, it was in the old Penal Code. Even though Article 236(2) was amended shortly afterwards the entry into force of the new Penal Code, the Council of Europe's GRECO was alarmed. It decided to apply Rule 34 of its Rules of Procedure, which allows for ad hoc procedures to be initiated in exceptional circumstances, e.g., if institutional reforms, legislative initiatives or procedural changes in a participating State could result in *serious violations* of the Council of Europe's anti-corruption standards (emphasis added). While the determination on the classification of criminal behaviour as well as on the severity of the threatened penalties should be considered a matter of State sovereignty, GRECO proceeded with the issuance of recommendations addressed to Greece. When these were not implemented (arguably there is no obligation under the rules of public international law to do so), it issued a follow-up Report in November 2020[227] and a Second Follow-up Report in March 2022.[228]

The passive and active bribery of court (judicial) officials is specifically envisaged in Article 237. A different form of corruption is envisaged in Article 237A, which is titled 'Trading in influence – Middlemen/Intermediaries'. It was added to the Penal Code in 2014 to implement Article 12 of the aforementioned Council of

227. *See* GRECO, *Follow-up Report to the Ad hoc Report on GREECE (Rule 34)*, adopted at its 86th Plenary Meeting (Strasbourg, 26–29 Oct. 2020), published on 27 Nov. 2020, Greco-AdHocRep(2020)1, at: https://rm.coe.int/follow-up-report-to-the-ad-hoc-report-on-greece-rule-34-adopted-by-gre/1680a081f4.

228. *See* GRECO, *Second Follow-up Report to the Ad hoc Report on GREECE (Rule 34)*, adopted at its 89th Plenary Meeting (Strasbourg, 29 Nov. – 3 Dec. 2021), published on 3 Mar. 2022, Greco-AdHocRep(2021)1, at: https://rm.coe.int/second-follow-up-report-to-the-ad-hoc-report-on-greece-rule-34-adopted/1680a5a14b.

Europe Criminal Law Convention on Corruption in the Greek legal order. Regardless of the form of bribery committed, the sentencing court of justice must always order the confiscation of the gift or the benefit received (Article 238).

*212.* As regards the second sub-Chapter, it sets out several misdemeanours which are committed by a civil servant who abuses or misuses his status or service. However, certain of these offences become serious crimes, if they were perpetrated for enriching oneself or for creating an illicit benefit to a third person or for illegally causing damage to a third person, provided that the benefit or damage in question exceeds the amount of EUR 120,000. These offences include: (a) blackmailing a witness or a defendant to extract a confession or a testimony orally or in writing, provided that it does not constitute torture under Article 137A (*supra* paragraphs 180 et seq.) (Article 239); infringing one's private residence (Article 241); issuing a public document or record which contains untrue facts and which has legal consequences (Article 242); notifying/announcing to a third person facts which were secret or which were entrusted to the offender on account of his service (Article 252); and disobeying a legal order, which was issued by a competent civil authority asking military or police officers to use the forces under the offender's command (Article 260).

*213.* When an offender has been sentenced pursuant to the aforementioned Articles, he shall automatically be deprived of his office (Article 263(1)). However, Article 263A, probably the longest provision in the whole of the Penal Code, envisages many measures which are favourable to Chapter XII offenders. Of particular interest is the provision of paragraph 4(a) of Article 263A, which is based on the offender's willingness to become akin to a whistle-blower: if an offender, who has been sentenced under Articles 235 et seq., or if someone, who has carried out acts for the legitimation of the proceeds directly emanating from such offences, offers evidence showing that current or past government ministers, or deputy ministers participated in them, the competent Judicial Council shall order the suspension of the criminal prosecution against him and the case file shall be transferred to Parliament. Depending on how the proceedings before Parliament will develop, the offender may eventually receive a lower penalty (Article 44(2)), which the sentencing court of justice is entitled to suspend. Arguably, Article 263A(4)(a) should have also covered offences allegedly committed by the President of the Republic, for otherwise, he appears to be above the law.

### *Chapter XIII. Common Dangerous Offences (Articles 264–289)*

*214.* Chapter XIII includes offences, whose common characteristic is that they concern criminal behaviour aimed at protected rights enjoyed by a very large number of persons, in other words, offences endangering the public at large. These offences are perpetrated, *inter alia*, through arson (Articles 264–265); flooding (Article 268); explosions (Articles 270–272A); destroying or damaging electrical installations or infrastructure designed to protect the public from natural and other disasters (Article 273); disabling safety devises in factories, mines or in other establishments (Article 275); causing a shipwreck (Article 277); poisoning dwells, water tanks, food provisions, etc. (Article 279); violating measures ordered by a public authority to prevent the spread of a contagious disease either to animals or to people (Article 285); and violating planning and construction regulations (Article 286).

*215.* Most Chapter XIII offences are misdemeanours. However, if their perpetration had the effect of putting human life in danger or resulted in the death of one or more people, they shall be treated as serious crimes. The criminal act of arson in the woods (Article 265) deserves particular mention. Since the 1980s, deliberate or negligent arson in forests and woodlands has become one of the Greek society's worst plagues with tens of thousands of acres being burned down every year and many human casualties. In the summer of 2018, negligent arson in a southern suburb of Athens led to the death of more than ninety people.[229] As forests and woodlands are in some instances deliberately destroyed by arson to be converted into land for cultivation or land for housing, Article 265(2) stipulates that if the offender aimed at acquiring for himself or for a third person an illegal pecuniary benefit, confinement in a penitentiary for up to ten years and a monetary penalty must be ordered.

*Chapter XIV. Offences Against Transportation, Telecommunications and Other Public Benefit Installations (Articles 290–298)*

*216.* This Chapter is divided into three sub-Chapters. The first concerns offences relating to dangerous disruptions in road traffic as well as in urban rail, maritime,[230] and aircraft transportation (Articles 290–292). The second concerns offences, *inter alia*, against the security of telephone communications, obstructing the operation of information systems, and violating the secrecy of public telecommunications (Articles 292A–292E). The third concerns offences relating to obstructing the operation of other public benefit installations (postal services, water, electricity, natural gas, heating, etc.) (Article 293). Generally speaking, the offences envisaged in this Chapter are misdemeanours but they shall be treated as serious crimes, if they resulted in heavy bodily injuries or in the death of a human being. Moreover, if reckless driving resulted in the death of a large number of people (the precise meaning of 'large number' is not given in the Penal Code), the court of justice is entitled to increase the punishment to confinement in a penitentiary for life (Article 290A(1)).

229. *See* 'Greek fires: Arson suspected in deadly Mati blaze', *BBC*, 27 Jul. 2018, at: https://www.bbc.com/news/world-europe-44971351; 'Arson Is Suspected in Deadly Fires in Greece, Government Says', *The New York Times*, 27 Jul. 2018, at: https://www.nytimes.com/2018/07/27/world/europe/arson-is-suspected-in-deadly-fires-in-greece-government-says.html.

230. *See* e.g., Convention for the Suppression of Unlawful Acts against the Safety of Maritime Navigation, adopted under the auspices of the International Maritime Organization on 10 Mar. 1988, entered into force on 1 Mar. 1992, 1678 *UNTS* 201. Greece ratified it under Act 4169/2013, FEK 2013 A' 162.

*217.* Article 291 envisages several acts, which are punishable because they lead to the disruption of the safety of urban rail, maritime or aircraft transportation. In addition, this provision criminalizes 'other, equally dangerous, acts for the safety of transportation. As Article 291 does not explain which these acts are, the question arises whether they include offences relating to aviation security, as these are specifically contained in Act 480/1976 on Prevention and Suppression of Certain Acts Against the Security of Aviation,[231] as currently in force. It should be noted that Greece has ratified several of the relevant international treaties, including the Convention on Offences and Certain Other Acts Committed on Board Aircraft (the Tokyo Convention),[232] the Convention for the Suppression of Unlawful Seizure of Aircraft (the Hague Convention),[233] and the Convention for the Suppression of Unlawful Acts against the Safety of Civil Aviation (the Montreal Convention).[234] Greece has not signed and is not a party to the Convention on the Suppression of Unlawful Acts relating to International Civil Aviation (the Beijing Convention).[235] Act 480/1976 principally deals with the illegal acts involving the use of or the threat to use force when occupying an aircraft or exercising control over it. Thus, the following serious crimes are, *inter alia*, created: forcefully seizing an aircraft in operation; using violence against persons in an aircraft or causing damage to it, thus endangering its security; and setting upon an aircraft any devise or substances, thus causing irreparable damage to it. They are all punishable with confinement in a penitentiary for at least ten years.

Article 1(4) of Act 480/1976 expressly stipulates that, as regards offences created by it, the provisions of Article 291 of the Penal Code shall not be applied. One important difference between the two provisions concerns the severity of punishment: while under Act 480/1976 all offences are threatened with confinement in a penitentiary of a minimum of ten years, pursuant to Article 291, this is envisaged only when the commission of the criminal act resulted in the death of a third person while, if no human life was threatened, a term of imprisonment of at least one year shall be imposed. Since 25 May 1991, Greece has been a contracting party to the Protocol for the Suppression of Unlawful Acts of Violence at Airports Serving International Civil Aviation, Supplementary to the Convention for the Suppression of Unlawful Acts Against the Safety of Civil Aviation.[236] Finally, as regards offences

231. FEK 1976 A' 314.

232. Signed on 14 Sep. 1963, entered into force on 4 Dec. 1969, 704 *UNTS* 220. For Greece it entered into force on 29 Aug. 1971.

233. Signed on 16 Dec. 1970, entered into force on 14 Oct. 1971, 860 *UNTS* 105, (1971) 10 *ILM* 133. For Greece it entered into force on 20 Sep. 1973. Greece has not signed the Protocol Supplementary to the Hague Convention, which was concluded in Beijing on 10 Sep. 2010 and entered into force on 1 Jan. 2018, (2011) 50 *ILM* 141.

234. Signed on 23 Sep. 1971, entered into force on 26 Jan. 1973, 974 *UNTS* 177, (1971) 10 *ILM* 1151. For Greece it entered into force on 15 Jan. 1974.

235. It was adopted on 10 Sep. 2010 by the International Conference on Air Law, which was held under the auspices of the International Civil Aviation Organization (ICAO), entered into force on 1 Jul. 2018, ICAO Doc. 9960, *UNTS* No. 55859, at: https://www.icao.int/secretariat/legal/Docs/beijing_convention_multi.pdf.

236. Signed on 24 Feb. 1988, entered into force on 6 Aug. 1989, 1589 *UNTS* 474, (1988) 27 *ILM* 627. *See* further Convention on the Marking of Plastic Explosives for the Purpose of Detection, signed

perpetrated against the safety of aviation, the question of the applicable law[237] as well as the choice of jurisdiction among different States will depend on a number of conditions, including the nationality of the offender, the nationality (i.e., the State of registration) of the aircraft, the nationality of those persons who were endangered, etc. However, these questions may also become the object of bilateral regulation. Thus, the relevant rules are to be found in the bilateral air transport agreements, which Greece has concluded with third (non-EU) States.[238]

*218.* The second sub-Chapter of Chapter XIV regulates cybercrime. As mentioned, Greece has ratified the Council of Europe Convention on Cybercrime (2001) and the Additional Protocol (2003) under Act 4411/2016, which also harmonized domestic legislation with EU Directive 2013/40 on attacks against information systems (2013). In particular, Article 292B provides that anyone who, without having the necessary rights to do so, seriously obstructs or interrupts the operation of an information system with the introduction, transmission, deletion, destruction, etc., of digital data or by blocking access to such data, shall be punished with a prison sentence of up to five years and a monetary penalty. In case the offence was perpetrated with tools designed primarily to carry out attacks targeting a large number of information systems or causing significant data loss and/or if the targeted information system formed part of an infrastructure supplying the population with vital goods or services, the perpetrator shall be imprisoned for three to five years and shall be ordered to pay a monetary penalty (Article 292B(2)). Moreover, Article 292C threatens with imprisonment of up to two years or a pecuniary fine anyone who, without the right to do so and with the intention of committing Article 292B offences, produces, sells, procures for use, imports, possesses, or distributes: (a) computer devices or programmes designed or adapted mainly for the purpose of committing the same or (b) passwords or access codes the use of which allows gaining access to an information system. Finally, Article 292D(1) provides that, anyone

---

on 1 Mar. 1991, entered into force on 21 Jun. 1998, 2122 *UNTS* 359, (1991) 30 *ILM* 721. Greece ratified it under Act 2264/1994, FEK 1994 A' 208.

237. Note that Greece must also comply with the relevant rules of EU law, namely (a) Regulation 300/2008 of the European Parliament and of the Council of 11 Mar. 2008 on common rules in the field of civil aviation security and repealing Regulation (EC) No 2320/2002, O.J. L 97, 9.4.2008, p. 72, as amended by Commission Regulation (EU) No 18/2010 of 8 Jan. 2010 amending Regulation (EC) No 300/2008 of the European Parliament and of the Council as far as specifications for national quality control programmes in the field of civil aviation security are concerned, OJ L 7, 12.1.2010, p. 3; and (b) Commission Implementing Regulation 2015/1998 of 5 Nov. 2015 laying down detailed measures for the implementation of the common basic standards on aviation security, O.J. L 299, 14.11.2015, p. 1, as amended by Commission Implementing Regulation (EU) 2021/255 of 18 Feb. 2021 amending Implementing Regulation (EU) 2015/1998 laying down detailed measures for the implementation of the common basic standards on aviation security, O.J. L 58, 19.2.2021, p. 23.

238. *See* e.g., the Air Transport Agreement between the Government of the Hellenic Republic and the Government of Ukraine, signed in Kiev on 15 Dec. 1997; Greece ratified it under Act 2982/2002, FEK 2002 A' 11. Note that, since 2004, the air service agreements concluded between individual EU Member States and third States must adhere to the relevant rules of EU law, *see* Regulation 847/2004 of the European Parliament and of the Council of 29 Apr. 2004 on the negotiation and implementation of air service agreements between Member States and third countries, O.J. L 157, 30.4.2004, p. 7.

who, without the right to do so, gains access to a connection or to a network providing telephone or electronic communication services to the public, or to a hardware or software system used to provide such services, if the act may result in risking the privacy of the content of telephone or electronic communications or their location or movement, shall be punished with a prison sentence of at least two years and a pecuniary penalty. However, if the perpetrator of the offence is a provider of telephone or electronic communication services or its employee or intends to provide himself or another an illegal financial benefit, he shall be imprisoned for at least three years and shall be ordered to pay a pecuniary penalty (Article 292D(2)).

*Chapter XV. Offences Against (Human) Life and Violations Against the Embryo (Articles 299–307)*

*219.* Apart from the serious crime of intentional homicide (Article 299), which is punishable with confinement in a penitentiary for life or with confinement for between ten and fifteen years, Chapter XV also covers the offence, which it describes as 'homicide on demand'. In particular, under Article 300, whoever decided and committed homicide after a serious and persistent demand by the victim, who suffered from an incurable disease, and, out of pity (mercy) for the victim, terminated his life, shall be punished with imprisonment. It follows that in this situation, even though the court of justice must always convict the offender, it has been endowed with a very wide margin of appreciation to determine the length of the custodial sentence. Thus, it could order the lowest ceiling of imprisonment, namely ten days. It follows from the wording of Article 300 that both facts must be present, i.e., the victim's persistent demand towards the offender and that the victim suffered from an incurable disease for the (intentional) homicide to be treated as misdemeanour. What constitutes 'serious and persistent demand' may be difficult to be substantiated given that the author of the demand will no longer be alive.

*220.* The Penal Code does not explain which diseases could and should be regarded as incurable. Presumably, this is a question to be answered by the medical profession depending on each case. Arguably, it is not required that the victim is terminally ill, but he was suffering from a disease from which he may never recover (e.g., cancer, poliomyelitis, Creutzfeldt–Jakob disease, Alzheimer's disease, etc.). However, committing homicide when the victim was in a state of total paralysis not on account of an incurable disease but on account of, e.g., a car accident may not be covered under Article 300. It should also be noted that the criminal legislator has (doubtlessly deliberately) not used the term 'euthanasia', even though, according to the criminal legislation of other States,[239] the constitutive elements of Article 300

239. As far as EU Member States are concerned, suffice to mention that the Netherlands legalized active/direct euthanasia in April 2002, Belgium in May 2002, Luxembourg in March 2009 (but only for certain terminal cases), while Sweden allowed passive euthanasia in 2010. In several other Member States, including Italy, Romania, Greece, Croatia, Poland, and Ireland, euthanasia is forbidden and is treated as homicide. Switzerland has allowed assisted suicide since 1942.

appear to cover some forms of it.[240] The Penal Code does not distinguish the person of the offender: he may be a close relative of the victim, or he may be a medical doctor or a health professional. In the latter cases, they should follow any medical protocols in place.[241]

*221.* The offence of participation in suicide is laid down in Article 301, whose constitutive elements go beyond what is known as 'assisted suicide'. Thus, whoever persuaded a third person to commit suicide, if the suicide was carried out or was attempted, as well as whoever gave his assistance while the suicide was being carried out, and which would have otherwise not been possible, shall be punished by imprisonment. Article 301 does not cover situations where the person, who committed suicide, did not do so on his free will but was brought to this decision, e.g., out of despair or where it was intentionally done by the perpetrator who persuaded the victim to cause his own death.

*Chapter XVI. Offences Against the Physical Integrity of Another (Articles 308–315A)*

*222.* Reference to the provisions of Articles 308 and 309, dealing, respectively, with causing bodily harm and causing dangerous bodily harm, has already been made (*supra* paragraphs 24, 49, 99, 115, 128, 139). As regards the offence of severe bodily harm, Article 310(2) defines it as 'the act causing to the victim a life-threatening risk, or a severe and long-term illness, or a serious mutilation or hindering him from using his body or mental capabilities for a long period of time'. According to Article 311, if the bodily harm sustained resulted in the death of the victim, the court of justice must sentence the offender to confinement in a penitentiary for a maximum of ten years. If the offender intended to cause severe bodily harm to the victim, who subsequently died, the punishment is confinement in a penitentiary of up to fifteen years.

*223.* Article 312, which is titled 'Physical harm to weak people', envisages offences perpetrated within a domestic or family environment, what is usually

240. Given that euthanasia is illegal in Greece, the following legal question may be raised which is linked to the so-called euthanasia tourism: if a person living in Greece asks a Greek medical doctor to perform euthanasia in another EU Member State, which permits it, and if he does so, given that, on account of the free movement of professionals in the EU, the doctor in question is allowed under EU law to perform medical services in another Member State, could he be prosecuted in Greece for having performed euthanasia in the other Member State?.

241. *See* e.g., Committee on Bioethics of the Council of Europe, *Guide on the decision-making process regarding medical treatment in end-of-life situations*, adopted in 2014. It facilitates the implementation of the principles enshrined in the Convention for the Protection of Human Rights and Dignity of the Human Being with regard to the Application of Biology and Medicine (the Oviedo Convention), signed on 4 Apr. 1997, entered into force on 1 Dec. 1999, ETS No. 164. Greece ratified it under Act 2619/1998, FEK 1998 A'132. *See* D. Veshi and G. Neitzke, 'Council of Europe: Guide on the Decision-Making Process Regarding Medical Treatment in End-of-Life Situations' (2016) 16 *Medical Law International* 94–102.

referred to as 'domestic violence'.[242] Domestic violence is significant in Greece.[243] According to Greek Police data, 13,700 cases of domestic violence (70% of them against women) were recorded in the period 2013–2017.[244] Under the first paragraph of Article 312, whoever causes bodily harm or harm to the health of (a) a minor or a person who cannot defend himself, provided that they were placed under the offender's supervision or protection, or (b) to persons who cohabit with the perpetrator or have entered into an employment relationship with him, shall be punished with a term of imprisonment or with confinement in a penitentiary, depending on the circumstances of the case. The second paragraph of Article 312 places even more importance on violent offences during cohabitation. It stipulates that the same penalties shall be imposed when the act was committed against the spouse during marriage or against a partner during cohabitation. Presumably, this provision will also be applied in the case of marital rape, when it does not fulfil the constitutive elements of rape as laid down in Article 336 (*infra* paragraph 230).[245] These provisions should be read in conjunction with Act 3500/2006 on addressing domestic violence,[246] as lastly amended under Act 4610/2019.[247]

*224.* In 2018, a new provision was added to the old Penal Code, Article 315B, which was renumbered Article 315 in the new Penal Code. Based on Article 38 of the Council of Europe Convention on Violence Against Women, it creates the offence of persuading a woman to have genital mutilation performed on her. Offenders face a term of imprisonment of up to five years. It should be noted that such acts are unknown in the Greek society. While the view has been expressed that girls in Greece might risk genital mutilation,[248] in reality, it rather concerns females coming from countries where it is performed (e.g., Egypt, Guinea and Somalia) and who live in Greece either as immigrants or as refugees.[249]

242. For a definition of domestic violence, *see* Art. 3 of the aforementioned Council of Europe Convention on Preventing and Combating Violence against Women and Domestic Violence.
243. *See* T. Kaldi-Koulikidou, 'Domestic Violence Against Women in Greece' in S.M. Asay et al. (eds), *Family Violence from a Global Perspective: A Strengths-Based Approach*, London: Sage, 2014, 94–107.
244. Generally, *see* Immigration and Refugee Board of Canada, *Greece: Domestic violence, including legislation; state protection and support services available to victims, including non-citizens (2009 – Apr. 2014)*, 30 Apr. 2014, GRC104858.E, available at: https://www.refworld.org/docid/53b137394.html.
245. For the situation in Greece, *see*, *inter alia*, United Nations Committee on the Elimination of Discrimination against Women, *Concluding observations on the seventh periodic report of Greece adopted by the Committee at its fifty fourth session (11 Feb. – 1 Mar. 2013)*, UN Doc. CEDAW/C/GRC/CO/7, 26 Mar. 2013.
246. FEK 2006 A' 232.
247. FEK 2019 A' 70.
248. *See* European Institute for Gender Equality, *Girls in Greece are at risk of female genital mutilation*, 22 Jun. 2018, at: https://eige.europa.eu/news/girls-greece-are-risk-female-genital-mutilation.
249. Generally, *see* Parliamentary Assembly of the Council of Europe, *Female genital mutilation in Europe*, Resolution 2135 (2016), 13 Oct. 2016; UNGA Resolution 71/168 of 19 Dec. 2016, *Intensifying global efforts for the elimination of female genital mutilation* as well as Resolution 53/117 of 9 Dec. 1998, *Traditional or customary practices affecting the health of women and girls*; and UN Human Rights Council, *Resolution on the Elimination of Female Genital Mutilation*, 8 Jul. 2022.

*Chapter XVII. Duel (Articles 316–321)*

*225.* The rather elaborate provisions on duel, a relic of a different era with its own societal values and morals, were abrogated by virtue of Act 3904/2010.

*Chapter XVIII. Offences Against Personal Freedom (Articles 322–335)*

*226.* Chapter XVIII includes the following criminal acts: (a) the serious crime of kidnapping (Article 322) and the misdemeanour of kidnapping minors. The latter, if aggravating circumstances are present (e.g., grave life or health threat), shall be treated as a serious crime (Article 324); (b) the serious crime of THB (Article 323A); (c) the misdemeanour of illegal detainment (Article 325); (d) the misdemeanour of coercion (Article 330); (e) the misdemeanour of taking the law into one's own hands (Article 331); (f) the misdemeanour of causing fear to another by threatening to use violence (Article 333); and (g) the misdemeanour of violating domestic peace (Article 334). The new Penal Code abrogated several of this Chapter's offences, including the serious crime of trading in slaves (Article 323 of the old Penal Code); the misdemeanour/serious crime of involuntary or voluntary abduction of females with the purpose of sexual intercourse or marriage (Articles 327–329); and the misdemeanour of using force or threats to compel another to participate in a collective work stoppage at a workplace (Article 332).

*227.* Article 322 (kidnapping) punishes those who, by using deception, violence or threat of violence, arrest, abduct or illegally detain a third person with the purpose of depriving him of the protection of the State, including taking someone as a hostage or depriving him of his freedom (liberty) in similar circumstances. Kidnapping is punishable with confinement in a penitentiary for up to ten years. But if the offence was perpetrated to force the victim or someone else to act in a certain way or to omit acting or to tolerate an act for which he had no obligation, confinement may be increased to fifteen years. According to Article 325, if not all the constitutive elements of Article 322 are present, but a person was nevertheless kidnapped or detained without his consent or his freedom of movement was denied, this is treated as a misdemeanour punishable by a term of imprisonment of up to five years and a monetary penalty. Illegal detention should also be regarded as a breach of one's personality and/or privacy, these being violations of the respective human rights and fundamental freedoms. Article 6 of the Constitution comes into play here because it sets maximum time limits to the detention of those arrested. According to Article 6(4) of the Constitution, the maximum duration of detention pending trial may never exceed one year in the case of serious crimes or six months in the case of misdemeanours, these limits are to be exceptionally extended by six months and three months respectively. Pursuant to the Constitutional provisions, whoever is responsible for the detainment of arrested persons must immediately release them when the envisaged time limits have lapsed. Moreover, under Article 6(3) of the Constitution, those who violate this stipulation 'shall be punished for illegal detention and shall be liable to restitution for any damage caused to the victim and shall pay him a monetary compensation for the pain and suffering, as specified in the legislation'.

Thus, Article 325 provides that detention in breach of Article 6 of the Constitution shall be punished with a term of imprisonment of between two and five years and a monetary penalty.

*228.* Article 323A defines THB as the use of violence, threat of violence or other coercive means to recruit, kidnap, transport, illegally detain, deliver, or receive a third person for the purpose of exploiting him. THB is a serious crime punishable by confinement in a penitentiary for up to ten years and a monetary penalty.[250] The term 'exploitation' is very broadly understood in the fifth paragraph of Article 323A. It concerns the acquisition of an illegal pecuniary benefit from the victim of THB, who was subjected to the following: (a) slavery and similar practices; (b) working as a drudge; (c) begging or another form of exploiting his work; (d) the commission of criminal acts; (e) the removal of cells, tissues, or body organs;[251] (f) the performance of sexual intercourse and, generally, exploitation for sexual purposes; and (g) forced marriage. The enumeration of the acts and activities that victims of THB may be obliged to perform appears to be exhaustive and not illustrative.

Article 323A deals with two other aspects of THB. The first is that the prosecution of THB offences is very difficult, especially when the recruitment or the delivery of the victims have taken place in a third country. The second is that THB victims are very often in violation of domestic legislation, e.g., because they are aliens who have no right to work or because they are engaged in prostitution without being licensed, etc. Therefore, the eighth paragraph of Article 323A stipulates that if someone files criminal complaints against third persons for having perpetrated THB offences against him, the public prosecutor may, if the complaints are well-founded, temporarily abstain from their criminal prosecution for having breached, e.g., the law on aliens or the law on paid prostitution, as well as for other infractions, provided, however, that participation in the latter was a direct consequence of being a THB victim.

The Penal Code does not address the question of the compensation owed to the victims of THB. The applicable European Union instrument, Directive 2011/36,[252] deals with compensation in the context of the Member States' duty to ensure that victims have access without delay, on the one hand, to legal representation for the purpose of claiming compensation (Article 12 of Directive 2011/36), including victims who are children (Article 15(2) thereof), and, on the other hand, to existing

250. Note that in the European Union, THB is prohibited under Art. 5(3) of the EU Charter. Moreover, pursuant to Art. 83 TFEU, it is a particularly serious form of organized crime whose combatting is linked to the EU Common Immigration Policy (Art. 79 thereof).

251. Note that at least in Europe trafficking in human organs is viewed as being a separate from THB, *see* Council of Europe Convention against Trafficking in Human Organs, signed on 25 Mar. 2015, entered into force on 1 Mar. 2018, CETS No. 216. Greece has signed but not ratified it. Generally, *see* K. Magliveras, 'A Critical Overview of the Council of Europe Convention Against Trafficking in Human Organs' (2015) 31 *International Enforcement Law Reporter* 370–373.

252. Directive 2011/36/EU of the European Parliament and of the Council of 5 Apr. 2011 on preventing and combating trafficking in human beings and protecting its victims, and replacing Council Framework Decision 2002/629/JHA, O.J. L 101, 5.4.2011, p. 1. It was transposed in the Greek legal order under Act 4198/2013, Prevention and combatting human trafficking and protection of its victims and other provisions, FEK 2013 A' 215, as amended under Act 4280/2014, FEK 2014 A' 159 and Act 4781/2021, FEK 2021 A' 31.

domestic schemes of compensation for victims of violent crimes which were perpetrated intentionally (Article 17 thereof). The EU has specific legislation protecting the victims of criminal acts,[253] pursuant to which Member States must ensure that they all receive appropriate information, support and protection and are able to participate in criminal proceedings.

In two cases relating to THB, the ECtHR held that Greece had violated Articles 4 and 6 of the ECHR, which enshrine, respectively, the prohibition of slavery and forced labour and the right to a fair trial.[254] In the second case, which is known as the '*Manolada* case', Greece was found to have breached Article 4(2) of the ECHR, which expressly prohibits forced labour, on the ground that the applicants had not received adequate protection by the competent public authorities. In 2013, the Office of the National Rapporteur on Trafficking in Human Beings was established within the Ministry of Foreign Affairs and was designated as the national co-ordinating body.[255] And in 2016, the National Referral Mechanism (NRM) for the protection and support of THB victims was formally established.[256] Thus, Greece complied with the relevant international and EU legal instruments by having a formal national identification and referral system for the THB victims and for securing their rights.[257] Finally, it should be mentioned that the Trafficking in Persons Report 2020, published by the US government, ranked Greece as a 'Tier 2' country (countries are ranked as Tier 1 (best ranking), Tier 2, Tier 2 Watch List and Tier 3 (worst ranking)).[258] The same ranking was given in the 2021[259] and 2022 Reports.[260]

253. Directive 2012/29/EU of the European Parliament and of the Council of 25 Oct. 2012 establishing minimum standards on the rights, support and protection of victims of crime, and replacing Council Framework Decision 2001/220/JHA, O.J. L 315, 14.11.2012, p. 57. *See* further, European Commission, Commission Staff Working Document, Evaluation of Directive 2012/29/EU of the European Parliament and of the Council of 25 Oct. 2012 establishing minimum standards on the rights, support and protection of victims of crime, and replacing Council Framework Decision 2001/220/JHA, SWD(2022) 179 final, 28 Jun. 2022.
254. *See* ECtHR, *L.E. v. Greece*, Application No. 71545/12, Judgment of 21 Jan. 2016; *Chowdury and others v. Greece*, Application No. 21884/15, Judgment of 30 Mar. 2017. For the execution of the latter judgment, *see* Council of Europe, Comité des Ministres, Communication de la Grèce concernant l'affaire Chowdury et autres c. Grèce (Requête n° 21884/15), DH-DD(2018)607, 13.6.2018, p. 12, at: http://hudoc.exec.coe.int/ENG?i=DH-DD(2018)607F.
255. *See* further, https://www.mfa.gr/en/foreign-policy/global-issues/human-trafficking.html.
256. Under Joint Ministerial Decision 30840/2016, FEK 2016 B' 3003.
257. *See* further, Council of Europe, *Group of Experts on Action against Trafficking in Human Beings, Report concerning the implementation of the Council of Europe Convention on Action against Trafficking in Human Beings by Greece – First evaluation round*, GRETA(2017)27, October 2017, at: https://rm.coe.int/greta-2017-27-fgr-gre-en/168075f2b6.
258. US Department of State, *Trafficking in Persons Report*, 25 Jun. 2020, at: https://www.state.gov/wp-content/uploads/2020/06/2020-TIP-Report-Complete-062420-FINAL.pdf.
259. US Department of State, *Trafficking in Persons Report*, June 2021, at: https://www.state.gov/reports/2021-trafficking-in-persons-report/greece/.
260. US Department of State, *Trafficking in Persons Report*, June 2022, at: https://www.state.gov/reports/2022-trafficking-in-persons-report/greece/.

*Chapter XIX. Offences Against Sexual Freedom and Offences Relating to the Economic Exploitation of Sexual Life (Articles 336–353)*

*229.* Chapter XIX deals with offences, which are committed against the sexual freedom that everyone must enjoy freely and without fear. It, *inter alia*, includes (a) the serious crime of rape (Article 336); (b) the misdemeanour of violating another person's sexual dignity (Article 337); (c) sexual acts with minors or performed in front of minors, which are either a serious crime or a misdemeanour depending on the minor's age (Article 339); (d) the misdemeanour of sexual acts committed between blood relatives of the ascending or descending lines or between brothers and sisters (incest, Article 345); and (e) the misdemeanour of violating another person's sexual decency (Article 353). Additionally, Chapter XIX covers offences which are perpetrated for the purpose of exploiting, mostly for profit, the sexual life of another. These include the misdemeanour of child pornography, which becomes a serious crime if committed, for example, as a profession (Article 348A – 348C); (f) pimping, namely serving the debauchery of others through the prostitution of minors (Article 349); and (g) sexual acts with a minor in exchange of payment (Article 351A).

*230.* According to Article 336(1), the crime of rape is perpetrated when someone, by using physical violence or threatening gravely and imminently the life or physical integrity of a third person, coerces such person to engage into a sexual act (defined as intercourse and other acts of equal gravity) or to tolerate such an act. Rape is punishable with confinement in a penitentiary for at least ten years. Article 336(4) stipulates that, even if the constitutive elements of rape are not fulfilled, to perform a sexual act without the consent of the victim is punishable by confinement in a penitentiary of up to 10 years.

*231.* The offence of violating one's sexual dignity (Article 337) covers various forms of sexual harassment, while the violation of sexual decency (Article 353) refers to acts against public morals (e.g., exhibitionism, sex in public places, etc.). In the new Penal Code, the latter provision replaced the previous Article 353, which criminalized causing a public scandal through acts of debauchery. Both Articles 337 and 353 arguably cover what is referred to as 'sexual harassment'. However, sexual harassment at the workplace is expressly envisaged in Article 337(4),[261] pursuant to which, anyone, who makes gestures of a sexual character or makes suggestions for performing sexual acts on a person whose employment depends on him or who takes advantage of a person's need to work, shall be punished with a term of imprisonment of up to three years or with a monetary penalty.[262] A monetary penalty might be inadequate when the offender has not only violated the victim's personality and

261. For a European Union soft law instrument covering harassment against the female population, *see EU Guidelines on Violence against Women and Girls and Combating all Forms of Discrimination against them*, which were adopted by the General Affairs Council of 8 Dec. 2008, available at: https://ec.europa.eu/anti-trafficking/sites/antitrafficking/files/eu_guidelines_on_violence_against_women_and_girls_1.pdf.

262. Generally, *see* K. Magliveras, 'The Regulation of Workplace Sexual Harassment in Greece' (2005) 7 *International Journal of Discrimination and the Law* 169–186. *See* further the data of the Global

sexual dignity but has also seriously abused his hierarchically superior position in a workplace. Moreover, to distinguish between male and female employees and to deny the former protection from sexual harassment coming from males and/or females, as is the case with UNGA Resolution 73/148,[263] the first-ever UN resolution on sexual harassment, is rather wrong. The Penal Code has correctly treated it as a gender-neutral offence. Finally, Greece has complied with the provisions of the principal EU legislation, namely Directive 2000/78[264] and Directive 2006/54[265] by virtue of, respectively, the aforementioned Act 4443/2016 and Act 3896/2010.[266]

### *Chapter XX. Offences Relating to Marriage and Family (Articles 354–360)*

*232.* Chapter XX deals with misdemeanours, which centre around the notions of 'marriage' and 'family'. However, they may not only be committed by members of a family but by third parties as well. Modern tendencies in how relationships between the two sexes are carried out as well as the introduction of the cohabitation agreement in the Greek legal order[267] made the provision of Article 355 of the old Penal Code redundant: it stipulated that it was an offence to deceitfully persuade another to enter into a marriage while being aware that such marriage would be null and void or voidable. The following offences are laid down in Chapter XX: disruption of family peace and order (Article 354); bigamy which concerns both an existing marriage and an existing cohabitation agreement (Article 356); violation of the obligation to subsistence recognized by a court of justice (Article 358); deserting a female person, who became pregnant by the offender, provided that she cannot make ends meet (Article 359); and neglecting the supervision of persons under the age of fifteen, if it resulted in the commission of a punishable act (Article 360). It should be noted that Article 360 covers anyone to whom supervision of minors has been entrusted; thus, not only parents and court-appointed custodians but also the director of a foster home.

### *Chapter XXI. Offences Against Honour (Articles 361–369)*

*233.* This Chapter is of fundamental importance not only for the freedom of the press but also for the protection of the public from the press. It covers the following

---

Database on Violence against Women, which is maintained by UN Women, at: https://evaw-global-database.unwomen.org/en/countries/europe/greece.

263. Resolution 73/148 of 17 Dec. 2018, *Intensification of efforts to prevent and eliminate all forms of violence against women and girls: sexual harassment*, with references to other relevant UN instruments.
264. Council Directive 2000/78/EC of 27 Nov. 2000 establishing a general framework for equal treatment in employment and occupation, O.J. L 303, 2.12.2000, p. 16.
265. Directive 2006/54/EC of the European Parliament and of the Council of 5 Jul. 2006 on the implementation of the principle of equal opportunities and equal treatment of men and women in matters of employment and occupation, O.J. L 204, 26.7.2006, p. 23.
266. FEK 2010 A' 207.
267. Generally, *see* H. Constandinidou-Stavropoulou and K. Stavropoulos, *Family Law in Greece: Overview*, Thomson Reuters Practical Law, 2020, at: https://uk.practicallaw.thomsonreuters.com.

misdemeanours: insult (Article 361); defamation (Article 362); slander (Article 363); and violating the memory of a dead person (Article 365). The offence of defamation of a public limited company (*société anonyme*), which was envisaged in Article 364 of the old Penal Code, was abrogated because, according to the Explanatory Memorandum, there was no substantive criminal wrongdoing and the allegedly defamed company could file a civil action pursuant to the provisions on unlawful acts (Articles 914 et seq. of the Civil Code, *supra* paragraph 16). However, it is debatable whether these were adequate reasons to delete this offence especially if the perpetrator had a clear intention to discredit a well-known company. Moreover, Article 12 of Act 146/1914 on Unfair Competition still punishes the spreading of false information that may damage a company (of any kind).

*234.* The general provisions contained in Articles 366 and 367 merit particular attention. According to Article 366, defamation shall not be punished if the defamatory facts are true. However, adducing evidence to prove the truthfulness of such facts is not allowed where these refer solely to family and/or private relations and are not in the public interest. Moreover, the defendant may still be punished for insult despite the truthfulness of the facts if a specific intent to insult can be shown. According to Article 367, the following does not give rise to criminal responsibility: (a) to express negative opinions for scientific, cultural, or professional work; (b) adverse opinions contained in the documents of a public authority, if they concern its activities; (c) acts which are carried out for the purpose of executing lawful duties as well as for enforcing or protecting legitimate interests and rights; and (d) in other similar cases. Finally, if the offences of Articles 361, 362, 363 and 365 were perpetrated publicly or on the Internet, the person who lodged the criminal complaint has the right to demand, and the competent court of justice has the discretion to order the publication of the judgment finding the accused guilty. Should the convicted person fail to carry out this obligation, he faces imprisonment of up to one year and a monetary penalty.

### *Chapter XXII. Offences Relating to Individual Secrecy and Communication (Articles 370–371)*

*235.* The Greek Constitution affords a great measure of protection to the privacy of individuals and guarantees secrecy, the latter being an emanation of the former. Suffice to mention the following Constitutional provisions: Article 5(3) (personal freedom shall be inviolable), Article 9(1) (the private and family life of all individuals shall be inviolable), and Article 19(1) (guaranteeing the secrecy of postal correspondence and the freedom of (tele)communications). Originally, Chapter XXII of the Penal Code criminalized solely the breach of post secrecy (Article 370) and of professional secrecy in the sense of confidentiality (Article 371). The criminal nature of the latter offence, which covers clerics, lawyers and jurists, notaries public, the medical profession and their assistants, is negated, if these persons have acted in fulfilling a legal duty or some important public or private interest which could not have been protected in another way (Article 371(4) in conjunction with Article 20).

*236.* However, with the rapid development of science, the evolution of telecommunications, the widespread use of listening and other eavesdropping devices, etc., since the 1990s the legislator has had to constantly intervene to safeguard the constitutionally protected right to privacy and to secrecy. Thus, it has not only introduced additional offences but has also updated the constitutive elements of existing offences. Presently, Chapter XXII covers the constitutive elements of the following offences: (a) trapping and taping telephone calls (Article 370A(1)); (b) eavesdropping and recording private conversations (Article 370(A)(2)); (c) accessing without authorization information systems or digital data, including scientific or professional secrets of a company belonging either to the public sector or to the private sector (Article 370B); (d) copying, using or revealing to a third person without authorization data or computer software where State, scientific, professional or company secrets are stored (Article 370C); (e) copying or using computer software without having the right to do so; if the offender was employed by the lawful holder of the software, his offence is punishable only if it is expressly prohibited by the holder's internal regulations (Article 370D); and (f) monitoring or capturing material from non-public data transmissions or electromagnetic emissions from, to or within an information system. The punishment for the latter offence is more severe than the previous ones, namely a term of imprisonment between three and five years and a monetary penalty.

### *Chapter XXIII. Offences Against Property Assets (Goods) (Articles 372–406)*

*237.* In the new Penal Code, the previous Chapter XXIII and Chapter XXIX were merged into the new Chapter XXIII, which now covers a whole range of offences perpetrated against property. It has been divided into two sub-Chapters, which respectively cover most of the provisions of each of the previous two Chapters. It should be also noted that the right to property is guaranteed by the Constitution. In particular, Article 17(1) thereof stipulates that property shall be protected by the State. This is in line with the First Protocol to the ECHR: 'Every natural or legal person is entitled to the peaceful enjoyment of his possessions'.[268]

*238.* The first sub-Chapter covers a range of offences against property (Articles 372–381), including various forms of theft (Articles 372–374A); embezzlement (Article 375); damage to another person's property (Article 378); and robbery (Article 380).

*239.* Theft is defined as wholly or partly removing from the possession of a third person (ownership is not a prerequisite) a moveable item (including electricity or other forms of energy) with intent to unlawfully appropriate it (i.e., without having

---

268. *See* Art. 1 to Protocol 1 to the Convention for the Protection of Human Rights and Fundamental Freedoms, signed on 20 Mar. 1952, entered into force on 18 May 1954, ETS No. 9. Originally, Greece deposited the instrument of ratification on 28 Mar. 1953, but the Protocol was denounced when Greece withdrew from the Council of Europe in 1970. On 28 Nov. 1974, Greece was re-admitted to the Council of Europe and on the same day Protocol 1 came into force for Greece.

legal title to do so). It is punishable with a term of imprisonment of up to three years or a monetary fine. In the case of petty theft, a monetary penalty or community service shall be inflicted, but if it was perpetrated out of need for immediate use or consumption, it is to the discretion of the court of justice not to punish the offender (Article 377). Even though theft is a misdemeanour, there are four instances laid down in Article 374(1) where it becomes a serious crime (aggravated theft) punishable with confinement in a penitentiary of up to ten years and a monetary penalty. These include the following circumstances: removing religious items or objects of archaeological, historical, cultural, or scientific importance, which were part of a collection open to the public; the theft was committed by two or more persons, who had organized themselves for this purpose; and/or the total value of the stolen objects exceeded the amount of EUR 120,000 (it was previously set at EUR 73,300).

*240.* The new Penal Code added a second paragraph to Article 374: if the theft is directly targeting the Greek State or legal persons governed by public law or local authorities and it amounted to more than EUR 120,000, it shall be treated as a serious crime punishable with confinement in a penitentiary for at least ten years and a monetary penalty of up to 1,000 daily units.

*241.* The serious crime of robbery (Article 380) is committed when someone, by using physical violence or threats together with imminent danger for the life or the physical integrity of another person, removes from the latter's possession an item (moveable object) or forces him to surrender it with intent to appropriating it illegally. In case the robbery resulted in the victim's death or in heavy bodily injuries or was carried out with cruelty, the offender faces confinement in a penitentiary for life or for a minimum of ten years and a monetary penalty.

*242.* The misdemeanour of damaging/harming another person's property is perpetrated through the intentional destruction in part or in whole of an object belonging to a third person or through any other means preventing its use (Article 378(1)). Aggravated forms are set out in both the first and second paragraphs of Article 378 and include the destruction of objects having a particularly large value, objects serving the welfare provided by the State, historical monuments, etc.

*243.* Finally, the misdemeanour of embezzlement (Article 375) is the unlawful appropriation of another person's movable property, which came to the offender's possession in any way. Embezzlement involving the misuse of a relationship based on special trust – for example, the offender had the legal status of a guardian, a trustee or the administrator of a third person's property – is considered aggravating circumstances. Embezzlement will become a serious crime if (a) the value of the appropriated property exceeds EUR 120,000 (Article 375(2)) and (b) it directly targeted the Greek State or legal persons governed by public law or local authorities and was valued at more than EUR 120,000 (Article 375(3)). The aforementioned provisions of Article 377 apply to petty embezzlement as well.

*244.* The second Sub-Chapter covers an array of offences perpetrated against the wealth (property/assets) of another person (Articles 385–405). They include blackmail (Article 385); fraud (Articles 386–388); intentionally causing loss to another person's wealth (breach of trust, Article 390);[269] accepting and disposing of proceeds derived from criminal acts (Article 394); defrauding creditors (Article 397); and loan sharking (Article 404). The new Penal Code deleted several offences, including deceitful bankruptcy (Article 398 of the old Penal Code), which is presently regulated in Article 197 of Act 4738/2020.[270]

*245.* The offence of blackmail (Article 385) is committed when someone, with the intention to obtain for himself or a third person an illicit monetary benefit, forces another to act or not to act, and, in this way, causes him (or to a third person) a monetary damage. Blackmail is a serious crime (punishable with confinement in a penitentiary), if the offender employed physical violence or threats accompanied by imminent physical violence, and a misdemeanour (imprisonment of between three and five years and a pecuniary penalty) if he threatened to cause damage to the victim's business or professional life. Article 385(1) expressly stipulates that it is applied to those criminal acts which do not come into the ambit of the aforementioned Article 380 (robbery). Although blackmail shares common characteristics with both robbery and fraud, there are also important differences. In the case of fraud, the pecuniary damage is suffered by an act or omission of the person towards whom the representation of untrue facts as true has taken place, whereas in blackmail through physical violence or threats. In the case of robbery, the common characteristic is that the offender employs coercive means (violence or threats against the victim). However, in the case of robbery, the intention is to remove or acquire a moveable object, whereas in blackmail the intention is to obtain a monetary benefit.

*246.* The misdemeanour of fraud (Article 386) is perpetrated when a person enriches oneself or a third person by knowingly representing untrue facts as being true and, in this way, persuades another to act or omit to act, thus causing him a pecuniary damage. In case the pecuniary damage exceeds the amount of EUR 120,000, the offender shall be confined in a penitentiary for up to ten years and ordered to pay a monetary penalty. In case the fraud was directed against the Greek State or against legal persons governed by public law or municipal authorities, this shall be treated as aggravating circumstances, and the offender shall face confinement of at least ten years and a monetary penalty of at least 1,000 daily units. This latter provision on aggravating circumstances could be considered 'general provisions' and applies to most instances of committing fraud. The misdemeanour of fraud in insurance policies, which was envisaged in Article 388 of the old Penal Code, was deleted under the new Penal Code. Fraudulent acts towards insurers and insurance companies shall be treated under Article 386.

---

269. *See* O. Lykou, 'Analyse und Kritik der Reform des griechischen Untreuestrafrechts' (2020) 132 *Zeitschrift für die gesamte Strafrechtswissenschaft* 473–501.
270. FEK 2020 A' 207.

Contemporary developments in fraudulent behaviour have led to the introduction of two specific offences in the Penal Code: fraud by using computers (Article 386A) and fraud in relation to subsidies/grants (Article 386B). According to the constitutive elements of the former offence, it is punishable with a term of imprisonment of up to five years and a monetary penalty to give oneself or another an illegal pecuniary benefit by causing damage to the property of a third person and by affecting the outcome of computer data processing through: (a) the incorrect configuration of a computer programme; (b) the unauthorized interference in the operation of a computer programme or a computer system; (c) the incorrect or incomplete use of computer data, in particular, identity identification data; (d) the unauthorized insertion, alteration, or deletion of computer data; or (e) the unauthorized use of software intended for the transfer of money. According to the constitutive elements of the latter offence, it is punishable with a term of imprisonment of between one and five years and a monetary penalty to submit a request to an authority, which is responsible for approving the award of a grant, when knowingly incorrect or incomplete information have been given or when facts have not been disclosed, even though it was required, and this led to the approval of the requested grant.

*247.* The offence of accepting and disposing the proceeds of criminal activity is laid down in Article 394: whoever hides, buys, receives as a pledge or otherwise accepts in his possession an object/item/thing, which came from the commission of an offence, or transfers its possession to a third person, or in any way ensures that its possession remains with a third person, faces a term of imprisonment of up to two years or a monetary penalty. If the item was of particular value, the person who accepted it, etc., faces imprisonment of up to five years and a monetary penalty. The convicted person shall be sentenced irrespective of whether the principal offender, i.e., the perpetrator of the offence from which the object originated, was punished or not.

Finally, reference should be made to Article 395 (obstruction of free competition in public procurement) and to Article 396 (accepting and giving bribes in the private sector). According to the first paragraph of Article 395, it is punishable with a term of imprisonment of at least three years and a monetary penalty for anyone to obstruct free competition in public procurement procedures by using concerted practices or agreements between undertakings or by using force or threats or by removing from such procedures competitors by offering them gifts or promises. *Mutatis mutandis,* these provisions apply to the second paragraph of Article 395, which concerns specifically public auctions (the threatened term of imprisonment here is more lenient).

The constitutive elements of the misdemeanour of bribery in the private sector under Article 396(1) are as follows: anyone, who is employed or provides services with any capacity or relationship in the private sector and, during a business activity, has requested or received or promised, directly or indirectly, any unjust benefit for himself or for another in exchange of performing an act or omitting an act and in violation of his duties as these are envisaged in the legislation or derive from the nature of his position. The threatened punishment is imprisonment of at least one year and a monetary penalty. Under Article 396(2), the same punishment is threatened to anyone who has bribed an employee in the private sector.

*Chapter XXIV. Begging and Vagrancy (Articles 407–410 of the Old Penal Code)*

*248.* This Chapter was abrogated in the new Penal Code. However, reference should be made to Article 409 of the old Penal Code, the misdemeanour of supplying minors to another for begging or forcing minors to beg. It now falls under Article 323A(7) of the new Penal Code and is punishable by imprisonment of up to five years and a monetary penalty. The so-called traffic-lights children have not been a phenomenon only in Greece but in several other European countries as well.[271]

*Chapter XXV. Petty Offences (Articles 411–459 of the Old Penal Code)*

*249.* As has been mentioned, the new Penal Code abolished the regulation of petty criminal acts and, therefore, this Chapter was abrogated. In September 2020, the Greek government announced that in a forthcoming draft law it will include provisions to substitute –only where necessary– the criminal sanctions, which were threatened for petty offences under the old Penal Code, with the imposition of administrative fines ranging from EUR 100 to 600.

*Chapter XXVI. Violation of Administrative and Police Regulations (Articles 458–459 of the Old Penal Code)*

*250.* This Chapter was abrogated in the new Penal Code.

## II. Criminal Offences in Special Penal Statutes

### A. Introduction

*251.* The Penal Code does not include all criminal offences. On the contrary, the legislator has opted to regulate criminal acts both at the level of the Special Part of the Penal Code and at the level of the so-called special criminal statutes. It is not immediately clear which criminal acts the legislator determines to regulate in the Penal Code and which in the special criminal statutes. Thus, trafficking of human beings has been criminalized under Article 323A of the Penal Code but money laundering, as will be explained, under Act 4557/2018. It could be argued that the Penal Code includes core offences, while the special criminal statutes deal with other forms of criminality, which tend to be subject to modifications more often than core crimes (tax evasion, money laundering, environmental crimes, drug trafficking etc.). Moreover, the regulation of behaviour, which has been criminalized pursuant to treaties ratified by Greece and/or under EU legislation, has often been done by virtue of special criminal statutes but this is not an absolute rule, as the above example

271. Generally, *see* the chapter on Greece in European Commission, *Report for the Study on Typology and Policy Responses to Child Begging in the EU*, JLS/2009/ISEC/PR/008-F2, December 2012, pp. 168 et seq.

shows. There is no hierarchy between the Penal Code and the special criminal statutes. Their main connecting provision appears to be Article 12 of the Penal Code according to which, the general principles of the General Part of the Penal Code shall apply to all special criminal statutes, unless the latter contain different stipulations, in which case they shall prevail. In the following paragraphs, a selection of special criminal statutes is presented and briefly analysed alongside references to pertinent international treaties and EU law.

### *B. Offences Relating to Cultural Property (Including Antiquities)*

*252.* Greece, being a country, whose uninterrupted history goes back to ancient times, is bound to be extremely sensitive in preserving and safeguarding its cultural heritage. Article 24 of the Constitution protects what it calls 'the cultural environment', which includes all moveable and immovable property constructed/built/created before the early 1830s, when the modern Greek State was established following a ten-year war of independence against the Ottoman Empire. Greece has repeatedly suffered from the illegal removal of archaeological and other cultural items, especially during the Ottoman occupation. The removal of the so-called Elgin marbles (also known as the 'Parthenon Sculptures') from the Acropolis in Athens by Thomas Bruce, 7th Earl of Elgin and 11th Earl of Kincardine, at the beginning of the nineteenth century has become a celebrated case. It has also acted as a catalyst for those countries seeking from third States the return of objects which they consider part of their cultural heritage. Greece is a contracting party to several relevant treaties, which have been concluded under the auspices of the following international organizations: (a) UNESCO, namely, the Convention on Means of Prohibiting and Preventing the Illicit Export, Import and Transfer of Ownership of Cultural Property;[272] (b) Council of Europe, namely, the Convention on the Protection of the Archaeological Heritage,[273] the Convention on the Protection of the Architectural Heritage of Europe,[274] and the Convention on the Protection of the Architectural Heritage of Europe (revised), which replaced the Convention of 1969;[275] and (c) UNIDROIT, namely the Convention on the Return of Stolen or Illegally Exported Cultural Goods.[276] Finally, the domestic legal system is subject to the relevant provisions of EU law, including Directive 2014/60.[277]

---

272. Concluded in Paris on 14 Nov. 1970, entered into force on 24 Apr. 1972, 823 *UNTS* 231. Greece ratified it under Act 1103/1980, FEK 1980 A' 297. Greece is not a party to the UNESCO Convention on the Protection of the Underwater Cultural Heritage, concluded in Paris on 2 Nov. 2001, entered into force on 2 Jan. 2009, 2562 *UNTS* 1.
273. Opened for signature on 6 May 1969, entered into force on 20 Nov. 1970, ETS No. 66. Greece ratified it in 1981.
274. Adopted on 3 Oct. 1985, entered into force on 1 Dec. 1987, CETS No. 121. Greece ratified it under Act 2039/1992, FEK 1992 A' 61.
275. Adopted on 16 Jan. 1992, entered into force on 25 May 1995, CETS No. 143. Greece ratified it under Act 3378/2005, FEK 2005 A' 203.
276. Adopted on 24 Jun. 1995, entered into force 1 Jul. 1998, 2421 *UNTS* 457. Greece ratified it under Act 3348/2005, FEK 2005 A' 144.
277. Directive 2014/60/EU of the European Parliament and of the Council of 15 May 2014 on the return of cultural objects unlawfully removed from the territory of a Member State and amending Regulation (EU) No 1024/2012, O.J. L 159, 28.5.2014, p. 1, transposed under Act 4355/2015, FEK 2015

*253.* Reference should also be made to the European Convention on Offences relating to Cultural Property. It was concluded under the auspices of the Council of Europe in Delphi, one of the most sacred sites in Ancient Greece, on 23 June 1985. The Convention was adopted as a multilateral legal instrument to promote co-operation among contracting parties in the prevention of offences relating to cultural property and in the discovery of cultural property removed.[278] This is quite progressive for the time it was concluded treaty has never entered into force even though only three ratifications are required. Until today, it has been signed by only six States (including Greece), but none has ratified it! Apparently undeterred by this failure, the Council of Europe negotiated a new treaty, the Convention on Offences Relating to Cultural Property. Concluded in Nicosia, Cyprus, on 19 May 2017, it aims, *inter alia*, at preventing and combatting the destruction and trafficking of cultural property by means of criminalizing certain acts.[279] It should be noted that the kind of behaviour envisaged in the 2017 Convention, if committed during an armed conflict, may constitute a war crime.[280] Already, the ICC has ruled on such a case.[281]

*254.* Antiquities are primarily protected under Act 3028/2002, which stipulates that they belong de jure to the Greek State.[282] Anyone, who comes into possession of such objects, even if he happened to accidentality find them, e.g., by excavating his land, must declare it without any delay to the Police or to the Archaeological Service, the competent public authority which is part of the Ministry of Culture (Article 8(1) thereof). Failure to do so is criminally punishable. Generally speaking, ownership in antiquities is only permitted, if they form part of a private collection, whose content has been catalogued by the competent public authority, and if some

A' 178. *See also* Regulation 2019/880 of the European Parliament and of the Council of 17 Apr. 2019 on the introduction and the import of cultural goods, O.J. L 151, 7.6.2019, p. 1.

278. ETS No. 119.

279. Entered into force 1 Apr. 2022, CETS No. 221. Greece ratified it under Act 4744/2020, FEK 2020 A' 213.

280. *See* e.g., UNESCO Convention for the Protection of Cultural Property in the Event of Armed Conflict with Regulations for the Execution of the Convention, signed on 14 May 1954, entered into force on 7 Aug. 1956, 249 *UNTS* 215, the First Protocol to the Convention, entered into force on the same day as the Convention, 249 *UNTS* 358, ratified under Act 1114/1981, FEK 1981 A' 6, and the Second Protocol to the Convention, adopted on 26 Mar. 1999, entered into force on 9 Mar. 2004, 2253 *UNTS* 172, (1999) 38 *ILM* 769, ratified under Act 3317/2005, FEK 2005 A' 45; International Guidelines for Crime Prevention and Criminal Justice Responses with Respect to Trafficking in Cultural Property and Other Related Offences, adopted under UNGA Resolution 69/196 of 18 Dec. 2014; UNESCO Declaration Concerning the Intentional Destruction of Cultural Heritage, adopted by the Thirty-Second Session of the UNESCO General Conference, Paris, 17 Oct. 2003.

281. *See* International Criminal Court, Trial Chamber VIII, *The Prosecutor v. Ahmad Al Faqi Al Mahdi*, Reparations Order, ICC-01/12-01/15-236, 17 Aug. 2017; K. Magliveras, 'The ICC Orders Wide-Ranging Reparations for Destroying Religious and Cultural Sites in the *Al Mahdi* Case' (2017) 33 *International Enforcement Law Reporter* 335–339. The Order was confirmed: Appeals Chamber, *Public redacted Judgment on the appeal of the victims against the 'Reparations Order'*, ICC-01/12-01/15-259-Red2, 8 Mar. 2018. *See* further, UN Security Council Resolution 2199(2015) of 12 Feb. 2015 and Resolution 2347(2017) of 24 Mar. 2017.

282. Act 3028/2002 on the protection of antiquities and cultural heritage in general, FEK 2002 A' 153, as last amended under Act 4761/2020, FEK 2020 A' 248.

of the objects are on public display. Despite efforts to combat trafficking in antiquities, it remains a thriving business. A matter which is difficult to regulate concerns the possession of objects, such as ancient coins or icons (religious paintings), which may form part or claim to be part of family heirlooms passed from one generation to the next.

The criminal law and criminal procedure provisions of Act 3028/2002 are laid down in Articles 53–72. Pursuant to Article 53(1), the commission of theft (Article 372 of the Penal Code) shall be punished with confinement of a penitentiary of up to ten years, if it concerned a monument of particularly high value or was removed from a stationary monument, from an excavated site, from a museum, from places where ancient finds are in storage or from places where antiquity collections are kept. In accordance with Article 63(1), the prohibited exportation or the attempt to export monuments or items of cultural property is a serious offence punishable with confinement in a penitentiary of up to ten years. Acquiring monuments in a criminal manner constitutes aggravating circumstances. Moreover, under Article 64, anyone importing into Greece cultural goods, within the meaning of the aforementioned UNESCO Convention on Means of Prohibiting and Preventing the Illicit Export, Import and Transfer of Ownership of Cultural Property, which have been illegally removed from museums or similar institutions or religious or public monuments located in the territory of the Convention's contracting parties, shall be punished by imprisonment of at least one year, unless punished more severely by other criminal statutes. Finally, pursuant to Article 69(1), it is obligatory to confiscate the cultural goods that are the object of the illegal exportation or the attempted exportation (including the means/instrumentalities of committing these offences), if they belonged to the perpetrator or to an accomplice.

### C. *Offences Relating to Narcotics*

*255.* As has been mentioned (*infra* paragraph 44), Greece has ratified the UN Convention against Illicit Traffic in Narcotic Drugs and Psychotropic Substances. In 1972, it acceded to the Single Convention on Narcotic Drugs (1961), and in 1985 it ratified the Amending Protocol (1972).[283] It has also ratified the UN Convention on Psychotropic Substances (1971).[284] Greece is also subject to the regulation of narcotics pursuant to the secondary EU legislation, namely Council Framework Decision 2004/757/JHA,[285] as currently in force.[286] The current domestic regulatory

283. The Convention was signed under UN auspices on 30 Mar. 1961, entered into force on 13 Dec. 1964, 520 *UNTS* 151, ratified under Legislative Decree 1105/1972, FEK 1971 A' 36. The Protocol was signed on 25 Mar. 1972, entered into force on 8 Aug. 1975, 976 *UNTS* 105, ratified under Act 1549/1985, FEK 1975 A' 93.
284. Signed on 21 Feb. 1971, entered into force on 16 Aug. 1976, 1019 *UNTS* 175, ratified under Act 348/1976, FEK 1976 A' 146.
285. Council Framework Decision 2004/757/JHA of 25 Oct. 2004 laying down minimum provisions on the constituent elements of criminal acts and penalties in the field of illicit drug trafficking, O.J. L 335, 11.11.2004, p. 8, transposed in Greek law under Act 3459/2006, FEK 2006 A' 103.
286. *See* Directive 2017/2103 of the European Parliament and of the Council of 15 Nov. 2017 amending Council Framework Decision 2004/757/JHA in order to include new psychoactive substances in the

regime is Act 4139/2013,[287] which compared to other European jurisdiction contains much harsher provisions.[288] It distinguishes between drug possession and the acquisition of narcotics for personal use, on the one hand, and the procurement of narcotics for business/profitable use (trafficking), on the other hand. The envisaged punishment varies accordingly. Thus, pursuant to Article 29 thereof, those using narcotics or obtaining or otherwise processing them solely for personal use and in quantities to satisfy their own needs, shall be sentenced to a term of imprisonment not exceeding five months. The commission of this offence shall not be entered into the convicted person's criminal record. The perpetrator of Article 29 offences may not be punished, if the court of justice, assessing the circumstances under which the offence was committed as well as his personality, takes the view that the offence was occasionally perpetrated and is unlikely to be repeated.

*256.* As regards those engaged in trafficking in narcotics, pursuant to Article 20 Act 4139/2013, they face confinement in a penitentiary for up to eight years and a maximum monetary penalty of EUR 300,000. More lenient sanctions are envisaged in Article 21 (a term of imprisonment of up to three years) when the offender has handled small quantities of narcotics to meet his daily individual needs, and he is an addict or when he has supplied narcotics to his relatives without making a profit and in order to cover their own immediate needs. And heavier sanctions (confinement in a penitentiary for at least ten years and a monetary penalty between EUR 50,000 and EUR 500,000 ) are threatened in Article 22, *inter alia*, in the following instances which are all considered aggravated circumstances: if the offender is a civil servant/employee of the public sector (Article 13 of the Penal Code) and, on account of his duties, he is involved in narcotics or if he trafficked narcotics to facilitate or to conceal the commission of other serious crimes or if he distributed drugs in armed forces' camps, in police detention centres, in penitentiaries, in schools and tertiary education institutes, etc., or if the trafficking was carried out in the context of a criminal organization (Article 187 of the Penal Code, *supra* paragraphs 69, 151, 194).

*257.* Finally, Article 23 Act 4139/2013 sets out several instances of what it calls 'notably aggravated circumstances', which include the following instances: (a) the criminal act involved drugs, which could cause serious bodily harm (Article 310(2) of the Penal Code, *supra* paragraph 222) and either caused serious bodily harm or death to a third person or damaged the health of many people (the threatened sanction is confinement in a penitentiary for life or for at least ten years and a monetary

definition of 'drug' and repealing Council Decision 2005/387/JHA, O.J. L 305, 21.11.2017, p. 12, and Commission Delegated Directive 2019/369 of 13 Dec. 2018 amending the Annex to Council Framework Decision 2004/757/JHA as regards the inclusion of new psychoactive substances in the definition of 'drug', O.J. L 66, 7.3.2019, p. 3; for transposition in Greek law, *see* FEK 2019 B' 2391 and FEK 2018 B' 4838.

287. Act 4139/2013, Law on Addictive Substances and other provisions, FEK 2013 A' 74, as amended by Act 4691/2020, FEK 2020 A' 108, and by Act 4982/2022, FEK 2022 A' 195.

288. For relevant statistical data, *see* the database of the European Monitoring Centre for Drugs and Drug Addiction, a decentralized agency of the European Union, at: https://www.emcdda.europa.eu/countries/drug-reports/2019/greece_en.

penalty ranging from EUR 50,000 to EUR 600,000), and (b) the offender financed as a profession the commission of acts of trafficking or was a professional drugs trafficker and the expected benefit of these acts exceed EUR 75,000 (confinement in a penitentiary for life and a monetary penalty between EUR 50,000 and EUR 1 million).

### *D. Offences Relating to Money Laundering*

*258.* Act 4557/2018 is the principal criminal statute on money laundering.[289] Its purpose was to transpose in the domestic legal order the then-relevant EU law, namely Directive 2015/849,[290] and to codify the existing provisions on money laundering. In June 2018, the EU adopted an updated anti-money laundering Directive (also known as Fifth EU Anti Money Laundering Directive or AMLD V).[291] It had to be transposed in the legal systems of Member States by 10 January 2020, but Greece did so in October 2020 under Act 4734/2020.[292] Finally, in July 2021, the EU adopted the Sixth Anti Money Laundering Directive or AMLD VI,[293] which was transposed pursuant to Act 4816/2021.[294]

It is submitted that the content of the Greek anti-money laundering legislation should also be compatible with the relevant treaties accepted by Greece (e.g., the Council of Europe Convention on Laundering, Search, Seizure and Confiscation of the Proceeds from Crime and on the Financing of Terrorism,[295] which Greece ratified in June 2017[296] subject to reservations)[297] as well as with other instruments

289. Act 4557/2018, Prevention and suppression of money laundering and terrorist financing (transposition of Directive 2015/849/EU) and other provisions, FEK 2018 A' 139; unofficial English translation at: http://www.hcmc.gr/en_US/web/portal/elib/lawslaws. Credit and financial institutions supervised by the Bank of Greece are also subject to Decision No. 281 Item 5 of 17 Mar. 2009 adopted by the Bank of Greece's Banking and Credit Committee, as last amended by Bank of Greece's Executive Committee Act no. 172/2/29.5.2020 and Executive Committee Act no. 188/1/26.4.2021. Generally, *see* https://www.bankofgreece.gr/en/main-tasks/supervision/prevention-of-money-laundering.
290. Directive (EU) 2015/849 of the European Parliament and of the Council of 20 May 2015 on the prevention of the use of the financial system for the purposes of money laundering or terrorist financing, amending Regulation (EU) No 648/2012 of the European Parliament and of the Council, and repealing Directive 2005/60/EC of the European Parliament and of the Council and Commission Directive 2006/70/EC, O.J. L 141, 5.6.2015, p. 73.
291. Directive 2018/843 of the European Parliament and of the Council of 30 May 2018 amending Directive (EU) 2015/849 on the prevention of the use of the financial system for the purposes of money laundering or terrorist financing, and amending Directives 2009/138/EC and 2013/36/EU, O.J. L 156, 19.6.2018, p. 43.
292. Act 4734/2020, Amendment of Law 4557/2018 for the prevention and suppression of money laundering and terrorist financing, incorporation into Greek legislation of Directive (EU) 2018/843 (L 156) and Art. 3 of the Directive (EU) 2019/2177 (L 334), and other provisions, FEK 2020 A' 196.
293. Directive (EU) 2018/1673 of the European Parliament and of the Council of 23 Oct. 2018 on combating money laundering by criminal law, O.J. L 284, 12.11.2018, p. 22.
294. FEK 2021 A' 118.
295. Opened for signature on 16 May 2005, entered into force on 1 May 2008, CETS No. 198, 2569 *UNTS* 91.
296. Under Act 4478/2017, FEK 2017 A' 91. Note that, in addition, Act 4478/2017 transposed into the domestic legal order two other EU instruments with a criminal law dimension, namely Directive

having the status of international soft law (e.g., the FATF 40 Recommendations).[298] However, the Report issued after the latest FATF mutual evaluation of Greece's regulatory regime on money laundering (October – November 2018) concluded that 'Greece has the foundations for effective action against money laundering and terrorist financing. However, it needs to improve prosecution of these crimes and focus more on the risks that face the non-financial sector.'[299] The question of weaknesses in the implementation in Greece of money laundering Directives was raised in a question put by a member of the European Parliament to the European Commission in February 2022.[300]

*259.* The constitutive elements of the offence of money laundering are quite extensively laid down in Act 4557/2018 and include the following:

(a) Knowingly converting or transferring property assets being the proceeds of crime in order to conceal their illegal source, or aiding any person involved in such an act in order to avoid being punished.
(b) Concealing the truth in relation to the nature, source, disposal, movement or use of assets, or the place from which they were acquired or in which they are located, or their ownership, while knowing that such assets are the proceeds of criminal acts or the proceeds of participation in criminal activities.
(c) Acquiring, possessing or using any assets knowing that they are the proceeds of criminal acts or the proceeds of participation in criminal activities.
(d) Using the financial sector to deposit or to transfer the proceeds of criminal activities so as to appear as having derived from a legitimate source.
(e) Forming an organization or a group consisting of at least two persons to perpetrate one or more of the previous acts or participating in such an organization or group.

---

2013/48/EU of the European Parliament and of the Council of 22 Oct. 2013 on the right of access to a lawyer in criminal proceedings and in European arrest warrant proceedings, and on the right to have a third party informed upon deprivation of liberty and to communicate with third persons and with consular authorities while deprived of liberty, O.J. L 294, 6.11.2013, p. 1, and Directive 2012/29/EU of the European Parliament and of the Council of 25 Oct. 2012 establishing minimum standards on the rights, support and protection of victims of crime, and replacing Council Framework Decision 2001/220/JHA, O.J. L 315, 14.11.2012, p. 57.

297. Available at: https://www.coe.int/en/web/conventions/full-list/-/conventions/treaty/198/declarations?p_auth=HZIuU6vR.

298. Financial Action Task Force, *Forty Recommendations against money laundering, terrorist financing and the financing of proliferation of weapons of mass destruction*, adopted in February 2012, as last amended in February 2023, at: https://www.fatf-gafi.org/en/publications/Fatfrecommendations/Fatf-recommendations.html. FATF claims to be an 'independent inter-governmental body' that develops and promotes policies to protect the global financial system form money laundering, the financing of terrorism and the financing of the proliferation of weapons of mass destruction.

299. *See* Financial Action Task Force, *Anti-money laundering and counter-terrorist financing measures – Greece, Fourth Round Mutual Evaluation Report*, September 2019, at: https://www.fatf-gafi.org/media/fatf/documents/reports/mer4/MER-Greece-2019.pdf.

300. *See* European Parliament, Parliamentary question E-000788/2022, 24 Feb. 2022, at: https://www.europarl.europa.eu/doceo/document/E-9-2022-000788_EN.html. For the European Commission's reply, *see* Parliamentary question E-000788/2022(ASW), 22 Apr. 2022, at: https://www.europarl.europa.eu/doceo/document/E-9-2022-000788-ASW_EN.html.

(f) Attempting to perpetrate, aiding, abetting, facilitating or advising a person to perpetrate any of the previous criminal acts.

*260.* The punishment of money laundering depends on the classification of the offences the proceeds of which were legitimized by the offender (the so-called predicate offences; in Act 4557/2018 they are called 'principal offences'). Article 4 thereof sets out in detail which are the predicate offences. Moreover, it provides that predicate offence shall also be any other offence, which is punishable by a custodial sentence of at least six months and from which a pecuniary benefit has derived. It should be noted that for a money laundering offence to be prosecuted and for the offender to be convicted it is not a *conditio sine qua non* that the perpetrator of the predicate offence has been prosecuted and/or convicted. Thus, while the criminal act of money laundering is hinged upon the prior commission of an offence and without the latter it cannot be perpetrated, for the legislator, it is of no consequence who carried out the prior (predicate) offence and whether he is culpable for it; what is of concern is that an offence has been carried out, which led to the illegal acquisition of proceeds and that these proceeds have been legitimized (laundered) by a third person.

*261.* Pursuant to Article 39(1) of Act 4557/2018, if the predicate offence is a misdemeanour, the offender shall be imprisoned for between one and five years and fined an amount between EUR 10,000 and EUR 500,000. But if the predicate offence is a felony, he faces a minimum term of imprisonment of one year and a maximum term of six years and a monetary penalty ranging between EUR 20,000 and EUR 1 million. Moreover, if the offender committed money laundering as a profession, or if his acts related to organized crime or to terrorist activities, these constitute aggravated circumstances and, therefore, he shall face confinement in a penitentiary of between ten and fifteen years and a monetary penalty ranging between EUR 50,000 and EUR 2 million. Other aggravated circumstances include the following: (a) the offence of money laundering was perpetrated by an employee of an entity, which is by law required to have in place anti-money laundering measures, and (b) where the predicate offence was the passive or active bribery of civil servants/public sector employees (including judges). In these instances, even if the predicate offences are misdemeanours, offenders face confinement in a penitentiary of between five and fifteen years as well as a monetary penalty of between EUR 30,000 and EUR 1.5 million.

*262.* One of the crucial aspects of the money laundering legislation is the obligation of certain legal persons and professionals to report transactions which may involve acts legitimating proceeds from criminal acts to the competent authorities (Articles 22 and 27 of Act 4557/2018). This is an obligation borne by banks and other financial institutions and intermediaries, auditing companies, tax consultants, auction houses, etc. It is very closely connected to the so-called know your customer (KYC) principle. The intentional failure by an employee of these companies to report any suspicious or unusual transactions or activities that have come or should have come to his attention, or the intentional supply of false or misleading information and data is punishable by imprisonment of up to two years or a monetary penalty. According to Article 40 of Act 4557/2018, assets derived from any of the predicate offences or from the offence of money laundering itself, as described in Articles 2 and 4 thereof, respectively, or assets acquired directly or indirectly from the proceeds of such offences or the means that were used or were intended to be used for committing these offences, must be seized. Moreover, if there is no legal basis to have such assets returned to their owner, they shall be compulsorily forfeited following the court's judgment. In case a money laundering offence was carried out on behalf or for the benefit of a company or a legal entity (corporate liability), Article 45 of 4557/2018 threatens the following sanctions: an administrative fine of between EUR 50,000 and EUR 10 million; the temporary (from one to twenty-four months) or the permanent suspension of company activities; the prohibition of pursuing certain business activities, of share capital increases, etc.; and banning the convicted company from being awarded or receiving public subsidies and other forms of public funding.

# Chapter 7. The Sanctioning System

## §1. Punishments

### I. The Principal Penalties

*263.* According to Article 50, there are three types of criminal penalties: (a) custodial penalties, or penalties depriving one's freedom, to use the precise wording of the Penal Code; (b) pecuniary (monetary) penalties; and (c) community service. As a general observation, the new Penal Code, as amended, has brought about considerable changes in the sanctioning system and has abolished certain characteristics of the Greek criminal justice system, e.g., the conversion of terms of imprisonment into pecuniary penalties.

#### A. The Death Penalty

*264.* Even though the death penalty has now been completely abolished in Greece, as is the case in most European States, it is interesting to briefly recount how this was achieved as it would appear to have been the outcome of concerted international action. The question of the abolition of the death penalty has always attracted much attention. It is also rather controversial because it is the sovereign right of each State to decide whether to retain capital punishment as the ultimate punishment or not. The international human rights instruments of the pre-World War II period avoided any direct reference to it because it was considered a delicate issue best left to be regulated by each State party separately. However, during the 1940s, several European States abrogated capital sentences as statutory punishment, including Denmark, the Netherlands, Latvia, Norway, Portugal, Romania and Switzerland. While the Greek criminal statutes included the death penalty, throughout the twentieth century its imposition and execution were rather rare and concerned criminal acts committed with particular cruelty. The last time a convicted to death person was executed by a firing squad was in August 1972; he had been convicted for having burned alive his wife, his mother-in-law and his two underaged children. Capital punishment was abolished by virtue of Article 33(1) of Act 2172/1993.[301] This provision was a rather interesting example of Greek legislative technique: instead of amending all relevant provisions in the criminal statutes, including the Penal Code, it stipulated: 'Whenever the death penalty is envisaged as sole punishment for a criminal act, confinement in a penitentiary for life is meant. If the imposition of the death penalty is envisaged as an alternative to another sanction, only the latter is meant.'

*265.* The promulgation of Act 2172/1993 allowed the ratification of two international human rights instruments dealing specifically with the abolition of capital punishment. The first was the Second Optional Protocol to the ICCPR aiming at

301. FEK 1993 A' 207.

abolishing the death penalty.[302] The second instrument was the Sixth Protocol to the ECHR Concerning the Abolition of the Death Penalty,[303] which was signed by Greece on May 2 1983 and ratified under Act 2610/1998.[304] Even though the death penalty has been abolished, it could still have been inflicted as a sanction for committing several military offences under Article 8 of the Military Penal Code (Act 2287/1995). The latter provided for the death penalty in the commission of, *inter alia*, the following offences: treason (Article 15); capitulation of a commanding officer to the enemy without exhausting all possible means of defence; evasion of draft during belligerency (Article 32); desertion during belligerency (Article 33); and mutiny during belligerency (Article 46). The Military Penal Code's provision on capital punishment was in conformity with the ICCPR Optional Protocol and the ECHR Sixth Protocol, as both instruments stipulate in Article 2 that State parties may prescribe the death penalty for acts which were committed in wartime or during an imminent threat of war. And it was also in line with the Constitution, whose Article 7(3) stipulates, following the constitutional amendments of 2001, that 'The death penalty is not imposed, except in cases provided for in the legislation for crimes committed in time of war and related to it.'

The situation changed radically, when Greece ratified the Thirteenth Protocol to the ECHR Concerning the Abolition of the Death Penalty in all Circumstances.[305] The operative text of the Thirteenth Protocol, which has been accepted by all Member States of the Council of Europe except three (Armenia, Azerbaijan and the Russian Federation (the latter was expelled from the Council of Europe in March 2022)), is very brief: Article 1 provides that 'The death penalty shall be abolished. No one shall be condemned to such penalty or executed', Article 2 prohibits derogations, and Article 3 prohibits reservations. Act 3289/2004 resulted in the abrogation of Article 8 of the Military Penal Code.

## *B. Custodial Penalties*

*266.* Article 51(1) of the Penal Code envisages the following three custodial penalties: confinement in a penitentiary (incarceration); imprisonment; and confinement in a special detention facility for young offenders. The amendments to the new Penal Code deleted the custodial penalties of confinement in special institutions and detention, which had been carried over from the old Penal Code.

### *Confinement in a Penitentiary*

*267.* According to Article 52, an offender shall be sentenced to a fixed term confinement and, only if expressly stipulated in the criminal statutes, to confinement for life. The duration of the fixed term is between five and fifteen years (twenty years

302. Adopted by the UN General Assembly on 15 Dec. 1989, entered into force on 11 Jul. 1991, 999 *UNTS* 171, ratified under the aforementioned Act 2462/1997.
303. Concluded on 28 Apr. 1983, entered into force on 1 Mar. 1985, ETS No. 114.
304. FEK 1998 A' 110.
305. Opened for signature on 3 May 2002, entered into force on 1 Jul. 2003, ETS No. 187. Greece ratified it under Act 3289/2004, FEK 2004 A' 227.

under the old Penal Code). Under the old Penal Code, in certain cases, if the offender had already been repeatedly convicted, the provisions of Article 52 were not applicable, but Article 90 was applicable. The latter had introduced the so-called confinement of indefinite duration, which meant that it was the court itself determining the minimum term of confinement. Article 90 was applied to those who had already been sentenced three times for serious crimes or for intentionally perpetrated misdemeanours and had committed another serious crime or misdemeanour. In this instance, the repeated offender was regarded as a habitual or by profession criminal who was dangerous to public safety. This type of sentencing, which had never been applied by Greek courts and was abolished under the new Penal Code, does recall the habitual offender laws, better known as 'three-strikes laws', which have been enforced in the USA since the mid-1990s.

*Imprisonment*

*268.* In accordance with Article 53, the minimum term of imprisonment is ten days, and the maximum is five years. When the Penal Code and the other criminal statutes stipulate 'imprisonment' as punishment without specifying its length (e.g., up to two years, a minimum of three years, etc.) the court may inflict any period within these limits, provided that the rules on the calculation/assessment of penalties (Articles 79 et seq.) have been followed.

*Confinement in Special Facilities (Institutions)*

*269.* Pursuant to Article 36, the courts must take into account that the defendant acted with diminished criminal responsibility due to psychological, mental or other conditions laid down in Article 34 and impose a mitigated penalty. Under Article 37 of the old Penal Code, such offenders in need of special treatment or care had to spend the custodial sentence in special facilities. Article 37, which had found no application in practice, was abolished by the new Penal Code. Moreover, the provisions on sentencing dangerous convicted persons with diminished responsibility to psychiatric institutions (Articles 38–41) had already been abrogated and replaced under Act 4509/2017.[306]

*Confinement in a Special Detention Facility for Young Offenders*

*270.* According to Article 54, the duration of confinement in a special detention facility for young offenders may not exceed five years and may not be less than six months, if the legislation threatens for the offence committed confinement in a penitentiary of up to ten years. Should the threatened punishment be life-long confinement or temporary confinement exceeding ten years, it shall range between two and eight years.

306. Act 4509/2017, Measures to treat people who are released from punishment due to mental or intellectual disorder, FEK 2017 A' 201.

### C. *Pecuniary (Monetary) Penalties*

*271.* Article 57 of the old Penal Code envisaged monetary sanctions and fines, the former ranged between EUR 150 and EUR 15,000, the latter between EUR 29 and EUR 590. These amounts had not changed during the last twenty-five years. Article 57(1) of the new Penal Code envisages only pecuniary penalties, which are no longer calculated in terms of monetary amounts but in terms of the so-called daily units. Each such daily unit has a particular value, which, subject to any special criminal provisions, has been set at EUR 1 minimum and EUR 100 maximum (Article 57(3)). Pursuant to the second paragraph of Article 57, the threatened pecuniary penalty may not be higher than (a) ninety daily units when it is the only criminal sanction envisaged or when it may be inflicted *in lieu* of community service; (b) 180 daily units when it is threatened *in lieu* of a custodial sentence; and (c) 360 daily units when it is threatened together with a custodial sentence.

*272.* According to Article 80(1)–(2), when the court of justice calculates/assesses the monetary penalty to be inflicted, it shall lay lawn in the judgment both the number of the daily units as well as the value of each unit. In order to decide the precise number of the daily units, the court may only take into account the severity of the offence committed and the degree of the offender's culpability. The court, in determining the value of each daily unit, must take into consideration the personal and financial situation of the offender, his net income from work, etc., other assets that he may hold, his obligations and commitments towards his family, and so on (Article 80(3)). Should the convicted person not be in the position to pay promptly the whole of the pecuniary penalty or if this would lead to his inability to pay the compensation awarded to the victim, the court is entitled to set out a deadline not exceeding three years to pay up the penalty in instalments.

*273.* The fact that an offence was committed out of a drive to enrich oneself is treated as aggravating circumstances. Thus, in the case of Article 324 dealing with the abduction/kidnapping of minors, should the abduction have been carried out for the purposes of extracting ransom from a third party (not necessarily the minor's parents or relatives) or forcing a third person to act or refrain from acting in a certain way, the offence's legal status changes from misdemeanour to serious crime and, therefore, confinement in a penitentiary shall be imposed (Article 324(3)). However, if the offender, on his own free will and before he received any ramson, freed and returned the minor unharmed, the aggravating circumstances will not be taken into account, presumably because the economic element of *dolus* is no longer present. In this instance, the offender shall be sentenced to imprisonment for a maximum of five years.

### D. *The Conversion of Imprisonment into Pecuniary Penalties*

*274.* One of the principal characteristics of the Greek criminal justice system under the old Penal Code was the conversion of terms of imprisonment into pecuniary penalties, which in certain instances was happening automatically and the sentencing court of justice had no discretion but to convert them. In particular, under Article 82 of the old Penal Code, custodial sentences not exceeding one year were obligatorily converted, while those between one and two years were converted unless the offender was a recidivist, and the court took the view that the non-conversion was necessary to prevent him from carrying out other criminal acts. Equally, custodial sentences between two and five years were also converted, unless the court had decided in a fully reasoned judgment not to convert them in order to prevent him from perpetrating other offences. It follows that in most cases the commission of misdemeanours was effectively punished by pecuniary penalties and the offender was never imprisoned. Finally, each concerted day of imprisonment was assessed between EUR 5 and EUR 100 maximum.

As stated in the Explanatory Memorandum, this system was abolished in the new Penal Code because conversion was considered unfair on two grounds: (a) it was understood differently by those having adequate financial means to pay the monetary penalty and by those who do not, and (b) when the criminal legislator threatened a custodial sentence for a certain offence, this means that the legislator believed that a pecuniary penalty on its own was not adequate punishment.

## *E. Community Service*

*275.* Since the early 1990s, the Greek legislator has played with the idea of introducing community service (public welfare work) as an alternative form of punishment. A first attempt was made under Act 1941/1991, which did not produce the desired results. Later on, Act 2408/1996 introduced in the sanctioning system the idea of converting certain custodial sentences into offering community service as a measure for a more humane rehabilitation of convicts. Under the old Penal Code, if the convicted person was declared unable to pay the monetary penalty of the converted imprisonment, the court of justice was directed to further convert the pecuniary penalty, wholly or partly, into community service. The following schedule was laid down: for a term of imprisonment of up to one year, the hours of community service were set between 100 and 240 hours; for imprisonment of between one and two years, between 241 and 480 hours; for imprisonment of between two and three years between 481 and 720 hours; and for the maximum period of imprisonment, i.e., four to five years, between 961 and 1,200 hours of community service.

*276.* According to Article 55 of the new Penal Code, community service becomes a principal punishment which can be inflicted as sole punishment, while it remains a criminal sanction in the case of converted custodial or pecuniary penalties. Moreover, the maximum number of community service hours has been reduced to 720 hours. Furthermore, Article 81(1)–(2) directs the court to take into consideration the offender's age, health as well as his professional and family obligations and restricts the maximum duration of community service to twenty-four months. Pursuant to Article 81(4), four hours of community service correspond to one day of imprisonment or to one daily unit of pecuniary penalty. According to Article 95(e) of the aforementioned Act 4623/2019 (it amended the new Penal Code), the designated places for carrying out community service shall be the legal entities belonging to the public sector or governed by public law, the local government organizations, other non-profit legal persons governed by private law, which will be laid down in a future joint ministerial decision.[307]

*277.* As has been mentioned (*infra* paragraph 20), the government that came into power in the summer of 2019 objected to several changes brought about by the new Penal Code– the extensive use of community service as punishment being one of them – on the grounds that the infrastructure required for its implementation was not available. Thus, Article 98 of the aforementioned Act 4623/2019 stipulates that the application of the Penal Code's provisions on community service either as principal punishment or as conversion of a custodial penalty or of a pecuniary penalty shall be suspended, while those misdemeanours, which are threatened with community service as the only punishment, shall be punished with pecuniary penalties.

### *F. The Conversion of Imprisonment in Community Service*

*278.* Article 104A allows the conversion of imprisonment into community service. In particular, when the imposed imprisonment does not exceed three years and Articles 99 and 100 (*infra* paragraphs 295–297) have not been applied, the sentence shall be converted to Article 81 community service (*supra* paragraph 276). The only exception is if the court of justice has considered that conversion will not be sufficient to prevent the perpetrator from committing further offences. Regarding the scale of conversion, each day of imprisonment corresponds to no more than three hours of community service, while the duration of community service may not exceed 2,000 hours or be longer than three years. As explained, by virtue of Act 4623/2019, the application of the new Penal Code's provisions on community service has been suspended.

## II. Accessory Penalties

*279.* Article 59 of the penal Code lays down the following five accessory penalties: deprivation of public positions and offices; prohibition of practising a profession; deprivation (revocation) of a driving license; publication of the criminal court judgment regarding the offender's conviction; and confiscation.

### *A. Deprivation of Public Positions and Offices*

*280.* Article 60 stipulates that if the offender has been sentenced to confinement in a penitentiary for any period of time, the court of justice may strip him of the

307. It appears that such a Decision has not yet been issued. The one which is apparently still in force (Joint Ministerial Decision 21325/31-10-2018, Framework for the implementation of the institution of community service for adults and compilation of a new list of bodies involved in its implementation, FEK 2018 B' 5315) envisages community service to be carried out in NGOs, and in entities of the so-called social solidarity economy.

public position or office or the local government position that he holds, provided that the offence perpetrated constituted a grave violation of his duties. It is not always clear which these positions or offices are, as they are not enumerated in the Penal Code. However, Article 152 titled 'Accessory penalties' provides that in the case of Chapter II (Articles 138–148, *supra* paragraphs 183 et seq.) offences, the court of justice must order the deprivation of public positions and offices together with the imposition of the punishment. Finally, the provisions in the old Penal Code regarding the deprivation of political rights as accessory penalty in the commission of specific serious crimes (e.g., torture and inhuman treatment; conspiracy, high treason and espionage; violence against the Parliament or the Government, etc.) have been abrogated.

### *B. Prohibition of Practicing a Profession*

*281.* This accessory penalty concerns those offenders who committed an offence by grossly violating the duties of their profession, provided that practising it requires the prior permission from a competent public authority (attorneys at law, notaries public, accountants/auditors, medical doctors, nurses, civil engineers, etc.) and that the imposed custodial sentence was of at least two years. In these cases, Article 65(1) allows the court to prohibit the offender from practicing his profession for a period of time ranging from one month to two years. According to Article 65(2), this accessory penalty commences as soon as the judgment becomes res judicata and, if the offender is in custody, it is calculated from the day following his release from prison.

### *C. Deprivation (Revocation) of a Driving License*

*282.* This is a new accessory penalty which is regulated in Article 66. It stipulates that if the perpetrator committed an offence, which was in direct connection to driving or to the operation (including the economic exploitation) of a means of transport and if he was sentenced to a custodial sentence of at least six months, the court may order, respectively, the revocation of the driving license that he holds for all or some types of means of transport or his license for operating them for a period between one month and one year. Arguably, this accessory penalty covers two different situations: the former concerns offences committed by anyone and involving, e.g., reckless driving which led to serious bodily harm of a third person, while the second offences carried out by someone holding a special driving license (e.g., a taxi driver, a lorry driver, a bus driver). Arguably, considering that holding a driving license is a necessary condition for being allowed to operate a taxi, a lorry, etc., is more closely connected to the aforementioned Article 65. And this is because to be deprived of the driving license means that the offender shall not be able to practice his profession. Pursuant to Article 66(2), the provision of Article 65(2) shall be applied here by analogy.

### *D. Publication of Conviction*

*283.* Article 67(1) stipulates that the court may also order the publication of the judgment convicting the offender, if the public interest so requires. The term 'public interest' is not defined in the Penal Code. Publication may only be ordered if so requested by the victim and only in the cases laid down in the legislation. The legitimate interest to be protected through the publication of the conviction is presumably the honour and dignity of an individual.[308] As far as the Penal Code is concerned, it refers, *inter alia*, to the following instances. First, Article 229(3) (wrongful incrimination). Second, Article 369, which extends to the following provisions: Article 361 (insult); Article 362 (defamation); Article 363 (slander); and Article 365 (slander or defamation of a dead person). According to Article 369(2), if the offence was carried out through the press or through the internet, it must be published in the same medium and include at least the relevant elements of the reasoning and the operative part of the judgment. Should this obligation not be complied with, it constitutes a separate offence punishable by imprisonment for up to one year or with a pecuniary penalty.

### *E. Confiscation*

*284.* According to Article 7(3) of the Greek Constitution, the general confiscation of one's property is prohibited. In the Penal Code, confiscation of the offence's instrumentalities or proceeds is envisaged as both an accessory penalty (Article 68) and as a security measure (Article 76).

*285.* Article 68(1) stipulates that objects or assets, which are the product (outcome) of a serious crime or of a misdemeanour committed with intent, as well as their value and any other object or asset acquired directly or indirectly therewith, and the objects or assets which were used or intended to be used for the commission of an offence are liable to confiscation if they belong to the perpetrator or to one of the participants. However, confiscation shall not be ordered when the court, on its own initiative or at the request of a litigant party or a third party, decides that this is disproportionate, e.g., when the convicted person or a third party, as well as their families, will be deprived of objects necessary for their livelihood or when it will cause them excessive and irreparable damage. Under Article 68(2), in these cases the court may substitute confiscation with a pecuniary penalty. Moreover, if the court cannot order confiscation because the objects or the assets do not exist or are not sufficient or belong in whole or in part to a third party, against whom confiscation may not be imposed, it may impose a pecuniary penalty which shall not exceed their value (Article 68(4)).

*286.* As regards the involvement of a third person with the objects or assets, which are the product of an offence, Article 68(5) stipulates that confiscation shall

308. As has been explained (*supra* para. 233), the offence of defaming a company (Art. 364 of the old Penal Code) was deleted.

be imposed on such third party if the objects or assets were transferred, directly or indirectly, from the perpetrator to him or if acquired by him or came to him in another way, provided that at the time of their acquisition he knew that they potentially derived from a serious crime or a misdemeanour and that the purpose of being transferred to him was to avoid confiscation. The judgment of the court must specifically explain how the third person had such knowledge. Arguably, the provision of Article 68(5) covers, at least indirectly, the constitutive elements of the offence of receiving stolen property and money laundering.

*287.* Finally, the Special Part of the Penal Code refers to confiscation in the following two instances. The first instance is Article 213(1) dealing with the compulsory confiscation of forged banknotes, coinage, other means of payment as well as of the instrumentalities used to perpetrate the criminal acts of Articles 207, 208A and 208B. In these cases, confiscation shall be ordered even if a certain person has not been prosecuted or convicted and irrespective of whether they belong to the principal offender or to an accessory. The second instance is Article 238, which forms part of Chapter XII dealing with the offences of giving and/or accepting bribes. In particular, Article 238 stipulates that if the offences of Articles 235–237A have been committed (e.g., Article 235 (passive bribery, i.e., a civil servant demands or accepts gifts for acting or omitting to act unlawfully); Article 236 (active bribery, i.e., a person offers or promises gifts/benefits to a civil servant for acting or omitting to act unlawfully); Article 237 (passive or active bribery of judges, arbitrators, etc.), and Article 237A (trading in influence – middlemen/intermediaries)), the court of justice shall also impose upon the convicted offender the accessory penalty of confiscation laid down in Article 68.

*288.* Special confiscation as a security (protective) measure is envisaged in Article 76(2). It takes the form of confiscating instrumentalities, proceeds, etc. It is ordered against the persons possessing them, if they pose a threat to public order and irrespective of whether there have been convictions. Confiscation is also executed against the heirs of the person against whom the confiscation order was made, but only if the relevant court decision had become res judicata at the time the convicted person was still alive. This possibility should be understood as an exception to the general rule that court sentences are never carried out against heirs; it is justified on the grounds of *ordre public*. A manifestation of this general rule is enshrined in Article 57(4): pecuniary penalties ordered against a convicted offender expire at the time of his death and may not be executed against his heirs. Finally, in all cases of confiscation, the court must decide whether the confiscated items should be destroyed (Article 76(3)) or could be used in other ways, e.g., for the public interest or for compensating victims.

### §2. Measures of Security

*289.* According to the general provision of Article 69, with the exception of the provisions of Articles 122 and 123, there are two measures of security: (a) those for the treatment of offenders suffering from a psychological or mental disruption/ disorder (Articles 69A–71), and (b) the confiscation envisaged in Article 76. Security measures may not be imposed when their enforcement violates the principle of proportionality, taking into account the gravity of the offence committed as well as the possibility that further offences may be perpetrated. If, from the day the court judgment imposing the Article 69A security measures became irrevocable (res judicata), three years have lapsed, and their execution has not yet commenced, they may no longer be enforced, unless the court that imposed them orders otherwise and provided that ten years from the original judgment have not lapsed. Notwithstanding this provision, Article 75(2) allows the court to order their execution if the purpose for which they were ordered is still present.

## I. Measures for the Treatment of Those Persons Who Were Not Sentenced on Account of a Psychological or Mental Disorder

*290.* According to the first paragraph of Article 69A, if a person, who has committed a criminal offence and is threatened with imprisonment for at least one year, is acquitted of the sentence due to mental or intellectual disorder (Article 34, *supra* paragraph 52), the court must order appropriate measures for its treatment. The court is under this obligation, if it deems that, on account of the offender's situation, there is a risk that, if released, he will commit further offences of at least similar gravity to those for which he was convicted. The second paragraph of Article 69A introduces certain variations to the rule that such measures may be imposed only as regards offences punishable with at least one-year imprisonment. In particular, it stipulates that Article 69(1) shall apply to all offences against the life or the psychical integrity of a third person punishable with imprisonment for a minimum period of three months. On the contrary, it does not apply to property offences that did not involve the use of force or did not threaten the use of violence. The Penal Code enumerates three appropriate therapeutic measures. First, hospitalization in a special ward of a public psychiatric or general hospital. Second, hospitalization in the psychiatric ward of a public psychiatric hospital or general hospital. Third, compulsory treatment and regular psychiatric follow-up sessions in an appropriate outpatient mental health unit or in an outpatient clinic of a psychiatric or general hospital.

*291.* Regarding the duration of the therapeutic measures, Article 70 provides that the court judgment ordering them must lay down their maximum length, which may not exceed two years in the case of misdemeanours and five years for serious crimes. At any rate, their total duration, including any prolongation of the measures under Article 70(1), may not exceed the duration of the penalty as stipulated in the relevant criminal legislation. It is noteworthy that Article 70 does not use the terms 'perpetrator' or 'offender' but the term 'patient' (the literal translation of the wording is 'he who receives a therapy').

*292.* Article 71 deals with those who committed an offence due to a psychological or mental disorder. Under Article 36(1), *infra* paragraph 52, this fact significantly reduces their imputation provided that the offence is punishable with a custodial sentence of at least one year. In these cases, the court, notwithstanding the infliction of a reduced sentence, shall order admission to the psychiatric ward of a detention facility. Should the sentence be suspended, the therapeutic measures of Article 69A may still be ordered, if the court believes there is a risk of committing further offences.

## II. Confiscation

*293.* Article 76(1) stipulates that the confiscation of the objects of Article 68(1) must be ordered against the person possessing them, even if he was not convicted of the offence accused of and provided that, by their nature, these objects pose a risk to public order. If the judgment was made irrevocable while he was still alive, the confiscation order shall be executed against the convicted person's heirs. Presumably, the rationale here is that the heirs should not (continue to) benefit from the deceased's criminal behaviour. Evidently, the court will have to distinguish the confiscated objects from any other assets/objects belonging to the inheritance. It is up to the court to decide whether the confiscated objects shall be destroyed or whether they can be used in the public interest or for social purposes or to be disbursed as satisfaction for the victims. Presumably, this enumeration of the possible uses of confiscated objects does not follow a hierarchical order. Arguably, to secure that victims will receive the compensation ordered by the judgment should be of greater importance.

### §3. Modes of Punishment

## I. Postponement of Sentencing

*294.* Postponement of sentencing is not envisaged in the Greek criminal justice system. The sentencing of offenders is done either right after a guilty verdict is pronounced or shortly thereafter.

## II. Suspension of the Execution of Criminal Sanctions

*295.* Reformed, compared to the old Penal Code, provisions on the suspension of the execution of criminal sanctions are contained in Articles 99 et seq. of the Penal Code, as currently in force. The basic provision is Article 99(1). It stipulates that, if a person is sentenced to imprisonment for a term not exceeding three years, the court shall order the suspension of the sentence for a period of one to three years, unless the court can give sufficient reasons why the execution of the sentence is absolutely necessary to prevent the convicted person from committing further criminal acts. It follows that the court should consider the personality of the offender and his previous behaviour.

*296.* Pursuant to Article 99(2), the court is allowed to set out the conditions under which the suspension of the sentence shall be granted. These conditions, which can be imposed either separately or cumulatively, include the following: (a) the restoration, wholly or partly, of the damage caused to the victim to the extent possible by the convicted person; (b) the revocation of the driving licence for up to one year, if the offence was linked with a serious violation of the road traffic rules; (c) the payment of an amount of up to EUR 10,000 for public benefit purposes; (d) the fulfilment of the offender's obligations as regards the maintenance or custody of other persons;[309] (f) the participation of the convicted person in sessions with a social welfare officer; (g) appearance at a police station at given intervals; and (h) prohibition of leaving the Greek territory. The latter condition is in line with Article 5(4) of the Constitution, which stipulates that individual administrative measures restrictive of free movement within Greece are prohibited. Article 5(4), which is compliant with the relevant international and regional human rights treaties, guarantees the right of Greek nationals to leave and enter the country. These restrictive measures may only be imposed as an accessory penalty by a criminal court judgment and only in order to prevent the perpetration of further offences.

*297.* Article 100(1) allows the suspension of only part of the sentence. In particular, if a person is sentenced to imprisonment not exceeding three years and if the court considers it necessary that he serve part of the custodial sentence (from ten days to three months), the court could suspend the execution of the remainder. According to Article 100(2), Article 99(2) will be applied by analogy. The Penal Code does not envisage the minimum amount to be paid for public benefit purposes, but it is obvious that its punitive nature must be maintained.

*298.* Both types of suspension may be lifted. This is laid down in Article 102: if during suspension, the convicted offender is again convicted of an offence, the court shall order the lifting of the suspension as soon as the new conviction has become irrevocable. The sentence, which was imposed under the new conviction, shall be executed after serving the suspended sentence. However, if the criminal intensity of the new misdemeanour is low, the court is empowered to order that the suspension should not be lifted. Should the suspension not have been revoked and lifted, the suspended punishment is considered as never having been imposed. Article 103 introduces an extraterritorial dimension in the operation of Article 102. In particular, it stipulates that, if the conviction provided for in Article 102 was rendered by a foreign court of justice, its consequences with regard to the lifting of the suspension shall be freely considered by the domestic court, unless otherwise specified in any international or European legal instruments that are binding on Greece.

309. For the rules of EU law as regards maintenance obligations, *see* Council Regulation 4/2009 of 18 Dec. 2008 on jurisdiction, applicable law, recognition and enforcement of decisions and cooperation in matters relating to maintenance obligations, O.J. L 7, 10.1.2009, p. 1, as currently in force.

§4. PRINCIPLES AND RULES CONCERNING SENTENCING

## I. General Principles

*299.* It follows from the legal principle *nulla poena sine lege* that the infliction of vague and imprecise punishment is prohibited. Pursuant to Article 79(1) of the Penal Code, the purpose of measuring criminal sanctions is to determine the appropriate and fair punishment of the offence committed based on its gravity and the degree of the offender's guilt. The Penal Code lays down the specific limits of the punishment to be inflicted on offenders, thus subscribing to the so-called system of relatively specific punishments. When the Penal Code lays down the sanctions for a particular offence, it follows a legal construction which could be summarized as follows:

(a) It foresees for each offence a typology of sanctions, which, depending on the nature and the intensity of the offence perpetrated, it may be confinement in a penitentiary, imprisonment, a pecuniary penalty, or community service.
(b) It always sets out the minimum and/or the maximum limits of each time applicable punishment, and, therefore, avoids vagueness. Usually, the Penal Code uses the following wording: 'imprisonment of at least three months' or 'imprisonment of up to two years' or 'imprisonment of at least three months and a maximum of two years'. There are other instances, where the threatened punishment is referred to as 'imprisonment', which means that, subject to any specific guidance given by the legislator, the court of justice may sentence the offender for any period lasting between ten days and five years.
(c) It often threatens alternatively more than one criminal sanctions: for example, imprisonment or a pecuniary penalty.
(d) It sometimes threatens cumulatively a custodial sentence and a pecuniary penalty.

## II. Guidance on Sentencing: Grounds for Increasing and Mitigating Punishment

*300.* Although, generally speaking, courts have a very wide discretion in determining punishment, the Penal Code contains specific guidance which judges must observe. Should they fail to do so, the sentencing judgment is open to appeal. The aforementioned Article 79(1) also stipulates that the court must weigh the facts and circumstances, which operate either in favour or to the detriment of the guilty party and must take into account the consequences of the punishment upon the offender and his family. Moreover, Article 79(2) provides that to assess the offence's gravity the court shall take into account the following: (a) the damage caused or the danger/risk involved in the commission of the offence; and (b) the nature, kind and object of the offence as well as all the circumstances regarding time, place and the means that accompanied its preparation or execution. Specifically, for the purpose of evaluating the degree of the offender's *dolus*, the court shall examine, pursuant to Article

79(3), the following parameters: (a) the intensity of the *dolus* or the degree of negligence; (b) the reasons that led him to perpetrate the offence and the purpose he aimed at; (c) his character and the degree of his development which affected the criminal act; (d) personal and social circumstances as well as his previous life insofar as they relate to the act perpetrated; (e) the extent of his ability and capability to do otherwise; and (f) his conduct during and after the offence and in particular the repentance which he showed and his willingness to redress its consequences.

*301*. Regarding the facts (evidence), which operate in favour and those operating to the detriment of the guilty party, these are set out, respectively, in Article 79(4) and Article 79(5). The former include that the offender had a subordinate role in the commission of an offence perpetrated by several persons; that he committed the act while being under a justifiable emotional situation; that he made himself available to the authorities with no undue delay, even though he could have escaped; and that he facilitated to a large measure the investigation of the offence. The latter include that the offence was perpetrated as a profession (habitually); that the offender showed particular cruelty; that he exploited the trust/confidence of the victim; that the victim could not have protected himself; and that the offender played a leading role in the criminal act which was perpetrated by several persons.

*302*. Reference should be made to Article 82A, which covers specifically criminal acts having racist and other similar characteristics (e.g., the race, colour, ethnic or national origin, religion, disability, sexual orientation, identity or gender characteristics of victims). Their perpetration is regarded as aggravating circumstances leading to the imposition of more severe custodial sentences. Thus, if an offence was perpetuated against a person and this person was selected on account of any of these characteristics, the offender shall receive the following punishment: in the case of misdemeanours, if the threatened sanction is imprisonment for up to one year, the minimum sentence shall be increased by six months, while in all other cases of misdemeanours, the minimum sentence shall be increased by one year. Finally, in the case of serious crimes, the minimum limit shall be increased by two years.

## III. Reduction of Threatened Punishment

*303*. Pursuant to Article 83, where the criminal legislation stipulates reduced sentences without any other indication (e.g., Article 49, *supra* paragraph. 172), the following schedule shall apply: (a) instead of confinement in a penitentiary for life, confinement of between five and fifteen years shall be imposed; (b) instead of confinement in a penitentiary for at least ten years, imprisonment of at least two years or confinement in a penitentiary for up to eight years shall be imposed; (c) instead of confinement in a penitentiary for up to ten years, imprisonment of at least one year or confinement in a penitentiary of up to six years shall be imposed; (d) in any other case, the court is authorized to reduce the sentence freely but not below the minimum level of the custodial sentence prescribed. And if the criminal legislation threatens cumulatively a custodial sentence and a pecuniary penalty, only the latter may be imposed.

*304.* Further reduction in punishment is envisaged in Article 84: the threatened sanctions shall be reduced as stipulated in Article 83 when mitigating circumstances are present. The second paragraph of Article 84 sets out what these mitigating circumstances are. Arguably, it does so in a non-exhaustive manner and, therefore, the sentencing court may take other relevant facts, circumstances or events into consideration. In particular, that (a) the perpetrator had lived without breaking the law until the time of the offence (convictions for minor misdemeanours do not render in themselves the perpetrator's previous life 'unlawful'); (b) he was driven to the offence by non-humble causes or by great poverty or under the influence of a serious threat or under the influence of a person to whom he owed obedience or with whom he was in a relationship of dependence; (c) he committed the offence on account of the inappropriate behaviour of the victim or out of anger or grief which was caused to him by a previous unjust act directed against him; (d) he showed sincere repentance after perpetrating the offence and sought to restrict its consequences; and (e) he has behaved well for a relatively long period following the perpetration of the offence, including any time spent in detention. Clearly, what constitutes a 'relatively long period of time' differs from case to case. However, given that criminal proceedings in Greece are extremely lengthy, at least compared to other European States, and that several years may have lapsed from perpetrating an offence until the alleged offender is tried, it will literally be a long period of time. Article 84(3) stipulates that the unreasonable length of the criminal proceedings shall also be considered as mitigating circumstances. This provision is in line with the case law of the ECtHR on Article 6(1) ECHR with respect to the right to be tried within reasonable time.[310] It should be noted that the Greek State is obliged to compensate litigant parties when court proceedings, including criminal trials, have exceeded a reasonable duration.[311]

*305.* The parallel application of Articles 83 and 84, on the one hand, and the parallel existence of several Article 84 mitigating circumstances, on the other hand, raise the obvious question of to which extent may the threatened punishment be reduced. And this is because the final penalty to be imposed on the offender must still serve and satisfy the primary functions of criminal sanctions. The answer to this question is given in Article 85, which deals with the accumulation of reasons leading to the reduction of the final sentence. In particular, the first paragraph of Article 85 stipulates that when there are several reasons for reducing the criminal sanction or when there exist one or more such reasons together with Article 84 mitigating circumstances or only more than one mitigating circumstances, the court of justice shall further reduce the lower threshold of the sentence already reduced under Article 83 as follows: (a) five years shall be reduced to three years; (b) two years to one year; (c) one year to six months; and (d) the already reduced term of imprisonment to community service or to a pecuniary penalty. Finally, these reduced sentences will also be applied in a situation which is not considered mitigating

---

310. *See*, *inter alia*, ECtHR, *Papargyriou v. Greece*, Application no. 55846/15, Judgment of 21 Nov. 2019; *Firat v. Greece*, Application no. 46005/11, Judgment of 9 Nov. 2017.
311. *See* Art. 7 of Act 4239/2014, Just satisfaction due to exceeding the reasonable duration of the trial, FEK 2014 A' 43.

circumstances. This is envisaged in Article 85(2) and concerns those who have been accused and who pleaded guilty during the pre-trial phase of the proceedings thus contributing to the timely award of justice.

## IV. Concurrence of Offences

*306.* In Article 94, the Penal Code distinguishes between the so-called real and 'ideal' concurrence of offences and establishes the rules for the overall (aggregate) custodial sentence to be imposed accordingly. According to Article 94(1), real concurrence concerns the commission by the same person of two or more offences which were perpetrated through two or more criminal acts. Ideal concurrence, according to the second paragraph of Article 94, exists when the offender, by perpetrating a single criminal act, has committed two or more offences. Under Article 94(1), the perpetrator of two or more offences, which were committed through several offences and are punishable by custodial sentences but not with confinement in a penitentiary for life, shall be punished with an overall sentence consisting of the heaviest of the applicable sentences augmented as follows. Should they be of the same type and of equal duration, the total sentence to be imposed shall be by increasing one of them. Moreover, the increase of the heavier sentence for each of the applicable sentences may not be greater than one-half of each of the applicable sentences, while the total sentence may not exceed twenty years, if the heaviest sentence is confinement in a penitentiary, and eight years in case it is imprisonment. And if the concurred offences were committed with one deed (criminal act), the court shall freely increase the heavier among the applicable sentences, but not beyond its upper threshold (Article 94(2)).

*307.* The aggregate sentence to be imposed in the case of concurrence of pecuniary penalties is regulated in Article 96, which again reflects the distinction between 'real' and 'ideal' concurrence. Thus, according to the first paragraph of Article 96, if there are more than one pecuniary penalties, the aggregate sentence to be imposed shall be the heaviest among them, increased depending on the financial situation of the convicted person. However, such increase may not exceed one-half of the sum of the remaining applicable pecuniary penalties. If the applicable pecuniary penalties are equal, the aggregate sentence shall be calculated by increasing one of them. As regards the 'ideal' concurrence of offences, Article 96(2) applies the aforementioned provision of Article 94(2). Finally, Article 96A deals with the aggregate sentence to be inflicted in case of concurrence of sentences imposing community service. However, since, as has been explained, the provisions of the Penal Code on community service have been suspended, the operation of Article 96A should also be considered as being in suspension.

*308.* The question of concurrence of offences also concerns continuous offences (*supra* paragraph 100). According to Article 98(1), if more than one criminal act of the same person constitutes a continuation of the same offence, the court may, instead of applying the provisions of Articles 94(1), 96(1) and 96A(1), impose a single sentence, for the calculation of which the totality of the individual offences shall be taken into account. Both the purpose (object) of the offence and the ensuing damage or the pecuniary gain resulting from its continued commission shall be considered if the perpetrator intended to this result by undertaking several criminal acts. In these cases, the criminal nature of the act shall be determined by taking into account the object and the pecuniary damage or pecuniary benefit, which was materialized or was aimed at. Arguably, the application of the latter provision could turn the commission of several misdemeanours into a serious crime. Therefore, the question arises if the fact that the offender did not intend to carry out a serious crime should be taken into consideration or not. Moreover, should the legislator allow the perpetration of a series of misdemeanours without calculating the total value of the criminal acts committed and deal with the offender accordingly? It is submitted that the legislator should not accept situations where an offender construes his criminal behaviour in such a way so that, even though his intention was to carry out a serious crime, he managed to conceal it by perpetrating several misdemeanours.

## V. Recidivism

*309.* The system of the old Penal Code (Articles 88–93) relating to recidivism as well as the criminal sanction of indeterminate confinement in a penitentiary, which was inflicted only in the case of recidivist offenders, was abrogated in the new Penal Code. Arguably, the abolition of special sanctions for recidivism indicates that the contemporary criminal legislator believes that such punishment as the indeterminate confinement is incompatible with a European State subscribing to the rule of law. Arguably, the new Penal Code places a lot of emphasis on penalties being proportionate, i.e., they fully reflect the degree of wrongfulness and do not punish the offender for his criminal past. Prior convictions shall be taken into account by the court of justice when fixing the specific sentence to be served within the margin of appreciation provided for under the applicable provisions.

# Part II. Criminal Procedure

## Chapter 1. Principles, Institutions, Stages

### §1. The Judicial Organization

*310.* Following the overview of the criminal justice system in the General Introduction (*supra*, paragraphs 25 et seq.) the details of the trial and the investigating jurisdictions are explained in this Part.[312,313]

The main body of rules that governs all stages of the criminal procedure can be found in the new CCP which entered into force on 1 July 2019 together with the new Penal Code. The new CCP, which is the result of reform initiatives going back to 1995, aims to establish a modern, transparent, and flexible model of criminal procedure within the continental tradition. It includes significant improvements to the former Code especially with respect to fair trial guarantees and the rights of suspects and accused persons in order to make sure that the Greek criminal procedure is compliant with the ECHR and the EU Charter and the case law of the European Court of Human Rights (ECtHR) and the Court of Justice of the European Union (CJEU). The new CCP has introduced important new legal instruments like the penal order or the plea negotiations while broadening the scope of existing ones (e.g., conditional refrainment from prosecution, criminal mediation). Their purposeful use by the competent prosecuting and judicial authorities would enable the acceleration of the notoriously sluggish criminal proceedings in Greece without sacrificing fair trial guarantees. Overall, the new CCP seeks to strike a fine balance between due process requirements and the need for an efficient criminal justice system.

312. All references to Articles in this Part are to Articles of the Code of Criminal Procedure unless stated otherwise. References to the male gender imply the female gender as well, unless otherwise indicated or becomes obvious from the text.

313. *See* e.g., T. Dalakouras, *Criminal Procedure Law*, Vol. I, 2nd ed., P.N. Sakkoulas, Athens, 2019 (in Greek), A. Karras, *Criminal Procedure Law*, 6th ed., Nomiki Bibliothiki, Athens, 2019 (in Greek), A. Papadamakis, *Criminal Procedure*, 10th ed., Sakkoulas, Athens/Thessaloniki, 2021 (in Greek); for a short overview of the procedure before criminal courts, *see* I. Anagnostopoulos, J. Zapanti and A. Tsagkalidis, 'Procedure Before Criminal Courts', in: Greek Law Digest, 3rd ed., Nomiki Bibliothiki, Athens, 2019, 57–64.

## I. Trial Courts

*311.* The Penal Code (Article 18) classifies criminal offences into two categories, misdemeanours and serious crimes (*supra*, paragraph 173). The organization of the trial courts follows the division of the offences.

*312.* The Single-Judge Misdemeanour Court deals with the less serious misdemeanours, i.e., those punishable by imprisonment not exceeding three years and/or by pecuniary sanctions and/or community service (Articles 5, 115). Some exceptions apply to the above rule in respect of offences which are considered more complex (e.g., perjury, bribery misdemeanours, breach of duties by public officials etc.) and fall under the jurisdiction of the Three-Member Court. However, the Single-Judge Court tries certain categories of misdemeanours that are rather frequent and/or less complex, irrespective of the sentence provided for in law (e.g., road traffic offences, non-payment of social security contributions, issue of uncovered cheques etc.) (Article 115(2)).

The Three-Member Misdemeanour Court is composed of three judges (Article 4(1)) and deals with all other misdemeanours except political offences, which are submitted to the Mixed Jury Court (Article 109), as well as – *ratione personae* – misdemeanours allegedly committed by certain categories of persons (judges, prosecutors, lawyers), which are heard by the Three– Member Court of Appeal as a first-instance court (Article 111(6)).

*313.* The Mixed Jury Court is composed of a presiding judge and two other professional judges of the Misdemeanour Court and four jurors (Article 7 (1)). The jurors are selected by lot. The selection procedure is described in Articles 379 et seq. At a local level, a list of Greek citizens who are eligible to sit as lay judges is made each year by the competent Judicial Council of the Misdemeanour Court and of the Court of Appeal respectively using electoral and other lists provided by local communities and other public authorities and institutions. After further selection procedures, the four jurors who shall participate in the Mixed Jury Court are drawn by lot at the beginning of each trial.

The Mixed Jury Court handles the more serious crimes (e.g., homicide, serious bodily harm, arson, rape, sexual abuse of children, high treason) which have not been submitted to the competence of the Court of Appeal as a first-instance court (Article 109 (1)). In the last five decades, the legislator has awarded the competence to try certain serious crimes such as drug trafficking, robbery, serious fraud, serious forgery and counterfeiting, theft, embezzlement, or extortion under aggravating circumstances, etc. to the competence of the Court of Appeal sitting as a first-instance court. As a result of this policy, which is motivated by the need to deal more effectively with an increasing number of such cases, the Mixed Jury Court has seen its competence seriously reduced. Critics point out that this development jeopardizes the primary competence of the Mixed Jury Court for serious crimes enshrined in Article 97(1) of the Constitution.

The Mixed Jury Court of Appeal consists of a presiding judge and two judges of the Court of Appeal and four jurors (Article 7(1)) and hears appeals against judgments of the Mixed Jury Court (Article 109(2)).

*314.* The Single-Judge Court of Appeal for Serious Crimes (Article 7(1)) handles as a first-instance court for specific categories of serious crimes, which are considered less complex, i.e., theft, non-aggravated robbery, non-aggravated drug trafficking, smuggling of migrants (Article 110). It also handles the sentencing in cases where the accused person has admitted the charges in accordance with Articles 301–303 (*infra*, paragraphs 517, 521).

The Three-Member Court of Appeal for Serious Crimes is composed of a presiding judge and two appellate judges (7(1)) and handles as a first-instance court the main bulk of serious crimes, i.e., those which do not fall under the competence of the Single-Judge Court of Appeal or the Mixed Jury Court (Article 111(1–5)). It also hears appeals against the judgments of Single-Judge Court of Appeal Article 111(7)).

*315.* The Court of Appeal for Misdemeanours is composed of a presiding judge and two appellate judges (Article 7(1)) and deals with appeals against judgments of the Three-Member Misdemeanour Court (Article 111(7)). As a first-instance court, it also handles *ratione personae* misdemeanours of the above-mentioned categories of persons (judges, prosecutors, lawyers) (Article 111(6)).

*316.* The Five-Member Court of Appeal, consisting of a presiding judge and four appellate judges (Article 7(1)), hears appeals against judgments of the Three-Member Court of Appeals for Serious Crimes (Article 111(B)). This Court is also competent to hear appeals against judgments of the Court of Appeal as a first-instance court for misdemeanours of said categories of persons.

*317.* The rules of the territorial competence of the above-mentioned Courts are set forth in Articles 122 et seq. The Court in whose territorial jurisdiction the alleged offence has been committed is primarily competent to try the case; alternatively, the territorial competence is attributed to the Court in whose territorial jurisdiction the defendant has or had his residence, or to the Courts of Athens if the defendant was never domiciled in Greece.

*318.* *Areios Pagos*, the country's Court of Cassation, comprises currently seven sections. Three of these are the criminal sections which hear appeals by way of cassation against judgments of all criminal courts or against indicting decisions of the Judicial Council (Article 10). *Areios Pagos* sits as a five-judge chamber presided by the President of the respective criminal section only on questions of law (Articles 504 et seq.) If a judgment is appealed by the General Prosecutor of *Areios Pagos* in the interests of law, the case is considered by the *Areios Pagos in pleno*; the same applies to cases which are considered of major importance or where the chamber's judgment is taken by a 3:2 vote (Article 10 (2)).

*319.* *Areios Pagos* also sits *in camera* on requests to reopen a case which has been finally judged by a Mixed Jury Court or by a Court of Appeal (Articles 528–529, *infra*, paragraph 509). If the final judgment was issued by a Court of Misdemeanours said appeals lie with the Court of Appeal.

*320.* Article 86 of the Constitution as amended stipulates that the members of the government, i.e., the prime minister, the ministers and the vice-ministers, are submitted to the jurisdiction of a Special Court which is composed of the President of *Areios Pagos* and twelve judges drawn by lot out of all judges of *Areios Pagos* and the Council of State (the country's Highest Administrative Court). This special jurisdiction is provided only for criminal offences allegedly committed by members of the government during the execution of their duties, while criminal offences which are unrelated to these duties are tried by the ordinary courts (Article 1 of Act 3126/2003 as amended). There is an ongoing debate in legal doctrine and case law in relation to the offences which are considered to have been committed 'during' or 'in' the execution of ministerial duties. For example, passive bribery in exchange for public procurement contracts is considered by the prevailing view as a 'ministerial' offence while the laundering of the bribes by the bribed minister is not. Article 86 of the Constitution and Act 3126/2003 on Criminal Liability of Ministers describes the rather complicated procedure which shall be followed for the criminal prosecution of the members of the government. The pre-trial proceedings are opened by a majority decision of the Parliament at the written request of at least thirty members of the Parliament (Article 5 of Act 3126/2003). The preliminary investigation is carried out by a twelve-member committee, which is composed of twelve members of the Parliament and is vested with all the powers of the Public Prosecutor (*infra*, paragraphs 453–457). The investigating committee submits a written report to the Parliament whose members decide by majority on the opening of a formal investigation. In the affirmative, a Judicial Council is established consisting of three judges of *Areios Pagos* and two judges of the Council of State and presided by the most senior *Areios Pagos*-Judge. This Council oversees the formal investigation and mandates one of its *Areios Pagos* Judges to conduct the same as a Special Investigating Judge who is vested with all relevant powers. However, the issue of an arrest warrant or a warrant of attachment as well as the pre-trial detention is not allowed with respect to acting or former ministers (Articles 8, 10 of Act 3126/2003). One of the Prosecutors with the Prosecutor's Office of *Areios Pagos* is selected by lot in order to represent the charges. After the closing of the formal investigation, the aforementioned Judicial Council, to which the Prosecutor submits a written recommendation, decides upon indictment or acquittal of the defendants. This decision is not subject to an appeal. The trial hearing follows the basic rules of the CCP (*infra*, paragraphs 459–471) if not otherwise stipulated by Act 3126/2003 (e.g., the defendant may always be represented by counsel, no ordinary legal remedies are provided against the judgment of the Court, etc.).

*321.* Military courts, i.e., courts martial, naval courts and air force courts, are special courts that are competent to try the military criminal offences included in the Military Criminal Code (Articles 15–166 of Act 2287/1995 as amended) by military personnel serving in the army, navy, or air force respectively. The procedure before these courts are described in Articles 167–228 of the Military Criminal Code and are modelled after the CCP.

*322*. Juvenile Courts hear cases of minor defendants, i.e., persons aged between 12 and 18, sitting as a single-judge or three-member court depending on the seriousness of the case (Articles 6, 113–114). Their members are selected among those judges who have an additional education on juvenile deviance (Article 30(5), (6) JC).

## II. Pre-trial Chambers

*323*. The Judicial Council, i.e., the pre-trial chamber, of the Misdemeanour Court is composed of a presiding judge and two other judges (Articles 4, 305). It deliberates *in camera* on issues such as the supervision of the length of pre-trial detention of the defendant (Articles 292 et seq.), resolving disputes between the investigating judge and the public prosecutor or the parties as well as between the parties and the public prosecutor with respect to pre-trial detention, orders of search and seizure, examination of witnesses, etc. (Article 307). The Judicial Council handles appeals of the defendant or the party supporting the charges against orders of the prosecutor or the investigating judge during the investigation. This Council also operates as an indicting chamber. After the closing of the formal investigation, the Public Prosecutor submits the case file to the Judicial Council with a written and reasoned recommendation on referral of the case to the competent trial court (Articles 308); if the Prosecutor considers the evidence insufficient to open a trial hearing or where the prosecution must be discontinued on other legal grounds (e.g., statute of limitation, withdrawal of the criminal complaint, res judicata), he recommends the acquittal of the defendant. The Judicial Council decides *in camera* on the above without being bound by the Prosecutor's recommendation (Articles 310–311), though in practice it often does. It may also refer the case to the investigating judge for further investigation (Article 310(3)) and, if it considers the evidence insufficient for a referral to trial, it may suspend the pre-trial proceedings and reopen them following the submission of new evidence by the Public Prosecutor (Article 312). A final acquittal decision of the Judicial Council has the effect of res judicata.

*324*. The Judicial Council of the Court of Appeal is composed of a presiding judge and two appellate judges (Articles 9, 316) and handles appeals of the public prosecutor or the defendant against decisions of the Judicial Council of the Misdemeanour Court where a right of appeal is given (Articles 317(1), 481). After referral of the case to a Mixed Jury Court or to a Court of Appeal for Serious Crimes, the Judicial Council of the Court of Appeal also decides on the continuation of the pre-trial detention (Articles 294, 315).

*325*. The Judicial Council of the Court of Appeal has a special jurisdiction in extradition or European Arrest Warrant (EAW) proceedings. It deals with such requests from foreign states as a first-instance court (Articles 449 et seq., *infra*, paragraphs 532–533).

*326.* The Judicial Council of *Areios Pagos* handles appeals by way of cassation for errors of law against decisions of the Judicial Council of the first or of the second instance (Articles 10, 483 et seq.) This Council also sits as a second instance Court of Appeals against decisions of the Judicial Council of the Court of Appeal in extradition or European arrest warrant proceedings (Article 451).

## §2. The Stages of the Criminal Procedure

### I. Basic Distinctions

*327.* The criminal procedure consists of two basic stages, the pre-trial proceedings and the trial hearing. Pre-trial proceedings vary depending on the seriousness of the offence under investigation and/or the complexity of the evidence. As a rule, the very first step is the opening of a preliminary investigation, which is ordered by the Public Prosecutor of the Misdemeanour Court (Articles 43, 243). After the closing of the preliminary investigation the Prosecutor has in principle the following options: (i) to discontinue the proceedings on factual or legal grounds by issuing a reasoned order, (ii) to open a formal investigation to be conducted by an investigating judge in cases of serious crimes where there is sufficient evidence, (iii) to refer the case for trial before the Court for Misdemeanours. In case of option (ii), a judicial council will decide upon indictment or acquittal of the defendant after the closing of the investigation (*supra*, paragraph 323). There are also some alternative forms of disposal of the proceedings available to the Prosecutor (conditional suspension of the prosecution etc.) which are discussed in the following sections (*infra*, paragraphs 354–362).

### II. The Pre-trial Stage

*328.* All pre-trial procedures have in principle an inquisitorial character, i.e., they are in writing, secret in respect to third parties and, as a rule, non-adversarial (Article 241). For every act of the investigating officials, i.e., the investigating judge, the public prosecutor, the investigating magistrate, police officers or officers of other special investigative agencies, a written record is drawn up and kept in the case file (Articles 241, 148 et seq.).

#### A. *The Formal Investigation*

*329.* The formal investigation is ordered by the Public Prosecutor, and it is carried out by the Investigating Judge but with an active role for the Prosecutor (Article 30(1)). The Investigating Judge is a professional judge of the Misdemeanour Court. He is appointed by Presidential Decree following a recommendation by the Council which heads the respective Court for a period of three years (Article 30(1) JC). The formal investigation is mandatory in all serious crimes; in misdemeanours, the Public Prosecutor orders this form of investigation only if coercive measures (e.g., restrictive measures, pre-trial detention etc.) may be taken against the defendant (Article 246).

1. The Beginning of the Formal Investigation

*330.* The Public Prosecutor requests the formal investigation in writing. In his request, he shall specify the criminal offence with respect to the facts and the law. The Prosecutor's order binds in principle the Investigating Judge. However, the latter may object to the Prosecutor's request for lack of jurisdiction or where, in his view, the prosecution lacks legal basis. The dispute between the Investigating Judge and the Prosecutor is resolved by the Judicial Council (Article 247).

*331.* The purpose of the investigation is to collect all the necessary evidence in order to allow the Judicial Council or the Public Prosecutor to decide whether the defendant has to stand trial for a criminal offence (Article 239). Within the factual framework specified in the Prosecutor's request, the Investigating Judge must carry out the inquiry in rem and involve all prima facie participants in the offence. If new criminal offences other than those mentioned in the Prosecutor's request are revealed in the course of the investigation, the Investigating Judge requests the Prosecutor to open criminal proceedings for them too (Article 250).

*332.* The Investigating Judge may conduct or order all necessary investigating measures such as the examination of witnesses, inspections of places, searches, expert opinions etc. He may ask other investigating officers or experts to carry out specific actions and to assist him in his task (Articles 248–249). The Investigating Judge has the power to seize documentary and digital evidence and freeze bank accounts or other assets which are related to the offences under investigation (Articles 261–265). Special investigating measures such as the use of undercover agents, the interception of communications, electronic surveillance or controlled deliveries shall be ordered by the Judicial Council with respect to specific crimes (e.g., organized crime, terrorism, human trafficking, drug trafficking, corruption), if they are considered strictly necessary (*infra*, paragraphs 438–439). In emergency cases, these special acts may also be ordered by the Investigating Judge or the Prosecutor who must submit their decision for confirmation to the Judicial Council within three days (Articles 253–254).

*333.* The Investigating Judge is primarily responsible for deciding which procedural actions shall be carried out during the investigation. The parties and the Prosecutor may also request such actions; if the Investigating Judge rejects their request, they can appeal to the Judicial Council which decides on the contested act (Articles 102, 307). Moreover, the Investigating Judge shall ask for the Prosecutor's written opinion or consent before ordering certain intrusive measures (internment for insanity, pre-trial detention or other restrictive measures, order of an expertise, freezing of bank accounts, etc.; *infra*, paragraphs 434, 436, 444–448). The general supervision of the formal investigation lies with the Public Prosecutor of the Court of Appeal (Article 32).

## 2. The Closing of the Formal Investigation

*334.* The formal investigation cannot be completed without prior notification of the defendant of the charges against him, unless the Investigating Judge takes the view that there is no evidentiary or legal basis for the alleged offences, in which case he may abstain from summoning the defendant (Article 270). After having concluded all actions he deems necessary, the Investigating Judge returns the case file to the Public Prosecutor of the Misdemeanour Court. The Investigating Judge is not entitled to comment on the results of the investigation or to recommend further proceedings. The Public Prosecutor reviews the case file and, if he is of the opinion that further investigative acts should be performed, he asks the Investigating Judge to initiate them (Article 308(1)). Otherwise, i.e., if he agrees with the Investigating Judge that the investigation can be closed, he prepares further proceedings, depending on the character of the offence.

*335.* In cases of misdemeanours, the Public Prosecutor can, with the consent of the Investigating Judge, refer the case to trial by issuing a writ of summons, if he believes that the charges are substantiated (Article 308(3)). The writ of summons is served on the defendant (*infra*, paragraphs 384–386). In misdemeanour cases to be tried by the Three-Member Court for Misdemeanours or the Court of Appeal for Misdemeanours, the defendant can appeal against his indictment before the Public Prosecutor of the Court of Appeal or the Judicial Council with the same Court respectively on factual and/or legal grounds (Article 322). In the opposite case, where the Public Prosecutor is of the opinion that there is no sufficient evidence against all or some of the defendants or that the case is not legally sound, he files a written request with the Judicial Council recommending the acquittal of the defendants (Article 308(1)). The Judicial Council may follow or reject –partly or wholly– the Prosecutor's recommendation; it may also decide to amend the charges within the limits prescribed by the law. In all cases, the decision of the Judicial Council shall be in writing and well-reasoned (Article 139). The decision of the Judicial Council has to define the charges with respect to the facts as well as to the law.

*336.* In cases of serious crimes, the Public Prosecutor files a written and reasoned request with the Judicial Council recommending the referral of the case to trial or the acquittal of all or some of the defendants for the above-mentioned reasons (Article 308(1)). The Judicial Council decides *in camera* by issuing a written and reasoned decision, which may follow or reject the Prosecutor's recommendation (Articles 310–313). The Judicial Council may exceptionally order the Prosecutor and the parties to appear before it in order to argue their case in a non-public session either on its own motion or at the request of the Public Prosecutor or the parties (Article 310(2)).

The defendant has a right to launch an appeal before the Judicial Council of Appeal against the indicting decision only on errors of law or for serious procedural deficiencies (Article 478). Such right of appeal, albeit without the above restrictions, is also awarded to the Public Prosecutor (Article 479 *infra*, paragraphs 485–487).

*337.* In certain categories of serious crimes such as theft, robbery, drug trafficking, contraband, migrant smuggling, tax fraud etc., which fall within the competence of the Court of Appeal for Serious Crimes as a first-instance court (*supra*, paragraph 314), the Public Prosecutor of the Misdemeanour Court forwards the case file after the closing of the formal investigation to the Public Prosecutor of the Court of Appeal. The latter reviews the file and, if he is of the view that the case shall be referred to trial, he requests written consent from the Presiding Judge of the Court of Appeal, following which he refers the case to the Court of Appeal issuing a writ of summons (Article 309(1)). The defendant has no right to appeal against such referral of the case to trial. If either the Public Prosecutor or the Presiding Judge of the Court of Appeal are of the opinion that the case is not substantiated or lacks legal basis, the case file is referred to the Judicial Council of the Court of Misdemeanours to decide upon indictment or acquittal following a written recommendation of the Public Prosecutor (Article 309(3)).

The above simplified indictment procedure as opposed to the standard one described in the previous paragraph was first introduced in the 1970s and has been officially justified by the need to deal more effectively with an increasing number of cases without complicated evidentiary and/or legal issues. However, the acceleration of the pre-trial phase for these crimes sometimes happens at the cost of a thorough investigation and undue referral to trial in these cases is not unusual resulting in overburdening the trial courts.

*338.* In all the above-mentioned cases of misdemeanours or serious crimes, the competent Judicial Council has the power to order further investigation mentioning the facts to be investigated and/or the acts to be carried out (Articles 310(3), 318).

### *B. The Summary Investigation*

*339.* The summary investigation is ordered by the Public Prosecutor of the Misdemeanour Court or of the Court of Appeal only in limited circumstances in cases of misdemeanours with the aim to supplement a previous preliminary or police investigation (Articles 43(2), 245(1)). Its purpose is no different from the formal investigation, i.e., to collect the evidence required to decide whether to refer the defendant to trial. It is conducted following the same basic procedural rules already mentioned (non-public, written, non-adversarial).

*340.* The summary investigation is carried out by the Public Prosecutor of the Misdemeanour Court, who may request the competent investigating magistrates and/or police officers to carry out all necessary acts with respect to the criminal offence specified in his order.

At the end of the summary investigation, the Public Prosecutor of the Misdemeanour Court reviews the case file and decides on further proceedings.

The Public Prosecutor has, according to Article 245(1), three options:

> First, he can refer the case to trial before the Misdemeanour Court by issuing a writ of summons which is served on the defendant. The latter may launch an appeal against his indictment before the Public Prosecutor of the Court of Appeal, if he is summoned before the Three-Member Misdemeanour Court (Art 322, *supra*, para 335). In cases referred to the Single-Judge Misdemeanour Court, no right of appeal is conferred on the defendant.
>
> Second, the Prosecutor can submit a request of acquittal on factual or legal grounds to the Judicial Council of the Misdemeanour Court, which in turn decides on the case issuing a written and reasoned decision.
>
> Third, the Public Prosecutor can order a formal investigation where he takes the view that the evidence collected indicates that the offence under investigation shall be considered a serious crime.

### *C. The Summary Investigation in Flagrant Offences and Other Emergency Cases*

*341.* As mentioned before, criminal proceedings generally open with an order of the Public Prosecutor of the Misdemeanour Court. However, there are emergency cases (e.g., flagrant offences, imminent risk of evidence loss, etc.) where evidence must be secured and/or other measures must be taken on the spot without the Prosecutor's prior order. For such situations, Article 245(2) provides that all investigating officers mentioned in Article 31 shall conduct all procedural actions which are necessary to secure evidence and locate the alleged perpetrator (e.g., searches, inspection of places, taking of fingerprints). The investigating officers shall inform the Public Prosecutor of the Misdemeanour Court as soon as possible of their acts and forward him the case file including the relevant records. The Investigating Judge is also empowered to conduct said actions with respect to offences revealed in the course of the formal investigation (Article 251(1)). It is then for the Public Prosecutor to decide whether or not to open formal criminal proceedings, i.e., to order a summary or a formal investigation, to refer the case to trial in case of misdemeanours, or to drop the case in pursuance to Articles 43 et seq. (*infra*, paragraph 355).

### *D. The Preliminary Investigation*

*342.* The preliminary investigation is, as already mentioned, the very first stage of pre-trial proceedings. It is ordered by the Public Prosecutor and aims at establishing whether there is sufficient evidence to open formal criminal proceedings, i.e., a formal investigation or a trial hearing in misdemeanour cases (Articles 30(1), 43(1), 243). The preliminary investigation is mandatory in cases of serious crimes or misdemeanours which are tried by the Three-Member Misdemeanour Court.

Exceptions to this rule are the above-mentioned emergency summary police investigations or cases where disciplinary administrative proceedings have already been conducted on the same facts which would constitute the criminal offence under investigation, and the competent administrative authorities have filed a report with their findings to the Public Prosecutor. In such cases, the Public Prosecutor may skip the preliminary investigation if he takes the view that the evidence collected in the above administrative proceedings is sufficient to open formal criminal proceedings. The preliminary investigation may also be ordered by the Prosecutor of the Court of Appeal or by the General Prosecutor of *Areios Pagos* (Article 32).

*343.* The preliminary investigation is conducted by the Public Prosecutor, who may request the investigating officers to carry out specific acts (examination of witnesses etc.) within their competence. Articles 240 et seq., which govern the formal or summary investigation, apply in principle to the preliminary investigation as well. However, coercive measures against suspects such as an arrest or pre-trial detention are not allowed. After the conclusion of the preliminary investigation, which shall be concluded, as a rule, within six months, the Public Prosecutor decides upon further proceedings having the three options mentioned above (*supra*, paragraph 340), i.e., to drop the case, to order a formal or a summary investigation, or to refer the case for trial before the Court of Misdemeanours).

## III. The Prosecution

### A. *The Right to Prosecute*

*344.* The right to prosecute a person for a criminal offence is reserved exclusively to the State. Private persons or entities may request the Public Prosecutor to open criminal proceedings by lodging a criminal complaint or report including their allegations and thus initiate prosecution. They are not entitled, however, to directly launch criminal proceedings against a person. This right is exercised by the Public Prosecutor of the Misdemeanour Court in the name of the State (Article 27).

*345.* Greece is divided into sixty-three judicial districts of first instance, in each of which an Office of Public Prosecutions is established. An Office of Public Prosecutions is also established in each of the nineteen Appellate Jurisdictions where a Court of Appeal resides. *Areios Pagos* has its own Prosecutions Office headed by the General Prosecutor with nationwide jurisdiction. Although Public Prosecutors are not 'judges' *stricto sensu*, they are Judicial Officials who enjoy independency vis-à-vis the Executive and the Legislature (Article 28(1) JC). Prosecutors are also independent towards the courts and may at every stage express freely their opinion following only the rules of law (Article 24(4) JC).

*346.* In the last decade, two separate Prosecutorial Offices have been established, specializing in the prosecution of economic crimes and corruption.

First, the Prosecutor for Economic Crime with powers to prosecute and supervise investigations of financial fraud, criminal tax offences, financial and economic crimes against the State, state-owned entities or of broader public interest. This Prosecutor was selected among the Prosecutors of the Court of Appeal and had a nationwide jurisdiction and was supported by a group of deputy prosecutors. He could request the co-operation of prosecutors from the first instant courts, the Police, other regulatory or administrative authorities and/or other enforcement agencies in the course of the investigations. In the exercise of his duties, the Prosecutor for Economic Crimes had broad powers including access to all kinds of physical or digital evidence and information except those protected under the lawyer-client privilege or the confidentiality of communication rules. The Prosecutor's Office for Economic Crimes was supervised by one of the Prosecutors with *Areios Pagos*.

Second, the Anti-Corruption Prosecutor, with powers to prosecute and supervise investigations of serious crimes resulting in financial loss for the State or state-owned entities involving government and public officials. The Anti-Corruption Prosecutor had two offices, one in Athens and one in Thessaloniki. Both offices were run by a Deputy Prosecutor with the Court of Appeal, who was supported by a team of prosecutors with the respective first-instance court and expert officials and were supervised by one of the Prosecutors with *Areios Pagos*. The Anti-Corruption Prosecutor had broad powers and could request the co-operation of other enforcement agencies as above. He could also order special investigative acts such as the use of undercover agents, the interception of communications or electronic surveillance with respect to bribery offences (Article 255).

Act 4475/2020 brought the above two prosecutorial offices under one umbrella, in an attempt to strengthen and streamline enforcement. Following the amended Articles 33–336 CCP, a special Department for Economic Crimes has been established within the Prosecutor's Office with the Court of Appeal of Athens, which is vested with all the above powers of the former two separate prosecutorial offices. The new Department is led by a Chief Prosecutor and comprises fourteen prosecutors (seven with Court of Appeal and eight with the First Instance Court) who are appointed for a three-year term.

Act 4506/2019 as amended by Act 4786/2021 has implemented the EU Regulation on the European Public Prosecutor's Office (EPPO) and established a special EPPO Office in Athens (*infra*, paragraph 540).

*347.* The organization and function of the Prosecution Service follow the principles of indivisibility and hierarchical subordination (Articles 28(2), (4) JC).

Indivisibility means that the Prosecutions Office is represented each time as a judicial authority by the prosecutor who acts in its name. All acts of a Public Prosecutor are considered acts of the Prosecution Service. From this principle follows that the Public Prosecutor may be substituted by a colleague of the same rank during various trial stages except the trial hearing. Hierarchical subordination means that every Public Prosecutor must comply with the instructions of his superiors, e.g., to open criminal proceedings, conduct a preliminary investigation, etc. On no occasion, however, may these instructions prejudice the Prosecutor's independency with respect to the merits of the case.

*348.* The Public Prosecutor opens criminal proceedings after receiving a *notitia criminis*, i.e., information that a criminal offence has been committed. Such information is usually provided by the person who files a criminal complaint stating the facts which constitute a criminal offence and the alleged perpetrators (Article 42). Other sources of information are reports by public officials, investigating officials, investigating judges and trial courts who are under an obligation to forward to the Public Prosecutor all information and the relevant documents with respect to alleged criminal offences of which they become aware during the execution of their duties (Articles 38–39). Private persons are under an obligation to report serious crimes which to their knowledge are about or have begun to be committed where they can be still prevented (Article 40, Article 232 PC). The Prosecutor may also start criminal proceedings ex officio for any criminal offence of which he is informed by other means, e.g., newspaper reports (Article 37).

*349.* Although private persons cannot prosecute criminal offences in their own right, for certain offences the filing of a criminal complaint by the alleged victim or his/her legal representative is necessary to start criminal proceedings (Article 53). Two categories of such offences exist. First, offences against persons (e.g., non-serious bodily harm, defamation, offences against private property etc.) where there is no strong public interest for prosecution. Second, offences which relate to the intimate sphere of victims (e.g., some forms of sexual harassment), where the State will not take action unless requested by the alleged victims, who have to lodge a criminal complaint within three months after they came to know the offence and the perpetrator (Article 114(1) PC). The rationale behind this rule is that in some cases the prosecution of a criminal offence will result in certain publicity that may cause more harm to the victim than the criminal offence itself.

*350.* In the execution of the right to prosecute, the Public Prosecutor of the Misdemeanour Court is independent (Article 27(2)). However, some exceptions apply to this principle.

First, the Plenary Court of Appeal has the power, after having heard the report by one of its members, to instruct the competent Public Prosecutor of the Misdemeanour Court or the Prosecutor of the Court of Appeal to prosecute criminal offences which are considered of high importance (Article 28). In such cases the formal investigation is carried out by an ad hoc appointed Judge of the Court of Appeal. In the last four decades, the Court of Appeal –mainly in Athens– has used this power to initiate criminal proceedings in some serious and widely publicized cases concerning serious economic, political or violent crimes.

Second, the Minister of Justice, with the consent of the Cabinet, can also adjourn or suspend prosecution of political offences as well as of offences involving the Greek State and foreign States where their prosecution would jeopardize the international relationships of the Greek State (Article 29) Such suspension or adjournment of the prosecution is not allowed in respect of bribery offences.

As a result of the above-mentioned principle of hierarchical subordination that governs the Prosecution Service, the Public Prosecutor of the Misdemeanour Court shall comply with the orders of his superiors, i.e., the Prosecutor of the Court of Appeal and the General Prosecutor of *Areios Pagos*, in respect to the opening of criminal proceedings. However, he is free to express his opinion on the merits of the case and the legal issues to be addressed according to the principle *'la plume est serve mais la parole est libre'*.

*351.* The importance of the Public Prosecutor's role in all stages of the criminal procedure cannot be overemphasized. No court decision, including those of the Judicial Council, and no significant order of the Investigating Judge (e.g., warrant of arrest, pre-trial detention, internment for reasons of insanity, freezing of assets etc.) is valid without prior hearing of the Public Prosecutor, who submits his reasoned opinion on the case with respect to the facts and the law (Articles 30(2)–(4) CCP, Article 29(1) JC).

The Prosecutor is not technically a party to the proceedings. Although he exercises the right to prosecute in the name of the State and represents the State throughout the criminal proceedings (Article 27), he is not under an obligation to support in all circumstances the charges and request the indictment or the conviction of the defendant. The Prosecutor is under a duty to consider each case on its merits and request the Judicial Council or the Court to acquit the defendant if the charges are not substantiated or legally sound. Moreover, he has the power to appeal a Court's decision not only against but also in favour of the defendant. Although no official statistics are available, it is not unusual in court practice for prosecutors to request an acquittal either on factual or legal grounds. As a matter of practice, Judicial Councils and Courts often accept the Prosecutor's recommendations. A possible drawback of this widespread consensus between Courts and Prosecutors, who sit together at trial as impartial judicial officials (notwithstanding the fact that the Prosecutor is the prosecuting party), is that it blurs the procedural roles and makes it more difficult for the defence to successfully argue their case where the Prosecutor requests a conviction.

While not a party to the proceedings, the Public Prosecutor's procedural rights are balanced against those of the defendant and of the party supporting the charges with regard to filing of requests with the Judicial Council or the Court, the examination of witnesses, the lodging of appeals, etc. The relevant procedural rules aimed at achieving an overall equality of arms between the parties *stricto sensu*, i.e., the defence and the party supporting the charges and the Public Prosecutor.

### *B. The Principle of Legality and Its Exceptions*

*352.* The prosecution of criminal offences is governed by the principle of legality. This means that, as a rule, the Public Prosecutor is obliged to open criminal proceedings by ordering a preliminary, summary, or formal investigation or referring the case to trial after receiving the criminal complaint or other information on criminal offence (Articles 37, 43(1)). The principle of legality is subject to certain restrictions, which are explained below.

*353.* The Prosecutor of the Misdemeanour Court may dismiss the case for lack of evidence that a criminal offence has been committed. He may do the same on legal grounds, e.g., limitation by time (*infra*, paragraphs 370–371), lack of a duly submitted criminal complaint by the alleged victim where this is required, res judicata, etc. In both cases, the Prosecutor shall issue a reasoned order which has to be confirmed by the competent Prosecutor of the Court of Appeal (Article 43(3)). If the latter does not share the former's view, he instructs him to open criminal proceedings specifying the elements of the alleged offence under the law. The dismissal order of the Public Prosecutor of the Misdemeanour Court is served on the criminal complainant (Article 51(2)) who has the right to file an appeal against the dismissal of the complaint before the Prosecutor of the Court of Appeal (Article 52). The latter may confirm or overturn the dismissal of the complaint and order the continuation of the criminal proceedings.

*354.* The Prosecutor of the Misdemeanour Court may, with the consent of the Prosecutor of the Court of Appeal, suspend the prosecution of a misdemeanour if the expected sentence in case of a conviction of the defendant is insignificant compared to an already passed sentence, which the defendant serves, or compared to an anticipated sentence for another offence already prosecuted (Article 44).

*355.* The Prosecutor of the Misdemeanour Court may refrain from prosecuting the alleged perpetrator of a criminal offence, where the latter is extorted by another person threatening him with the revelation of said criminal offence. The Public Prosecutor has the same power with respect to fraud if the alleged victim of fraud could be incriminated of fraud or an offence linked thereto. In both cases, the refrainment from prosecution requires that the offence in question is of minor seriousness compared to that of the extortion or fraud and its prosecution is not necessary to protect the public interest. The decision of the Public Prosecutor of the Misdemeanour Court requires the consent of the Prosecutor of the Court of Appeal (Article 45(1)).

*356.* Refrainment from prosecution as above is also allowed for lesser misdemeanours, i.e., those punishable with imprisonment up to one year or with monetary sanctions or community service, where there is no public interest to prosecute the offence in view of its specific circumstances (e.g., the victim's behaviour, the age or health of the suspect or his compensation efforts, etc., Article 45(2). Moreover, in cases of juvenile misdemeanours prosecution is also not obligatory if it is not considered necessary by the Prosecutor for Juveniles in order to prevent the defendant from committing new offences (Article 46). The refrainment from prosecution may be combined with supervisory and/or educational measures provided for in Article 122(1) PC.

*357.* Whistle-blowers ('witnesses in the public interest' in the CCP's terminology) may be exempted from prosecution in cases of bribery offences and related acts (Article 47). Notably, persons who provide an essential contribution to the investigation and prosecution of bribery offences without being a participant in them and do not pursue financial benefits for their contribution may be classified as witnesses in the public interest by order of the Prosecutor for Economic Crimes (*infra*, paragraph 416). If a criminal complaint is filed against such witnesses for false accusation, perjury, defamation, breach of secrecy or breach of personal data in connection with the bribery offences, the above Prosecutor may instruct the competent Public Prosecutor of the Misdemeanour Court to refrain from prosecuting the whistle-blower for the above offences where he is of the view that such prosecution is not necessary in the public interest.

*358.* The Penal Code stipulates (Article 187Γ (1)) that refrainment from prosecution shall be ordered by the Prosecutor of the Misdemeanour Court in relation to persons who are members of criminal or a terrorist organization (Articles 187, 187A PC) and have informed the authorities of a planned crime which has been prevented as a result of such information or who have essentially contributed to the disbandment of such organization. The order of the Prosecutor must be submitted to the Prosecutor of the Court of Appeal for confirmation, who may decide otherwise.

*359.* A conditional refrainment from prosecution for offences under the legislation on migration or on prostitution may be ordered in relation to persons who have informed the authorities in a reliable manner of their victimization by a criminal organization. The refrainment order is issued by the Prosecutor of the Misdemeanour Court with the consent of the Prosecutor of the Court of Appeal and becomes final after it is established by a final court judgment that the information on the offences against such persons have been confirmed (Article 187Γ (3)).

Moreover, a conditional refrainment from prosecution of the above offences as well as of other related crimes is possible according to Article 323A (8) PC following the above procedure in respect of persons who inform the authorities that they are victims of human trafficking. Such order becomes final after the offences against such persons have been confirmed by a final court judgment. Article 323A (8) PC also applies to cases of pornography or sexual exploitation of minors (Article 350A PC).

*360.* For misdemeanours punishable with imprisonment not exceeding three years, the Public Prosecutor of the Misdemeanour Court may abstain from the prosecution of the offence with the consent of the competent Judge of the First Instance Court, if the suspect agrees to fulfil certain conditions such as a serious effort to reconcile with the victim, the payment of an amount of money to charity organizations, the attendance of educational programs, full compensation of the victim, etc. After the fulfilment of the conditions by the suspect, the Prosecutor proceeds with a final refrainment from prosecution order (Article 48).

Article 344 PC empowers the Public Prosecutor to refrain from prosecution in cases of rape or some forms of sexual abuse if the alleged victim files a declaration that he does not wish the criminal prosecution of the suspect.

*361.* Conditional refrainment from prosecution is also possible for certain serious crimes of a prevailing financial character (fraud, embezzlement, breach of fiduciary duties, money laundering, criminal tax, etc.) under Article 49. In these cases, the Prosecutor of the Misdemeanour Court can, with the consent of the competent Judge of the First Instance Court, decide not to prosecute if the suspect agrees to fully compensate the victim within a time frame of eight to twelve months. After fulfilment of such compensation, the Prosecutor proceeds with a final refrainment from prosecution order.

*362.* In most crimes against property, the Prosecutor of the Misdemeanour Court refrains from prosecution with the consent of the Prosecutor of the Court of Appeal if the alleged perpetrator has returned the property to its legitimate owner or has fully compensated the victim before the opening of formal criminal proceedings (Article 50). A limited number of offences such as robbery or extortion are exempted from this procedure.

### *C. The Object of the Right to Prosecute*

*363.* As has been explained (*supra*, paragraph 51), criminal behaviour is understood in Article 14 PC as an outgoing human behaviour which can be attributed to the perpetrator's culpability. Only natural persons may therefore be prosecuted for a criminal offence. Legal entities do not bear criminal responsibility (*supra*, paragraphs 54 et seq.) but are subject to various administrative sanctions (fines, debarment from public contacts, revocation of business license, etc.) and may bear civil liability in relation to offences committed by their employees in breach of their duties and/or for the benefit of the legal entity.

### *D. Conditions on the Right to Prosecute*

*364.* As a rule, all persons can be held criminally liable for offences that fall within the competence of Greek criminal courts. Exceptions based on national or international public law have already been explained (*supra*, paragraphs 76–81). To initiate prosecution against Members of the Parliament for offences they committed during the legislative period, the Public Prosecutor seeks leave to prosecute from the Parliament (Article 62 of the Constitution). An exception applies to serious crimes caught *in flagrante*. The Parliament must comply with the Prosecutor's request where the offence in question is unrelated to the exercise of the parliamentary duties or the political activity of the Parliament's member.

*365.* Article 10(2) of the Constitution states that no person shall be prosecuted for criminal offences allegedly committed with respect to submitting a complaint to public authorities including allegations against state officials for actions or omissions in the execution of their duties. In said cases, a permission by the authority to which the complaint had been filed is required to start prosecution against the complainant.

*366.* For certain offences, the Penal Code or special statutes provide that prosecution may be started only if a request to this end has been submitted to the Public Prosecutor by a competent authority (Article 41). Such a request by a foreign government is, for example, necessary to prosecute criminal offences against the honour of heads or diplomatic representatives of foreign states. A request by the foreign government or a complaint by the alleged victim is also required to establish territorial jurisdiction of Greek criminal courts with respect to most misdemeanours committed by foreigners against Greeks or by Greeks against foreigners in a foreign country, as already explained (*supra*, paragraphs 69–71) (Articles 6(3), 7(2) PC).

### *E. Dissolution of the Right to Prosecute*

#### 1. Decriminalization, Amnesty, Death of the Defendant

*367.* The principle of retroactivity of the milder criminal statute (*supra*, paragraphs 61–6344) means that prosecution or further prosecution of an offence is precluded if this offence has ceased to be punishable by virtue of a subsequent law. Article 2(2) PC provides that in such cases also the execution of the sentence imposed must be terminated.

Granting amnesty for political offences (Article 47(3) of the Constitution, Articles 311(1), 368 CCP) results in the termination of the right to prosecute.

The death of the defendant at any stage of the proceedings results in their termination. The defendant's heirs may only be civilly liable for claims arising from the damage inflicted by the criminal offence.

#### 2. Withdrawal of Complaint, Compensation of the Victim

*368.* Withdrawal of complaint or waiver of the right to lodge a complaint result in the termination of the right to prosecute, if filing of such a complaint is required by law (*supra*, paragraph 349).

*369.* Compensation of the victim may result in the termination of the right to prosecute and the closing of criminal proceedings in those cases expressly provided by law. Such is the case with most offences against property. Articles 381(2), 405(2) PC provide that theft, embezzlement, breach of fiduciary duties and fraud shall not be punishable if the perpetrator has returned the stolen property or has compensated the victim on his own free will before being questioned by the authorities as a suspect about the offence. The same applies to the above-mentioned offences, if the defendant fully compensates, including interest, the alleged victim until the indictment or, in cases of misdemeanours, until the closing of the evidence hearing before the Court of First Instance (Articles 381(3), 405(3)).[314] Various special criminal statutes (e.g., Act 2960/2001 (Customs Code), Act 86/1967 on Social Security, etc.)

314. *See* A. Tzannetis, 'Von der ‚tätigen Reue' zum ‚Täter-Opfer-Ausgleich'– Zielsetzungen und dogmatische Grundlagen des Schadenswiedergutmachungssystems im neuen griechischen Strafrecht', ZIS 4/2012, 134 et seq.

mandate the termination of criminal proceedings for the respective offences (non-aggravated contraband, non-payment of social security contributions, etc.) upon full payment of the amounts due including interest, imposed fines, etc.

Moreover, the Code of Criminal Procedure establishes a separate criminal mediation procedure for certain categories of crimes (Articles 301–302) which will be discussed in the following chapter (*infra*, paragraphs 515–518).

## 3. Limitation by Time

*370.* Criminal prosecution cannot start or continue if the offence in question is time-barred (Articles 311(1), 368). Limitation by time starts on the day a criminal offence is committed unless otherwise stated by law (Article 112 PC). In cases of continuous offences, limitation by time starts after the last act or omission was committed. The right to prosecute serious crimes is precluded for twenty years (if punishable by life sentence, or for some serious crimes against the property of the State or state entities) or fifteen years (if punishable by confinement in a penitentiary) after commission of the crime (Article 111 PC). Misdemeanours are time-barred five years after their commission. The limitation by time continues to run during the pre-trial proceedings. It is suspended for five years in cases of serious crimes and for three years in cases of misdemeanours only after the defendant has been duly summoned to appear before the trial court (Article 113 PC). After completion of the suspension period, it continues to run from the point it had been suspended.

*371.* It is also worth noting that limitation by time is considered an institution of the substantive criminal law and not simply a procedural bar. In other words, non-limitation by time is considered a negative element of the crime itself. This approach has far-reaching consequences with respect to the retroactivity of the milder criminal statute (*supra*, paragraphs 61–63). For example, an offence, which at the time of its prosecution constituted a serious crime, may be time-barred, if it is downgraded to a misdemeanour and five years have passed since its commission or eight years have passed since summoning the defendant, and no final judgement is issued in the case. The same applies if the Court rules that the offence in question constitutes a misdemeanour and not a serious crime as initially alleged in the indictment, for example, because no aggravating circumstances which render the offence a serious crime have been proven in court.[315]

## 4. *Non Bis in Idem*

*372.* The *non bis in idem* principle is enshrined in Article 57 CCP, Article 4(1) of the Protocol No. 7 to the ECHR (ratified by Law 1705/87) and Article 14(7) of the ICCPR (ratified by Act 2462/97).[316] It provides that no person who has been finally convicted or acquitted for an offence shall be prosecuted anew for the same

315. Cf. the CJEU judgment in *M.A.S., M.B.* (C-42/17) of 5.12.2017, at 49 et seq.
316. Il. Anagnostopoulos, 'Non bis in idem in Greece', RIDP 2002, 965 et seq.

offence. *Idem* is understood as the same act, i.e., 'the same or essentially the same facts' according to ECtHR case law.[317] A final conviction by a court judgment or a final acquittal by a decision of the Judicial Council bars a new prosecution for the same act even under a different legal qualification (Article 57(1)). A final acquittal may be reversed only in exceptional circumstances under Article 527 (*infra*, paragraph 508). A final refrainment from criminal prosecution by a Prosecutor's order in the above-mentioned cases (*supra*, paragraphs 355–362) also bars a new prosecution. In cases where the Prosecutor has dropped the case by issuing an order for lack of evidence, he may reopen the case only on the basis of new evidence which justifies such re-opening (Article 43(6)).

Article 57(3) empowers the Public Prosecutor to refrain from prosecution of an act if it is established that the latter is being prosecuted in another Member State of the European Union. This newly introduced provision is in line with recent efforts in the EU to avoid parallel prosecutions on the same facts within the common judicial area.

*373.* Greece is party to the Convention on the Implementation of the Schengen Agreement (CISA – ratified by Act 2514/1997) and has also ratified the Lisbon Treaty and the Charter of Fundamental Rights of the European Union (Act 3671/2008). Article 54 CISA and Article 50 of the Charter establish a cross-border *non bis in idem* principle in the common judicial area. Accordingly, persons who have been finally convicted or acquitted in a Member State shall not be prosecuted or convicted for the same act in another Member State. The Court of Justice of the European Union has issued an impressive body of judgments on *non bis in idem* which adopt a generous interpretation of '*bis*' to include not only court judgments but also alternative forms of termination of criminal proceedings (e.g., disposal of proceedings via a prosecutorial order imposing a fine). Moreover, it adopted a broad interpretation of '*idem*' to include not only those facts considered by the judicial authority who issued the decision in question but also those 'inextricably connected' to the facts considered.[318]

*374.* *Areios Pagos* issued in 2011 an important judgment *in pleno* (No 1/2011) on *non bis in idem* within the European Union. The Court held that after the entry into force of the Lisbon Treaty and the Charter reservations filed by Member States (including Greece, which had filed a reservation in relation to, *inter alia*, drug trafficking offences) with respect to said principle for certain crimes under Article 55 CISA are no more valid.

In all cases where prosecution of the offence is precluded on *non bis in idem* grounds, the Public Prosecutor shall dismiss the case by issuing an order (*supra*, paragraph 353); after the opening of formal proceedings, the decision to terminate

317. *See* the ECtHR judgment in *Zolotukhin v. Russia* of 10 Feb. 2009, at 70 et seq.

318. *See* the CJEU judgments in *Gözütok and Brügge* of 11 Feb. 2003 (C-187/01 and C-385/01) and *van Esbroeck* of 9 Mar. 2006 (C-436/04); Il. Anagnostopoulos, 'Ne bis in idem in der Europäischen Union – Offene Fragen', *in:* Festschrift für W. Hassemer, C.F. Müller Verlag, Heidelberg, 2010, 1123 et seq.

proceedings on such grounds falls within the competence of the Judicial Council or the trial court before or after referral of the case to trial respectively (Articles 311, 368).

## IV. The Trial Stage

### *A. General Characteristics*

*375.* As explained, pre-trial proceedings are non-public and, as a rule, non-adversarial. The decisions taken during these proceedings are based on the records drawn up for every investigating act and on the written submissions by the Public Prosecutor and the parties. In contrast to the above structure of the pre-trial proceedings, the inquiry in court is public, oral and moderately adversarial.

*376.* Article 93(2) of the Constitution and Article 329 CCP state that all trials in court are held in public and that all decisions of courts are pronounced in public. Any breach of this fundamental principle results in the nullity of the whole trial hearing (Article 510(1)). The public character of the trial means that all adult citizens have an unrestricted right to be in the courtroom during the trial. No discrimination based on race, gender, profession, etc., of the persons who wish to attend the trial is allowed. In cases that may attract a bigger number of attendants than the courtroom can seat, the Judge in co-operation with the Public Prosecutor defines the number of persons that can be indiscriminately admitted until the courtroom is full.

*377.* There are two exceptions to the above principle. First, the trial can be conducted behind closed doors to protect public morals (Article 330(1) CCP, Article 93(2) of the Constitution). Second, the same may be decided by the Court to protect the personal or family life of the parties. In cases of rape or other sexual offences, the Court may conduct the trial non-publicly, if it is of the opinion that a public trial would inflict undue suffering upon the alleged victim or would expose him to public disparagement, especially where the victim is a minor. The exclusion of the public can be decided by the Court *proprio motu* or at the request of the Public Prosecutor or the parties and may be decided for the whole of the trial hearing or for a part of it (e.g., testimony of the alleged victim, of certain witnesses, etc.). In all cases, the Court prior to deciding has to hear the Public Prosecutor and the parties and pronounce in public a reasoned decision in this respect.

On the contrary, trials of juveniles are always non-public (Article 96(3) of the Constitution, Article 1 of Act 3315/55).

*378.* In regard to media publicity, Article 8(1) of Act 3090/2002 prohibits videotaping or broadcasting of trial hearings. In exceptional cases videotaping or broadcasting may be allowed by the court if it is in the public interest and only with the consent of the Public Prosecutor and the parties. Moreover, Article 8(2) of the above Act bars the taking of photographs, videotaping, or broadcasting of defendants who appear before the investigating authorities without their consent. A breach of the above rules is a criminal offence punishable by imprisonment of up to three years and a fine of up to EUR 200,000. Despite such sanctions, private television channels do not always comply with the above rules in search of sensation in widely publicized cases.

*379.* Article 331 provides that the trial in court is conducted orally. The principle of orality means that the Court's judgment shall rely on the evidence which has been introduced during the trial hearing. Witnesses including the alleged victim are examined by the Court and the parties, all relevant documents are read out, and the Public Prosecutor as well as counsel for the parties address the Court orally. The Court cannot rely on any document of the case file made up during the pre-trial investigation if this is not read out in court and subjected to comments or objections of the parties. A breach of this rule results in the nullity of the trial hearing (Articles 171(1), 510(1)). Written statements of witnesses at the pre-trial stage may be read out in court only if the witnesses have died or cannot appear before the court or if the defendant consents thereto (Article 363). The use of parts of pre-trial written statements of witnesses is allowed in court only to point out inconsistencies or to help the memory of the examined person (Article 357(4)). Parts of the defendant's pre-trial statement may be read out in court only to point out inconsistencies between those and his statement in court (Article 365(2)). Though the Code of Criminal Procedure proclaims the primacy of the trial hearing and restricts the referral to the case file during trial, the courts tend sometimes to overestimate the probative value of pre-trial evidence due to its proximity to the facts and its alleged 'spontaneous' character.

*380.* The inquiry in court is of moderately adversarial character. It differs from a pure adversarial model in that the Presiding Judge has a rather dominant role during the whole trial. Not only does he direct the proceedings but he also has priority vis-à-vis all other participants in the trial with respect to the examination of the witnesses and the defendant (Articles 333, 357, 365). This 'presidential' character of the trial is mitigated by the fact that the Public Prosecutor and the parties have a wide range of rights regarding access, presentation or objection to evidence and can address the Court on any factual or legal issue, including the appeal of procedural decisions of the Presiding Judge (*infra*, paragraphs 466–479).

### *B. The Judge: An Active but Impartial Adjudicator*

*381.* The foregoing remarks demonstrate the delicate balance of the judge's position in the trial: On the one hand, he has to be active throughout the procedure in search of the true facts which shall be the basis of his judgement; on the other hand, he must stay impartial in all circumstances and show no emotional involvement in the case. Article 332 provides that judges must treat all persons participating in the trial in an impartial, decent, composed, and unemotional way. The breach of this duty may trigger the judge's excuse and is considered a serious disciplinary offence. The Code of Criminal Procedure comprises a number of provisions which secure impartiality of the judge. For example, the investigating judge of a case cannot be a member of the Judicial Council that decides on referral of the case to trial

(Article 14(2)); a judge who was a member of the judicial council that issued an indicting decision cannot sit, as a rule, as a judge at the trial hearing; a judge, who sat with the court of the first instance, cannot be a member of the appellate court or *Areios Pagos* in the same case (Article 14(3)); all members of a court or a judicial council, whose decision has been quashed by *Areios Pagos*, cannot sit with the court which retries or the judicial council which reconsiders the case (Articles 522, 485), etc.

### *C. The Trial Hearing*

#### 1. The Preparation of the Trial Hearing

*382.* In the section on the pre-trial stage, mention has been made of the various ways in which a case can be referred to a trial court that depend on the gravity of the alleged offence (*misdemeanours v. serious crimes*), on the form of pre-trial procedures (preliminary investigation, formal investigation or summary investigation) and on the court the case is referred to (Single-Judge or Three-Member Misdemeanour Court, Mixed Jury Court, Single-Judge or Three-Member Court of Appeal for Serious Crimes or Court of Appeal for Misdemeanours as first-instance courts). As already explained, referral to trial is being made either through a decision of a Judicial Council or through a writ of summons issued by the Public Prosecutor with the competent Court. Summoning of the defendant is regulated accordingly.

*383.* If a Judicial Council refers the case to trial, it always issues a written decision consisting of two parts (Articles 306, 139). In its first part, the provisions of substantive and procedural law which apply to the case are referenced and interpreted, the facts of the case are stated, the relevant evidence is summed up and the reasoning of the chamber is set out. In its second (operational) part, the formal counts are stated, i.e., the criminal acts the defendant is called to account for, with respect to the facts and the applicable laws.

A clear description of the accusation is dictated by Article 321 in compliance with Article 6(3)(a) ECHR.

The decision of the Judicial Council and a summons issued by the Public Prosecutor with the competent court stating the defendant's name, the trial date, the Court he has to appear before, the number of the Judicial Council's indicting decision and the witnesses called by the Public Prosecutor are served by a bailiff or a policeman on the defendant at the residence he has declared before the investigating authorities at the pre-trial stage (Articles 156, 320, 321, 326, 273). Foreign defendants, who do not understand the Greek language, also receive a translation of the indicting decision and the summons in a language they understand (Articles 101, 237). A translation of other essential documents or essential parts of the same shall also be provided.

The indicting decision and the summons may be served on a person who lives with the defendant or on the doorman at his residence or on a person who works with him at his workplace; if none of them are found, the bailiff has to hang up the documents on the defendant's house-door (Article 155). In the latter case, a copy of the documents must be served on the lawfully appointed attorney of the defendant (usually his defence counsel). The same applies, if the above-mentioned persons (fellow lodgers, etc.) refuse to receive the documents to be served and/or to sign the bailiff's certificate of summons.

If the residence of the defendant is unknown and cannot be found using the available sources of information, an effort must be made to serve the summons on the defendant's spouse or, failing such, on his parents or brothers or sisters, provided that they are not the victims of the acts in question or minors or mentally ill or intoxicated. If such effort is unsuccessful, the documents are 'served' on the secretary of the Prosecutor's Office with the court where the pre-trial proceedings have taken place (Article 157). Defendants who reside in a foreign country are invited when examined during the pre-trial stage to appoint an attorney residing in the court's district on whom all documents are served. If they appoint defence counsel, such documents are served on the latter (Article 156(4)). Failure of the defendant who resides abroad to appoint defence counsel or an attorney for receiving the above documents, results in the 'serving' of the documents only on the secretary of the Prosecutor's Office where the pre-trial proceedings have taken place. This provision, which serves 'practical' needs of the Greek authorities sparing them with the time-consuming judicial assistance procedures, raises compatibility issues with Articles 6 ECHR and 48(2) of the Charter.[319]

*384.* The Public Prosecutor who refers a case to trial issues a writ of summons (Article 321). This document states the accusations – identical to the second part of the Judicial Council's decision mentioned above – and the name of the defendant, the trial date, etc., like the aforementioned summons. The writ of summons is served on the defendant following the same rules already explained with respect to the Judicial Council's decision and the summons.

*385.* Notification of the defendant must be made fifteen days before the trial date at the latest not including the day of the notification and the day of the trial (Article 166). For persons domiciled in European or Mediterranean countries, a period of thirty days is stipulated, and for residents in any other country the relevant period is extended to sixty days.

*386.* The fulfilment of the above requirements is essential for the validity of the court hearing. If a defendant who was not duly summoned fails to appear, the Court shall adjourn the hearing and order a new summons (Article 176(3)). The defendant who appears in court has the right to object to the beginning of the trial for procedural irregularities that occurred at the preparatory stage. For example, he may argue that the Judicial Council's decision does not include a clear description of the alleged offences, that it does not refer properly to the applicable laws or that it has not been duly served on him. Furthermore, he may object to the summons's validity, if it does not include all necessary details or if the bailiff's certificate is not duly signed, etc. The Court adjourns the hearing should the defendant's objections be

319. Cf. the CJEU judgment in *Covaci* of, 15 Oct. 2015 (C-216/14) at 62–63.

sustained, in order for the deficiencies to be remedied; otherwise, it orders the continuation of the hearing. An error of the Court in this respect results in the invalidity of the trial, which can be declared by the appellate instance (Article 502(4)) or by *Areios Pagos* (Article 510(1)) (*infra*, paragraph 504). However, the voluntary appearance of a defendant in court who does not object to the beginning of the trial, cures the above procedural irregularities (Article 175(2)).

## 2. The Closing of the Trial Hearing

*387.* After the closing of the evidence hearing and the closing arguments of the parties, the Court retires to deliberate *in camera* on the issue of guilt (Article 369(3)). Multi-Member Courts of all instances decide unanimously or by absolute majority. Judges who are of a lower rank or are younger in the same rank vote first, while the presiding judge of the court votes last. In case of more than two opinions between the judges, those who voted less favourably for the defendant must adhere to the next favourable vote for the defendant until a majority builds up (Article 369(2)). All members of the court vote on all relevant issues, i.e., with respect to the facts and the law. The same applies to the mixed jury courts, where judges and jurors deliberate and vote in common on all issues except for purely procedural ones (Articles 404–405).

The Court delivers a verdict of guilty if *actus reus* and *mens rea* are established and punishment is not precluded on legal grounds (Article 368). The Court acquits the defendant if the facts which constitute a criminal offence and/or *mens rea* are not proven beyond reasonable doubt or if other reasons of impunity are established.

All decisions must be pronounced in public (Article 93(2) of the Constitution, Article 369(1) CCP). In cases of decisions taken by majority, the Court shall name the members who formed the majority and those who dissented (Article 370).

After a verdict of guilty, the Public Prosecutor and the defendant and/or his counsel make their oral arguments on the sentence they deem appropriate (Article 369(3)). The Court retires again to deliberate following the aforementioned rules with respect to voting, etc. and returns its decision on the sentence to be passed. In practice, this part of the procedure follows the guilty verdict on the spot and is short. Critics point out that such practice undermines the fairness of this important phase of the trial hearing.

*388.* The minutes of the trial hearing and the decision of the court on both guilt and sentence are laid down in one document signed by the presiding judge and the secretary of the court (Articles 140–142). The trial record only includes a summary of the debates in court and does not always accurately reflect the same, which in turn does not allow a proper assessment of the judgments of the first-instance courts by the appellate instances. More recently, audiotaping of the trial hearings has been introduced (Article 143) and has been widely practised since 2021 in courts for serious crimes.

As already mentioned, judgments must be reasoned with respect to the facts and the law (Article 93(3) of the Constitution, Article 139 CCP). Reasoning is also required for the sentence passed according to Article 79(7) PC. However, in practice, most courts help themselves with a standard wording of reasoning which is supposed to justify the sentence imposed. As a result, defendants as well as higher courts can hardly follow the 'real' reasons which would explain the sentence imposed in each specific case. Unfortunately, this unsatisfactory and sharply criticized practice has been upheld by *Areios Pagos*.

## §3. The Legal Position of the Accused and the Injured Party

### I. Introductory Remarks

*389.* A criminal offence is always regarded as an infringement on public interests. The State has the right to prosecute criminal offenders in order to protect vital interests of society and to strengthen confidence in the rule of law. The importance of the legal position of the defendant, who is the object of the State's right to prosecute, is self-evident. He is the person who must be effectively protected against abuse of power and erroneous decisions.

A criminal offence, however, does not only create a relationship between the prosecuting State and the alleged perpetrator. At the same time, it may infringe on another person's rights by causing material and/or moral damage. The natural or legal persons who are the victims of the alleged criminal offence, i.e., those who have suffered direct harm from it, can ask for compensation by filing a civil action against the perpetrator before the civil courts (Articles 914 et seq. CC). In parallel, the injured party has the right to participate as a party in all stages of the criminal proceedings in support of the charges against the defendant. Though the victim of the offence cannot directly claim damages before the criminal court, the latter has the power to order the return of assets, which had been confiscated or seized pretrial and are the proceeds of the offence in question, to the victim of the same after convicting the defendant or after termination of the proceedings due to the death of the defendant or on prescription or admissibility grounds (Articles 372–373).

Civil action can always be brought before the civil courts which are competent to adjudicate civil claims arising from the commission of a criminal offence. Criminal prosecution of the wrongful act is not a prerequisite for the establishment of civil jurisdiction. In case of offences prosecuted only on the alleged victim's criminal complaint (*supra*, paragraph 349), the victim may sue the perpetrator for civil claims before the civil courts and refrain (for tactical, financial, or other reasons) from lodging a criminal complaint against him, thus barring the execution of the State's right to prosecute.

The decision of the injured party to actively participate in the criminal proceedings has far-reaching implications with respect to the structure of the criminal trial and the balancing of parties' rights.

## II. The Legal Position of the Defendant

### *A. The Provisions in the Code of Criminal Procedure and the Constitution*

*390.* During the preliminary investigation (*supra*, paragraphs 342–343), the 'suspect' is the person who allegedly committed the offence under investigation (Article 244). After the opening of a formal or summary investigation (*supra*, paragraphs 329 et seq., 339 et seq.), the alleged perpetrator of the offence under investigation is called the 'accused' (Article 72); the same term is used in the CCP after indictment and during the trial hearing for the individual charged with the respective criminal offence. For the purpose of avoiding multiple terminology, the term 'defendant' will be used throughout Part II of this monograph for the person who is a suspect or an accused in the various stages of criminal proceedings.

On the one hand, becoming a defendant might seem an undesirable situation, since nobody strives to get entangled in a criminal investigation as the alleged perpetrator of an offence. On the other hand, the defendant status becomes advantageous with respect to a wide range of procedural rights, which the law provides only for defendants. These rights operate in connection with the presumption of innocence (Article 6(2) ECHR, Article 71 CCP) and ensure the effective protection of the individual's fundamental rights.

*391.* The Code of Criminal Procedure provides a well-developed system of defendant's rights at the pre-trial as well as at the trial stage, which are in line with the ECHR and the Charter as well as with the EU Directives on procedural rights in criminal and European Arrest Warrant proceedings. The basic catalogue of these rights applies to all kinds of investigations or trials, while some rights are specific to certain forms of procedure.

The list of the defendant's rights at the pre-trial stage includes, *inter alia*:

(i) the right to be informed by the Prosecutor or the investigating police or judicial authorities of his basic procedural rights, i.e., the right to counsel and to legal aid, the right to information, the right to interpretation and translation, the right to silence and against self-incrimination (Article 95). Persons in custody must be provided with a 'Letter of Rights' in a language they understand on the above rights as well on their additional rights, i.e., the right of access to the case file, the right to communicate with the consular authorities of the defendant's home state and with a person of his choice, the right to receive medical care and the applicable time limits with respect to his detention (Article 96);

(ii) the right to be informed of the factual and legal basis of the offence of which he is suspected and receive copies of the evidence in the case file and ask for an adequate time (which cannot be less than forty-eight hours) to prepare his defence (Articles 100, 103, 274);

(iii) the right to remain silent and to non-self-incrimination; the right to submit a written defence statement as well as evidence in his defence (Articles 104, 106, 244(1), 273(2)) including expert evidence;

(iv) the right of access to a lawyer (no more than two) and the right to legal aid where applicable from the beginning of the police or judicial investigation and before his first examination and to communicate with counsel at any stage of the investigation (Articles 89, 91, 99, 105(2), 106);
(v) the right to attend the acts of the investigation, save the examination of witnesses, to request the taking of evidence including expert evidence and submit comments on the evidence collected (Articles 92, 94, 102, 274);
(vi) the right to interpretation and translation of essential documents for those defendants who do not understand the language of the court (Articles 101, 233–238);
(vii) the right to promptly notify a person of his choice after detention and communicate with such person during detention and the right to communicate with the consular authorities of his home country.

At the trial stage, the defendant has some further rights including:

(i) the right to call witnesses or experts of his choice and ask the Public Prosecutor to call witnesses he wishes (one witness in misdemeanour trials before the Three-Member Misdemeanour Court and two in serious crimes trials (Articles 326(3), 327(2));
(ii) the right to directly examine witnesses and experts and to comment on all evidence submitted during the trial hearing (Articles 357(3), 358); and the right to introduce new evidence in his defence (Article 362);
(iii) the right to defend himself in person and/or through his counsel (up to three) and to always have the last word (Articles 365–367, 333(3));
(iv) the right to appeal against conviction and sentence by a first-instance court (Article 489, *infra*, paragraph 491).

*392*. The above-mentioned provisions of the Code of Criminal Procedure are complemented by provisions of the Constitution, which include directly applicable procedural law. The following provisions of the Constitution should be mentioned:

Article 7(2) of the Constitution stipulates that no person shall be submitted to torture or other inhuman or degrading treatment infringing his dignity (*supra*, paragraph 182); in Article 2(1) of the Constitution, the protection of human dignity is proclaimed to be a fundamental duty of all state authorities.

Article 6 of the Constitution provides that nobody shall be arrested but only upon a duly issued and reasoned warrant of arrest which shall mention the offence charged and the reasons justifying the arrest. The arrested person must be informed upon his arrest of its reasons and must be brought promptly and no later than twenty-four hours before the Public Prosecutor and the Investigating Judge, who must decide within the next three days upon releasing him or remanding him in pre-trial custody according to the law (*infra*, paragraphs 442–443). The length of pre-trial detention cannot exceed nine months in misdemeanour cases and eighteen months in serious crime cases.

Article 9 of the Constitution states that a person's private sphere deserves strong protection, and his home can be searched only in accordance with the law (Articles 253 et seq. CCP, *infra*, paragraphs 424–425) and always in the presence of a judge or a public prosecutor, while Article 19 proclaims the protection of the secrecy of correspondence or other forms of confidential communication.

Access to the courts and the right to be heard are guaranteed as fundamental rights (Article 20(1)), while respect for the proportionality principle is established as a duty of all state authorities (Article 25(1)).[320]

The Constitution also includes an important exclusionary rule with respect to evidence acquired in breach of the right to confidential communications and/or of the rules for the protection of personal data in Article 19(3) (*infra*, paragraph 417).

### *B. The Provisions of the European Convention of Human Rights, the EU Charter and the International Covenant on Civil and Political Rights*

*393.* The above-mentioned provisions of the Code of Criminal Procedure and the Constitution with respect to the rights of the defendant are in line with the corresponding provisions of the European Convention of Human Rights, the EU Charter and the International Covenant on Civil and Political Rights (ICCPR). These international statutes hold an important position within the Greek legal system. After their ratification they not only form part of national law, but they also prevail over conflicting provisions of national law pursuant to Article 28(1) of the Constitution. The catalogue of the defendant's rights set out in the Constitution and the Code of Criminal Procedure is complemented by said European or international statutes, especially in respect of rights not expressly stated in domestic law.

For example, the right to a fair hearing within reasonable time is not mentioned as such in the Constitution or the CCP, though fairness of the criminal proceedings is pursued in domestic law through a series of provisions guaranteeing the fair character of pre-trial and trial proceedings. The explicit establishment of a fundamental right to a fair trial in the above statutes has far-reaching implications for the interpretation of the domestic provisions on the defendant's rights, the admissibility of evidence, the overall fairness of the proceedings, etc.

The European Convention on Human Rights, the EU Directives on procedural rights, and the EU Charter as interpreted by the ECtHR and the CJEU play an increasingly significant role in Greek criminal legislation and court practice.[321]

## III. The Legal Position of the Injured Party

*394.* The criminal procedure is primarily a case between the prosecuting State, on the one hand, and the defendant, on the other. However, the victim of the alleged

320. *See* Sp. Vlachopoulos, 'The Procedural Aspects of the Proportionality Principle in the Greek Legal Order', in: *Human rights in times of illiberal democracies*, Liber Amicorum in Memoriam of Stavros Tsakyrakis, Nomiki Bibliothiki, Athens, 2020, 81 et seq.

321. *See* the contributions of L. Karelos, M. Tsirli and E. Salamoura, in: Athens Bar Association (ed.), *European Court of Human Rights – 50 years*, Athens, 2020, 91, 101, 166; M. Kaiafa-Gbandi, 'ECJ's Recent Case-Law on Criminal Matters: Protection of fundamental Rights in EU Law and its Importance for Member States' National Judiciary', EuCLR 3/2017, 219 et seq.

offence also deserves a role in the criminal proceedings. Under the Code of Criminal Procedure, the injured party, i.e., the individual or the legal entity who claims that they have suffered harm as a result of the offence in question, is vested with a wide range of rights through all stages of the proceedings. Unlike the legal systems of other countries where the alleged victim of the criminal offence cannot acquire the status of a party to the proceedings or has an ancillary position in them, it has been a long tradition in Greece to allow the injured party to become an active participant in the proceedings, who can influence the course of the investigation and the outcome of the trial.

The injured party's participation in the criminal procedure aims at supporting the charges against the defendant whose conviction would also serve the injured party's claims for compensation, which the latter is allowed to raise before the civil courts either in parallel to or after the closing of the criminal proceedings. This 'double nature' of the injured party's role in the criminal proceedings has been highlighted in legal doctrine.

*395.* By Act 4478/2017, Greece has implemented the EU Directive 2012/29 on establishing minimum standards on the rights, support and protection of victims of crime.[322] Apart from amending and supplementing the provisions of the Penal Code and the Code of Criminal Procedure, which were then in force, the above Act also established a significant number of rights for the victims of criminal offences, which relate to the criminal procedure and may be exercised irrespective of whether the alleged victim has constituted himself party to the proceedings in support of the charges under the CCP (*infra*, paragraph 396). These rights include the right to be informed in a simple and understandable language of the status of pending procedures in their various stages and of the respective rights conferred on victims, the right to have access to certain essential documents of the case, the right to legal aid and psychological or other expert support, the possibility of mediation, etc.

### A. *General Observations*

*396.* A person or an entity can constitute themselves parties in support of the charges only if they have suffered material and/or moral damage resulting directly from the alleged criminal offence (e.g., the victim of the rape or the bodily harm, the owner of the stolen or embezzled goods, the victim of the fraud, etc. (Article 63)). The courts tend to interpret rather narrowly the term 'directly damaged person', not allowing the participation of natural persons or legal entities who suffered indirect losses, e.g., insurance companies who have compensated the damage inflicted on the victim, shareholders who suffer indirect losses as a result of a criminal offence committed against the company, etc. The use of the 'direct damage' criterion, which originates from tort law, in order to define those entitled to participate in the criminal proceedings in support of the charges, may weaken the otherwise purely 'criminal' character of the proceedings.

322. *See* I. Androulakis, 'European Perspectives on Rights for Victims of Crime', eucrim 2014, 111 et seq.

The heirs of the alleged victim of the criminal offence may constitute themselves a party for moral damages in a pending criminal procedure only if the inherited person had duly constituted himself party while alive (Article 64). The same rule applies in respect of legal entities in cases of mergers and acquisitions, i.e., the acquiring succeeds the acquired entity as an injured party. In cases of homicide or other offences resulting in the death of a person, the members of the victim's family (spouses, children, siblings, parents, grandparents) also have the right to participate in the proceedings against the alleged perpetrator of the offence.

*397.* The right to participate as an injured party in the criminal proceedings lapses five years after the commission of the criminal offence. However, if the latter is subject to a longer limitation by time, this also applies to the injured party's right. This rule applies to all serious crimes which, as already mentioned, are subject to a statute of limitation of fifteen or twenty years (*supra*, paragraphs 370–371).

### B. *The Injured Party at the Pre-trial Stage*

*398.* The injured party may participate in support of the charges both pre-trial and at the trial hearing including appellate procedures filing a declaration to this end. At the pre-trial stage, it may do so from the opening of the investigation until the closing of the same (Article 83(1). The declaration must state the core facts which constitute the wrongful act and the harm it caused (Article 84). In its declaration, the injured party has the right to appoint counsel, to whom all documents of the trial are served. The declaration can be submitted (orally or in writing) to any competent investigating official (police officer, investigating magistrate, investigating judge) or public prosecutor who handles the case. A widespread practice for criminal complainants is to attach an injured party's declaration in support of the charges to their criminal complaint filed with the Public Prosecutor or other competent authority or to include such a declaration in their witness testimony before the investigating authorities.

*399.* The defendant has the right to object to the injured party's participation by filing a written submission in which the grounds of the objection are set out (Articles 85–86). For example, the defendant may argue that the person who filed the declaration is not considered a directly damaged person under the law, or that the declaration does not properly describe the alleged offence etc. The objections of the defendant are considered by the Judicial Council, which, when admitting them, orders the exclusion of the person from the proceedings (Article 86). The Judicial Council may also do so at the Public Prosecutor's request or on its own motion (Article 87).

*400.* After constituting themselves party in support of the charges, the injured person or entity acquires an important position at the pre-trial stage, as they are vested with a wide range of procedural rights which equal in many respects those attributed to the defendant, e.g., the right of access to a lawyer, the right of access to the case file, the right to present or request evidence, to appoint experts on their behalf, etc.

### *C. The Injured Party at the Trial Stage*

*401.* At the trial hearing, the injured person has the right to become a party in support of the charges until the beginning of the evidence hearing (Articles 67, 83(2)). To this purpose, an oral declaration of the same content as at the pre-trial stage is required. An injured party's declaration is not admissible before an appellate court if it has not been lawfully submitted before the first-instance court.

*402.* The defendant has the right to object to the injured party's participation on the same grounds as pre-trial. Moreover, the court must exclude the person who claims to be an injured party if the requirements of the law are not met. The unlawful participation of a person in support of the charges results in the nullity of the proceedings (Article 171(3)).

*403.* The person who participates at the trial hearing in support of the charges has a wide range of rights, which are equal in many respects to those conferred on the defendant, including the examination of witnesses. However, the injured party is not allowed to directly examine the defendant in court or to make submissions with respect to the sentence to be passed. Moreover, it has no right to appeal an acquittal judgment.

## §4. The Rules of Evidence

*404.* The Code of Criminal Procedure sets the basic rules of evidence which apply to all kinds of criminal investigations and trials. In general, these provisions combine the rules of evidence with the powers of the investigating authorities and the trial court on the one hand and the defendant's rights on the other thus creating a rather complex system of evidentiary law. Moreover, the mitigated inquisitorial character of the pre-trial and the moderately adversarial character of the trial proceedings (*supra*, paragraphs 328, 375) allow the courts' room to adjust the law to the particularities of each case.

## I. The Principles of Evidentiary Law

*405.* The presumption of innocence (Article 71 CCP, Article 6(2) ECHR, Article 48(1) of the Charter, Article 14(2) ICCPR) is a fundamental principle which governs the criminal procedure. Until found guilty by a trial court, the prosecuting State must treat the defendant as a presumably innocent person and not as an anticipated guilty person. In a system based on the presumption of innocence, the burden of proof lies with the prosecuting State. The defendant is not under any obligation to prove his innocence and is fully protected against self-incrimination (Article 14(3)(g) ICCPR, Article 104 CCP). Moreover, he benefits from any doubts regarding his guilt; the principle *in dubio pro reo* is expressly established in Article 178(3) of the CCP.

Article 178(2) mandates judges and prosecutors to carefully consider all incriminating or exonerating evidence as well as the claims of the defendant in respect of essential facts of the case. Though the defendant bears technically no burden of proof in relation to his claims, his chances of achieving a positive outcome increase when he is able to present evidence which supports his defences, for example, that he acted in self-defence, under coercion, in a state of mental illness, that he was entrapped etc. Indeed, the Court is under an obligation to explain the reasons for rejecting the defences which have been put forward by the defendant; however, such an obligation does not apply in relation to defences that the defendant did not invoke and which were not otherwise indicated by the evidence produced.

*406.* The defendant is free to organize his defence in a manner he and his counsel feel appropriate and is not under an obligation to disclose to the Public Prosecutor and/or the party supporting the charges his evidence (witnesses, documents etc.) before the trial (Articles 326(3), 362(1)). On the contrary, the Public Prosecutor must serve on the defendant before the trial (five days at the latest) a catalogue of the witnesses he intends to examine (Article 326(1)). The same obligation applies to the party supporting the charges (Article 326(2)). The Prosecutor and the parties are allowed to introduce new documentary evidence during the trial hearing. However, in cases of essential new documents, the opposing party may ask for an adjournment of the hearing for up to fifteen days in order to evaluate the newly introduced evidence (Article 362(3)). The Court has the power to call new witnesses, if necessary, during the trial hearing. If the Court makes use of such power, the defendant has the right to request an adjournment of the hearing for up to fifteen days (Article 353(1)).

*407.* In regard to the means of proof which are admissible in the criminal proceedings, the CCP stipulates that every lawfully acquired evidence is in principle admissible and can be adduced by the Public Prosecutor or the parties (Articles 177, 178(1)). The investigating authorities and the courts have a duty to search for the truth (Articles 177(1), 178(2), 351(1), 357(1)). The courts do not confine themselves to the evidence presented by the Public Prosecutor or the parties but are entitled to initiate any investigating act or take other appropriate measures with respect to any evidence deemed necessary to find the truth.

*408.* The CCP does not establish general rules in respect of the probative value of the various means of proof. All lawfully acquired evidence is subject to the court's free evaluation (Article 177(1)). The court may, for example, acquit a defendant who confesses a crime, if it concludes that the confession is outweighed by other compelling evidence; or to reject an expert's opinion which it considers wrong etc.

However, some restrictions apply to the court's freedom to evaluate the weight of the evidence. Article 211, for example, provides that a conviction cannot be based solely on a co-defendant's testimony but needs to be corroborated by other evidence; Article 152 stipulates that records drawn up by investigating authorities with regard to investigating acts they carried out prove the facts referred to unless evidence to the contrary is produced. Moreover, it is firmly established in case law that a court, which declines to follow a unanimous opinion of forensic experts on crucial issues of the case (e.g., on the insanity of the defendant), must give detailed reasons for its adverse judgment.

The CCP does not exclude hearsay evidence and does not contain the best evidence rule. Still, in various provisions preference for the best evidence is expressed. Article 224, for example, states that a witness must identify the source of his information; if he fails to do so, his testimony cannot be the basis for a conviction.

*409.* The court must mention in its judgment the means of proof on which it relied. However, according to *Areios Pagos's* case law, the court has in principle no obligation to separately address each piece of evidence and its probative value against that of other evidence. An exception applies with respect to scientific evidence or evidence of high relevance (e.g., alibi, eyewitness testimony), which the court, depending on the specifics of the case, may have to address separately.

## II. The Means of Proof

*410.* Article 178(1) mentions the most common means of proof: indices, inspection of persons, places and objects, expert reports, confessions, statements of witnesses, and documents.

*411.* The term 'indices' in the CCP does not indicate a specific category of evidence but refers in general to all means of proof that fall under the so-called indirect or circumstantial evidence. For example, the fact that the defendant was seen armed with a rifle in the garden of the victim's home a few minutes after the robbery, is an indication that he may have participated in the robbery. In legal doctrine and in case law it is well established that even if indices do not prove guilt each in itself, a series of indices in conjunction with other evidence can meet the standard of proof, i.e., they can prove guilt beyond reasonable doubt.

*412.* Inspections of persons, places and objects are carried out by all competent investigating authorities, i.e., the investigating judge, the investigating magistrates or police or investigative agencies officers and the public prosecutor. Inspections, especially those of the crime scene, may play an important role, as they often are the basis of scientific evidence (hair or fingerprint analysis, blood or DNA testing, etc.). For every inspection the investigating official must keep a written record, where his acts and findings are stated. As already explained, these records are presumed truthful with respect to the facts mentioned therein, unless proof to the contrary has been produced (Article 152), without prejudice to the judge's freedom to evaluate them against other pieces of evidence.

*413.* Experts are appointed by the investigating judge or by other investigating officials, whenever the proper assessment of relevant facts requires scientific or technical expertise (Article 183). Experts can also be appointed by the judicial council or the trial court for the same purpose. Experts give on oath their opinion on the issues defined by the authority who appoints them (Articles 194 et seq.). The parties can request the appointment of an expert; their request may be rejected, where the appointment of an expert is not deemed necessary. The parties have the right to appeal against the rejection of their request by the prosecutor, the investigating judge, or other investigative authorities before the judicial council (Article 307). Whenever an expert is appointed in the course of a preliminary, summary or formal investigation, the parties must be notified of the appointment and are granted the right to appoint expert advisors to act on their behalf (Article 204). The expert advisors of the parties are entitled to be present at the acts carried out by the experts appointed by the investigating authorities and to take knowledge of all the documents the latter have access to (Article 207). Experts file their report with comments on their expertise in writing with the competent authority (Article 198). Experts may be called to testify in Court with respect to the issues addressed in their opinion (Article 360). Technical advisors of the parties do not testify under oath.

*414.* Mention has been made of the defendant's confession as a means of proof in criminal proceedings (*supra*, paragraph 418). A confession is commonly considered strong evidence of the defendant's guilt. However, it is subjected, like all other evidence, to the court's evaluation. The court may, therefore, acquit a defendant who pleads guilty, if his confession is outweighed by other compelling evidence.

A defendant's confession incriminating a co-defendant has a restricted probative value and cannot prove guilt of the incriminated defendant if not corroborated by other evidence (Article 211, *supra*, paragraph 418).

*415.* Witnesses are an indispensable means of proof in criminal proceedings, albeit an often unreliable one. At the pre-trial stage, the investigating officials call and examine all witnesses to facts relevant to the case under investigation. The examination of witnesses at this stage is carried out by the competent investigating official and is not adversarial, i.e., the parties have no right to be present at the witness' examination nor to put questions to him orally or in writing. A written record of the witness' testimony is drawn up by the investigating official and the secretary and is signed by them and the witness. The written witness statements form part of the case file.

In preparation of the trial hearing, the Public Prosecutor calls all material witnesses and notifies the defendant of their names five days before the trial at the latest (Articles 326(1), 327(1)). The injured party supporting the charges has the same obligation regarding the witnesses it wishes to call (Article 326(2)). Within five days from his summoning to trial, the defendant has a right to request the Public Prosecutor to call one witness, in cases of misdemeanours before the Three-Member Court, or two witnesses, in cases of serious crimes, over and above to those already summoned by the Public Prosecutor (Article 327(2)). Moreover, the defendant may call at trial witnesses to his defence without prior notice to the parties or the Court

(Article 326(3)). All witnesses are examined orally by the Court, the Public Prosecutor, and the parties (Articles 333, 357). The Presiding Judge of the Court can dismiss questions put by the Public Prosecutor or the parties only if he deems them irrelevant to the case (Article 333(2)). A right to appeal before the trial court against such decision is provided for in Article 335(2).

Witnesses testify in principle under oath (Article 219). However, for certain categories of persons (e.g., persons under the age of seventeen, mentally weakened etc.) the Code of Criminal Procedure provides that they do not testify under oath. The same applies to the injured party supporting the charges (Article 221). A witness cannot, in principle, refuse to testify unless he falls under one of the categories explicitly mentioned in law (e.g., spouses or close relatives of the defendant (Article 222)). Witnesses are also protected against self-incrimination (Article 223(4)), since they are not obliged to reveal facts which might incriminate them with regard to a criminal offence. Article 210 provides that investigating judges, public prosecutors, investigating officials and their secretaries are incompetent to testify before the trial court on a case they were involved at the pre-trial stage. The same applies for a person who has been found guilty in connection with the same offence. Some professionals (e.g., lawyers, doctors, etc.) are not competent to testify with respect to facts entrusted to them by their clients, and they can refuse to testify on facts they came to know while exercising their profession. The same is true in relation to clerics (Article 212).

*416.* Article 218 provides that in proceedings for certain categories of crimes, i.e., criminal or terrorist organizations, human trafficking, migration offences, a series of measures may be taken by the authorities in order to protect victims and/or witnesses or their relatives against intimidation or retaliation. Protection measures may also be afforded in proceedings for bribery offences to witnesses or witnesses in the public interest (whistle-blowers) (*supra*, paragraph 357), undercover agents or informants.

Protective measures include, *inter alia*, anonymous or pseudonymous testimony, the use of voice-altering technology, change of residence and/or identity, etc. At the trial hearing, protected witnesses may testify under their altered identity. Their testimony, however, cannot be the basis for a conviction. Moreover, the court has the power to order the witness to reveal his real identity and personal details if it deems it necessary.

## III. The Exclusion of Evidence

*417.* The principle of the free evaluation of evidence enshrined in Article 177(1) applies to lawfully acquired evidence. Therefore, a conviction cannot be based on illegally obtained evidence.

Article 177(2) provides that evidence acquired through criminal acts or resulting from them must be excluded from criminal proceedings. Moreover, Article 19(3) of the Constitution states that evidence acquired in violation of the fundamental rights enshrined in Articles 9 (protection of home and privacy), 9A (protection of personal data) and 19 (confidentiality of correspondence or other forms of private communication) must be excluded as evidence in criminal or other proceedings.

*418.* In a most remarkable judgment (No. 2/99) *Areios Pagos* ruled *in pleno*, that disregard of the exclusionary rule enshrined in Article 177(2) by the trial court may trigger the nullity of the trial because it entails a serious infringement on the defendant's fundamental rights according to Article 171(1d). The Court held that such nullity occurs when a witness statement of a person during the police investigation, who was later criminally prosecuted for the offence he had testified, is relied on by the trial court to convict him.

*419.* An exception to the above exclusionary rules was introduced by Article 14 of Act 4637/2019. According to this controversial provision, in cases of serious crimes which fall within the competence of the Prosecutor's Office for Economic Crimes unlawfully obtained evidence, to which said Prosecutors could have had lawful access under Articles 34(1) or 36(3) CCP respectively (*supra*, paragraph 346), may be taken into account as evidence in criminal proceedings if the following three conditions are fulfilled: (i) the criminal act by which the evidence had been acquired did not infringe on human dignity; (ii) the criminal act that such evidence proves is more serious than the act by which it was obtained; (iii) the unlawfully acquired evidence is the sole or decisive proof of the criminal act under investigation.

*420.* Despite the rigid wording of the aforementioned provisions of the CCP and the Constitution, courts tend to adopt a more flexible approach towards improperly obtained evidence which leaves some room for exceptions to the exclusionary rules.

Notably, courts have repeatedly ruled (*see*, e.g., *Areios Pagos* Judgment No. 1323/2011) that such evidence may be allowed in criminal proceedings to prove the defendant's innocence if no other means of proof are available to him to rebut the charges. In its judgment No. 1351/1997, *Areios Pagos* held that an illegally recorded tape which contains exonerating information for one defendant and incriminating information for another can be taken into consideration by the court only with respect to its exonerating contents while its incriminating information must be excluded.

Moreover, the use of improperly obtained evidence may also be exceptionally allowed to prove the defendant's guilt following a proportionality test assessing the seriousness of the offence to be proved which must far outweigh the seriousness of the unlawful act by which the evidence in question was obtained (*see*, e.g., *Areios Pagos* Judgment No. 653/2013).

The rigidness of the exclusionary rule is being further mitigated in case law by a tendency to narrow the scope of privacy rights. For example, videotapes from a secretly installed camera in a shop showing an employee committing theft have been admitted in evidence on the basis that the employee's privacy rights had not been infringed (*Areios Pagos* Judgment No. 874/2004). Also, it is accepted that privacy rights are not protected in situations where such rights are used in order to commit a criminal offence, for example, when extortion is attempted during a telephone call, and the victim secretly records the threats of violence.[323]

323. For a comparative approach of exclusionary rules with a focus on the United States, Greece, France and England and Wales, *see* D. Giannoulopoulos, *Improperly Obtained Evidence in Anglo-American and Continental Law*, Hart Publishing, Oxford, 2019, 17 et seq.

# Chapter 2. Powers, Rights and Duties in the Pre-trial Proceedings

*421.* The Code of Criminal Procedure contains a body of provisions with respect to the investigating acts which may be carried out in the course of the formal investigation. These provisions apply to a large extent to the summary investigation, the investigation in flagrant offences or the emergency investigation, and the preliminary investigation. It is therefore appropriate to outline the powers and duties of the competent authorities and the rights of the defendant in the formal investigation; an overview of the provisions governing the pre-trial detention of the defendant and its alternatives will follow; in the third part of this chapter the above powers and rights within the other forms of pre-trial proceedings are discussed.

## §1. The Powers and Duties of the Investigating Judge: The Rights of the Defendant in the Formal Investigation

### I. Introductory Remarks

*422.* The formal investigation is ordered in writing by the Public Prosecutor of the Misdemeanour Court (Article 246, *supra*, paragraphs 329–330). The Investigating Judge initiates any act he deems necessary to reveal the facts constituting the criminal offence under investigation and the persons involved therein (Article 248). In the execution of his powers, the Investigating Judge can act *ratione loci* not only within the judicial district of the Misdemeanour Court he belongs to but, if necessary, in the districts of other such courts as well with the consent of the Public Prosecutor of the Misdemeanour Court. He can even act in the judicial district of a Court of Appeal other than the one he comes under with the consent of the Public Prosecutor of the Court of Appeal, notifying the Public Prosecutor of the Court of Appeal within whose judicial district he intends to operate (Article 249). The Investigating Judge can also request investigating judges or investigating officers anywhere in the country to conduct specific acts (e.g., interrogation of witnesses or defendants, seizure of documents, etc.).

Article 251 CCP states that the Investigating Judge and the investigating officers must respect the fundamental principle of proportionality when conducting any investigative act.

### II. The Powers of Inspection, Entry, Search and Seizure

*423.* Articles 180 and 252 CCP empower the Investigating Judge to inspect places and (let) secure any evidence, including the taking of fingerprints, hair or blood samples, taking of photographs or drawing diagrams of the scene of the crime, etc., which is prima facie related to the criminal offence under investigation.

*424.* Articles 253 et seq. CCP in conjunction with Article 9 of the Constitution set forth the conditions under which searches of places and persons may be conducted in the course of an investigation for a serious crime or a misdemeanour.

Searches are allowed, if it can be reasonably assumed that these are necessary to reveal a criminal offence and/or the perpetrators of the same and no other more lenient means seem appropriate to this end.

*425.* A person's home may be searched only in the presence of a judge or a public prosecutor (Article 9 of the Constitution). If the resident of the house to be searched refuses to allow entrance to the judge and the investigating officers accompanying him or if no residents are present, reasonable force may be used to enter the house. The resident of the house, or in his absence, a neighbour, is called to be present at the search. The resident of the house has the right to receive a copy of the search record (Article 256).

Additional conditions are prescribed in Article 256 with regard to the search of houses during the night, i.e., from 8 p.m. to 6 a.m. or from 9 p.m. to 5 a.m. for the period from 1 October to 31 March and from 1 April to 30 September respectively. Notably, a house search during the night is allowed only in the following cases: to arrest a person, who is criminally prosecuted according to the law, i.e., by virtue of a warrant of arrest or in *flagranti crimine*; to arrest a person committing a misdemeanour or a serious crime in the house; if there is a gathering of people for the purpose of illegal gambling or if the house is used for forbidden lewd activities. Article 256 stipulates that publicity must be avoided during the search of a house while care must be taken to protect the reputation and privacy of the residents and to conduct the search in a decent and polite way.

It should be noted that neither the Constitution nor the Code of Criminal Procedure requires the issue of a detailed search warrant in order to search homes or other premises or seize evidence therein. The mandatory presence of a judge or prosecutor during the search may guarantee that it will be properly conducted. However, the lack of a properly detailed search warrant that would define the scope of the search and/or the physical evidence to be seized creates uncertainty. The authorities tend to stretch the extent of searches and seizures to their limits thus transforming them from focused investigative acts to disproportionate fishing expeditions.

The above practice has triggered the conviction of Greece by the ECtHR for violation of Article 8 ECHR rights.[324]

*426.* The search of the defendant is allowed if the Investigating Judge believes that it is strongly indicated for establishing the facts of the case. Third persons may be searched only if their search is deemed indispensable to secure material evidence with respect to the investigated case (Article 257). Persons shall be searched separately in a way that does not infringe on their feeling of decency.

*427.* In the course of the search, documents or other items which are relevant to the case under investigation can be seized. All such items must be mentioned in the search record drawn up by the Investigating Judge and put under official custody. Not only items found during the search of a house or a person but also any other

324. *See*, for example, the Court's judgments in *Modestou v. Greece* of 16 Mar. 2017, *Leotsakos v. Greece* of 4 Oct. 2018.

documents or items which constitute evidence with respect to the offence in question may, in principle, be seized. To this purpose, the Investigating Judge calls public employees or private persons who are in possession of such items, to handle them over. The latter may exceptionally refuse to do so, for example, in cases of documents containing diplomatic or military secrets related to national security or documents protected under a professional secrecy statute according to Article 212 CCP (Article 263). In the event that the Investigating Judge disputes the professional secrecy affirmation, he secures the documents to be seized without taking knowledge of their contents; thereafter, he forwards the document to the Minster of Justice in case of a state's secret declaration or to the competent professional association in case of a professional secrecy declaration (e.g., the Bar Association or the Medical Association of which the professional is a member). The professional association notifies the Investigating Judge on the truthfulness of the declaration, failing which may result in the professional's criminal liability (Article 264).

Persons who were in the possession of the seized documents have the right to receive copies of the same. Alternatively, the Investigating Judge takes copies of the seized documents and returns the originals to their owners (Article 267).

*428.* The seizure of digital evidence is regulated in Article 265 CCP. Such seizure may be ordered with respect to computer systems and data stored therein or in another storage medium to which the investigating officer has access. The same applies to remote computer systems or storage mediums which are interconnected to the above. Data stored in the Cloud are also subject to seizure. The seizure must be conducted by using the appropriate technology for the purpose of producing authenticated copies of the seized data; the latter shall be stored in one storage medium that forms part of the case file.

## III. The Powers to Examine the Defendant and the Witnesses

*429.* The Code of Criminal Procedure describes the procedure to be followed for the examination of the defendant (Articles 270 et seq.) and the witnesses (Articles 209 et seq.). Non-respect of the relevant provisions may trigger the nullity of the respective procedural act or stage.

### A. *The Interrogation of the Defendant*

*430.* The formal investigation cannot be closed without prior notification of the defendant, who is summoned to appear for examination before the Investigating Judge. An exception can be made if the investigation does not reveal any evidence against the defendant (Article 270), in which case the Investigating Judge terminates the investigation without summoning the defendant. Should the defendant, though duly summoned, fail to appear, the Investigating Judge has the power to issue a warrant of attachment or a warrant of arrest (*infra*, paragraphs 441–442).

The defendant must be summoned twenty-four hours before the date of the interrogation at the latest (Article 271). The summons is served on him according to the procedure described above (*supra*, paragraph 383). After appearing before the Investigating Judge, the defendant may exercise all his rights proclaimed in Articles 89 et seq., i.e., the right to be informed of the charges brought against him and of his rights in a language he understands, to ask for a period of at least forty-eight hours to prepare his defence, to appoint counsel of his choosing or to have counsel appointed and to obtain copies of all the documents of the case file etc. (*supra*, paragraph 391).

*431.* The defendant has the right not to answer the charges brought against him, i.e., to remain silent (Articles 104, 273(2)). In practice, however, defendants very rarely make use of their right to silence due to the rather inquisitorial character of the pre-trial proceedings and the disadvantages such tactics might entail, especially with regard to pre-trial detention and other coercive measures. Notwithstanding the fact that the Investigating Judge must search on his own motion for all evidence against or in favour of the defendant (Articles 239(2), 274) and that the burden of proof is on the State (Article 178), a defendant who remains silent and presents no evidence in his defence takes the risk of being judged on the basis of the evidence adduced by the Public Prosecutor and the injured party. The defendant can answer the charges either orally or in writing filing a defence submission, which, on most occasions, is written by his counsel, with the Investigating Judge. The latter may ask the defendant questions with respect to the charges and the contents of his defence submission (Article 273(2)). The defendant's counsel has the right to be present at the interrogation and to submit any comments (Articles 99, 100). However, the defendant cannot consult his counsel before answering the questions put to him by the Investigating Judge. A written record of the defendant's examination including all questions, answers and comments is drawn up by the Investigating Judge and his secretary and is signed by the same; the defendant and his counsel sign said record as well after checking its content. The defendant has the right to submit evidence in his defence and to have witnesses examined by the Investigating Judge or ask for other evidence to be collected (Article 102). The Investigating Judge has a duty to carefully evaluate all relevant facts and evidence put forward by the defendant (Article 274).

### *B. The Interrogation of Witnesses*

*432.* The Investigating Judge calls all material witnesses. In cases opened after a plaintiff's criminal complaint (*supra*, paragraph 349), it is common practice to first call the witnesses named by the plaintiff in his complaint. The Investigating Judge is free to summon any other person who he thinks is a material witness to the case in the course of the investigation. Persons summoned to testify must appear before the Investigating Judge and give their testimony taking an oath that they will tell the whole truth (Articles 209, 213, 219, 220). If a witness fails to appear without good reasons, the Investigating Judge can issue a warrant of attachment and impose a fine on him (Articles 229–230).

Witnesses are examined by the Investigating Judge separately and not in the presence of the defendant or other parties; the Investigating Judge may, however, call the defendant or other witnesses in order to confront them with the witness he interrogated on specific facts of the case (Article 225), especially in cases of fully contradictory statements. Moreover, the Investigating Judge calls the parties to be present at the interrogation of a witness if it can be reasonably assumed that the witness will not be able to appear in the trial court (Article 220(2)).

The Code of Criminal Procedure includes special provisions (Articles 214–216) with respect to the examination of certain categories of witnesses (ministers, high-ranking clerics, diplomats, etc.).

The witness' testimony is laid down on a written record by the Investigating Judge and his secretary and is signed by the same and the witness after being read out (Articles 151, 226).

Incompetence of some categories of persons to testify, statements given not under oath, statements of protected witnesses, the right to refuse to testify on professional confidentiality grounds, protection against self-incrimination, the best evidence rule and the limited probative value of a co-defendant's statement, have been discussed above in the context of the law of evidence (*supra*, paragraphs 415–416).

*433*. Article 227 CCP regulates the interrogation of minors who are considered victims of certain crimes making them vulnerable (human trafficking, abduction, rape or other forms of sexual abuse or sexual exploitation). These persons shall receive, first, advice with respect to their upcoming interrogation by an expert psychologist or psychiatrist from those employed by the Office for the Protection of Minors. To this end, the expert cooperates with the Investigating Judge or other investigating officers as well as the defendant's experts and prepares a report on the cognitive abilities and the mental state of the minor witness. The interrogation of the minor takes place at the above Office's premises or other specially prepared premises without the presence of the parties or the defendant's experts and shall not be unduly prolonged. The lawyers of the parties have the right to submit to the Investigating Judge their questions to be put to the minor. The expert who advises the minor can exclude questions that may have an adverse impact on the psycho-mental state of the minor. The minor's parents or other legal representatives have the right to be present during the interrogation but may be excluded by order of the Investigating Judge in cases of conflicting interests or where they are suspected of being involved in the acts under investigation. The minor's interrogation shall be video-recorded and is introduced at the trial hearing in lieu of his examination in court. The Prosecutor and the parties may ask the Court to order further questioning of the minor witness. If their request is admitted, the supplemental interrogation of the witness is conducted by an investigative officer appointed by the Court and follows the above-described procedure (presence of an expert, pre-submitted questions of the parties etc.).

A similar procedure as above is followed for the interrogation of adult witnesses who are considered victims of human trafficking (Article 228).

## IV. Miscellaneous

### A. Mental Examination of the Defendant

*434.* According to Articles 80 and 200 CCP, the Investigating Judge can order a mental examination of the defendant, if there are reasons to believe that he may be mentally ill. To this purpose, the Investigating Judge issues a written and reasoned order for the defendant's internment in a public mental hospital. Before issuing the order, the Investigating Judge must ask for the Public Prosecutor's consent. The consent of the two appointed psychiatric experts is also needed. The internment order shall be served on the defendant and his counsel who must be heard before the issue of the order; if the defendant has no counsel, the Investigating Judge shall appoint one on his own motion. Within three days after the service of the internment order, the defendant and/or his counsel may appeal against it before the Judicial Council which decides finally on the interment. The lodging of an appeal suspends the execution of the appealed order. After internment, the necessary mental examination of the defendant is carried out by the appointed experts who submit a written report. The interment period cannot exceed three months. The criminal proceedings against a defendant who has been found mentally ill are suspended until he recovers. The Investigating Judge can, however, initiate all acts which are necessary to secure evidence with respect to the criminal offence.

### B. Interception of Communications

*435.* Act 2295/1994 on the Protection of the Freedom of Correspondence and Communication as amended allows the interference with the right to correspondence and communication (e.g., opening of letters, wiretapping, etc.) by state authorities in the course of a criminal pre-trial investigation, if it is necessary for the purposes of the investigation in relation to broad categories of crimes mentioned in Article 4-(1a) (e.g., high treason, bribery, organized crime, terrorism, human trafficking, sexual offences, homicide, robbery, drug trafficking, antiquities trafficking, intellectual property offences, etc.). The competence to order wiretapping etc., lies with the Judicial Council of the Misdemeanour Court or of the Court of Appeal which is competent *ratione materiae* for the criminal offence under investigation. At the request of the Public Prosecutor, who carries out a preliminary or a summary investigation, or at the request of the Investigating Judge, who carries out a formal investigation, the Judicial Council, after hearing the Public Prosecutor, issues a reasoned order stating the person(s) whose communications shall be intercepted, the purpose of the interception, the means of communications (letters, telephone communications, electronic communications, etc.) to be traced, the territory and the period of time for which the order will be enforced. This period of time cannot exceed two months; it may, however, be prolonged following the same procedure for no more than two months each time until it reaches a maximum of ten months (Article 5(2), (6) of the above Act). In emergency cases, the Public Prosecutor or the Investigating Judge have the power to issue a provisory interception order; thereafter, they must submit the case to the Judicial Council to decide upon the order within three days from issuance of the provisory order (Article 4(6) of Act 2295/94).

The state officers of the competent organization draw up a detailed record of the ordered investigative acts and their findings. These are forwarded to the Public Prosecutor or the Investigating Judge, as the case may be, and the Judicial Council which issued the order. All evidence collected during the execution of the aforesaid order shall be included in the case file and be accessible to the parties. If the findings are irrelevant to the case under investigation, they are returned to the persons with whom they concern following a decision of the Hellenic Authority for Communication Security and Privacy, an independent agency established according to Article 19 paragraph 2 of the Constitution. Alternatively, if the notification of the persons involved and return of the collected data would put in danger the purpose for which the Judicial Council's order had been issued, they shall be destructed in the presence of the judicial authority which ordered their collection (Article 5(9) of Act 2295/1994).

### C. *Freezing of Assets*

*436.* Article 248(6) CCP empowers the Investigating Judge in cases of serious crimes to scrutinize the assets of the defendant if there is evidence that he may have enriched himself through the commission of the crimes under investigation. In such cases the Investigating Judge with the consent of the Prosecutor can access all relevant data kept with public authorities or private organizations including banks or other financial institutions with the exception of data, which are protected pursuant to the lawyer-client privilege or the confidentiality of communications statutes.

Following the above scrutiny of the defendant's assets, the Investigating Judge, with the Prosecutor's consent, may order the freezing of any alleged proceeds of the offence under investigation or other (tangible or intangible) assets originating from the same owned by the defendant or by third parties to which they had been transferred with the purpose of avoiding their confiscation. The freezing order is valid from the day it is served on all involved individuals or entities in possession of the assets without prior notification of the defendant or the above third parties. The sums of money which are necessary for the living expenses of the defendant or the third parties and their families as well as those needed for running costs of the frozen property and for legal fees with respect to the case are exempted from the freezing order (Article 261).

The freezing order must be served on the defendant and/or the third party within twenty days after its issuance, who have the right to file an appeal against the same to the competent Judicial Council. The latter has the power to quash or amend the freezing order (Article 262(2)). However, in practice, freezing orders are routinely confirmed. Freezing orders may be lifted or amended during the investigation by the Investigating Judge depending on its findings either *proprio motu* or at the request of the affected persons. The freezing order is automatically lifted if no court judgment is issued on the case within five years from its issuance (Article 262(4)).

According to Article 68 of the Penal Code, in case of a guilty verdict, all direct or indirect proceeds of an intentional criminal offence are subject to confiscation. In case these assets have been 'mixed' with lawfully obtained assets, confiscation applies to assets up to the value of the assets that derived from the offence. Confiscation of assets may not be imposed if it would be disproportionate, for example, if it would deprive the defendant or his family or third parties of living essentials. Confiscation of 'clean' assets of the convicted person may also be imposed up to the value of the proceeds of crime if the latter have not been found; alternatively, the Court may impose a monetary penalty of equal value.

*437.* Moreover, proceeds of crime may be subject to confiscation even when criminal proceedings have not been initiated or have been terminated because of the death, unavailability, etc., of the offender, or if the prosecution was terminated or declared inadmissible on other grounds. In these cases, confiscation shall be ordered by the Judicial Council or the Court (Article 40(3) of Act 4557/2018 on Money Laundering). These decisions are subject to appeal on the merits and on points of law according to Articles 495 and 504(3) CCP.

Act 4557/2018 as amended is the basic legal statute on money laundering, which implemented the EU Directive 2015/849. The main offence of laundering the proceeds of crime has a broad scope covering all forms of such conduct including criminal organizations. The offence requires knowledge with respect to the criminal source of the assets and the intention to conceal or cover up their true origin.

According to Article 47 of the above Act, the Hellenic Financial Intelligence Unit (FIU), which has seventeen members and is chaired by an acting or retired Deputy Prosecutor of *Areios Pagos*, is the competent authority to collect information from reports on suspicious transactions or any other source and make use of information communicated by foreign authorities. It also releases guidelines to natural persons or businesses covered by Act 4557/2018. The Hellenic FIU is a member of the FIU-Net and the Egmont Group and files its annual report with the Commission on Transparency of the Hellenic Parliament, the Ministry of Finance, the Ministry of Justice, and the Ministry of Citizens Protection.

The Chair of the FIU may issue, if necessary, a provisional freezing order of bank accounts or other suspicious assets even before the opening of criminal proceedings (Article 42(5) of the above Act). The freezing order is served on the persons or entities involved who have the right to file an appeal against the order within twenty days from its service before the competent Judicial Council. The freezing order together with the FIU case file shall be subsequently forwarded to the Public Prosecutor for further actions. The provisional freezing order of the FIU Chair cannot exceed nine months; in exceptional circumstances, it may be prolonged for another eight months, after the passing of which it is automatically lifted.

### *D. Special Investigative Acts*

*438.* Article 254 CCP regulates special investigative acts which may be ordered for a specific period of time by the Judicial Council, i.e., the use of undercover persons (police or investigative officers or private persons), with respect to criminal or terrorist organizations, counterfeiting, human trafficking or sexual abuse or exploitation of minors. In emergency situations, such measures may also be ordered by the Public Prosecutor or the Investigating Judge, who must submit their order within three days to the Judicial Council for confirmation.

The undercover activity may involve the facilitation of offences that the perpetrator had pre-decided to commit as well as the participation in routine activities of a criminal or terrorist organization. It may also involve controlled deliveries of narcotic substances according to Article 38 of Act 2145/1993, the interception of communications (*supra*, paragraph 435), the electronic surveillance of activities of individuals outside their home and the collection of personal data. Such activities may affect not only suspects but also third parties to the extent that it is necessary to uncover the above criminal acts. Data on third parties which are not related to the offences under investigation must be destroyed after the expiration of the special investigative measure except in cases where they prove the commission of certain unrelated serious offences by the third party (homicide, grievous bodily harm, sexual offences, high treason, offences against national security).

Undercover persons are supervised in their activities by the Public Prosecutor. All actions of the undercover persons must be taken on record in sufficient detail. Evidence acquired during the undercover activity which is not mentioned in the respective record cannot be relied upon for the conviction of the defendant.

*439.* Article 255 CCP allows the above acts with respect to bribery offences which are not envisaged or committed by a criminal organization if it is considered strictly necessary to uncover such offences. The respective order is issued by the Prosecutor for Economic Crimes (*supra*, paragraph 346) for a maximum period of three months which may be prolonged for another three months. All evidence collected can be used only in relation to the offences under investigation.

## §2. Powers, Rights and Duties Within the Framework of Arrest and Pre-trial Detention

### I. Introductory Remarks

*440.* The arrest and pre-trial detention of persons follow the rules enshrined in the Constitution (Articles 6 et seq.) and the Code of Criminal Procedure (Articles 275 et seq.). These provisions meet the requirements set out in Article 5 ECHR.

### II. The Warrants of Attachment and of Arrest

#### A. *The Warrant of Attachment*

*441.* Under Articles 270 and 272 CCP, the Investigating Judge may issue a warrant of attachment against the defendant who, though duly summoned, does not appear for interrogation without good reasons. The warrant of attachment is enforceable in the entire territory of the State, and all police authorities have a duty to bring the defendant before the Investigating Judge using reasonable force, if he refuses to comply with the warrant. After being brought before the Investigating Judge, the defendant has all the rights and the Investigating Judge all the powers already mentioned. Article 270(2) allows the Investigating Judge to close the formal investigation after issuing the warrant of attachment, i.e., without awaiting its enforcement.

*B. The Warrant of Arrest*

*442.* Article 6 of the Constitution and Article 276 CCP state that no person shall be deprived of his liberty unless upon a duly issued warrant of arrest. An arrest without a warrant is allowed only in cases of flagrant criminal offences (*infra*, paragraph 455). The warrant of arrest is issued by the Investigating Judge only in cases where pre-trial detention would be justified, i.e., on strong evidence that the person to be arrested committed a serious crime and only if his arrest is absolutely necessary to prevent him from fleeing or committing criminal offences (*infra*, paragraph 448). The Investigating Judge must consult the Public Prosecutor before issuing the warrant of arrest. The warrant of arrest must contain the name, the residence, and a description of the person to be arrested, the criminal offence he is charged with as well as the reasons which justify the arrest. The warrant is enforceable by all police authorities in the whole territory of the State under the orders of the Public Prosecutor (Article 277). Those who enforce the warrant of arrest must treat politely and show respect for the arrested person; reasonable force may be used only if necessary and putting of handcuffs is allowed on reasonable suspicion that the arrestee would escape (Article 278(2)). The details of the arrest (the place, the date, the hour, etc.) are laid down on a record drawn up by the police officers who carried out the arrest.

The arrest of a person is not allowed during a religious ceremony in a church or other place of worship, nor during the night in someone's residence unless the requirements of Article 256 are met (*supra*, paragraph 425).

*443.* Within twenty-four hours from his arrest or, if arrested outside the judicial district of the Investigating Judge, within the absolutely necessary time for his transport, the arrested person shall be brought before the Public Prosecutor who refers him to the Investigating Judge (Article 6 of the Constitution, Article 279 CCP).

The above strict time limits aim at ensuring that the arrested person's fundamental right to be promptly brought before a judge (Article 5(1)(c) ECHR) is respected and discourages improper police practices.[325]

The Investigating Judge acts as prescribed in Article 273 (*supra*, paragraph 431). After the examination of the defendant the Investigating Judge decides with the consent of the Public Prosecutor upon imposing restrictive measures or pre-trial detention on the defendant.

---

325. In *Kortesis v. Greece*, (Judgment of 12 Jun. 2012, at 52–54), the ECtHR found a breach of the applicant's right to be promptly brought before a judge because the police authorities, which had arrested him on suspicion of terrorist acts, manipulated the real time of his arrest in their respective report.

## III. Restrictive Measures on the Defendant

*444.* Article 282 CCP provides that during the formal investigation restrictive measures of varying intensity may be imposed on the defendant by the Investigating Judge with the Public Prosecutor's consent, if they are considered necessary to secure his presence at the proceedings and the enforcement of the sentence, if convicted, and/or to prevent him from committing other offences.

The restrictive measures may include the deposition of a surety by the defendant or a third person in his favour, the obligation to regularly appear at the police station of his residence or before other state authorities including Greek consular authorities in the home country of the defendant, the prohibition to travel outside the country, to visit certain places or to communicate with certain persons, etc. (Article 283(1)).

The imposition of the above measures is allowed only in cases of serious crimes or misdemeanours punishable by imprisonment of at least three months and only if there are serious indications that the defendant has committed the crime under investigation. According to the fundamental principle of proportionality, the Investigating Judge shall choose the less intrusive measure that fulfils the above purposes and shall specify it taking into account the circumstances of each case, the family and financial status of the defendant, etc.

*445.* The restrictive measures may be imposed by the Investigating Judge only after the interrogation of the defendant after consulting with the Prosecutor on their necessity. In case of a disagreement between the Investigating Judge and the Prosecutor, the matter is resolved by the Judicial Council. The restrictive measures are imposed by an order of the Investigating Judge, which states the reasons for their issuance. The order is served on the defendant, who has the right to appeal against it within ten days from notification before the Judicial Council which decides finally on the matter. The Judicial Council can confirm, amend, or reverse the order of the Investigating Judge (Article 290).

The defendant who fails to comply with the imposed conditions or to appear though duly summoned can be remanded in custody (Article 296).

*446.* The restrictive measures may be lifted or amended depending on the findings of the investigation, the passing of time and/or the defendant's conduct etc. The amendment or the lifting of the measures can be decided by the Investigating Judge during the formal investigation after hearing the Public Prosecutor, who submits a written recommendation, or by the Judicial Council which is competent to decide upon referral of the case to trial after the closing of the investigation, on their own initiative or at the defendant's or the Public Prosecutor's request (Article 291). The defendant and the Public Prosecutor can appeal against the order of the Investigating Judge rejecting their request within ten days from notification. They can also appeal before said Judicial Council against an order of the Investigating Judge which substitutes the restrictive measures with pre-trial detention (Article 291(3)) within ten days from notification or issue of the order respectively. The Judicial Council which refers the case to trial must always rule on continuation, amendment or lifting of the imposed measures until the trial hearing. It may also substitute the restrictive measures with pre-trial detention if it deems it necessary and the legal requirements thereto are fulfilled (Article 315). The trial court may lift or replace the pre-trial detention of the defendant with restrictive conditions during the trial hearing and whenever it postpones the trial hearing (Article 294).

Greece has implemented (by Act 4307/2014) the European Council Framework Decision 2009/829/JHA on the European Supervision Order, which allows the supervision of pre-trial restrictive measures on defendants who reside in another EU Member Sate by the authorities of his home country thus avoiding unnecessary pre-trial detention of non-residents.

## IV. House Arrest under Electronic Surveillance and Pre-trial Detention

### A. *House Arrest*

*447.* Article 284 CCP states that the Investigating Judge may decide the house arrest of the defendant under electronic surveillance, if in his view the above-mentioned less intrusive restrictive measures would not prevent him from fleeing or from committing new crimes. In his order, the Investigating Judge specifies the building or complex of buildings which is home of the defendant and the area around them in which he is allowed to freely move for his daily needs (food etc.). The defendant shall not interfere with the electronic device which is put on him and must pay in advance the cost of his surveillance for a period of six months. An exception applies if the defendant cannot afford the costs which will be on the State (Article 285).

House arrest is allowed in cases of serious crimes if there are sufficient indications that the defendant has committed the offence under investigation. It may also be imposed exceptionally in cases of homicide by negligence with multiple victims.

The house arrest cannot exceed six months; in cases of serious crimes, it may be prolonged for another six months with a maximum limit of eighteen months.

The above-described procedure (*supra*, paragraph 446) with respect to the lifting or replacement of the restrictive measures and the available legal remedies applies to house arrest as well. A violation of the conditions imposed on the defendant under house arrest may lead to his detention. The latter is mandatory if the defendant destroys or otherwise manipulates the electronic surveillance device (Article 284(6)).

### B. *Pre-trial Detention*

*448.* Pre-trial detention of the defendant is an exceptional measure, which is allowed in cases of serious crimes or in cases of homicide by negligence with multiple victims, only if neither the aforementioned restrictive measures nor the house arrest under electronic surveillance would ensure the defendant's presence at trial and/or the non-commission of new crimes.

According to Article 286 CCP, the defendant may be remanded in pre-trial detention on serious indications that he committed the crime under investigation and only if he is a flight risk based on the fact that he has no domicile or has made preparations to flee or has been a fugitive from justice in the past or has been convicted for escaping from prison or has violated restrictions with regard to his residence. Pre-trial detention may also be ordered to prevent the defendant from committing new crimes in view of his past or of the specifics of the criminal offence under investigation. The seriousness of the alleged crime alone can never justify the pre-trial detention of the defendant.

The detailed wording of Article 286 is evidence of the legislator's effort to tackle the persisting overuse of pre-trial detention in criminal practice.[326]

*449.* The Investigating Judge issues a pre-trial detention order after the examination of the defendant and with the consent of the Public Prosecutor, who also hears the defendant and his counsel prior to deciding whether he consents to the pre-trial detention (Article 288). A disagreement between the Investigating Judge and the Public Prosecutor is finally resolved by the Judicial Council within eight days. Pending the decision of the Judicial Council, the Investigating Judge orders the house arrest of the defendant; alternatively, he may order the defendant to surrender his passport and stay in the country.

The pre-trial detention order of the Investigating Judge or the decision of the Judicial Council must clearly state the reasons which make necessary the remand in custody of the defendant. The latter may appeal against the Investigating Judge's order before the Judicial Council within ten days from notification (Article 290). The appeal does not suspend the execution of the order. The above– described procedure with regard to the lifting or substituting of the restrictive measures imposed on the defendant by the Investigating Judge, the Judicial Council or the Court (Articles 291, 294 – *supra*, paragraph 446) also applies to the pre-trial detention.

*450.* Article 6(4) of the Constitution and Article 292(2) CCP stipulate that the pre-trial detention can under no circumstances exceed eighteen months in cases of serious crimes and nine months in cases of misdemeanours for which it is allowed. These are strict time limits which cannot be exceeded irrespective of the complexity of the case or other circumstances which may delay the proceedings. In other words, the defendant, who has been detained for the above-mentioned periods of time, must be released even before or during the trial hearing. This rule complies with the exceptional character of the pre-trial detention stated in Article 286 and the right of the defendant to a trial hearing within reasonable time (Article 6(1) ECHR).

The Code of Criminal Procedure sets strict time limits to the maximum length of pre-trial detention but also provides for the control of its continuation by the competent Judicial Council during the formal investigation and after indictment. Notably, Article 292 stipulates that six months after remanding the defendant to pre-trial detention (or three months in case of a misdemeanour) the Judicial Council shall

326. I. Anagnostopoulos, 'Untersuchungshaft und Verfahrensbeschleunigung – Das Beispiel Griechenlands', StraFo 2013, 454 et seq.; E. Lambropoulou, 'Pre-Trial detention in Greece: the Achilles heel of the prison system', in: P.H. van Kempen (ed.), *Pre-trial Detention, Human Rights, Criminal Procedural Law and Penitentiary Law, Comparative Law*, Intersentia, Cambridge etc., 2012, 425 et seq.

decide on its own motion upon continuation of the pre-trial detention. To this end, the Public Prosecutor submits a written recommendation and the defendant or his counsel is notified to submit the defendant's views in writing. The Judicial Council may call the Prosecutor, the defendant and his counsel to appear in person if it considers it necessary before taking a decision on continuation of the pre-trial detention. The once prolonged pre-trial detention shall be reviewed again ex officio after six months by the Judicial Council following the same procedure and may be prolonged again only in cases of serious crimes punishable with incarceration of up to fifteen years.

*451.* Article 293 CCP deals with the issue of the 'multiple' pre-trial detention ordered in cases where the defendant is accused of more than one criminal offence. In cases of concurrent offences committed by one act the time for the pre-trial detention runs from the day it was imposed even for one of them. The same rule applies in cases of two or more offences committed by two or more acts, if on the basis of the available evidence it would have been possible to examine the defendant on all offences. A second pre-trial order is only allowed if the evidence indicating the new offence was not available at the time of the first pre-trial order nor during the execution of the latter and until the last three months before its expiration. Second pre-trial detention cannot exceed twelve months. In cases of a series of the same criminal offence the time of the pre-trial detention runs from the first day of detention irrespective of the simultaneous or successive examination of the defendant on his various acts.

## §3. The Powers and Duties of the Public Prosecutor and the Investigating Officers in the Summary Investigation and the Preliminary Investigation

### I. Introductory Remarks

*452.* The above-discussed rules which govern the formal investigation also apply to the summary and the preliminary investigation. However, some highly intrusive measures (e.g., arrest, pre-trial detention, internment for a mental examination of the defendant, etc.) may be ordered only within the framework of the formal investigation.

### II. Powers in the Summary Investigation

*453.* Inspections of the crime scene, searches of places and persons, the seizure of evidence and the examination of witnesses are carried out in the summary investigation following the same rules set forth by the above-mentioned provisions of the Code of Criminal Procedure. The summary investigation is conducted by the Public Prosecutor who may personally carry out the investigative acts or commission the investigating officers, i.e., the district magistrates, police officers or officers of other special units to accomplish them (Articles 31(1), 243(1), 251). Mention has been made that a person's home cannot be searched but only in the presence of a judge or a public prosecutor (*supra*, paragraph 425). It follows that if such a search is deemed necessary in the course of the summary investigation, the investigating officers have to request a member of a judicial authority to be present at the search.

*454.* The examination of the defendant is conducted in the summary investigation according to the provisions which govern the formal investigation (Article 106). However, there are two exceptions to this rule. First, the defendant is not obliged to appear in person before the investigating officer; he may be represented by his counsel who files on his behalf defence submissions. The investigating officer can nevertheless call the defendant to appear in person, if he believes that this is necessary for the purposes of the investigation. Second, the defendant has the right to have counsel appointed only if he is indigent.

After the closing of the summary investigation the Public Prosecutor evaluates the evidence and decides upon further proceedings pursuant to Article 245, i.e., to refer the case to trial, to order a formal investigation, or to file a recommendation for acquittal with the Judicial Council, (*supra*, paragraph 340).

## III. Powers in the Investigation of Flagrant Offences and in Other Emergency Cases

*455.* A person may be arrested only upon a duly issued warrant of arrest (*supra*, paragraph 432). An exception to this basic principle enshrined in the Constitution (Article 6(2)) and the Code of Criminal Procedure (Article 276(1)) applies to flagrant offences. Article 242 stipulates that a criminal offence is *in flagranti* if it is caught while being committed. An offence is also considered flagrant while the state authorities or the public are in hot pursuit of the suspect or when he is caught shortly after the crime with traces or items connected to it. An offence ceases to be flagrant if a whole day after the day of its commission has passed.

If the *in flagranti* requirements are met, all investigating officers and all policemen have a duty, and every citizen has a right to arrest the suspect (Article 275). In cases of criminal offences which can be prosecuted only at the victim's request (*supra*, paragraph 349), he who intends to arrest the perpetrator must call the alleged victim to declare orally or in writing his/her wish that the perpetrator shall be prosecuted. Moreover, the Public Prosecutor has the power to issue a warrant of arrest against the alleged perpetrator of a flagrant offence. The person arrested *in flagranti* must be brought before the Public Prosecutor within the strict time limits set forth by Article 279 CCP and Article 6 of the Constitution discussed above (*supra*, paragraphs 442–443).

*456.* In all flagrant offences as well as in other emergency cases where any delay could result in the loss of evidence etc., the police and other investigating officers must take all appropriate measures and carry out all the necessary acts in order to secure the evidence and to identify the perpetrators of the criminal offence (e.g., search and seizure, taking of fingerprints, inspection of the scene of the crime, etc.)

and notify the soonest possible the Public Prosecutor of the Misdemeanour Court to whom they forward the case file with all the evidence secured so far (Article 245(2), *supra*, paragraph 341).

## IV. Powers in the Preliminary Investigation

*457.* In the preliminary investigation, the Public Prosecutor and/or the investigating officers who assist him, perform the acts which are necessary to collect the evidence which is required in order to decide upon criminal prosecution (Article 243). The preliminary investigation is conducted in a similar way to the summary investigation. The suspect is invited to submit his views with respect to the act under investigation and has all the basic rights mentioned above (Article 244 – *supra*, paragraph 391). A witness testimony of a person during the preliminary investigation who became a defendant in respect of the same act at a later stage must be removed from the case file and is excluded as evidence against him (Article 244(3)).

# Chapter 3. The Inquiry in Court

*458.* In previous chapters, the basic rules which apply to all stages of the criminal procedure with respect to the powers and duties of the Public Prosecutor and the Court, the evidence and the rights of the parties have been explained.

In this chapter, the most important of the specific rules which govern the trial in court are set forth.

## §1. The Trial in the Misdemeanour Courts

### I. The Attendance of the Parties

*459.* The defendant, who was duly summoned shall appear in person before the Court (Article 340(1)).[327] Alternatively, he may choose not to appear in person but empower in writing a lawyer to represent him at the trial (Article 340(3)). A power of attorney must state the defendant's permanent residence and have his signature certified by a public authority or a lawyer. The Court has the power to order the defendant to appear in person if it deems such presence necessary for the truth-finding process. The failure of the defendant to comply with the Court's order may trigger the issue of a warrant of attachment against him (Article 340(3)). In court practice, defendants often make use of their right to be represented by a lawyer during the trial hearing or part thereof, especially in lengthy trial hearings and/or when they reside in a foreign country.

*460.* The defendant who fails to appear in Court though duly summoned, is tried *in absentia* (Articles 340(4)). Before proceeding with the hearing in the defendant's absence the Court must establish that the defendant has been duly summoned (*supra*, paragraph 386) including his information that his failure to appear will result in him being tried *in absentia*. The Court shall adjourn the hearing and order a proper notification of the defendant, if the latter was not summoned at all or in case of procedural irregularities with respect to his summons (e.g., errors in the writ of summons, errors in the bailiff's certificate etc.). The Court can also adjourn the hearing if the absent defendant notifies the Court by any appropriate means (e.g., through another person appearing in Court who testifies with regard to the reasons of the defendant's absence, by telegram, facsimile, letter, etc.) of the good reasons that prevented him from appearing before Court and asks for an adjournment of the hearing (Article 349(1)).

The absence of the defendant has no legal influence on the burden of proof, i.e., the burden to prove the defendant's guilt beyond reasonable doubt is on the prosecuting State (*supra*, paragraph 405). However, the chances of an absent defendant, who cannot present evidence in his defence or otherwise rebut the charges against him in court assisted by counsel, to be acquitted on the merits are diminished.

327. *See* E. Billis/P. Gkaniatsos, 'Report on Greece', in: S. Quattrocolo/ S. Ruggeri (eds.), *Personal Participation in Criminal Proceedings*, Springer, Cham, 2019, 182 et seq.

*461*. Article 341 CCP gives the defendant who could not appear before the Court on good reasons nor was he able to notify the Court thereof, the right to oppose a guilty judgment issued in his absence and request a re-trial of the case. To this purpose the defendant has to lodge an appeal with the Secretary of the Court which issued the appealed judgment within fifteen days after its delivery stating the reasons (force majeure or other good reasons) for which he could not appear before the Court or notify the same of the reasons of his absence. The appeal does not suspend the enforcement of the judgment; however, the Public Prosecutor may order the suspension of the execution of the judgment until the appeal has been dealt with. If the Prosecutor declines to suspend the execution of the judgment, the defendant has the right to challenge within two days the Prosecutor's decision before the Judicial Council. The defendant's appeal against the judgment *in absentia* shall be dealt with on a priority basis and if admitted the judgment is quashed and a re-trial of the case is ordered. In misdemeanour cases, the above right to appeal the judgment *in absentia* is granted only if the judgment is not appealable before a second instance court (Article 341(2)).

*462*. A similar remedy is provided to defendants who had been considered persons of unknown residence (Article 157, *supra*, paragraph 383) and were convicted *in absentia* for a misdemeanour. They have the right to challenge the judgment if the latter cannot be challenged by an ordinary appeal and request its annulment before its execution or within eight days after its execution on the basis that they had been wrongly considered persons of unknown residence (Article 430 CCP). The appeal does not suspend the execution of the sentence imposed; however, the Public Prosecutor may order its suspension until the competent court decides thereupon. The appeal shall be dealt with on a priority basis by the Court and if successful, a re-trial of the case is ordered (Article 431).

*463*. The defendant has the right to attend and actively participate in the hearing. The hearing shall continue if the defendant deliberately leaves the courtroom. The Court may allow defence counsel to represent the defendant who left the courtroom for good reasons. The Court may also order the defendant to be removed from the courtroom and be represented by his counsel if he insists on disturbing the order in the courtroom through inappropriate acts despite the presiding judge's warning about such removal (Article 347). The defendant is allowed to re-enter the courtroom before his oral submission to the court at the latest and take knowledge of the trial's summary transcript which is read out by the Court's secretary. The Court may re-order the defendant's removal from the courtroom if after his return he insists on behaving inappropriately.

In the case of a serious health problem, which seems to prevent the defendant from further attending the hearing, the Court shall order his examination by an expert. Should the expert confirm the defendant's inability to attend the trial, the Court may adjourn the hearing. If it is expected that the health problem of the defendant will persist for a long period of time, the Court may order the trial to be continued in his absence and his representation by defence counsel (Article 348).

*464*. The defendant has the right to appoint up to three lawyers of his choice (Article 89(1)). In cases of misdemeanours punishable by a maximum sentence exceeding two years indigent defendants have the right to have counsel appointed (Article 91 CCP, Article 6 (2) of Act 3226/2004 on Legal Aid as amended). The Court appoints defence counsel on its own motion in the above-discussed cases of the defendant's inability to (further) attend the hearing because of health problems or other good reasons (Articles 344 and 348).

*465*. The injured party supporting the charges may be represented in court by a duly appointed lawyer (up to three). For indigent persons, legal aid is provided with respect to offences punishable by a maximum sentence exceeding two years (Article 6(6) of Law Act 3226/2004 as amended). A duty to appear in person applies when the injured party is an individual who has been summoned to testify as a witness in court. Such testimony is not given under oath (Article 221).

All summoned witnesses have a duty to appear in court. Failure to do so for no good reasons, may trigger the issue of a warrant of attachment against them and a fine (Articles 231, 353). The Court can adjourn the hearing if material witnesses fail to appear (Article 352).

## II. The Course of the Trial

*466*. The trial before the misdemeanour courts follows the basic principles set forth in previous chapters, i.e., it is public, oral and moderately adversarial (*supra*, paragraphs 375–380). The court hearing starts with the announcement of the defendant's name. The Presiding Judge asks the defendant his name, date of birth, family status, domicile, profession, and any other information regarding his identity and informs him of his right to defend himself against the charges brought and submit his comments after the examination of each witness as well as after the presentation of any other piece of evidence (Articles 342, 343). Thereafter, the injured party, if any, constitutes itself party to the trial proceedings according to the law (*supra*, paragraph 401) and the Public Prosecutor reads out a summary of the charges. The Presiding Judge asks the defendant how he pleads to the charges and informs him that he will have the opportunity to answer them as he deems appropriate orally after the closing of the examination of the evidence (Article 343).

*467*. Objections of the defendant to the progress of the trial on procedural grounds with respect to the contents of the writ of summons, the notification of the defendant or other procedural errors must be put forward at this stage; otherwise, the defendant's claims for such errors are procedurally defaulted (*supra*, paragraph 386). The same applies in respect of the Court's competence *ratione loci* (Article 126(1)), while the Court shall examine on its own motion at any stage of the trial its competence *ratione materiae* and shall refer the case to the competent court if it lacks jurisdiction (Article 120). Claims of dissolution of the right to prosecute such as limitation by time, withdrawal of the criminal complaint etc. (*supra*, paragraphs

367–374) are usually discussed at the beginning of the trial hearing for practical reasons, though the parties and the Court are not prevented from addressing them at a later stage of the trial.

*468.* After the examination of the above objections the evidence hearing starts. It includes the examination of witnesses and experts (Articles 350 et seq.), which is conducted according to the rules of evidence already mentioned (*supra*, paragraphs 404–409), as well as the reading out of all written evidence (e.g., reports of the investigative officers, statements of witnesses who cannot appear, documents or other pieces of evidence presented by the parties etc.). Other relevant evidence (e.g., photographs, audio and video tapes, etc.) shall also be presented in the appropriate manner (Articles 362–363).

*469.* The last stage of the evidence hearing is the statement of the defendant who is called to answer the charges (Article 365). The defendant has the right to remain silent (Article 104). In practice, defendants rarely use this right, primarily for tactical reasons (*supra*, paragraph 405). The defendant takes no oath and answers the charges orally and is free to put forward any facts or arguments which, in his view, rebut the charges. The defendant shall not be interrupted while addressing the Court except if he insists on stating facts irrelevant to the case. The Presiding Judge, the Public Prosecutor and the members of the Court may put questions to the defendant or ask for clarifications after he has finished his statement. The other parties are not allowed to directly question the defendant; they may only ask the Presiding Judge to put questions to the defendant. An exception applies with respect to co-defendants who have been incriminated by the defendant's statement; they have the right to directly question the defendant, albeit only on the incriminating facts he has stated. This exception is in line with the right to confront witnesses under Article 6 (3)(d) ECHR and the relevant case law of the Strasbourg Court.[328]

During the trial hearing, the defendant has the right to communicate with counsel but is not allowed to consult him before answering a question (Article 364). The defendant's statement(s) in the pre-trial proceedings are not read out in court. Parts of the defendant's statements may, however, be read out in court, if the facts stated therein are inconsistent with his oral statement before the Court (Article 365(2)).

*470.* The defendant's oral statement is followed by the closing arguments of the Public Prosecutor and those of counsel for the injured party supporting the charges and counsel for the defendant. The Public Prosecutor and the defendant or one of his counsels may answer each other's closing arguments in which case also the injured party has the same right (Article 367). The defendant and his counsel have always the right to speak the last word.

*471.* The Court retires to deliberate on the issue of guilt and returns its verdict in public (Articles 368–369, *supra*, paragraph 387). If the defendant is found guilty, the Public Prosecutor recommends the sentence to be imposed on him and the Court

328. *See*, for example, the ECtHR judgment in *Oddone and Pecci v. San Marino* of 17 Oct. 2019, at 93 et seq.

hears the defendant's and his counsel's submissions on the matter including mitigating factors (Article 369(3). The injured party has no right to speak at this stage. The Court retires again to deliberate and pronounces in public its decision on the sentence. If there are other issues to be dealt with (e.g., confiscation or return of assets, return of bail sums etc.), a decision on these follows the passing of the sentence (Articles 372–373). Assets which were seized during the proceedings are returned to the victim of the offence to compensate the damage inflicted, if it is established that they originate from the offence (Article 373(3)).

## III. Special Rules in Trials for Flagrant Misdemeanours

*472.* In flagrant misdemeanours (*supra*, paragraphs 341, 455–456), the police officer or other investigating officer who arrested the alleged perpetrator must promptly bring him before the Public Prosecutor and submit a report on the arrest together with any evidence gathered. The Public Prosecutor has the power to directly refer the case for trial before the competent Misdemeanour Curt, if he is of the view that the evidence justifies such referral (Articles 417–418).

The apprehended defendant shall be orally informed by the Prosecutor of the charges against him (a written record must be drawn up in this respect) and the case is referred for trial before the Single-Judge or the Three-Member Misdemeanour Court on the same day or the next day at the latest. The Public Prosecutor may order the detention of the defendant at a police station until the trial takes place but for no longer than twenty-four hours since he was brought before the Prosecutor (Article 419).

*473.* Witnesses and co-defendants are orally invited to attend the trial hearing (Articles 420–421), while the injured party supporting the charges may call witnesses in court with no obligation of prior notifying the defendant. The defendant has the right to request the adjournment of the trial hearing for three days with the purpose of preparing his defence and to have counsel appointed by the Court if he wishes so (Article 423). In this case, the Court decides on continuation of the defendant's detention. The Court may adjourn the hearing for a second time for up to fifteen days if further evidence is needed, in which case the detention of the defendant shall be lifted or replaced by other restrictive measures if necessary (Article 424, *supra*, paragraphs 444–446).

In all other respects, the trial hearing before the competent Misdemeanour Court in flagrant misdemeanours follows the above-described rules.

## §2. The Trial in the Courts for Serious Crimes

## I. The Trial in the Mixed Jury Courts

*474.* The trial in the mixed jury courts, which consist of three professional judges and four jurors and are competent to try certain categories of capital or serious crimes (homicide, rape, serious arson etc., *supra*, paragraph 313), follows the same basic rules already explained with respect to the misdemeanour courts, i.e., i is a public, oral and moderately adversarial procedure.

*475.* Articles 377 et seq. set out the procedure to be followed for the selection o the four jurors who will sit with the three professional judges. At the final stage, the four jurors are drawn successively by lot out of ten at the beginning of the hearing (Article 394). After the pronouncement of the name of each juror the Public Prosecutor and the defendant or his counsel have the right to request the juror's recusal with no obligation to state the grounds for such request. The challenged juror is excused and the next is drawn by lot. The Public Prosecutor and the defendant cannot, however, challenge more than two jurors each (Article 396). The jurors take their seats on the bench joining the judges, and they give an oath, the wording of which is provided in Article 398.

*476.* The procedure begins with the reading out of the charges by the Public Prosecutor; thereafter, the names of the witnesses called by the Public Prosecutor, by the defendant and the injured party as well as the indictment, which is contained in the judicial council's decision (*supra*, paragraph 383), are read out (Article 403). The next step is the examination of the witnesses followed by the presentation of all other evidence, the oral submission by the defendant and the closing arguments by the Public Prosecutor and counsel for the parties in accordance with the rules mentioned above.

*477.* The defendant has the right to appoint up to three defence counsel of his choice. The defendant is also entitled to ask before the trial to have counsel appointed irrespective of his indigence by sending a letter to the Public Prosecutor (Article 340(1)). The appointment of counsel to defendants who appear in court with no lawyer is mandatory irrespective of their financial situation. The appointed lawyer shall be given the time required to prepare the defence of the accused person; for this purpose the court schedules a new session within a month.

The defence lawyer is taken from a list in alphabetical order provided on a monthly basis by the Bar Association in the Court' district. In cases which are expected to last for a long time two or three lawyers from the above list may be appointed to the defendant in order to ensure that all of the court sessions will be attended by at least one of them (Article 340(2)). All lawyers admitted to the Bar Association may be included in the above list upon their request provided that they have participated as defence counsel or counsel for the injured party supporting the charges in at least five cases with no need to demonstrate any other special education and/or experience in criminal defence (Article 3(3) of Act 3226/2004 as amended). The defendant has no right to participate *pro se* in the trial hearings for serious crimes. Non-appearance of the defendant and/or his counsel or withdrawal of the latter in subsequent court sessions for no good reasons does not prevent the trial form continuing in their absence.

If the defendant fails to appear in court though duly summoned at his known residence, he is tried *in absentia* (Article 432(2)). In cases of defendants of unknown residence who are not apprehended after indictment, the procedure shall be suspended until their arrest or surrender (Article 432(1)). As in misdemeanour cases (*supra* paragraph 461), a special legal remedy against *in absentia* convictions is provided to those defendants who failed to appear in court for good reasons, which, if successful, results in a re-trial of the case (Article 435).

*478.* The professional judges and the jurors decide together on the issue of guilt by absolute majority; if the defendant is found guilty, they also decide by absolute majority on the sentence to be imposed (Article 404). The professional judges decide alone on procedural issues such as the competence of the Court, the dissolution of the right to prosecute, irregularities with respect to the notification of the defendant, and other issues set out in Article 405.

*479.* All the rules stated above also apply to the Mixed Jury Court of Appeal which handles the appeals against the decisions of the Mixed Jury (Article 408, *supra*, paragraph 313).

## II. The Trial in the Courts of Appeal for Serious Crimes

*480.* The greatest part of serious crimes (serious theft or embezzlement, serious fraud, robbery, drug trafficking, etc.) are tried by the Court of Appeal for Serious Crimes as a first-instance court. This Court sits either as a single-judge court or as a three-member court depending on the offence (*supra*, paragraph 314). The procedural rules which apply to the mixed jury court (bar those concerning the jurors) are in principle applicable to this courts as well.

*481.* Appeals against the judgments of the Single-Judge Court of Appeal are heard by the Three-Member Court of Appeal, while appeals against judgments of the latter are heard by the Five-Member Court of Appeal following the same procedural rules.

# §3. The Legal Remedies

## I. Introductory Remarks

*482.* The Code of Criminal Procedure provides a wide range of legal remedies with respect to court judgments and a rather limited one with respect to decisions of judicial councils (Articles 477 et seq.). The ordinary legal remedies, i.e., the appeal and the appeal by way of cassation may be employed against judgments of the courts and to a limited extent against decisions of the judicial councils. Moreover, various special legal remedies, such as the appeal against a conviction *in absentia*, the appeal against the writ of summons, the appeal against the decision of pre-trial detention, etc., have been discussed in the context of the relevant procedures (*supra*, paragraphs 335, 449, 461–462).

*483*. Some general principles apply to all legal remedies unless stated otherwise in the applicable provisions (Article 463). The general principles enshrined in Articles 462–476 are the following:

(i) A legal remedy is admissible only when it is expressly granted by law and may be lodged only by whoever has a lawful interest in challenging the decision (Article 464). For example, a defendant has no right, as a rule, to appeal against an acquittal decision of a judicial council or a trial court.

(ii) Legal remedies are admissible only if they have been lodged within the time limits and following the formalities prescribed by the law (Article 473). As a rule, legal remedies must be lodged within ten days after the pronouncement of the decision of the trial court or after the decision was served on the party entitled thereto in cases of trial by default. The decisions of the judicial councils can be challenged within the same term after they have been served on the party entitled thereto (Article 473). If the appellant is domiciled in a foreign country and was tried *in absentia*, he may lodge the legal remedy within thirty days. As a rule, legal remedies are lodged before the Secretary of the Court or the Judicial Council that issued the decision in question. The person entitled to appeal the decision may also lodge his appeal before the Secretary of the District Court of his domicile or before the competent Greek consular authority if he resides in a foreign country or before the Director of the Penitentiary where he is detained (Article 474). The Public Prosecutor may also lodge the legal remedy by facsimile or e-mail. The Secretary before whom the legal remedy is lodged shall draft a report including the grounds on which said remedy is based (Article 474(2)). If no such grounds are mentioned therein, the legal remedy will be rejected as inadmissible. Alternatively, the legal remedy may be drafted on a separate document which is handed over to the above Secretary who certifies its deposition.

(iii) A duly lodged legal remedy transfers the case to the competent court only to the extent that the decision of the first-instance court was challenged (*tantum devolotum quantum appellatum*, Article 502(2)). For example, the Court of Appeal will review only the sentence imposed on the defendant, if the latter has appealed the sentencing decision of the Court of First Instance, but not the guilty verdict. However, Article 469 stipulates that the overturn or amendment of the first instance decision by the appellate court in favour of the appellant defendant extends also to his co-defendants who did not appeal the decision, provided that the quashing or amending of the latter was not based on grounds exclusively related to the person of the appellant (e.g., acquittal by reason of insanity, etc.).

(iv) The principle of *non reformatio in peius* applies to legal remedies lodged by the convicted defendant or the Public Prosecutor in his favour against the judgments of the first-instance court. The same principle does not apply if a legal remedy was lodged (also) against the defendant nor with respect to decisions of the judicial councils (Article 470).

(v) The legal remedies have a suspensive effect except stated otherwise in law or decided otherwise by the trial court (Article 471). A case becomes res judicata either if no legal remedy has been lodged within the applicable time limits or after the judgment of the last appellate court has been issued.

*484*. Legal remedies which are considered inadmissible for any reason (e.g., lack of lawful interest, non-compliance with the formalities, non-appealable decisions, etc.) are dealt with *in camera* by the competent Judicial Council or the competent Court after hearing the Public Prosecutor and the parties concerned (Article 476).

## II. The Ordinary Legal Remedies Against the Decisions of the Judicial Councils

### A. *Appeal*

*485*. The defendant has the right to appeal against an indicting decision of the Judicial Council of the Misdemeanour Court for a serious crime only on procedural nullities grounds or for errors with respect to the applicable substantive laws (Article 478).

*486*. The Public Prosecutor of the Court of Appeal may appeal against any decision of the Judicial Council of the Misdemeanour Court either against or in favour of the defendant on legal or factual grounds. The appeal must be lodged within one month from the issuance of the decision (Article 479).

*487*. All aforementioned appeals are heard by the Judicial Council of the Court of Appeal in the judicial district of which sits the Judicial Council of the Misdemeanour Court that issued the appealed decision (Article 481). The appellate Judicial Council decides *in camera* as a three-member council (Article 9) on the appeal after considering the Public Prosecutor's written recommendation and the appellant's submissions, and has the power to quash, amend or confirm the appealed decision. The Judicial Council may exceptionally call the parties and the Prosecutor to appear in person in order to argue their case (Articles 310(2), 318).

### B. *Appeal by Way of Cassation*

*488*. A right to appeal by way of cassation against decisions of the Judicial Council is granted only to the Public Prosecutor, while the defendant has no such right.

The Public Prosecutor of the Misdemeanour Court may appeal by way of cassation indicting or acquittal decisions of the Judicial Council of the above Court on serious crimes charges against or in favour of the defendant (Article 483(1)).

The same right is conferred on the Public Prosecutor of the Court of Appeal with respect to the decisions issued by the Judicial Council of the above Court (Article 483(2)).

The General Prosecutor of *Areios Pagos* has the right to appeal by way of cassation any decision of any Judicial Council of the first or the appellate instance for an error of law within thirty days after the issue of the decision (Article 483(3)). It should be noted that the time limits for the appeal by way of cassation run after the expiration of those provided for the appeal.

The General Prosecutor of *Areios Pagos* may also appeal by way of cassation in the interests of law against any decision of any Judicial Council for an error of law including the infringement of procedural provisions after the passing of the above time limits (Articles 483(3). The appeal by way of cassation in the interests of law which shall be considered by *Areios Pagos in pleno* does not affect res judicata and the interests of the parties in the case involved.

*489.* The errors of law which can sustain an appeal before *Areios Pagos* are mentioned in Article 484(1). These are: the infringement of procedural provisions under pain of nullity; the erroneous interpretation or application of the relevant substantive criminal provisions; res judicata; lack of sufficient reasoning of the decision; erroneous rejection of the appeal as inadmissible; and exercise of jurisdiction *ultra vires*.

*490.* *Areios Pagos* decides sitting *in camera* as a three-member council (Articles 10(1), 485) after considering the Public Prosecutor's written recommendation and the parties' submissions. *Areios Pagos* may exceptionally call the Prosecutor and the parties to appear in person in order to argue their case. Appeals in the interests of law lodged by the General Prosecutor of *Areios Pagos* are handled by the Court's plenary session (Article 10(2)).

## III. The Ordinary Legal Remedies Against the Decisions of the Courts

### A. *Appeal*

*491.* According to Article 489, the defendant has the right to appeal against the convicting judgment of a One-Member Misdemeanour Court, which imposes imprisonment exceeding two months or a pecuniary sentence higher than EUR 2,000 or community service exceeding 240 hours. Decisions of the Three-Member Misdemeanour Court or the Court of Appeal for Misdemeanours as a first-instance court (*supra*, paragraphs 312, 315) may be appealed by the defendant, if he has been convicted to imprisonment exceeding four months or to a pecuniary sentence higher than EUR 3,000 or to community service exceeding 480 hours. The defendant who has been convicted by the Mixed Jury Court or the Court of Appeal for Serious Crimes may appeal its judgment if the sentence imposed is a life sentence or imprisonment exceeding two years or in case of conviction for a misdemeanour imprisonment exceeding one year.

*492.* The Public Prosecutor of the Misdemeanour Court has the right to appeal against all the above-mentioned decisions under the same terms as the defendant either in favour or against the latter. Furthermore, the Public Prosecutor of the Misdemeanour Court may appeal against any conviction the Single-Judge Misdemeanour Court of his judicial district in favour or against the defendant, while the

Public Prosecutor of the Court of Appeal has the same right with respect to any such convicting decision of the Three-Member Misdemeanour Court of his judicial district (Article 491). The Public Prosecutor of the Court of Appeal has the right to appeal in favour or against the defendant against convictions by the Mixed Jury Court or of the Court of Appeal for Serious Crimes or for Misdemeanours of his judicial district. The appeals lodged by the Public Prosecutor against acquittal judgments or against convictions to the detriment of the convicted defendant (e.g., requesting a more severe conviction and/or sentence) must be sufficiently reasoned, i.e., they shall clearly state the errors of the appealed judgment; otherwise they will be rejected as inadmissible (Articles 487, 491(2)). This requirement seeks to prevent an overuse of the Prosecutor's power to appeal court judgments against defendants who have already been submitted to a trial hearing.

*493*. The defendant may appeal an acquittal decision only if the acquittal was based on remorse after the criminal offence (*supra*, paragraph 369) or if the reasons contained in the decision unnecessarily damage the defendant's reputation (Article 486).

*494*. The Public Prosecutor of the Misdemeanour Court has the right to appeal against acquittal decisions of the Misdemeanour Courts in his judicial district, while the Public Prosecutor of the Court of Appeal has the same right with respect to the decisions of the Misdemeanour Courts in his judicial district (Article 486(1).

Unanimous acquittal decisions of the Mixed Jury Court or of the Three-Member Court of Appeal for Serious Crimes cannot be appealed against. The Public Prosecutor of the Court of Appeal may appeal acquittal decisions of said courts taken by majority only if the dissenting member(s) of the court found the defendant guilty (Article 486(2)).

*495*. Article 488 confers a right on the defendant and the Public Prosecutor to appeal against a court's decision which declined to handle the case *ratione materiae* and referred the case to another court. A right of appeal is also provided to the defendant, the injured party supporting the charges and third parties with respect to court decisions on confiscation of items or assets related to the criminal offence or their return (Article 495).

*496*. The trial hearing before the appellate courts follows in principle the same basic rules that have been already explained (*supra*, paragraphs 466–471). However, one should take note of the following three specific provisions in the appellate proceedings:

First, the Appellate Court shall reject the appeal and confirm the appealed decision if the appellant fails to appear in court though duly summoned (Article 501(1)). However, a duly lodged appeal must be handled even in the absence of the appellant, if Article 368 lit. b, c, applies, i.e., where the proceedings must be terminated on limitation by time or res judicata or amnesty grounds or because the required criminal complaint has been withdrawn or the defendant has died.

Second, the Appellate Court reviews the case only within limits set by the grounds on which the appeal is based (*tantum devolutum quantum appellatum*) (Article 502(2) *supra*, paragraph 483).

Third, if the Appellate Court quashes the decision of the first-instance Court for procedural errors (*supra*, paragraph 386), it shall not refer the case for re-trial before the first-instance Court but will try the case issuing a non-appealable judgment (Article 502(4)).

*B. Appeal by Way of Cassation*

*497.* As a rule, an appeal by way of cassation before *Areios Pagos* may be lodged against judgments of the first-instance courts which cannot be appealed before an appellate court as well as against decisions of the appellate courts (Article 504).

*498.* The defendant has the right to appeal by way of cassation against a conviction within twenty days after the engrossed judgment has been registered lodging his appeal before the Secretary of the Court which issued the decision. He may also lodge his appeal by way of cassation or supplement the same by serving a document through a bailiff on the General Prosecutor of *Areios Pagos* within the same time limits (Articles 505(1), 473(2)).

*499.* The Public Prosecutor of the Misdemeanour Court may appeal by way of cassation against judgments of the Three-Member or Single-Judge Misdemeanour Courts in his judicial district. The Public Prosecutor of the Court of Appeal may appeal by way of cassation against judgments of the Court of Appeal, the Mixed Jury Courts of Appeal, the Mixed Jury Courts and the Misdemeanour Courts in his judicial district (Article 505(1)). The above appeals must be lodged within twenty days after the engrossed judgment has been registered (Article 507).

The General Prosecutor of *Areios Pagos* may appeal by way of cassation against any decision of any Court within thirty days after an engrossed copy of the decision has been registered (Articles 505(2), 507). Thereafter, he may lodge an appeal by way of cassation only in the interests of law, which is handled by *Areios Pagos in pleno* and does not affect res judicata or the interests of the parties in the case involved.

*500.* The defendant may appeal by way of cassation against an acquittal decision only if the acquittal is based on remorse after the criminal offence (Article 506).

*501.* The Public Prosecutors of the Courts mentioned above (*supra*, paragraph 345) may appeal against acquittal decisions only for erroneous interpretation or application of the relevant substantive criminal provisions (Article 506).

*502.* An appeal by way of cassation is also provided for the defendant and the Public Prosecutor against the decision of a Court which declined its competence *ratione materiae* and referred the case to another court, if said decision cannot be challenged before an appellate court (Article 504(2)). A right of appeal by way of cassation is also granted to the defendant, the injured party supporting the charges and third parties with respect to court decisions on confiscation of items or assets related to the criminal offence if such decisions are not appealable before an appellate court (Article 504(3)).

*503.* The Criminal Section of *Areios Pagos* sits as a Five-Member Court presided by one of its Vice-Presidents and hears the appeals in public (Articles 10, 515). The defendant and the injured party supporting the charges must be represented by counsel. The Court hears oral arguments by the Prosecutor, the injured party's counsel and the defendant's counsel and returns its judgment in writing at a later point. The representation of the parties by counsel before *Areios Pagos* is mandatory (Article 512(3)) given that the Court sits only on questions of law. Indigent defendants may request the appointment of counsel (Articles 3, 7 of Act 3226/2004 on Legal Aid as amended). The same applies to injured parties who are victims of certain categories of crimes (e.g., terrorism, torture, human trafficking, sexual abuse or exploitation, racism, homicide, crimes against property, etc.). If the appellant does not appear before the Court though duly summoned, the appeal is rejected (Article 514). However, *Areios Pagos* shall apply the milder statute which entered into force after the pronouncement of the appealed decision even in the appellant's absence.

*504.* *Areios Pagos* considers only errors of law that are mentioned in Article 510 (1): infringement of procedural provisions under pain of nullity in the course of the trial hearing; violation of the public character of the trial hearing; lack of sufficient reasoning of the Court's decision; erroneous interpretation or application of the relevant provisions of the substantive criminal law; res judicata; lack of competence *ratione materiae*; and exercise of jurisdiction *ultra vires*.

The appellant defendant has the right to submit a supplementary document of appeal fifteen days before the Court hearing at the latest, in which he may invoke errors of law not included in the initial appeal or further argue those already stated (Article 509).

*505.* *Areios Pagos* quashes the appealed decision for one or more errors of law mentioned above. Whenever *Areios Pagos* vacates a decision on the grounds of res judicata or exercise of jurisdiction *ultra vires*, it orders the termination of the proceedings (Article 517), while in cases of lack of competence *ratione materiae* it refers the case for trial before the competent Court (Article 516). In cases of erroneous interpretation or application of substantive criminal law *Areios Pagos* acquits the appellant if the acts do not constitute a criminal offence according to the law; otherwise, it refers the case for a new trial to the same Court consisting of other judges than those who issued the quashed decision or to another Court of the same rank (Articles 518, 519, 522). The same applies to all other errors of law. If the appealed decision is quashed only with respect to the confiscation or return of items or assets related to the criminal offence and their ownership is disputed, the case shall be referred to the civil division of the appellate court (Article 520).

The trial Court which tries the case after its referral by *Areios Pagos* is bound to the principle of *non reformatio in peius* (*supra*, paragraph 483), if the appeal by way of cassation was lodged by the defendant or in his favour (Article 524).

## IV. Extraordinary Legal Remedies

*506.* A final conviction or acquittal judgment bars any new prosecution or conviction with respect to the same act (*non bis in idem, supra*, paragraphs 372–374).

The re-opening of a finally adjudicated case in favour of the convicted person is possible under the Code of Criminal Procedure only in exceptional circumstances, while such re-opening against a finally acquitted person is allowed under even more stringent conditions.

*507.* According to Article 525(1) CCP, the criminal procedure may be re-opened in favour of a finally convicted person when:

(i) Two persons have been convicted for the same act where it is certain that one of them is innocent.
(ii) New facts and/or evidence, which were not known to the court which issued the conviction, make it apparent (either on themselves or in combination with other known facts and/or evidence) that the convicted person was innocent or had committed a lesser offence.
(iii) The conviction had been influenced by false witness statements or false expert opinions or false or forged documents or exhibits introduced at the trial hearing.
(iv) One or more members of the court (judges or laymen) had been bribed or otherwise breached their judicial duties.
(v) The convicted person has been finally acquitted by a subsequent judgment for the same act.
(vi) Greece has been convicted by the European Court for Human Rights for a breach of the convicted person's fundamental right to a fair trial or with respect to the provision of the substantive law which was applied to the case at hand irrespective of whether the violation found by the ECtHR had negatively influenced the domestic court's decision.

The re-opening of the case under Article 525(1) (iii)-(iv) requires a final conviction on the merits of the perpetrators of the perjury, forgery, false certification or fraudulent procurement thereof, bribery, or breach of duties except for cases in which the Court was prevented on legal grounds from considering the facts of the case or where the criminal prosecution was suspended on legal grounds (Article 525(2)). In the latter cases, a separate procedure shall be followed in this respect (*infra*, paragraph 510).

*508.* Article 527 CCP allows the re-opening of a criminal procedure against a finally acquitted person, only if it is established that the acquittal judgment of the

Court or the acquittal decision of the Judicial Council had been substantially influenced by forged documents or exhibits or by the bribery of court members (judges or laymen) or by the breach of their judicial duties. The application for the re-opening of the case can be filed only by the Public Prosecutor with the Court or the Judicial Council which issued the acquittal decision.

The re-opening of the case requires a final conviction of the perpetrators for the above acts (forgery etc.) and, also, that the offence in question is not time-barred.

*509.* An application for the re-opening of the case in favour of the convicted person may be filed by the convicted person himself or by his spouse or registered partner or his parents or siblings or by the Public Prosecutor of the Court which decided the conviction and is allowed even after the sentence imposed has been fully served or time-barred as well as after the convicted person's death (Article 528(1)). There is also no limitation as to the number of the applications that may be successively filed.

The application shall be filed with the Prosecutor of the Court of Appeal if it challenges a final decision of a Misdemeanour Court or with the Prosecutor of *Areios Pagos* if it challenges decisions of other courts and must state the reasons for which the re-opening of the case is requested and be accompanied by all supporting evidence. The Public Prosecutor shall evaluate the application and the evidence submitted and may also ask an Investigating Judge to do so; thereafter he submits a written recommendation to the competent Judicial Council (Article 528(3)).

The Judicial Council of the Court of Appeal or of *Areios Pagos* hears oral arguments by the Public Prosecutor and the person who filed the request and/or his lawyer before issuing its decision. It may quash the conviction or refer the case to the Court which had issued the quashed judgment consisting of other judges for re-trial. The decision of the Judicial Council of the Court of Appeal may be appealed by way of cassation both by the requesting person or the Prosecutor (Article 529).

*510.* As mentioned above (*supra*, paragraph 507) the re-opening of the case in favour of the convicted person is possible under Article 525(1) (iii)–(iv) CCP without a prior conviction for forgery, bribery etc., which had influenced the conviction if such conviction was barred on legal grounds.

Article 530 CCP sets out the procedure to be followed in order to ascertain the commission of the above offences and their influence on the conviction. The hearing takes place before the Court of Appeal which summons the convicted person or the person requesting the re-opening of the case, the parties who participated in the trial hearing resulting in the conviction as well as the person(s) who allegedly committed the forgery or bribery etc. The latter is not obliged to appear at the hearing. A public hearing is held with the purpose of establishing whether the offences in question had been committed and a final decision is issued by the Court of Appeal in this matter.

If the commission of the above offence(s) is confirmed, the Judicial Council of the Court of Appeal or of *Areios Pagos* respectively decide whether the confirmed offence(s) have substantially contributed to the conviction and in the affirmative they quash the conviction or order a re-trial of the case as above.

*511.* A successful application for the re-opening of the case in favour of the convicted person extends to his co-defendants who had been convicted provided that the grounds for the re-opening of the case do not exclusively refer to the person in whose favour it was decided (Article 533).

The Court that retries the case following the admission of an application of the convicted person or an application in his favour cannot convict him anew for a more serious offence or impose a harsher sentence (*non reformatio in peius* – Article 534).

## §4. Shortened and Alternative Forms of Procedure

*512.* Mention has been made above (*supra*, paragraphs 360–362) of the Public Prosecutor's power to refrain from prosecution of the defendant in certain categories of criminal offences subject to the fulfilment of certain conditions imposed on him or after full compensation of the victim.

The Code of Criminal Procedure provides three further alternatives to the traditional model of criminal procedure, i.e., the penal order, the criminal mediation, and the negotiated pleas.

### I. Penal Order

*513.* A penal order may be issued for offences subject to the jurisdiction of the Single-Judge Misdemeanour Court (*supra*, paragraphs 355–362) which are punishable by imprisonment not exceeding one year and/or by a monetary penalty. The Public Prosecutor of the Misdemeanour Court files a request to issue a penal order to a Judge if, in his view, the evidence against the defendant need not be examined in a trial hearing (Article 409).

The Judge who receives the Prosecutor's request shall evaluate it and proceeds with the issuance of a penal order if he agrees with the assessment of the evidence. The penal order, which is issued without prior summons or hearing of the defendant, may impose a monetary penalty which shall not exceed one-third of the sentence that may be imposed following a trial hearing or a suspended imprisonment not exceeding three months (Article 410).

If the Judge disagrees with the Public Prosecutor's assessment of the evidence, the case shall be scheduled for trial.

*514.* The penal order must clearly state the offence for which it has been issued and must be served on the defendant (Article 411). The latter has the right to file an appeal with the Court's Secretary against the order within fifteen days from its service (Article 412). The appeal results in the reversal of the penal order and the referral of the case to a trial court. Such 'automatic' reversal of the penal order ensures that the *in-absentia* procedure which is followed for its issuance does not infringe the fundamental right of the defendant to be informed of the charges against him and have the benefit of a fair hearing in accordance with the ECHR and the EU Directive 2012/13 on the right to information.[329]

The trial court is free to impose a sentence which is higher than the sentence which had been imposed by the reversed penal order if the defendant is found guilty (Articles 413, 415).

## II. Criminal Mediation

*515.* Criminal mediation is possible for certain categories of non-violent serious crimes of a prevailing financial character (crimes against property, tax crimes, money laundering etc.) and may be pursued pre-trial until the closing of the formal investigation or after indictment prior to or during the trial hearing (Articles 301–302).

*516.* The criminal mediation must be initiated pre-trial by the defendant who may file during the formal investigation an application to this end with the Public Prosecutor of the Misdemeanour Court. The latter invites the defendant and the injured party to appear with their lawyers before him and grants them a period of fifteen days to settle the case between them which may be prolonged for another fifteen days. If the parties have no lawyer, they will have lawyers appointed to them. A written record of the settlement shall be drafted which includes the defendant's admission to the charges and the injured party's declaration on return of the stolen etc. items or full compensation (Article 301(2)–(3)).

Should the negotiations between the parties fail to achieve a settlement, the procedure returns to its normal course, and any documents related to the failed settlement must be destroyed and excluded from evidence in further proceedings. (Article 301(5)).

*517.* The Public Prosecutor forwards the settlement agreement within five days from its receipt to the Public Prosecutor of the Court of Appeal who refers the case to the Single-Judge Court of Appeal for Serious Crimes for sentencing (Article 301(7). The sentencing hearing, to which the defendant and the injured party are summoned to appear, takes place before the above Court.

The Court evaluates the settlement agreement and makes a legal assessment of the case which may lead to the termination of the proceedings with no conviction on legal grounds provided in Article 368 (b)–(c) CCP (e.g., limitation by time, *non bis in idem*, etc., *supra*, paragraphs 367–374). The Court may also change the legal qualification of the offence in favour of the defendant but not against him. If no legal grounds prevent a conviction, the Court imposes a sentence which cannot exceed one year or in aggravating circumstances two years. The sentence shall be suspended or commuted to community service according to the relevant provisions of the Penal Code (Article 301(8)).

The decision of the Court is appealable only by way of cassation before *Areios Pagos* (Article 301(9)).

329. *See* in this respect the CJEU judgment in *Covaci* of 15 Oct. 2015 (C-216/14) at 58–62.

*518.* After the closing of the formal investigation and before indictment the defendant may file an application for criminal mediation. In such a case, the case file is returned to the Public Prosecutor for the settlement procedure to take place as described above (Article 302(1)). An application for mediation is also possible to the defendant after indictment or during the trial hearing until the closing of the evidence hearing.

The Court of First Instance which is competent to try the case will adjourn the hearing for fifteen days for the purpose of achieving a settlement between the parties under the same terms mentioned above with respect to the pre-trial stage (*supra*, paragraph 516). If settlement is achieved, the sentence to be imposed shall not exceed two years or three years in aggravating circumstances and shall be suspended or commuted to community service as above (Article 302(7)).

Should the parties fail to achieve settlement, the proceedings will continue, while any documents or other evidence related to the failed attempt to settle will be destroyed and excluded from the trial evidence (Article 302(5)).

Criminal mediation in court is also possible in misdemeanour cases involving the above-mentioned criminal offences (*supra*, paragraph 515). The Court of First Instance shall proceed as described with respect to serious crimes and impose a suspended or commutable sentence of up to six months or up to twelve months in aggravating circumstances (Article 302(4), (7)).

*519.* In misdemeanour cases of domestic violence, Articles 11–13 of Act 3500/2006 as amended establish the possibility of a mediation procedure before the Public Prosecutor. The opening of the mediation procedure requires a declaration by the defendant that he will not commit any such offences in the future and will comply with the conditions to be imposed on him including the attendance of an advisory-therapeutic programme. If the defendant complies with all conditions imposed for a period of three years, the case is closed by an order of the Public Prosecutor.[330]

## III. Negotiated Pleas

*520.* The new Code of Criminal Procedure, which entered into force on 1 July 2019, introduced a procedure of negotiated pleas in Article 303.[331]

Plea negotiations are allowed until the closing of the formal investigation or the summary investigation for all offences except those punishable by life sentence, terrorist offences and sexual abuse or sexual exploitation offences (Article 303(1)). To this end, the defendant must file an application with the Public Prosecutor of the

---

330. On restorative justice procedures from a comparative perspective including Greece, *see* E. Symeonidou-Kastanidou, 'Restorative Justice as an Alternative to Penal Sanctions', in: D. Brown, J. Turner and B. Weisser (eds), *The Oxford Handbook of Criminal Process*, Oxford University Press, New York, 2019, 911, 915 et seq.

331. For a critical discussion of bargain practices and their compatibility with the ECHR fundamental values, *see* C. Mylonopoulos, 'Bargain Practices and the Fundamental Values of the ECHR' in U. Sieber/V. Mitsilegas/C. Mylonopoulos/E. Billis/N. Knust (eds), *Alternative Systems of Crime Control, National, Transnational, and International Dimensions*, Duncker & Humblot, Berlin, 2018, 89 et seq.

Misdemeanour Court in misdemeanour cases or with the Public Prosecutor of the Appeal Court in serious crimes cases. Prosecutors cannot initiate plea negotiations on their own motion.

*521.* After receiving the above application, the Prosecutor decides whether the case is suitable for a plea negotiation based on its specific characteristics and the defendant's personality. In the affirmative, the Prosecutor invites the defendant to appear with counsel or appoints him counsel if he has not one in order to negotiate the plea (Article 303(2)). The Public Prosecutor may also invite the injured party to be heard or ask the defendant to fully compensate the latter before entering into negotiations.

The negotiations refer both to the criminal offence, with respect to which the defendant must plead guilty, and the sentence to be imposed and are conducted between the latter (with counsel) and the Prosecutor with no involvement of a judge.

Should the negotiation fail, all documents or other evidence related to it must be destroyed and cannot be introduced in evidence in proceedings to follow or any other (Article 303(3)).

After successful negotiation, a written record shall be drafted including the guilty plea together with the recommended sentence and its proposed enforcement (Article 303(4)). The recommended sentence cannot exceed five years if the offence is punishable by a sentence of up to ten years or seven years if the maximum sentence would be fifteen years or two years if the offence is a misdemeanour.

The case is then referred to the Single-Judge Member Court of Misdemeanours or to the Single-Judge Court of Appeal for Serious Crimes respectively. The hearing takes place in public in the presence of the defendant and his lawyer before the competent Court, which may impose a lesser sentence if appropriate but has no power to impose a higher sentence than the one recommended. It may also change the legal qualification of the act in favour of the defendant or terminate the proceedings with no conviction on legal grounds provided in Article 368 (b)–(c) CCP (e.g., limitation by time, *non bis in idem*, etc.) (Article 303(6)). The Court's decision may be appealed only by way of cassation before *Areios Pagos* (Article 303(9)).

*522.* Plea negotiations are also allowed at the trial hearing before the Court of First Instance until the beginning of the evidence hearing (Article 303(7)). Upon such request of the defendant the Court shall adjourn or postpone the hearing. After a successful negotiation between the Public Prosecutor and the defendant and his counsel, the above-described procedure is followed, while on failure of the same, all related documents will be destroyed and are excluded from further proceedings.

# Chapter 4. Extradition and Mutual Assistance

## §1. Extradition and European Arrest Warrant Procedures

*523.* Greece is party to bilateral or multilateral extradition treaties with many countries.[332] Where no such treaty exists, Articles 436 to 457 CCP regulate extradition proceedings following the principle of reciprocity. Moreover, the CCP provisions apply with respect to matters not covered by the above treaties subject to their compatibility with the latter (Article 436).

European Arrest Warrant (EAW) proceedings are regulated by Act 3251/2004 as amended, which implemented the Council Framework Decision of 13 June 2002 on the European arrest warrant and the surrender procedures between Member States (FD EAW) and its subsequent amendments.[333]

Greece has ratified the Rome Statute of the International Criminal Court (ICC) by Act 3003/2002 and implemented its provisions with respect to the international crimes and the relevant co-operation and surrender procedures by Act 3948/2011.

*524.* The offences for which extradition is allowed vary depending on the applicable legal instrument. If a surrender request is filed through the EAW mechanism, the offences for which surrender is allowed are listed in the FD EAW. Outside EAW proceedings, extraditable offences under the Code of Criminal Procedure are in principle those punishable by deprivation of liberty the maximum of which exceeds two years. Extradition requests for the execution of a sentence are admissible if the sentence imposed is no less than three months. (Article 437). Certain categories of offences, i.e., political, military, press or tax offences, may be exempted from extradition depending on the legal extradition instrument that governs each case (Article 438).

*525.* Dual criminality is a fundamental principle in all extradition proceedings except those with state parties to the EAW mechanism.

The dual criminality test includes two phases. First, it must be established whether the act stated in the extradition request would constitute a criminal offence under Greek law irrespective of their different legal qualification. Second, it must be determined whether the criminal prosecution of the specific act is barred either under the laws of the requesting state or the laws of Greece (e.g., limitation by time, double jeopardy, etc.) (Article 438).

---

332. The laws that ratify extradition treaties are published in the Official Government Gazette. A list of the international treaties Greece has entered into can be found on the website of the Ministry of Justice, Transparency and Human Rights www.ministryofjustice.gr/site/en/EuropeanInternational Cooperation/InternationalJudicialCooperationinCriminalMat.aspx.

333. *See* e.g., Y. Naziris, 'First Periodic Country Report: Greece', in: STREAM (Strengthening Trust in the European Criminal Justice Area Through Mutual Recognition and the Streamlined Application of the European Arrest Warrant), 2021, https://stream-eaw.eu/wp-content/uploads/2022/01/STREAM_Country-Report_Greece.pdf, Il. Anagnostopoulos, 'Proportionality Issues in European Arrest Warrant Proceedings – Three Stories From the Field', in: E. Billis, N. Knust & J. P. Rui (eds), *Proportionality in Crime Control and Criminal Justice*, Hart Publishing, Oxford, 2021, 337 et seq.

In EAW proceedings, dual criminality does not apply with respect to a broad catalogue of thirty-two offences, provided that the maximum of the applicable sentence exceeds three years. For non-listed offences, the above dual criminality test is mandatory.

*526.* An extradition request shall include the judicial decision or the domestic arrest warrant that is the basis of the request, a statement of the offences for which extradition is sought, a description of the time, place and other circumstances of the offence, its legal classification, a reference and a copy of the relevant legal provisions and an accurate identification of the requested person, with any other information that will help establish his identity and nationality. Where the CCP provisions apply, the extradition requests must be supported by all necessary documents which indicate the commission of the offence by the requested person (Article 443). However, in most extradition treaties to which Greece is a party, the non-inquiry rule is established which bars the application of Article 443 CCP in this respect.

In EAW proceedings, the surrender request must be translated into Greek and provide the standardized information included in the Annex to the FD EAW.

*527.* Extradition proceedings include two stages, i.e., a judicial stage, where the Judicial Council rules against or in favour of the extradition, followed in the latter case by an administrative stage, in which the Minister of Justice decides upon satisfying the extradition request. Humanitarian, foreign policy or other factors may influence the decision of the Minister of Justice. EAW proceedings only involve a judicial stage not followed by an administrative stage.

*528.* A provisional arrest of the requested person is allowed in emergency cases following a notification by the requesting state by virtue of an order issued by the Prosecutor's Extradition Office with the competent Court of Appeal in order to prevent the person from fleeing. The Prosecutor must notify the Minister of Justice who may order the release of the arrested person. The Prosecutor's arrest order expires if the issuing state does not file a formal extradition request within thirty days from the arrest. As soon as the President of the Court of Appeal receives the formal extradition request, he decides upon arrest of the requested person by issuing an arrest warrant (Article 445).

While under arrest, the requested person has the right to be promptly informed in a language he understands of the reasons for his arrest, to appoint a lawyer, to access the case file and receive copies of the documents included therein (Article 447).

In EAW proceedings, a Letter of Rights must immediately be made available to the arrested person in a language he understands. The requested person has the right to inform and communicate with a third party and the consular authorities of the state of which he is a national.

*529.* Instead of a detention order, less intrusive restrictive measures may be imposed by the Extradition Prosecutor on the requested person pending the extradition proceedings, such as the prohibition to leave the country, the appearance at the police station of his residence or bail. The requested person has the right to appeal his detention or restrictive measures before the Judicial Council of the Court of Appeal, which may lift or amend the same (Article 449(4)). The detention for extradition purposes shall not exceed twenty-four months or exceptionally thirty months; after the passing of these deadlines, the requested person must be released (Article 452(2)).

*530.* Refusal grounds of an extradition request vary depending on the legal framework which applies to the proceedings. Generally, the most common refusal grounds are the following (Article 438):

(i) Greek nationality of the requested person at the time of the offence (Article 438). An exception to this rule applies with respect to EAW requests provided that the person is not being prosecuted for the same act in Greece. Greek nationality or the permanent residence of the requested person in Greece does not bar the execution of an EAW. However, the Court can order that persons surrendered under the EAW provisions, if convicted, must be returned to Greece in order to serve the sentence imposed on them in the issuing state.
(ii) Jurisdiction of the Greek Courts over the offence for which the extradition is sought. If the offence or part of it was committed on Greek territory, the extradition is barred with no further inquiry on whether the requesting state would be a more appropriate forum for the adjudication of the offence. This refusal ground is optional in EAW proceedings.
(iii) The political, military, press or tax-related nature of the offence; in many extradition treaties as well as in EAW proceedings the above offences are extraditable.
(iv) *Non bis in idem* or other grounds which bar the prosecution of the offence or the execution of the sentence under the laws of the requesting state or under the laws of Greece. In EAW proceedings, *non bis in idem* bar applies to all judicial decisions issued in Member States, while with respect to third states it constitutes an optional refusal ground.
(v) If there are reasons to believe that the requested person would be prosecuted in the issuing state for a different act to the one for which extradition is sought in breach of the specialty principle. Such prosecution will be possible if the Greek State subsequently consents to it (Article 440).
(vi) If there are substantial grounds to believe that the extradition request was made for the purpose of prosecuting or punishing a person on account of his race, religion, ethnic identity, nationality, language, sexual orientation or political opinion, his activities for freedom or that the person's position may be prejudiced for any of these reasons.
(vii) If a death sentence may be imposed for the offence in the requesting state or if it is likely that the requested person will be subject to otherwise inhuman or degrading punishment.
(viii) If it is likely that the requested person's human rights will be violated.
(ix) If the requested person had been convicted *in absentia* without being duly summoned to appear.

*531.* The extraditee can consent to his surrender. Such informed consent is given by the requested person accompanied by his lawyer (and an interpreter if need be) before the President of the Court of Appeal and is irrevocable (Article 448). Following such consent, the decision on extradition lies with the President of the Court of Appeal who must refuse it if the above refusal grounds apply.

*532.* Extradition and EAW surrender requests are handled by the Judicial Council of the competent Court of Appeal as a first-instance court. The hearing is held publicly except if the extraditee requests a non-public hearing. The extraditee has a right of full access to the case file as well as to submit any relevant evidence (documents, witnesses, etc.) to the Court. He also has the right to interpretation and to have counsel of his choice or to have counsel appointed by the Court. The Court hears evidence and oral arguments by the Public Prosecutor and the requested person's counsel, while the requesting state is not a party to the proceedings and has no right to be represented by a lawyer at the hearing (Articles 449–450).

*533.* The Judicial Council of the Court of Appeal shall issue a reasoned decision on the extradition request. It may also ask the requesting state to provide within tight time limits any supplemental information and/or documents which are considered necessary. If the Judicial Council rules in favour of the extradition, the requested person may lodge an appeal against the decision within five days from its delivery. The Public Prosecutor may also appeal the decision of the Judicial Council ruling either in favour or against the extradition within the same time limits. (Article 451). In EAW proceedings, the appeal must be lodged within twenty- four hours from delivery of the decision.

An appeal is also allowed both by the Public Prosecutor and the extraditee against a decision for extradition of the President of the Court of Appeal following the consent of the requested person if the above-mentioned refusal grounds apply (*supra*, paragraph 530).

The appeals are heard by *Areios Pagos* sitting as a second instance court. In the appellate proceedings a full rehearing of the case takes place which may lead to the confirmation, the amendment or the quashing of the appealed decision. *Areios Pagos's* decision finally terminates the judicial stage of the extradition proceedings.

*534.* In cases of concurring extradition requests from different states priority shall be given to the state of the requested person's nationality or to the state where the offence has been committed. If the concurring requests refer to different offences, priority shall be given to the state of the more serious offence under Greek law; where the offences are of equal seriousness, the request which was filed first shall have priority (Article 439).

A new request for the same offence by the same state is allowed even after the final refusal of the previous one on the condition that it is based on new evidence which had not been submitted to the Judicial Council which refused the extradition (Article 454).

*535.* Extradition requests from Greece are issued by the Extradition Office of the competent Prosecutor with the Court of Appeal and are forwarded to the authorities of the requested state through the Greek Ministry of Foreign Affairs. In EAW proceedings, the requests are directly sent to the competent judicial authority of the requested state.

Time spent in extradition detention in the requested state shall be deducted from the sentence to be imposed in Greece (Article 456).

## §2. Judicial Co-operation: Mutual Assistance

*536.* Greece is a party to numerous international and European conventions covering aspects of cross-border judicial co-operation such as the European Convention on Mutual Assistance in Criminal Matters (1959), the European Convention on the Suppression of Terrorism (1977), the Convention of the Council of Europe on Laundering, Search, Seizure and Confiscation of the Proceeds from Crime (1990), the UN Convention against Transnational Organized Crime (2000), the UN Convention against Corruption (2003), the Council of Europe Convention on Laundering, Search, Seizure and Confiscation of the Proceeds from Crime and on the Financing of Terrorism (2005). Greece also has bilateral mutual assistance agreements with countries like the United States, Canada, China, Mexico and others.

Within the EU area, Greece has implemented (Act 4489/2017) the EU Directive 2014/41 on the European Investigation Order, an innovative legal instrument which greatly facilitates judicial co-operation within the common area. Indeed, the EIO allows a direct and speedy co-operation between the prosecutorial and/or judicial authorities of EU countries with respect to the transfer of evidence or other investigative measures (search and seizure, examination of witnesses or suspects, etc.).

Articles 458 to 461 CCP establish some basic rules on judicial assistance which are applicable where no multilateral or bilateral agreements are in place or to complement the latter.

*537.* Requests for judicial assistance from Greece, which may seek the service of summonses or other court documents on individuals, the examination of witnesses or suspects, etc., are submitted by the competent Public Prosecutor of the Court of Appeal to the Greek Ministry of Justice and then forwarded to the Ministry of Foreign Affairs which is responsible for submitting them to the competent foreign authorities (Article 458). In emergency cases such requests may be directly forwarded to the Greek consular authorities only with respect to acts they are allowed to perform in the respective foreign country (e.g., the taking of testimony of a Greek citizen residing in the foreign country).

*538.* Requests for judicial assistance from foreign countries to Greece with respect to investigative acts (e.g., examination of witnesses or suspects) are transmitted through the Greek Ministry of Justice to the competent Public Prosecutor of the Court of Appeal who forwards them to the Investigating Judge for execution. The Public Prosecutor of the Misdemeanour Court is responsible for the execution of simple procedural acts (e.g., service of court decisions or documents, summonses to witnesses or suspects, etc.) (Article 459(1)–(2)).

The Minister of Justice may refuse the execution of the requested act with the consent of the Judicial Council of the Court of Appeal, if the request relates to offences for which extradition would be barred under Articles 437 and 438 CCP (*supra*, paragraph 530) or where the extradition would not be mandatory under the applicable treaties (Article 459(3)).

The Judicial Council of the Court of Appeal is competent to resolve any disputes in respect of judicial assistance requests; its decisions are appealable by way of cassation before *Areios Pagos* by the Public Prosecutor and the affected party (Article 459(4)).

*539.* Co-operation with law enforcement or prosecutorial authorities of other countries has become common practice in large-scale investigations. Special law enforcement agencies, such as the Economic Crime Unit or the Financial Intelligence Unit have entered into agreements with foreign counterparts, which enable an efficient direct exchange of information. In recent times, there has been a marked increase in the co-operation of special prosecuting and investigating task forces with the corresponding authorities in other countries (especially in Germany and Switzerland) by adopting more flexible and expeditious procedures.

Greek prosecutorial and judicial authorities also co-operate with those of other EU Member States through the Eurojust agency.

### §3. The European Public Prosecutor's Office

*540.* Greece is among the EU countries which participate in the European Public Prosecutor's mechanism. Notably, Act 4506/2019 has ratified the EU Regulation 2017/1939 on the European Public Prosecutor's Office (EPPO) with the competence to investigate, prosecute and bring to judgment crimes against the EU budget, such as fraud, corruption, or serious cross-border VAT fraud. Act 4596/2019 as amended by Acts 4786/2021 and 5026/2023 established a special EPPO Office in Athens whose selected prosecutors are responsible for overseeing and coordinating the conduct of the EPPO investigations. In an effort to integrate the EPPO into the domestic procedural system, the Greek legislator has assigned to the EPPO Office in the relevant cases the investigative powers of the Investigating Judge during the formal investigation (*supra*, Chapter 2, paragraphs 329 et seq.) with the exception of the interrogation of the defendant, the arrest, the pre-trial detention, the house arrest, or other restrictive measures on the defendant. It remains to be seen how smoothly this 'mixed' model of prosecutorial and judicial powers will work in practice.[334]

334. Cf. the EPPO model adopted in Belgium; *see* A. Claes, A. Werding and V. Franssen, 'The Belgian Juge d'Instruction and the EPPO Regulation: (Ir)reconcilable?', European Papers, Vol. 6 (2021), 366 et seq.

# Part III. Execution and Extinction of Sanctions

## Chapter 1. The Domestic and International Sources of Penitentiary Law

*541.* Greek penitentiary law has many different direct and indirect sources, namely the following: (a) the Constitution; (b) the Penal Code; (c) the Code of Criminal Procedure; (d) the Penitentiary Code; (e) ratified global and regional treaties; and (f) global and regional soft law instruments adopted under the auspices of international organizations in which Greece participates. The European Union has not adopted any specific mandatory rules and regulations as the penitentiary system falls primarily within the regulatory domain of the Member States.[335] However, there are some relevant EU law provisions including: (a) Article 4 of the EU Charter prohibiting torture and inhuman or degrading treatment; (b) Council Framework Decision of 13 June 2002 on the European arrest warrant and the surrender procedures between Member States (2002/584/JHA);[336] and (c) Directive 2008/115 of the European Parliament and of the Council of 16 December 2008 on common standards and procedures in Member States for returning illegally staying third-country nationals.[337]

*542.* Regarding the provisions in the Constitution, reference should be made to the following: Article 2(1), which reads 'Respect and protection of the value of the

335. For an overview of the penitentiary systems in the EU Member States, *see* European Union Agency for Fundamental Rights, *Criminal Detention Conditions in the European Union: Rules and Reality*, Luxembourg: Publications Office of the European Union, 2019, available at: https://fra.europa.eu/sites/default/files/fra_uploads/fra-2019-criminal-detention-conditions-in-the-eu_en.pdf.

336. O.J. L 190, 18.7.2002, p. 1. *See* European Union Agency for Fundamental Rights, *Criminal detention conditions in the European Union, ibid.*

337. O.J. L 348, 24.12.2008, p. 98. Greece transposed it under Act 3907/2011, Establishment of an Asylum Service and a First Reception Service, adaptation of Greek legislation to the provisions of Directive 2008/115/EC 'on common rules and procedures in the Member States for the return of illegally staying third-country nationals' and other provisions, FEK 2011 A' 7, as last amended under Act 4825/2021, Reform of procedures for deportations and returns of third-country nationals, attracting investors and digital nomads, issues of residence permits and procedures for granting international protection, provisions of the competence of the Ministry of Immigration and Asylum and of the Ministry of Citizen Protection and other urgent provisions, FEK 2021 A' 57.

human being constitute the primary obligation of the State'; Article 5, which guarantees the inviolability of personal freedom, and, in particular, Article 5(3) ('Personal liberty is inviolable. No one shall be prosecuted, arrested, imprisoned or otherwise confined except when and as the law provides'); Article 6, which deals with the conditions permitting the arrest and imprisonment of civilians and the maximum period of their detention pending trial; Article 7, which, as has been explained, embodies the *nullum crimen nulla poena sine lege* principle, and stipulates the obligation of the State to indemnify those who were unjustly or illegally convicted or detained pending trial, or otherwise deprived of their personal freedom;[338] Article 8, which embodies the principle of one's natural judge' ('No person shall be deprived of the judge assigned to him by law against his will'); Article 10, which recognizes the right of all citizens to address the State as well as public authorities in a written form and the obligation of the latter to reply to requests for information for the supply of documents; and, finally, Article 47(1) on pardoning offenders and convictions, which is discussed *infra* at paragraph 557.

*543*. Regarding the relevant treaties ratified by Greece, they have been primarily adopted under UN and Council of Europe auspices. The former include the ICCPR, and the Convention against Torture and Other Cruel, Inhuman or Degrading Treatment or Punishment.[339] The latter include the following: (a) the ECHR and especially the Seventh Protocol thereto, which extended the list of protected rights by adding the right of aliens to procedural guarantees if expelled from the territory of a contracting party; the right of those convicted of a criminal offence to have the conviction or sentence reviewed by a higher court of justice; the right to compensation in the event of a miscarriage of justice; and the introduction of the principle *non bis in idem*;[340] (b) the European Convention for the Prevention of Torture and Inhuman or Degrading Treatment or Punishment;[341] (c) the European Convention on the Transfer of Sentenced Persons;[342] (d) the European Convention on Extradition,[343] which is not applicable to those contracting parties which are at the same

338. This provision is in compliance with Art. 9(5) ICCPR. For details, *see* Arts 535 et seq. of the Code of Criminal Procedure.
339. Signed on 10 Dec. 1984, it entered into force on 26 Jun. 1987, 1465 *UNTS* 85. Greece ratified it under Act 1782/1988, FEK 1988 A' 116. Greece has also ratified the Optional Protocol to the Convention, signed on 18 Dec. 2002, entered into force on 22 Jun. 2006, 2375 *UNTS* 237.
340. Signed on 22 Nov. 1984, it entered into force on 1 Nov. 1988, ETS No.117. Greece ratified it promptly under Act 1705/1987, FEK 1987 A' 89.
341. Signed on 26 Nov. 1987, it entered into force on 1 Feb. 1989, ETS No.126. Greece ratified it under Act 1949/1991, FEK 1991 A' 83.
342. Signed on 21 Mar. 1983, it entered into force on 1 Jul. 1985, ETS No. 112. Greece ratified it under Act 1708/1987, FEK 1987 A' 108. In September 2005, Greece ratified the Additional Protocol to the Convention, ETS No. 167, which was signed on 18 Dec. 1997 and entered into force on 1 Jun. 2000. Greece has not signed the Protocol amending the Additional Protocol to the Convention on the Transfer of Sentenced Persons, CETS No. 222, which was opened for signature on 22 Nov. 2017 (not yet in force).
343. Signed on 13 Dec. 1957, it entered into force on 18 Apr. 1960, ETS No. 24. Greece ratified it under Legislative Decree 4165/1961, FEK 1961 A' 75. Greece signed in June 1980 but has not ratified the Additional Protocol of 15 Oct. 1975 (ETS No. 86) as well as the Second Additional Protocol of 17 Mar. 1978 (ETS No 98). It signed in September 2012 the Third Additional Protocol of 10 Nov. 2010

time EU Member States;[344] and (e) the European Convention on Mutual Legal Assistance in Penal Matters.[345] Greece has signed but not ratified the following two relevant treaties: (a) the European Convention on the Supervision of Conditionally Sentenced or Conditionally Released Offenders (1964),[346] and (b) the Convention on Compensation of the Victims of Violent Crimes.[347] Finally, as regards the transfer of sentenced persons, Greece must comply with the relevant rules of EU law,[348] has ratified the Council of Europe Convention on the Transfer of Sentenced Persons,[349] and has entered into bilateral Agreements with Albania,[350] Egypt[351] and Cyprus.[352]

*544.* As regards international and regional soft law instruments, these have also been adopted under the auspices of the United Nations, the Council of Europe, and the EU. Regarding UN instruments, reference can be made to: (a) the Standard Minimum Rules for the Treatment of Prisoners (1955),[353] and the revised Rules,

---

(CETS 209, entered into force on 1 May 2012). It has not signed the Fourth Additional Protocol of 20 Sep. 2012 (CETS No. 212, entered into force on 1 Jun. 2014).

344. *See* the Declaration submitted by Greece on 12 Oct. 2006: 'In accordance with Article 28, paragraph 3, of the European Convention on Extradition, the Hellenic Republic notifies that on 9 July 2004 the law nr. 3251/2004 has entered into force, implementing the Framework Decision of the Council of the European Union of 13 June 2002 on the European arrest warrant and the surrender procedures between Member States (2002/584/JHA). The Hellenic Republic shall apply this law in relations to Contracting Parties which are Member States of the European Union and have also implemented the Framework Decision on the European arrest warrant'.
345. Signed on 20 Apr. 1959, it entered into force on 12 Jun. 1962, ETS No. 30, ratified under Legislative Decree 4218/1961, FEK 1961 A' 171. Greece has made two reservations with regard, respectively, to Art. 4 and Art. 11 of the Convention, because they were incompatible with the Code of Criminal Procedure. Greece ratified the Additional Protocol of 17 Mar. 1978, ETS No. 99, under Act 1129/1981, FEK 1981 A' 42.
346. Opened for signature on 30 Nov. 1964, entered into force on 22 Aug. 1975, ETS No. 51. Greece signed it on 27 Aug. 1979.
347. It entered into force on 1 Feb. 1988, ETS No. 116. Greece signed on the very day it was opened for signature (24 Nov. 1983).
348. Council Framework Decision 2008/909/JHA of 27 Nov. 2008 on the application of the principle of mutual recognition to judgments in criminal matters imposing custodial sentences or measures involving deprivation of liberty for the purpose of their enforcement in the European Union, O.J. L 327, 5.12.2008, p. 27, as amended by Council Framework Decision 2009/299/JHA of 26 Feb. 2009 on trials in absentia, O.J. L 81, 27.3.2009, p. 24. Generally, *see* European Commission, *Commission notice – Handbook on the transfer of sentenced persons and custodial sentences in the European Union* (2019/C 403/02), O.J. C 403, 29.11.2019, p. 2.
349. Adopted on 21 Mar. 1983, entered into force on 1 Jul. 1985, ETS 112, ratified under Act 1708/1987, FEK 1987 A' 108. Greece has also ratified the Additional Protocol, signed on 18 Dec. 1997, entered into force on 1 Jun. 2000, ETS 167, under Act 3351/2005, FEK 2005 A' 147.
350. Signed on 17 May 1993, ratified under Act 2313/1995, FEK 1995 A' 121. The Agreement was discussed by the ECtHR in Applications nos 11546/05, 33285/05 and 33288/05, *Vezir Plepi, Fersilet Plepi and Miaftoni Zeka v. Albania and Greece*, Judgment of 4 May 2010.
351. Signed on 17 May 1993, ratified under Act 1765/1988, FEK 1988 A' 58.
352. Signed on 5 Mar. 1984, entered into force on 25 Aug. 1985, ratified by Act 1548/1985, FEK 1985 A' 95.
353. Adopted by the First UN Congress on the Prevention of Crime and the Treatment of Offenders and approved by the Economic and Social Council under Resolutions 663 C (XXIV) of 31 Jul. 1957 and 2076 (LXII) of 13 May 1977.

which were adopted as the 'Nelson Mandela Rules' (2015);[354] (b) the Basic Principles for the Treatment of Prisoners (1990);[355] (c) the Standard Minimum Rules for Non-custodial Measures (the Tokyo Rules, 1990);[356] (d) the Principles and Guidelines on Access to Legal Aid in Criminal Justice Systems;[357] and (e) the Body of Principles for the Protection of All Persons under Any Form of Detention or Imprisonment.[358] Regarding the Council of Europe, suffice to mention that in 2020 its Committee of Ministers adopted a Recommendation[359] to update the European Prison Rules, which were originally approved in 2006.[360] The other relevant Council of Europe recommendations are quite numerous to be mentioned but the interested reader can find them at its website.[361] Finally, as regards the EU, the European Parliament Resolution on prisons (2017) should be mentioned.[362]

354. Adopted under UNGA Resolution 70/175 of 17 Dec. 2015.
355. Adopted under UNGA Resolution 45/111 of 14 Dec. 1990.
356. Adopted under UNGA Resolution 45/110 of 14 Dec. 1990.
357. Adopted under UNGA Resolution 67/187 of 20 Dec. 2012.
358. Adopted under UNGA Resolution 43/173 of 9 Dec. 1988.
359. *See* Recommendation Rec(2006)2-rev of the Committee of Ministers to Member States on the European Prison Rules, as revised and amended by the Committee of Ministers on 1 Jul. 2020.
360. The 2006 Rules are available at: https://rm.coe.int/european-prison-rules-978-92-871-5982-3/16806ab9ae.
361. *See* https://www.coe.int/en/web/prison/conventions-recommendations.
362. European Parliament resolution of 5 Oct. 2017 on prison systems and conditions (2015/2062(INI)), O.J. C 346, 27.9.2018, p. 94.

# Chapter 2. The Protection Afforded to and the Rights of Prisoners and Detainees under the Penitentiary Code

*545.* The Penitentiary Code is embodied in Act 2776/1999,[363] as currently in force having been amended by Act 4596/2019,[364] by Act 4625/2019,[365] and lastly by Act 4985/2022.[366] As stated in Article 1(1) of the Penitentiary Code, the terms and conditions relating to the execution of penalties and security measures affecting one's personal freedom must be in accordance with the Constitution, with the international conventions ratified by Greece as well as with the laws and regulations which have been issued under their authority. Moreover, Article 2(1) of the Penitentiary Code provides specifies that the human dignity of prisoners must be ensured, while their self-respect and sense of social responsibility must also be strengthened. The equal treatment of prisoners, regardless of whether they are Greek nationals or foreigners, is guaranteed under Article 3(1). It stipulates: 'All forms of discrimination against detainees, in particular those based on race, colour, ethnic or social origin, religion, property or ideological beliefs, shall be prohibited.' Special treatment is possible, however, when it is justified by the prevailing circumstances *vis-à-vis* different groups of detainees, for example, *persons awaiting trial (pre-trial detainees)*[367] *v. convicted offenders, married v. unmarried convicts, minors v. adult prisoners, male v. female prisoners*, persons detained for the enforcement of commercial claims, etc. There is also special treatment when detainees have to observe religious or other duties. The provision of Article 4 lays down the general rule that, during the execution of custodial sentences, the rights of prisoners shall not be restricted, except the right to personal liberty. Thus, they shall not be prevented, only by reason of their detention, to freely develop their personality and to exercise those rights which are recognized by law and to which they are entitled, either in person or through a representative.

---

363. FEK 1999 A' 291.
364. FEK 2019 A' 32. Note that Act 4596/2019 is another of those multiplex Acts that the Greek Parliament has been adopting as of late. Thus, over and above amending the Penitentiary Code, it is also the ratification instrument of a treaty (namely, Protocol No. 16 of the ECHR), it transposed/harmonized/implemented in the domestic legal order three EU secondary legislation instruments (namely, Directive 2016/343 on the strengthening of certain aspects of the presumption of innocence and of the right to be present at the trial in criminal proceedings, O.J. L 65, 11.3.2016, p. 1; Council Framework Decision 2009/299/JHA amending Framework Decisions 2002/584/JHA, 2005/214/JHA, 2006/783/JHA, 2008/909/JHA and 2008/947/JHA, thereby enhancing the procedural rights of persons and fostering the application of the principle of mutual recognition to decisions rendered in the absence of the person concerned at the trial, O.J. L 81, 27.3.2009, p. 24; and Council Regulation 2017/1939 implementing enhanced cooperation on the establishment of the European Public Prosecutor's Office, O.J. L 283, 31.10.2017, p. 1) and, finally, amended certain legislative provisions concerning the domestic justice system.
365. FEK 2019 A' 139.
366. FEK 2022 A' 203.
367. Generally, *see* Z. Bahtiyar, 'Greece' in M. van Kalmthout, M.M. Knapen and C. Morgenstern (eds), *Pre-trial Detention in the European Union: An Analysis of Minimum Standards in Pre-trial Detention and the Grounds for Regular Review in the Member States of the EU*, Wolf Legal Publishers, 2009, 435–464; Lambropoulou, 'Pre-trial Detention in Greece: The Achilles Heel of the Prison System' in van Kempen, *supra*, 415–462.

*546.* As regards the right to vote during national (parliamentary) elections and during the elections for the members of the European Parliament (EP), Article 5 of the Penitentiary Code provides that prisoners will vote within their prison on the basis of special electoral rolls. The details are provided in the electoral legislation, namely Presidential Decree 55/1999, as currently in force.[368] A combined reading of the criminal legislation, the Penitentiary Code and Articles 51(3) and 55 of the Constitution leads to the conclusion that, apart from certain exceptions, prisoners should not be deprived of the right to stand as candidates for national elections.

*547.* The legal protection afforded to prisoners is laid down in Article 6 of the Penitentiary Code. Thus, if an unlawful act was carried out against them or an unlawful order was issued which affected them directly, prisoners have the right to file a report in writing and within a reasonable time to the Prison Board.[369] Should the request be rejected or if within one month of submitting the report no decision has been issued, prisoners have the right to appeal to the Court of Execution of Sentences. The latter, if it accepts the appeal in substance, shall rectify the effects of the illegal action or order. It should be noted that, in 2016, a National Mechanism for the investigation of incidents of ill-treatment by law enforcement officers (the Police, the Coast Guard, and the Fire Brigade) and by detention facility officers was established within the office of the Greek Ombudsman. The latter, one of the independent public authorities envisaged in the Constitution,[370] is competent to resolve complaints lodged by the population against the State and against public authorities alleging illegal actions, malpractice, refusal to follow the law, etc.[371] The National Mechanism has been authorized to investigate and evaluate allegations by the general population (including detainees and prisoners) that they have been the victim of the following: (a) torture and other insults to human dignity within the meaning of Article 137A of the Penal Code (*supra* paragraph 182); (b) unlawful intentional infringement on their life or on their bodily integrity or on their health or on their personal or sexual liberty; (c) illegal use of a firearm; and (d) unlawful conduct for which there are indications that it was committed with a racist motive or involving other forms of discrimination on the grounds of race, nationality, ethnic origin, religion, disability, sexual orientation, gender, etc.[372] The Ombudsman also deals with

368. Note that Art. 5 of the Penitentiary Code refers to the 'elections for the Greek members of the European Parliament'. This is rather incorrect, because EU law allows the nationals of Member States not only to vote in EP elections in their Member State of residence but also to stand as candidates in EP elections under the same conditions as a Member State's nationals.
369. This right has as its legal basis on Art. 20(2) of the Constitution: 'The right of a person to a prior hearing [by a competent public authority] … applies in any administrative action or measure which was adopted at the expense of his rights or [legal] interests'.
370. *See* Art. 103(9) of the Constitution.
371. Under Art. 56 of Act 4443/2016, FEK 2016 A' 232.
372. For more details, *see* The Greek Ombudsman, *National Mechanism for the Investigation of Arbitrary Incidents Report 2019*, Athens, 2020. According to the US Department of State, in the course of 2020 the Mechanism received 263 complaints, *see* Bureau of Democracy, Human Rights, and Labor, *2021 Country Reports on Human Rights Practices: Greece*, at: https://www.state.gov/reports/2021-country-reports-on-human-rights-practices/greece/. For the 2022 Report, *see* https://www.state.gov/reports/2022-country-reports-on-human-rights-practices/greece/.

cases where the ECtHR has determined that Greece breached the ECHR and identified crucial deficiencies in the disciplinary procedure against law enforcement officers.

*548.* The question of the acceptable restrictions on the rights and freedoms enjoyed by prisoners is addressed in Article 7 of the Penitentiary Code. It stipulates that they shall bear no other obligations or be subjected to any other restrictions on their rights, except as expressly provided for in the Penitentiary Code and in the regulatory acts, which have been adopted under its authority. Finally, the measures that are necessary to guard prisoners and to ensure the smooth operation of detention facilities cannot preclude the exercise of the constitutionally guaranteed individual and political rights of detainees, within the meaning of the aforementioned Article 4 of the Penitentiary Code.

## Chapter 3. Problems and Issues Surrounding the Penitentiary System in Greece

*549.* Even though the provisions of the Penitentiary Code, as currently in force, appear to be favourable for those convicted and for those serving custodial sentences, the reality is very different, as is often the case.[373] Several international institutions and international bodies have recorded and complained about the unacceptable conditions prevailing in the Greek penitentiary system.[374] This situation has on several occasions led to Greece being found by the ECtHR to be in violation of its obligations under the ECHR. Moreover, the UN Committee against Torture was very critical of the prevailing situation in the country when in July 2019 it examined[375] the Seventh Periodic Report that Greece had submitted as a contracting party to the UN Convention against Torture.[376] However, this state of affairs should not be attributed to Greece being 'a country that may be taking its international human rights obligations lightly', as has rather improperly and without adequate evidence been argued.[377] It has more to do with a country that for arguably a very long period has set the wrong priorities and has not invested enough in public infrastructure and has not offered adequate and quality services. This is a situation that applies to anything from state schools to hospitals to courts to public transportation and, unfortunately, does extend to the criminal justice system as well.

*550.* The case of *Nisiotis v. Greece* was one of those instances where the unacceptable conditions in Greek detention centres were exposed forcing the government to take remedial action. The applicant, a Greek national, had been sentenced to six years of imprisonment for drug trafficking. He complained before the ECtHR that the conditions of his detention in an overcrowded facility amounted to a violation of his human rights: he was held in a dilapidated cell of 50 square meters holding thirty inmates with no access to fresh air. The ECtHR found a violation of

---

373. Generally, *see* L. Cheliotis and S. Xenakis (eds), *Crime and Punishment in Contemporary Greece: International Comparative Perspectives*, Oxford: Peter Lang, 2011.

374. For details on conditions in Greek penitentiaries, *see* N.K. Koulouris and W. Aloskofis, *Prison Conditions in Greece*, European Prison Observatory, Rome: Antigone Edizioni, 2013, at: http://www.prisonobservatory.org/upload/PrisonconditionsGreece.pdf; V. Karydis and N.K. Koulouris, 'Greece: Prisons Are Bad but Necessary (and Expanding), Policies Are Necessary but Bad (and Declining)' in V. Ruggiero et al. (eds), *Punishment in Europe: A Critical Anatomy of Penal Systems*, London: Palgrave Macmillan, 2013, 263–286.

375. *See* UN Office of the High Commissioner on Human Rights, *Committee against Torture concludes its consideration of the report of Greece*, 25 Jul. 2019, at: https://www.ohchr.org/EN/NewsEvents/Pages/DisplayNews.aspx?NewsID=24853&LangID=E.

376. *See* United Nations Committee against Torture, *Seventh periodic report submitted by Greece under article 19 of the Convention pursuant to the optional reporting procedure, due in 2016*, UN Doc. CAT/C/GRC/7, 5 Nov. 2018.

377. *See* D. Giannounopoulos, 'Falling on Deaf Ears': Looking for the Salduz Jurisprudence in Greece' in J. Jackson & S. Summers (eds), *Obstacles to Fairness in Criminal Proceedings: Individual Rights and Institutional Forms*, Oxford: Hart Publishing, 2018, pp. 155–178.

Article 3 of the ECHR (prohibition of inhuman or degrading treatment).[378] Overcrowding is a very serious problem in Greek prisons. As argued in a Council of Europe Report published in 2019, even though the Greek State did adopt certain measures to address this issue, these measures proved to be 'more contingent than strategic, i.e., not able to provide for a solid and structural change in the system'.[379] The measures adopted by Greece have been described in detail in the information that the government sent to the Council of Europe in July 2018 relating to the execution of ECtHR' judgments in a series of cases concerning detention conditions,[380] which are collectively referred to as 'Group Nisiotis'.[381] Finally, another Council of Europe Report, also issued in 2019, painted a rather negative picture as regards the conditions of patients in psychiatric establishments and foreign nationals who had been deprived of their liberty pursuant to the Greek legislation on aliens.[382]

*551.* More specifically, the measures that the Greek State has taken since 2015 to ameliorate the conditions in Greek prisons include the following: (a) the abolition of the high-security prisons pursuant to Act 4322/2015;[383] (b) the reduction of the duration of juvenile detention under Act 4322/2015, which was deemed necessary to implement the provisions of the UN Convention on the Rights of the Child stipulating that arrest, detention or imprisonment of minors is only a measure of last resort and should be inflicted for the minimum period of time necessary; and (c) the reduction in the prison population through the adoption of emergency measures allowing the earlier release of a large number of prisoners. The validity of these measures, which have not always gotten the approval of segments of the

378. ECtHR, *Nisiotis v. Greece*, Application No. 34704/08, Judgment of 10 Feb. 2011. Generally, *see* D. Anagnostou & D. Skleparis, 'Human Rights in European Prisons: Can the Implementation of Strasbourg Court Judgments Influence Penitentiary Reform Domestically?' in T. Daems & L. Robert (eds), *Europe in Prisons: Assessing the Impact of European Institutions on National Prison Systems*, Cham: Palgrave Macmillan, 2017, 37–77.

379. *See* General of Human Rights and Rule of Law, Action against Crime Department, Criminal Law Co-operation Unit, *Reducing Prison Overcrowding in Greece*, Report, March 2019, at: https://theartofcrime.gr/wp-content/uploads/2019/05/REDUCING-PRISON-OVERCROWDING-IN-GREECE.pdf.

380. *See* Council of Europe, Secretariat of the Committee of Ministers, DH-DD(2018)716, 11 Jul. 2018; Council of Europe, *The implementation of judgments of the European Court of Human Rights (2018)*, Strasbourg, February 2018.

381. For further details, *see* the website of the, Council of Europe Committee of Ministers, at: https://rm.coe.int/168070e7dc.

382. *See* Report to the Greek Government on the visit to Greece carried out by the European Committee for the Prevention of Torture and Inhuman or Degrading Treatment or Punishment (CPT) from 10 to 19 Apr. 2018, Strasbourg, 19 Feb. 2019, CPT/Inf (2019) 4, at: https://rm.coe.int/1680930c9a. *See* further, Report to the Greek Government on the ad hoc visit to Greece carried out by the European Committee for the Prevention of Torture and Inhuman or Degrading Treatment or Punishment (CPT) from 22 Nov. 2021 to 1 Dec. 2021, 2 Sep. 2022, CPT/Inf (2022) 16, at: https://rm.coe.int/1680a7ce96. For the Greek Government's reply, *see* CPT/Inf (2022) 17, at: https://rm.coe.int/1680a7ce98.

383. FEK 2015 A' 42.

population, was prolonged under Act 4411/2016,[384] Act 4489/2017,[385] and Act 4571/2018.[386]

384. FEK 2016 A' 142.
385. FEK 2017 A' 140.
386. FEK 2018 A' 186.

## Chapter 4. Serving of Custodial Sentences on Humanitarian Grounds

*552.* Article 105 of the Penitentiary Code permits a convicted offender not to serve the custodial sentence in prison but at his residence if humanitarian grounds can be shown. In particular, Article 105(1) stipulates that, whoever has been sentenced to a custodial sentence for up to fifteen years and has reached the age of 70, will serve (the remainder of) his sentence at his residence, unless the competent court for the execution of the sentence, on the basis of a specific reasoning, considers that the serving in a detention centre is absolutely necessary to prevent the commission of other crimes of a similar gravity. Following the second paragraph of Article 105, this favourable regime shall also apply, regardless of the imposed sentence, to mothers who have the custody of children under the age of eight; and without the conditions of paragraph 1, it shall also apply to those who are quadriplegic, who suffer from final-stage acquired immune deficiency syndrome (AIDS), from chronic renal failure, from persistent tuberculosis, from cirrhosis of the liver and have a disability exceeding 67%, from senile dementia, or from final-stage malignant neoplasms. The enumeration of the illnesses and diseases is exhaustive. However, the Ministers of Justice and of Health have the discretion to add additional ones of comparable gravity. If the custodial sentence was converted to being served at the convicted person's residence, the competent court of justice, under Article 105(3), is entitled to (a) impose at its discretion and depending on the circumstances of the case the conditions envisaged in the aforementioned Article 99(2)(d–f) (i.e., fulfilment of the offender's obligations vis-à-vis the maintenance or custody of other persons; participation in sessions with a social welfare officer; participation in therapeutic programmes with his consent) and (b) order electronic surveillance. It goes without saying that if it is revealed that the conditions of Article 105(2) are not met, serving the sentence at the offender's residence shall be revoked.

## Chapter 5. Conditional Release from Prison

*553.* In the Greek criminal justice system, it is almost axiomatic that most convicted persons will not serve their custodial sentence in full and will be released at a certain stage. The Penal Code sets out the requirements, conditions, procedures, etc., for such an early release of convicted persons. It distinguishes between the release from prison subject to the imposition of conditions (Articles 105B et seq.) and the release subject to the condition of serving the remainder of the custodial sentence at one's residence with electronic surveillance (Article 110A).

*554.* Pursuant to Article 105B(1) of the Penal Code, those who were sentenced to a 'deprivation of liberty penalty' may be released subject to revocation, provided that they have already served two-fifths of the sentence in case of imprisonment; three-fifths in case of confinement in a penitentiary; and at least 20 years in case of life imprisonment (generally, *supra* paragraphs 269–270). However, the actual period of time required for early release may be reduced if the convicted offender works in the prison facility or suffers from certain illnesses. Thus, under Article 46 of the Penitentiary Code prisoners, who do any kind of work or who are engaged in programmes of vocational education or training, may have their sentencing days beneficially calculated on a proposal from the Prisoners' Labour Council and a decision of the competent judicial officer. The particular details on the calculation are laid down in a series of Presidential Decrees, e.g., in Decrees 342/2000[387] and 378/2001[388] relating to prison work, and in Decree 107/2001,[389] as lastly amended by Decree 240/2007,[390] relating to vocational education or training. As regards prisoners who suffer from the illnesses envisaged in the aforementioned Article 105(2), in accordance with, each day of detention shall be calculated as two days of sentence served (Article 105B(4)). The same beneficial calculation is also applicable to prisoners with a disability rate of at least 50% and who are unable to work if their stay in the detention centre becomes particularly burdensome due to their inability to be self-served as well as to prisoners with a disability rate of at least 67%.

Pursuant to Article 106 of the Penal Code, prisoners do not have an automatic right to conditional release. Thus, it may be refused if it is considered (specific grounds must be given) that, on account of the convicted person's conduct in prison, it is necessary to continue his detention to prevent him from committing new criminal acts. On the conditionally released prisoner certain obligations may be imposed concerning his way of life and his place of residence, which if not observed could lead to the release being revoked (Article 107). According to Article 108, the release shall be revoked if, within the period which is provided for in Article 109, the person in question were to commit a criminal act with *dolus* and for which he was convicted irrevocably with a custodial sentence exceeding one year of imprisonment. In this case, he must serve cumulatively the entire remainder of the previous custodial sentence, which he would have served had he not been released from prison.

387. FEK 2000 A' 296.
388. FEK 2001 A' 252.
389. FEK 2001 A' 97.
390. FEK 2007 A' 97.

The provision of Article 109 deals with the consequences of a conditional release which has not been recalled or revoked. Thus, if the period of the custodial sentence, which was left to be served at the time of release and which exceeded three years, has expired without being recalled or revoked, the sentence is considered to have been fully served. In all other cases, it will be considered served provided that three years have expired. The procedure for granting conditional release and for recalling it is laid down in Article 110. The application for the conditional release is filed ex officio by the director of the prison where the convicted person serves his sentence and not by the convicted person himself.

*555.* Article 110A of the Penal Code provides that those who have been sentenced to a custodial sentence may, at their request and in accordance with the provisions of Article 106(1) thereof, be released subject to 'house arrest' with electronic surveillance, as defined in Article 284 CCP. Before such request can be lodged, the convicted person must have served one-fifth of the custodial sentence in case of imprisonment; two-fifths in case of confinement in a penitentiary; or at least fourteen years in case of life imprisonment. House arrest does not necessarily mean that the convicted person must be always inside his residence. Article 110A(6) stipulates that at predetermined times he is allowed to leave it for any of the following reasons: work, education or vocational training, to participate in an approved programme for rehabilitation from drugs or alcohol or to fulfil duties imposed upon him. This type of release can also be revoked if the convicted person does not comply with the obligations imposed and, in view of the gravity of the breach of its obligations, there exists the probability that he will not meet them in the future. Should this happen, the period that lapsed from the release until the new arrest shall not count as time served. However, Article 110A(8) makes it clear that the convicted person retains the right to be conditionally dismissed under the provisions of Article 105B.

# Chapter 6. Termination of the Execution of Criminal Sanctions and the Extinction of Sanctions

*556.* According to Article 564 CCP, the execution of sanctions is terminated with the death of the convicted offender or if he is pardoned. Moreover, following Article 565 CCP, criminal sanctions shall expire through the application of the statute of limitations, as laid down in Articles 111–113 of the Penal Code, or with the award of amnesty.

## §1. Pardon by the President of the Republic and Amnesty

*557.* The conditions for pardoning convicted offenders are not regulated in the Penal Code but in Article 47(1) of the Constitution. It stipulates that the President of the Republic enjoys the right to grant pardons, to convert (commute) or to reduce the (severity of) sentences pronounced by the criminal courts as well as to revoke all consequences resulting from sentences which have been inflicted and served. However, the President does not have the right to initiate the pardoning procedure. This rests either with the Minister of Justice (now the Minister of Justice, Transparency and Human Rights) or with the convicted offender himself who must file an application to that effect. In either case, the Minister of Justice is mandated by Article 47(1) of the Constitution to request the opinion of a special Committee, the Board of Pardons, which was set up under Legislative Decree 68/1968.[391] The Board is chaired by the General Secretary of the Ministry of Justice and comprises six members, most of them judges. As has been mentioned (*supra* paragraph 320), government ministers, who were convicted under Article 86 of the Constitution, may be pardoned only if the Parliament has already given its consent, as laid down in Article 47(2) of the Constitution.

The opinion of the Board of Pardons may be accepted or not by the Minister of Justice, but it is ultimately the decision of the President of the Republic whether the pardon will be granted, in which case, a Presidential Decree will be published in the Government Gazette. The pardon, which is meant to be an extraordinary measure, is of a personal character and may be granted only when the sentencing judgment has reached the stage of res judicata. Even if a convicted offender was pardoned, this does neither abrogate the criminal judgment nor the stigma associated with having committed a criminal act. However, the granting of pardon results in pardoning the sentence inflicted and, therefore, if a custodial sentence had been imposed and was only partly served, the remainder shall not be served. And in case the criminal penalty has already been executed, the act of pardoning results in lifting the consequences deriving from the penalty, e.g., the inability to be employed in the public sector. It is not fully clear which criteria are to be taken into consideration before the Minister of Justice sets the pardoning process in motion, which criteria are relevant for the Board of Pardons to form its opinion, for the Minister of Justice to

391. As lastly amended under Art. 34 of Act 4640/2019, FEK 2019 A' 190.

accept or reject the Board's recommendation and, of course, for the President of the Republic to agree or not with the Minister's opinion.

The following events, which took place in November 2017, highlight the rather opaque character of the pardoning process. At the time, the Minister of Justice was heavily criticized for having proposed to the President of the Republic to pardon a person who in 2008 had been convicted to a two-year suspended custodial sentence for possession and sale of cannabis and who wanted to be employed by the Public Power Corporation, the leading electricity company in Greece. According to the Minister, all those involved in the pardoning process correctly consented to lift the consequences of the criminal sanction imposed by pardoning the offender. And he added: '[t]he deliberate disinformation, man-eating and the creation of impressions through ludicrous publications in the press must finally come to an end. This is the first and the final time that I make a statement to restore the truth in relation to pardoning and I call upon everybody to protect this irreproachable process and, above all, the status of the institution of the President of the Republic'.

*558.* Pursuant to Article 47(3) of the Constitution, amnesty is given only for political crimes under an Act of Parliament approved by a plenary session of Parliament with a three-fifths majority of the total number of Members (i.e., 180 Members of Parliament out of the current total of 300). The philosophy behind the award of amnesty changed fundamentally when the Constitution was amended in 1986. Originally, it had envisaged that amnesty was to be granted through a presidential decree based on a government recommendation. Thus, the authority and power to grant amnesty was withdrawn from the President of the Republic and was awarded to the Parliament. The voting requirement of three-fifths means that, if the government of the day does not control such a large majority in Parliament, it will require the assistance of parties in the Opposition to secure its passage. Finally, Article 47(4) of the Constitution prohibits amnesty for common criminal acts, even if an Act of Parliament has granted it.

## §2. The Statute of Limitation

*559.* The Penal Code envisages two kinds of limitation periods. The first prevents the State from exercising its right of criminal prosecution for the commission of offences (Articles 111–113, *supra* paragraph 173). The second prevents the State from demanding the enforcement or the execution of the imposed criminal sanctions (Articles 118–120 of the Penal Code and Article 565 CCP).

*560.* According to Article 118, criminal sanctions that were inflicted by a res judicata judgment and were not executed within a certain period of time, are time-barred. The limitation period commences on the day the judgment became res judicata (Article 119). The relevant period of time is proportionate to the gravity of the criminal offence. Thus, Article 118 stipulates that confinement in a penitentiary for life shall be time-barred after thirty years; confinement in a penitentiary shall be time-barred after twenty years; imprisonment, monetary penalties and confinement in a correctional institution for youth shall be time-barred after ten years; community service after five years; and, finally, accessory penalties shall be time-barred at the same time as the principal penalties. According to Article 120, the running of the limitation period under Article 118 shall be suspended in the following two instances: (a) for as long as the imposed criminal sanction cannot commence or cannot be carried out; and (b) for as long as the execution of the sanction imposed has been suspended (Articles 99 and 100, *supra* paragraphs 295 et seq.) or the court of justice has allowed the payment of the inflicted monetary penalty by instalments.

# Conclusion

*561.* The *tour d'horizon* of Greek criminal law in this monograph demonstrates that its foundations are strong. Substantive criminal law benefits from a long scholarly tradition and adaptive case law, while criminal procedure follows the continental model enriched with a wide range of rights conferred on both the defendant and the alleged victim of the offence.

Greek criminal law is liberal, pro-European and receptive to international trends. The Constitution establishes in Article 28(1) the supremacy of international treaties over contrary domestic legislation and the Greek legislator shows a diachronic will to comply with European and/or international legal instruments.

However, in its practical implementation Greek criminal law is not unproblematic. The criminal justice system has structural and administrative deficiencies, which are responsible, *inter alia*, for undue delays, while prison overpopulation and inhumane detention conditions pose a permanent challenge.

Moreover, the legislator is sometimes too fast in producing new laws in an effort to comply with EU obligations or to serve short-term crime policy goals, which distorts the balance of the two Codes and creates difficult legal issues to be resolved by usually overloaded courts.

The future will show whether the above problems can be addressed in a more efficient manner, which will allow full utilization of the new Codes' remarkable potential.

# Selected Bibliography

## Introductory Note

There are several Greek law journals either devoted to domestic criminal law and criminal procedure or which publish articles on these topics as well as commentaries on criminal courts' judgments. These journals are published in Greek and include the following: *Poinika Chronika*, *Criminal Justice*, *Praksi and Logos of Criminal Law*, *Elliniki Dikaiosini*, *Nomiko Vima* – The Journal of the Athens Bar Association, *Armenopoulos* – The Journal of the Thessaloniki Bar Association, etc.

## §1. Legislation

According to the Constitution, all Acts of Parliament, Presidential Decrees, Ministerial Decision, etc. shall be published in the Official Gazette of the Greek State) (*Εφημερίς της Κυβερνήσεως της Ελληνικής Δημοκρατίας*). All legislative instruments promulgated since the establishment of the modern Greek State (1833) are available on line at: https://www.et.gr/, which is only available in Greek. Legislative instruments are also published as a supplement to *Nomiko Vima* – The Journal of the Athens Bar Association. There is no policy to translate Greek legislation to other languages; however occasionally the websites of Ministries and other public authorities may upload translations of legislation of their purview. The Ministry of Justice has a very basic website in English (https://ministryofjustice.gr/English/) and the Ministry of Citizen Protection an even more basic website (https://www.minocp.gov.gr/en/). As regards immigration and the position of migrants and asylum seekers in Greece, the website of the Ministry of Migration and Asylum (https://migration.gov.gr/en/) provides some information on the relevant legislation and the applicable procedures.

## §2. Case Law

As regards websites with the texts of judgments rendered by Greek criminal courts, the following might be useful:

– https://www.gov.gr/upourgeia/upourgeio-dikaiosunes/dikaiosunes/elektronikes-dikastikes-apophaseis.
– https://e-justice.europa.eu/13/EN/national_case_law?GREECE&member=1, https://www.taxheaven.gr/dikastikes/2022, and, for the judgments of Areios Pagos: http://www.areiospagos.gr/.

## Selected Bibliography

### §3. Legal Doctrine

Preliminary note: The following is an indicative list of articles or book chapters on Greek criminal law in English or German; more contributions are to be found in the footnotes.

Il. Anagnostopoulos, 'Ne bis in idem in der Europäischen Union – Offene Fragen', *in:* Festschrift für W. Hassemer, C.F. Müller Verlag, Heidelberg, 2010, 1123 et seq.

I. Anagnostopoulos, 'Untersuchungshaft und Verfahrensbeschleunigung – Das Beispiel Griechenlands', StraFo 2013, 454.

Z. Bahtiyar, 'Greece' in M. van Kalmthout, M.M. Knapen & C. Morgenstern (eds), Pre-trial Detention in the European Union. An Analysis of Minimum Standards in Pre-trial Detention and the Grounds for Regular Review in the Member States of the EU, Oisterwijk: Wolf Legal Publishers, 2009, 435.

E. Billis & P. Gkaniatsos, 'Report on Greece' in: S. Quattrocolo & S. Ruggeri (eds), *Personal Participation in Criminal Proceedings*, Cham: Springer, 2019, 182.

E. Billis (ed.), *The Greek Penal Code*, English translation by V. Chalkiadaki and E. Billis, Berlin: Duncker & Humblot, 2017.

L. Cheliotis & S. Xenakis (eds), Crime and Punishment in Contemporary Greece – International Comparative Perspectives, Oxford: Peter Lang, 2011.

R. Da Silva Athayde Barbosa, V. Glerum, H. Kijlstra, A. Klip, C. Peristeridou, M. Wąsek-Wiaderek & A. Zbiciak, *European Arrest Warrant: Practice in Greece, the Netherlands and Poland*, Den Haag: Boom Juridisch, 2022.

D. Giannounopoulos, '"Falling on Deaf Ears": Looking for the Salduz Jurisprudence in Greece' in J. Jackson & S. Summers (eds), *Obstacles to Fairness in Criminal Proceedings: Individual Rights and Institutional Forms*, Oxford: Hart Publishing, 2018, 155.

T. Kaldi-Koulikidou, 'Domestic Violence Against Women in Greece' in S.M. Asay et al (eds), *Family Violence from a Global Perspective: A Strengths-Based Approach*, London: Sage, 2014, 94.

N. Kanellopoulou Malouchou, 'De la protection des animaux (en droit Grec): Vers un droit subjectif fondamental?' (2017) VII *Revue Méditerranéenne de Droit Public* 163.

V. Karydis & N.K. Koulouris, 'Greece: Prisons Are Bad but Necessary (and Expanding), Policies Are Necessary but Bad (and Declining)' in V. Ruggiero et al. (eds), *Punishment in Europe: A Critical Anatomy of Penal Systems*, London: Palgrave Macmillan, 2013, 263.

N.K. Koulouris & W. Aloskofis, *Prison Conditions in Greece*, European Prison Observatory, Rome: Antigone Edizioni, 2013.

E. Lambropoulou, 'Pre-trial detention in Greece: the Achilles heel of the prison system', in: P.H. van Kempen (ed.), *Pre-trial Detention, Human Rights, Criminal Procedural Law and Penitentiary Law, Comparative Law*, Cambridge: Intersentia, 2012, 425.

O. Lykou, 'Analyse und Kritik der Reform des griechischen Untreuestrafrechts' (2020) 132 *Zeitschrift für die gesamte Strafrechtswissenschaft* 473.

A. Tzannetis, 'Von der ‚tätigen Reue' zum ‚Täter-Opfer-Ausgleich'– Zielsetzungen und dogmatische Grundlagen des Schadenswiedergutmachungssystems im neuen griechischen Strafrecht', ZIS 4/2012, 134.

K. Vathiotis, 'Konvergenzen und Divergenzen zwischen dem neuen griechischen StGB und dem deutschen StGB im Bereich der Strafrechtsdogmatik' (2019) 131 *Zeitschrift für die gesamte Strafrechtswissenschaft* 1205.

S. Vlachopoulos, 'The Procedural Aspects of the Proportionality Principle in the Greek Legal Order', in: *Human rights in times of illiberal democracies, Liber Amicorum in Memoriam of Stavros Tsakyrakis*, Athens: Nomiki Bibliothiki, 2020, 81.

## Selected Bibliography

# Index

*The numbers here refer to paragraph numbers.*

## Index

## Index

## Index

www.ingramcontent.com/pod-product-compliance
Lightning Source LLC
Chambersburg PA
CBHW071431230926
51846CB00001B/192
*9789403538570*